Reason, Reality, and

Speculative Philosophy

Arthur Edward Murphy

Reason, Reality, and Speculative Philosophy

Arthur E. Murphy

Edited, with an Introduction, by
Marcus G. Singer

The University of Wisconsin Press

The University of Wisconsin Press
114 North Murray Street
Madison, Wisconsin 53715

3 Henrietta Street
London WC2E 8LU, England

Library of Congress Cataloging-in-Publication Data
Murphy, Arthur Edward, 1901–1962.
    Reason, reality, and speculative philosophy / Arthur E. Murphy:
edited, with an introduction, by Marcus G. Singer.
        330p.   cm.
    Includes bibliographical references and index.
    ISBN 0-299-15040-2 (alk. paper)
    1. Philosophy.   2. Reason.   3. Philosophy, Modern—20th century.
4. Philosophy, Modern—19th century.   I. Singer, Marcus George,
1926—   . II. Title.
B945.M963R43   1996
190'.9'04—dc20   96-5988

To
Frederick Ludwig Will
who introduced me to the work of Arthur Murphy
to
William Henry Hay
who shares my interest in it
and to
Abraham Irving Melden (1910–1991)
who provided advice insight and information

Contents

Preface

The present work brings to publication the main part of a long book manuscript that the author, Arthur E. Murphy, completed in 1940 and never published. It was in some ways a casualty of World War II, since the author's main interests and concerns were redirected so dramatically by that war and what he perceived as the needs of the time.

The title the author gave to his completed but unpublished book was "Contemporary Philosophy." To be sure, what was contemporary in 1940 is now no longer so. Nothing stays contemporary very long, and the astute reader will always check the reference of that word against the publication date of the work having that word in its title. And in this case the publication date has to be corrected by the date of writing. To adapt a remark that the author made about another work that was delayed in publication, "[T]he climate of philosophical opinion has changed so markedly in the last [five] decades that both the problems presented and the author's way of handling them" may be "now uncongenial to widely current habits of thought" ("McGilvary's Perspective Realism," 1959, *RCG,* p. 79).[1] Arthur Murphy died in 1962, and there have been further changes in habits of thought and climate of opinion since 1940. Yet these merely temporal facts indicate very little about the present work. Let it not, therefore, be labeled "contemporary," a label always subject to fairly rapid dating; the half-life of "recent," however, is somewhat greater. And what the author says about "the present situation in philosophy" may in general, with the appropriate translation into more up-to-date idiom, still obtain. For this

---

1. *RCG* abbreviates *Reason and the Common Good: Selected Essays of Arthur E. Murphy* (1963). *CP* abbreviates *Contemporary Philosophy,* the title of the original manuscript from which this book has been derived, and *CP,* accordingly, will be used to indicate that I am quoting or referring to some portion of the original not printed here or elsewhere. (References to *RCG* and other works cited in an abbreviated way, as by date only, are provided in the bibliographical notes starting on page 259.)

---

reason, I considered changing the title to "Recent Philosophy," but eventually decided that this title would be even more misleading. Nonetheless, I have retained the title "Recent Speculative Philosophy," the author's original title, for the chapters in which that is the subject of discussion; it should be clear that this title refers to speculative philosophy recent from the perspective of 1940, and also recent from the perspective of, say, Hegel's time.

It is probably best to avoid such indexical terms altogether. This is, in part, a study of dominant and overarching philosophical trends in the period from approximately 1890 to 1940, trends which, though certainly not identical with present trends, are, many of them, still of the same type, though of course the terminology now used, being up-to-date, is quite different. It is, as the title I have given it implies, a study *inter alia* of speculative philosophy, and speculative philosophy is actually present today in greater abundance and variety than it was fifty or even thirty years ago. For the period of the dominance of analytical and anti-metaphysical philosophy has now receded, giving way to other though not necessarily newer trends and prospects. As such the present work, especially in its now somewhat more streamlined form, has a contemporary relevance it might not have had at the time of its author's death, or even in 1940.

In November 1961 my colleague Bill Hay and I arranged to edit a collection of Murphy's essays (*Reason and the Common Good,* 1963). At the time Murphy was preoccupied with preparing for publication his Carus lectures, *The Theory of Practical Reason* (1965), and therefore said that he was not much interested in publishing a collection of his essays; nonetheless, in fairly short time he developed some enthusiasm for the idea. However, in less than a month he was ill—quite seriously ill, as it turned out. I quote from the preface to *Reason and the Common Good:*

> On December 13, 1961, he wrote from a hospital bed, in his "first try at letter writing": "I'm all for going ahead with the project. In fact it was one of the more cheerful things I thought about as they were probing my insides." And as things went along, he did more work on "the project" than he had originally anticipated. During the period of his convalescence at home, he spent a good deal of his free time looking over manuscripts and papers and trying to decide what should be included and what should not. This process was facilitated by the fact that [I] was able to visit him for a few days in February and to discuss with him, through thick clouds of cigar smoke ("One of the few vices left me") various details connected with the book. . . . This enthusiasm and interest remained with him until his death . . . [May 11, 1962].
>
> One of the bright sides of this short-lived recuperation period was Professor Murphy's discovery of a larger number of unpublished essays (in

the piles of boxes and cartons surrounding his bed) than he originally had thought he had; he was able to make some revisions, in some instances fairly extensive, of all of them for [the collection of essays].

This "great mass of documents, manuscripts, articles, books, notes, and papers" in those piles of boxes and cartons had been transported to Murphy's home from his office by Murphy's colleague and former student Daniel Kading. It was in this enormous and disarranged stock of materials that I came across the very long and heavy and somewhat disarranged manuscript of the present book. There were, as it turned out, two complete copies of the typescript and one incomplete one, a ribbon copy and two carbons, though this was not immediately obvious. It was arranged by chapter, the chapters were numbered in sequence, and the pages were consecutively numbered in each chapter, but otherwise it was not in sequence, since the chapters were out of order and there were extra pages with revisions on them scattered throughout. When I pulled this mass of material out and asked what it was, Murphy was genuinely puzzled at first—so it seemed to me at the time, though that in itself is puzzling—but after a moment or two he recollected and told me the story, or a bit of it. It was a book manuscript on Contemporary Philosophy that he had finished in 1940 and then put aside. However, once this discovery was made, Murphy started looking through it again and made a number of revisions in the typescript. He also pulled out the last section of the chapter on perceptual knowledge, retitled it "What Happened to Objective Relativism," revised it somewhat, and sent it to us for the volume of essays, where it duly appears. Although he told me the manuscript had been looked over by one or two people, he never told me why he had never published or even tried to publish it, though he did mention that he had used some ideas from it here and there in later pieces. I took one complete copy of the typescript home with me, along with masses of other materials, and put it aside while I dealt with other matters.

On March 7, 1962, Murphy wrote me, "I've been reading the big manuscript you disinterred." As I found out later, he had not just been reading it, he had been revising it. He also continued revising his Carus lectures, and it turned out that he had finished his last paper, a critical study of a book by Brand Blanshard,[2] which curiously enough I knew nothing about, since I neither saw it nor heard anything about it either during my stay in Austin or later. On March 23rd he wrote me (for the last time, as it turned out): "I have a complete

2. "Blanshard on Good in General," edited by A. I. Melden, *The Philosophical Review,* 1963, pp. 228–41. The manuscript—now in my possession—for some reason was written in red ink. Murphy had always before written in blue ink. His letter to me of December 13, 1961, written from a hospital bed, was also in red ink. It is possible that he wrote the Blanshard paper from a hospital bed, but naturally that is only speculation.

copy of the 1940 manuscript of 880 pages (God save us all!). Maybe I'll use some of it some day in a short book on 'Speculative Philosophy' (Alexander, McTaggart, Peirce, Whitehead, Collingwood, etc.). . . . The pencilled comments are those of Ralph Blake (now deceased)." He never answered the letters I sent him after that. The explanation came soon enough. Frederick H. Ginascol, Murphy's friend and colleague and the executor of his estate, told me in a letter of April 26: "Arthur has had serious relapse. Has been on 'extremely critical' list for 10 days, and constantly verging on comatose state. Can't conduct any business." On Friday May 11 he sent me a telegram saying, "Regret inform you death Arthur Murphy Funeral Saturday pm May 12th Austin—Ginascol."

I said above that I had not known anything about this "missing" manuscript which I "disinterred," but it may be that my memory had been deceiving me, for I later remembered that when I was a graduate student at Cornell, from 1948 to 1952, every once in a while I would hear some speculation about the "big book" that Murphy was reputed to have been or to be still working on. Not long ago Joel Feinberg told me that when Murphy was visiting at Michigan in 1952 there was similar speculation there among both students and faculty about the "great work" Murphy was reputed to have finished or to be working on, and he noted that at one time Murphy was regarded by some people as the logical successor to Dewey in American philosophy. That regard may now seem somewhat excessive and, obviously, Murphy never attained this stature, and his reputation after his death went into precipitous decline (something that also happened to Dewey's for a time, though only for a time). In any case, however, I am pretty sure that the present work is, in essence, the book these people were talking about.

It was not until 1964 that I was able to think again about this manuscript that had been entrusted to my care. In March 1964, Ginascol wrote me: "About that MS, it seemed that Arthur had sent an advance copy to Ernest Nagel, received an extensive criticism, most of it very flattering—but that Arthur decided to shelve the project. After Arthur's death I sent for the MS, and also asked Nagel's opinion as to the present possibility for publication. I have some letters in which Nagel repeated his admiration for the MS, marvelling that it had not been put out, and urging that it be done." I have not come across any comments on the manuscript by Nagel, nor have I come across any letters from Nagel to Murphy or seen any letters Nagel sent to Ginascol. Unfortunately, I never asked Nagel about this matter when I was able to. Although from time to time I came back to this manuscript, I was not able to do much about it until early 1984 when I travelled to Austin to retrieve the Murphy papers that had been promised me. Very late in my stay I discovered that the bulk of the Murphy papers had been deposited with the Humanities Research Center (HRC), and I was able to do some work on them then, though my remaining time was limited. In the spring of 1988 I went to Austin again; at that time I was able to compare the copies of the manuscript of this book in the HRC with my own copy, and was able to revise the manuscript I was working from in accordance with the revisions that Murphy—his handwriting was unmistakable—had made in the copy he had been reading in the period just before his death. I also at that time found masses of unpublished manuscripts the existence of which I had not suspected before, some of which I had heard about but had not seen, and there is now enough such material to make another collection of essays.[3]

Even though in his March 23rd letter Murphy mentioned Collingwood, there is nothing about Collingwood in the manuscript in question, nor is there anything extensive about other speculative philosophers in whom Murphy had an interest, such as Bergson and Royce, and there is naturally room for speculation about what is involved in that "etc." On this matter, after taking advice, I am reasonably certain that there is nothing published here that is not within the confines of the commission, as I interpreted it, which the author had given to me.[4]

As already indicated, portions of the manuscript now published here did receive careful revision by the author on various occasions in the past, and especially in the brief period between its resurrection in February 1962 and his death in May, in his sixty-first year. Other portions received no revisions at all, may not even have been looked at. The manuscript presented some problems. There are places where there are blank spaces left by the typist struggling with the author's handwriting, others where the author has inserted handwritten words or phrases—some of them filling in these blank spaces, others constituting revisions of the text—and not all of these late insertions were completely legible. The hand of one other person, at least, is to be discerned in the revisions. Murphy's friend Ralph M. Blake entered grammatical revisions and queries and comments for the author, and on occasion altered sentence structure.

Some sentences had to be adjusted, and in some instances I had to guess at what word or sequence of words was intended. I have indicated these places by editorial notes or by enclosing the word or phrase in square brackets. I have altered punctuation when this seemed necessary to display the meaning more perspicuously, but I have tried not to impose my own style on the text. Murphy had his own distinctive style of writing—though some readers complained that

3. One of these, evidently a speech the author gave many years ago and then forgot about, has since been published as "Emerson in Contemporary Thought," 1988.

4. And, it appears, only to me. Melden, who edited the Carus Lectures, knew nothing about this work at the time, just as I was not involved in editing the Carus Lectures. And Ginascol knew nothing about it until I informed him about it, after which he turned up copies of the manuscript.

his written work was difficult to follow, others thought he wrote beautifully—
and I am pretty sure this style has remained through the few transformations
effected by Ralph Blake (some of which I have expunged, in order to re-
gain the author's original wording and sentence structure). Occasionally, where
some word seemed clearly wrong—the result of a typist's error—I have si-
lently modified it to what seemed beyond question the word intended; where
there was room for doubt, I have inserted an editorial footnote. All numbered
footnotes in the text are those of the author. Editorial notes are indicated by
other symbols or, when appearing in the author's notes, are enclosed in brackets, as are words inserted editorially. In addition, the original footnotes have
been edited for consistency throughout this volume.

The work from which the present text has been extracted was arranged as
follows (I list the number of pages to give an idea of how large a book this was):

1. An Hypothesis to be Tested   35 pp.
2. Idealism   86 pp.
3. Pragmatism   124 pp.
4. Realism   83 pp.
5. The Problems of Perceptual Knowledge   80 pp.
6. The "Problem" of Moral Value   81 pp.
7. Recent Speculative Philosophy   160 pp.
8. Philosophical Analysis   161 pp.
9. The Standpoint of Philosophy   72 pp.

The general arrangement of the original text has been retained here. Chapter 1
of the original is also chapter 1 here. Chapter 3 has been published elsewhere
as "Pragmatism and the Context of Rationality" (1993); its last section is present chapter 3. Chapters 2 and 4 are the same here. Chapters 5, 6, and 8 of the
original are not included here; original chapter 7 has been split into two parts,
present chapters 5 and 6, to make it more manageable. The last three sections
of chapter 9, the discussion of Santayana and the final two sections, have been
included here as chapters 7 and 8.

The scope of the work now brought to publication is indicated in the title,
and for this purpose the discussions of idealism, chapter 2, and realism, chapter 4, count as discussions of speculative philosophy, just as they provide occasions for the author to develop his conceptions of reason and "reality." That
Bradley is discussed in the chapter on idealism rather than in the chapters on
speculative philosophy is of no consequence, for the author clearly wanted
what he had written on Bradley to be included, and clearly Bradley was, as we
shall see, a speculative philosopher as well as a metaphysician. This goes for
the other idealists and realists discussed also, at least on Murphy's understanding of speculative philosophy. For on this understanding, even if these philos-

ophers did not represent forms of speculative philosophy per se, they exhibited many of the same features and led to it. Both idealism and realism, two of the three most prominent competing philosophical isms of the period (the third was pragmatism), were attempts to determine the nature of reality—ultimate reality—by the power of reason, the one from an ontological orientation, the other from an epistemological orientation. The author's conception of reason—when, as he often puts it, about its proper business—does not correspond to that of the idealists or the realists or the pragmatists, though it has some significant affinities with the latter two, and the author is deeply suspicious of attempts to give an account of reality, especially ultimate reality, when it is treated as something other or deeper than or behind or underneath or veiled by the world that people live in and deal with in their everyday lives or that scientists deal with in their scientific lives. In this way we get a rival conception of the office and function of reason and of philosophy, a conception radically different from that of the philosophers Murphy discusses here. Indeed, the author was deeply suspicious of all "ultimates," whether ultimate reality, ultimate truth, ultimate meaning, or ultimate principles. This was a skepticism he arrived at by careful and sympathetic consideration of various attempts to arrive at ultimate reality or ultimacy of one sort or another, and by careful reconsideration of his own earlier attempt to formulate and establish a speculative hypothesis. One of the things he was fond of saying was "In the last analysis, there is no last analysis." It is not hard to transpose this into "Ultimately, there is nothing ultimate."

One problem the manuscript presented was the need to check all quotations and page references. In the present text, every one of these has been checked against the originals, and I was able, with assistance, to identify and check all but two, which are identified in the editorial notes. Murphy had an excellent, indeed astounding, memory. I never recall him bringing lecture notes to class, and I remember him often quoting from memory. Unfortunately, this facility with memory, so serviceable in lectures and oral presentations, turned out to have some problems when dealing with the written word. Someone, like Toscanini, who conducts from memory must have each and every detail of the score absolutely accurate in his head. Murphy's memory was not in this way photographically accurate. It was absolutely accurate as to the ideas, but not as to each and every word. And it appeared early on that, when he quoted, Murphy was often going from memory rather than from careful checking of a written text before him. Thus I needed to check each and every quotation for word-for-word accuracy. Also, the citations were occasionally off. Usually this was explained by the fact that Murphy did not correct the citations in the footnotes, even where he had corrected the typing in the body of the manuscript. On some occasions the explanation was rather that the author was quoting from or citing some earlier edition, one not now readily obtainable, and it was judged better, where this could be done, to provide citations to some currently more accessible edition; at least access to the latter was necessary to check the accuracy of the quotation. But in not one instance did I find a quotation that was not absolutely accurate as to meaning, and the paraphrases were not only right on target but more often than not were uncannily penetrating. I have also supplied full references to works Murphy referred to only in passing.

Items cited in the preface, the memoir, and the introduction are typically cited by year of writing or publication and may be located when not otherwise identified in the bibliographical notes.

For the rather daunting task of checking quotations and references I had the invaluable assistance of Dr. Michael F. McFall, a doctoral candidate at the University of Wisconsin and my research assistant for most of the time this work was in process. I am also pleased to acknowledge assistance or advice received at various times from the following former students or colleagues of Arthur Murphy, three of whom are given special acknowledgment in the dedication: Frederick H. Ginascol, Thomas F. Green, Bill Hay, Daniel Kading, Abe Melden (deceased), Ernest Schlaretzki, J. B. Schneewind, John R. Silber, and Fred Will. I also received invaluable assistance and advice from my late lamented friends Konstantin Kolenda and Edmund Pincoffs, both former students of Murphy's at Cornell, who were very interested in this project but did not live to see it completed. I am also pleased to acknowledge useful advice received from an anonymous referee for the University of Wisconsin Press—even if in the end I was unable to follow every one of this person's suggestions—and Peter Hare, also a referee and a source of advice and encouragement throughout. The manuscript has been much improved by the superb copyediting of Sylvan Esh, who helped improve the wording, and the sense, of a number of intractable sentences. Finally, my wife, Blanche Ladenson Singer, as she has done so often in the past, combed what I have written with her usual acute eye for obscurities, infelicities of style, and redundancies. Any such defects that remain must be ones she didn't catch.

MGS

June 1995

Memoir

Arthur Edward Murphy was born September 1, 1901, in Ithaca, New York, the second child of Emily Atkinson, a school teacher, and Edward Charles Murphy, an engineer. His father, then a professor at Cornell University, had previously been a professor at the University of Kansas, and was later "called back to Cornell University in recognition of his pioneer work in aerodynamics." [1] Edward Murphy entered the Geological Survey in 1903 and shortly thereafter was transferred to the West Coast, where the family lived in Napa, close to San Francisco and the University of California.

Arthur Murphy's older sister, Gladys, had been born in Kansas. In 1920 she graduated from the University of California with degrees in "Philosophy and Public Speaking and went on to teach and to do graduate work in both fields." In December 1921 she married Malbone Graham. "From that point on, her interests widened appreciably, embracing not only pioneering research in the speech field, as well as exploratory work in the purposive molding of public opinion, but all phases of education." Later in life she became very ill, and lived for a number of years in Santa Monica, California, as a nearly helpless invalid. Murphy had a high regard for his sister, and for many years, until she died in March 1957, spent every summer in Santa Monica.

Murphy went to Napa High School and won the state debating prize, and

1. The information provided about Edward Murphy and Gladys Murphy Graham is derived from a brief sketch of Arthur Murphy's sister found in the Murphy papers, from which some quotations are taken. On two occasions Murphy wrote me something about his sister and his relations with her, but only on those occasions. Other friends and former students have remarked that, although he loved to engage in conversation and to talk about people, and would always inquire how people's lives were going, he said very little about his own personal life. I know nothing about his mother, except that she was a teacher, and it is mere accident that I learned a little bit more about his father.

then to the University of California, from which he graduated valedictorian in 1923 with degrees in philosophy and political science, and was awarded the University of California Gold Medal as the most distinguished student in the 1923 graduating class. He had been a highly regarded member of the California debating team,[2] and had originally contemplated going into law. However, as he wrote in 1934:

> In the spring of 1922, during my junior year at the University of California, I read for the first time Santayana's *Life of Reason.* The effect of that great book was somewhat complicated by an attack of influenza which developed just as I was completing volume one, and it is difficult to assess in retrospect the respective contributions of fever and intellectual excitement in what for me was a decisive experience. A growing but rather superficial interest in philosophy, a subject I had elected as a not too arduous preliminary to the study of law, was then transformed into the major business of life and such it has remained during the succeeding years.[3]

Murphy received his Ph.D. in December 1925, after serving as an assistant in philosophy in 1923–24 and again in late 1925, and immediately was appointed instructor in philosophy. His dissertation was entitled "The Metaphysics of Space-Time." The thesis, as a physical object only and without reference to the content, gives the impression of having been typed very quickly to face a final oral defense that was very likely a pro forma affair, suggesting that his appointment as instructor had already been arranged and was contingent on his receiving the degree. (Thus the page numbers of the introduction, pages 1 through 11, are repeated in chapter one, so that later references to one of those page numbers are ambiguous, there are obvious mistypings if not misspellings, and there are no margins to speak of.) This was Murphy's own venture into speculative metaphysics, and his work for the Ph.D. supplied him with his main philosophical interests—metaphysics, epistemology, speculative philosophy, contemporary philosophical tendencies, and the view he labelled "objective relativism"—for at least fifteen more years, through the writing of the original text of the present book, after which his main interests shifted dramatically though predictably, without his earlier interests altogether disappearing.

Murphy taught as an instructor at the University of California until June 1927, then as instructor at the University of Chicago for a year, after which he went to Cornell University as assistant professor for a year, and returned to Chicago as an associate professor in 1929. He left the University of Chicago in 1931, as a result of some unpleasant events involving the Department of Phi-

2. *Berkeley Daily Gazette,* May 16, 1923, pp. 1, 11.
3. "A Program for a Philosophy," in *American Philosophy Today and Tomorrow,* 1935, p. 357.

losophy, President Robert M. Hutchins, and Mortimer Adler,[4] and at the age of twenty-nine went to Brown University as a full professor. He stayed at Brown until 1939; he undoubtedly was happy there, just as he had been at the University of Chicago, since he had a group of congenial friends and colleagues, including C. J. Ducasse, Ralph M. Blake, and Charles A. Baylis, and enjoyed the fellowship, friendship, and esteem of his fellow members of the Plymouth-Union Congregational Church. (Later on he was a Unitarian, and then, in the manner of Emerson, still later was not.) But in 1939 he went to the University of Illinois as department head, and thus began a career as administrator and department builder. In 1945 he went to Cornell again, this time as department chairman; in 1953 he went to the University of Washington as chairman, and in 1958 to the University of Texas in the same capacity. He thus in a way re-enacted the saga of the mobile American. He lived and worked and taught in every section of the country, lectured all over, and served on various commissions and committees. When he went to the University of Chicago for the second time, in 1929, he already had a national reputation. Later on, about the time he went to Illinois, his reputation was established outside of philosophy, and outside of academia as well.

During his career he held several visiting posts: at Columbia in the summer of 1930, Stanford in summer 1940, University of California at Los Angeles in summer 1946, University of Washington in 1948–49, University of Michigan in 1952, and University of Texas in 1957–58. He travelled to Europe twice, the

---

4. Murphy resigned February 5, 1931, along with E. A. Burtt, who went to Cornell, and George Herbert Mead—then in his first and only year as chairman of the department, who retired and was invited to Columbia the next year but actually did not live much longer—as a result of what they regarded as President Hutchins' unwarranted interference in the affairs of the Department of Philosophy. In the introduction to "Pragmatism and the Context of Rationality" (1993), p. 125, I gave an account of what occurred at the University of Chicago that was not altogether accurate. I had heard the story quite a number of years ago, about 1951, from Murphy himself, and later on checked it out with two or three other people, and had not checked any printed account. For a full and no doubt accurate account, and one of considerable interest, see Gary A. Cook, *George Herbert Mead: The Making of a Social Pragmatist* (Urbana: University of Illinois Press, 1993), "Epilogue: Mead and the Hutchins Controversy," pp. 183–94, 212–14. I am indebted to Terry Sheldahl and to Professor Cook himself for calling this account to my attention. Another account, from a different perspective, though it does not differ on any material facts, is in Harry S. Ashmore, *Unseasonable Truths: The Life of Robert Maynard Hutchins* (Boston: Little, Brown and Company, 1989), pp. 85–87, 90 ff. Murphy of course, at the age of twenty-nine, was a relatively minor player in this incident. Mead was the major player, Mead along with Mortimer Adler. According to Ashmore, Adler considered the Philosophy Department at Chicago "to be hopelessly mired in pragmatism." Mead and Burtt were certainly pragmatists; and this point indicates that Murphy at that time was also regarded as a pragmatist. Whether he regarded himself as one I do not know. Certainly Max Otto did not regard him as one in 1943, nor was he one later in life.

first time in 1924–25 on a Sigmund Heller Travelling Fellowship, when he got
to know Samuel Alexander, about whom he was then writing, and other British
philosophers in whom he was interested. He went again in 1937–38; 1937 was
the year in which he "read the *Blue Book,*" which made a profound impression
on him.[5] He gave two series of Matchette Lectures, once at Purdue in 1948 and
then at Brooklyn College in 1952, and gave the Carus Lectures in December
1955 in Berkeley, California. He was editor of the Prentice-Hall Philosophy
Series from 1936 until his death, a book editor of *The Journal of Philosophy*
from 1934 to 1939, on the editorial committee of *The International Journal of
Ethics* (later *Ethics*) from 1931 until his death, and editor of *The Philosophical Review* from 1949 to 1953, when he left Cornell. He was a Fellow of the
American Academy of Arts and Sciences, and served as president of the East-
ern Division of the American Philosophical Association in 1950.

Murphy also served as chairman of the American Philosophical Association's Commission on the Function of Philosophy in American Education from
its organization in 1943 until its termination in 1946. In this capacity he was
co-author of *Philosophy in American Education,* along with his colleagues
on the commission, Brand Blanshard, C. J. Ducasse, Charles W. Hendel, and
Max C. Otto. This team travelled around the country in 1943–44 and held
meetings with philosophers and others in every part of the country in prepara-
tion for its report. I have heard second-hand reports of this commission's activities travels and inquiries from various sources. One of the members, Brand
Blanshard, has given an account of the activities of this commission in his auto-
biography. Blanshard tells us the commission was to report on "the function
of philosophy in liberal education and in the development of a free and reflective life in the community. . . . The commission set out to gather facts, opinions,
and advice from philosophers in every part of the country." Blanshard goes on
to say:

> I enjoyed the months of service on this commission. They might have been
> debilitating if the members had been prickly toward each other, for we had
> to travel thousands of miles in each other's company, crossing the conti-
> nent twice by train. One member [Max Otto] . . . did not make these long
> trips with us. . . . The four who did make the circuit together formed a
> congenial group. Arthur Murphy, stoutish, pink-cheeked, jolly and cheru-

5. The "*Blue Book,*" as philosophical readers will know, refers to lectures of Wittgenstein's that
were then circulating bound in blue covers; it in no way refers to the John Birch Society's "1958
classic of global-government conspiracism" or to the "sacred text" of the Militia of Montana.
Some conspiracy theorists may, naturally, find some analogy. The latter organization boasts,
"When we take someone on a trip through 'The Blue Book' they cannot argue—all they can do is
say we are right or they just simply RUN AWAY!!!" (Michael Kelly, "The Road to Paranoia," *The
New Yorker,* 71.17 (19 June 1995): 60–61, italics omitted.)

bic, had an irrepressible sense of humor, and when he and Ducasse, his former colleague at Brown, fell to exchanging banter with each other, I wished that a recorder had been on hand. Murphy had a rare gift of extempore speech, and when called on for his views on a philosophical matter, could pour out his thought in a sequence of elaborate but well knit sentences that were impressive both at the time and in review.[6]

Murphy was a marvelous extempore speaker, and also a marvelous speaker when he had a prepared text in front of him. He would often write out what he was going to say, and his memory was such that he could deliver the speech with hardly a reference to the written words in front of him, even when he was quoting. He almost always quoted from memory, both in speaking and in writing. He spoke as he wrote and wrote as he spoke, a trait that is not very common. But, later in life at any rate, he wrote in long involved sentences with rounded periods and dependent clause within dependent clause. This often provided the effect that generated the humor. But it also may be the source of the trouble some people have had reading him, even those who would never miss a Murphy oral performance. For them the silver tongue and the platform manner conveyed the ideas, to an extent, and certainly provided the entertainment. In 1953 he presented the lead paper in a heavily attended APA Western Division symposium on "Reasons in Ethics" (*RCG*, pp. 35–46); this was a study that later eventuated in the view presented in his Carus lectures, *The Theory of Practical Reason,* it was sharply against established tradition in ethical theory, and it was not easily assimilated at one sitting. When the session ended, by prearrangement I was waiting for him in the back of the hall, and near me was a group of elder philosophical statesmen, clucking their tongues and shaking their heads and saying things like "What is Murphy up to now? Did you understand that? What will he be saying next?" After a bit he strolled up the aisle and as he approached this group of elder critics, said with a big grin, "W-e-l-l, was that sound doctrine?" The response was a sort of embarrassed silence and a group-nodding of heads and congratulations and handshakes all around. I found this so funny that I had to move away a bit. He knew just what he

---

6. Brand Blanshard, *The Philosophy of Brand Blanshard,* edited by Paul Arthur Schilpp (La Salle, Illinois: Open Court, 1980), pp. 93–94. Blanshard's further discussion of the work of the commission is of considerable interest. It should be realized that the commission carried on its work in wartime, when travel was difficult and sometimes restricted, and regular passenger trains, which had low priority, were sometimes sidetracked for long periods of time to make way for troop trains. See Blanshard on the suspension "by reason of restrictions on war travel" of APA meetings in 1943 and 1944. For a fuller account of the commission's charge and activities and conferences see the Preface to *Philosophy in American Education* (New York: Harper and Brothers, 1945), which Murphy was involved in writing, though it is not attributed to any one member of the commission, and also chapter 1, by Blanshard.

was doing and he was deliberately teasing. This illustrates the impish side of him. He often began both statements and questions with an expostulated "W-e-l-l. . . ." His cheerful "W-e-l-l" was often the prelude to some quip or mischievous remark or teasing question.

In his earliest papers his style was much more direct. His essays from 1926 to 1931 or so have the character of flashing self-confident though not arrogant brilliance. His sentences are direct, staccato, do not have the lilt and sweep of his later writing, and he wrote in the third person, not in the first person he moved to later.

Murphy suffered several serious philosophical disillusionments. His first enthusiasm was for the Santayana of *The Life of Reason;* but then the Santayana of *Skepticism and Animal Faith* and *The Realms of Being* led to disillusionment, for reasons explained in chapter 7. He also had great admiration for Whitehead, the Whitehead of *The Principles of Natural Knowledge, The Concept of Nature,* and *The Principle of Relativity.* But his early excitement about Whitehead ran into disillusionment when *Process and Reality* appeared in 1929, for reasons detailed in chapter 6 and in a brilliant but little-known paper entitled "The Development of Whitehead's Philosophy" (1930, in *RCG,* pp. 126–41, esp. pp. 128–34). The gist of his disappointment was that Whitehead, who early on "had maintained a policy of magnificent isolation with respect to the traditional metaphysical issues"—which Murphy regarded as dead ends and the source of interminable disputes and not a source of philosophical wisdom and enlightenment—had now gone on to immerse himself in the dialectics of traditional and endless metaphysical disputes, and somehow lost track of his original object, to bring down "the most rarified abstractions to the point of their intersection with the perceptible course of events" and "to correct the abstractions of contemporary physics by reference to their basis in occurrent reality" (*RCG,* p. 129). Later, however, Whitehead, while progressively developing "his contact with dialectics . . . at the same time lost something of his hold upon events. . . . In short, here is [just] another system of philosophy" and "however devious its argument and however close the dialectical network, this system is in the end a net to catch the wind" (*RCG,* pp. 136, 140, 141).[7]

A third philosopher to whom Murphy was greatly attracted and with whom he later became somewhat disillusioned was Dewey (cf. "Dewey's Epistemology and Metaphysics," 1939, and "John Dewey and American Liberal-

---

7. Murphy's 1929 review of Whitehead's *Symbolism, Its Meaning and Effect,* lamented "the progressive complication and diffusion of a philosophical insight second to none in this generation. The turning point in this philosophy seems to have occurred when analysis was supplanted by analogy and metaphor took the place of mathematics . . ." (*The Journal of Philosophy* 26 [1929]: 489).

ism," 1960; some might say that in the latter piece he actually turned on Dewey). He retained a life-long admiration for Bradley, though a somewhat exasperated one. Another philosopher for whom he had great admiration was William James, and Murphy was at work on a book on James—the manuscript, or what there is of it, is now in my possession—for some time prior to his death; I do not know which publisher had commissioned the work. What Murphy especially liked about James was the largeness of James' vision and his openness to new perspectives.

In conversation his sense of humor and his gift for extempore exposition were in constant operation. My friend the late Bill Marshall used to say that Murphy would wind long serpentine coils of words and sentences around you and before you knew what was happening you found yourself agreeing with him, if only because you couldn't see how to avoid doing so. Murphy had a knack that was almost uncanny of getting directly at the essence of what someone was saying and stating it in such a way as to bring out its connections with other thinkers and other problems and other areas of life. This practically unrivalled ability was manifested in his writing, is manifested in this book in connection with philosophical views that are not always easy to assimilate—one who reads Murphy on the idealists and the realists and the speculative philosophers will get an understanding of some first-rate and profound thinkers not otherwise obtainable. Murphy could get inside some other view and see it as its holder saw it, sometimes better—only he could engage in this act of appreciation and understanding without being convinced. This knack is a very special gift for a teacher of philosophy to have, and as a commentator of this sort Murphy had few rivals. He flew where others trod. It is probably for this reason that he is most often remembered mainly as a critic of the views of others; however, though he was often critical, it is more accurate to regard him as an interpreter of unusual insight. In this book, he is in large part serving the part of commentator and interpreter and critic. What it is important to see is that there is a positive view of some pith and moment underlying the pattern of criticisms he levels against the doctrines he considers in this work. Naturally, other writers on whom he was reporting did not always agree with his accounts of what they were saying, and this led to some notable controversies in the journals. Dewey's reply to Murphy in the Schilpp Dewey volume (1939) is especially bitter in its complaints that Murphy had misunderstood him, though Murphy was not convinced by Dewey's reply (see *RCG*, p. xiii).

On one occasion in Ithaca, some graduate students threw a party, a rather large party, to which Murphy was invited along with Max Black and I think no other members of the faculty. Black and Murphy had different groups of students around them whom they kept entertained with stories, mostly about philosophy and philosophers. (Somebody later came up with the thesis that they were competing with each other for laughs.) Black went home relatively early,

Murphy stayed on. He was having quite a time laughing and telling stories and, of course, drinking. When it came time to say goodbye to his host and hostess, they offered him his hat. He insisted he hadn't worn a hat, they insisted he had, but he said no he hadn't brought a hat, and walked on home. (He never drove, always walked, rain or shine, even up and down the steep hills of Ithaca.) A few days later, he saw his host, Bill Marshall, in Goldwin Smith Hall, and said, "W-e-l-l, that was quite a party. I'm still cheerful." A day or two later he was asking, "Has anyone seen my hat?"

In a preface to the 1934 paper I quoted from earlier, Murphy provides a brief autobiographical statement from which we can glean other insights:

> Though a native of New York State . . . my early geographical background was mainly that of rural California and the San Francisco region. From my undergraduate and graduate days I recall . . . an earnest moral idealism—the period was that of "the social gospel" and the League of Nations—a series of debates in which my preference was for the negative side of almost any question, and a growing interest in philosophy, aroused and guided by such teachers as Adams, Lovejoy, and Kemp Smith. In the eight years since that time I have learned something of my chosen subject, of human nature and of the contemporary American scene from sojourns at the University of Chicago, at Cornell and now at Brown in what is surely the most congenial of philosophical environments. I should perhaps also mention an abiding delight in motion pictures—even rather bad motion pictures—and a conviction that a sense of humor is an important adjunct to philosophic understanding. (1935, p. 356)

His sense of humor was not just a matter of conviction but an integral part of his personality and his philosophical style, and it was combined with a rare sense of irony. It was manifested in his writings, his lectures, and his conversation, and even in his comments on student papers, and it had the quality of philosophic wisdom. For he not only saw humor in situations where others did not until he pointed it out, he also had the ability to laugh at himself, and his occasionally sharp critical comments were smoothed over by humor. He was neither egocentric nor egotistical, and took a genuine interest in the lives, problems, and careers of his students.

I perhaps should mention that although I had many conversations with Murphy, and he was the chairman of my thesis committee, I had only two courses with him, both graduate seminars (both very large—too large really for seminars): one on Bradley, Bergson, and Whitehead, the other on Dewey and Mead. Although I met him early on, he was gone my first year at Cornell, 1948–49, and in my third year I was engaged in thesis research, but I sat in on the Collingwood part of his seminar on Peirce, Royce, and Collingwood. (At the same time I attended sessions of another seminar in which Collingwood was also being discussed; in the latter, a good presentation of more than ordinary competence, Collingwood's aims and motives remained largely dark; in Murphy's, Collingwood's strange metaphysics was lit up, as though from within.) That year or the next he also gave a seminar in ethics and value theory entitled "Can There Be a General Theory of Value?", in which one main text was R. B. Perry's *General Theory of Value* (and another, I think, was C. I. Lewis's *Analysis of Knowledge and Valuation*). He told me that the answer was no, but that there were a few other things to be said and naturally the interesting thing was how you get to the answer. At Cornell he regularly gave undergraduate courses on American Philosophy and on ethics. I never assisted him, but one of my friends (I don't recall who it was) assigned to assist him in an undergraduate course reported to me the following interchange with him: "Professor Murphy, what do you want me to do in this course?" "W-e-l-l, let's see. I should like you to accompany me to the door of the room, open the door for me, and then, after I've gone in, close it behind me." I was told that he regularly graded and commented on all student papers himself, even though he always had a graduate assistant. He wrote on a paper of mine, on Bradley, "A sensible discussion," nothing more. I went to see him to find out what this meant. He said, "W-e-l-l now, isn't that clear enough? 'Sensible' is pretty good. I should like to see more sensible discussions. There isn't enough good sense in the world and you've just added to the store." Later that term he commented on a long paper on Bergson, "Your criticism of Bergson's moral theory seems to me well founded. I'm not convinced by what you say about the way in which the intellect and intuition are each to know its own absolute while only intuition is adequate to 'things as a whole.' If matter is part of the whole and is known by intellect, *not* intuition, then how can intuition know 'reality as a whole'? This is more than a slip of the pen on Bergson's part; it's a slip of the mind." Next term I attached to a paper on Mead my own critique of it. He wrote: "Your comments on this paper are judicious (since you object to 'sensible' I won't use that word). What grade did you have in mind for it?"

In the summer of 1949 Wittgenstein came to Ithaca to stay with Norman Malcolm and his wife Lee, and possibly (I do not know—I never asked) Murphy got to see Wittgenstein that fall at one or another of the discussions then going on between Wittgenstein and some of the Cornell faculty. (In the early fall Wittgenstein came to a meeting of the Discussion Club, the first meeting of the new year, when Gregory Vlastos read a paper, and after that held two special meetings for graduate students alone—but that's another story.) Ed Gettier was then a graduate student at Cornell and a student of Malcolm's, who, as philosophers should know, was a friend and disciple of Wittgenstein's. One day Gettier came laughing into the Assistants' room and said, "Arthur Murphy just said to me: 'You sound like an echo of an echo.'" This generated laughter all around—Murphy's quips by this time were famous. In 1951 Murphy said to me about the first draft of my dissertation, about which he was unhappy: "I knew something was wrong when I noticed there were no quips in it." I hadn't agreed that it was all that bad, but that remark got me laughing. In a letter of January 1956, he said: "I expect I do owe you a letter—I owe one to practically everybody except Mamie Eisenhower. . . . The lectures [referring to the Carus lectures] are over and the winter quarter [is] well started here. I'm doing scholastic metaphysics, with special reference to Gilson's *Being and Some Philosophers,* and am simply bursting with Being." Such remarks were second nature to him, seemed to pour out of him. In a note of December 1952 he said: "I've been quoting Dr. Singer in public lectures recently—in Brooklyn. The light of reason shines in dark places." Again: "Ithaca is cold, as usual, and language is being torn apart, also as usual." In a letter of May 1953, commenting on a paper sent him for comments, he said, "I'm rereading the paper. I'm again impressed with the fact that it is good stuff, that it hasn't been said before (so far as I know) and that it ought to be published. It isn't very exciting and it seems at times, as Henry James, Sr., is alleged to have said of somebody's work, to be 'insipid with veracity.' But that, I suspect, is because it is much more exciting to say that $2 + 2 = 5$ than to reaffirm the elementary rules that show them to be 4." In the same letter he remarked about some student that he "is by all means the best of the current crop in 'discussion'—which goes on and on." I suspect that one reason he left Ithaca was that he got impatient with what he regarded as interminable discussion, and that it was his experience with the Cornell department that led him to the view expressed later that in contemporary philosophy "the love of argument has supplanted the love of wisdom" (*TPR,* 368).

He loved to laugh. (And discussions at Cornell tended to be very serious, almost solemn, with tensions high.) As mentioned, he loved to go to the movies. He also took great delight in musical comedies, and on occasion would make a special trip to New York City to take some in. On Friday afternoons in Ithaca we could almost regularly if we were looking see Arthur Murphy walking past our house down Buffalo Street, a very steep hill, on his way to the movies. If he caught sight of one of us he would wave and yell a cheerful "Well, hello" and keep walking without breaking stride. He once told me that he had observed the filming, in Ithaca's dells and gorges, of episodes of the *Perils of Pauline,* one of the first thriller serial films, which may have helped develop his love of motion pictures.

One Christmas season in New York City, some time after my Cornell years, he took my wife and me to the movies and to dinner. The main film was preceded by an animated cartoon, one of the episodes of "The Nearsighted Mr. Magoo," during which Murphy laughed and laughed. At one slight break in the proceedings, he leaned over and whispered, "Isn't this silly?" and continued laughing. But his favorite modern novelist was Faulkner, who was not always very funny. His enjoyment of motion pictures went along with a considerable distaste for "cinematic aesthetes"; he once remarked that the measure of one's aesthetic sophistication was apparently "to like as little as possible." He had the same somewhat amused distaste for aesthetes of all kinds. If something was meant to be enjoyed and was worth enjoying he intended to enjoy it. His critical guard was up in philosophy and on matters of social policy, but not in the area of entertainment.

He had charm, in abundance, along with the gift of tongues. He was a witty very funny philosopher, but he was also a very serious philosopher with a deep sense of philosophy's importance, both in itself, as the embodiment of inquiry and as the expression of the need to understand, and in relation to the civilization in which it could flower and to which, in his view, if it is to be civilization, it is essential. He was a short round man with twinkly eyes and a voice like a bell. He had an almost pixie quality, with a constant undertone of irony. If you remember Joseph Welch, the Army attorney in the famous Army-McCarthy hearings, you will get some sense of what Murphy sounded like. With his wit and sense of humor, constant smile rhetorical gifts and high-pitched voice, he also sounded on occasion like Adlai Stevenson, and occasionally Daniel Patrick Moynihan reminds me of him.

His style was often epigrammatic, his writing framed by elaborate allegories or extended analogies, by which he invoked some recent event or historical occurrence or some incident in fiction to frame some general philosophical point. His lectures and conversations were laced with such devices. I was surprised to notice this trait in his earliest writings. Indeed, it can be seen in his address as valedictorian in 1923, entitled "Babbitt and Educational Ideals," an early effort at giving an account of education and the university which culminated in his remarkable Honors Day Address of 1945, "The Rewards of Learning," in which the pungent Murphy wit can be seen at its best (*RCG,* pp. 385–97, esp. 395–97). There are many examples of the use of allegory in Murphy's writing, so many in fact, that there is no point in pointing to any particular examples here and now,[8] and the reader will find a number of examples in this book.

Murphy's practice was to rise very early and write for several hours, until it was time to head for class or his office. He always wrote in long hand with a

8. However, I cannot resist referring to the use Murphy made of the analogy between Woodrow Wilson's reception in Paris in 1919 and what happened to the great hopes generated for a League of Nations, and Whitehead's move from the enlightenment and philosophical progress foretold in his earlier works to the disappointing surrender—in Murphy's view—to philosophical orthodoxy exhibited in *Process and Reality.* See "The Development of Whitehead's Philosophy" (1930).

fountain pen on unlined paper—quite often stationery, on occasion hotel stationery—and his writing, especially in later years, tended to form an arc heading downward at the right-hand side of the page. He rarely crossed out a word,
though on occasion he did revise extensively. He seemed to have everything he
wanted to say clear in his head as he was writing. Occasionally he wrote out an
outline, and occasionally he would make a fresh start on the same topic rather
than merely revising what he had written before—thus there exist two or more
different versions of some papers on the same topic—and often he finished a
paper on the same day he started writing it. On more than one occasion he
prepared a lecture or an address, gave it, and then put the manuscript away and
forgot that he had written it. He had his writings typed from his handwriting,
which, though usually clear, would occasionally give even the most expert typist trouble deciphering. But there seem to be just as many handwritten manuscripts, which he may never have had typed. Thus, after Hay and I published
Reason and the Common Good, and well after Murphy had discovered at the
end of chapter 5 of the original version of this book the section on "What
Happened to Objective Relativism" which he revised for publication in that
collection, I came across a paper of some twenty pages in longhand entitled
"Objective Relativism Reconsidered," written judging from internal evidence
in 1932 or 1933. I have no real doubt, apart from the fact that it was a reconsidered defense of objective relativism, that he had by 1962 forgotten all about it.
He had given up objective relativism by 1936.

    He spent years revising the Carus lectures for publication, something very
unusual for him, so several copies remain of the draft chapters. They seemed
to present special difficulties for him. The first title he chose for them was "The
Theory of Practical Reason," the title under which they were eventually published. But when they were delivered the title was "An Inquiry Concerning
Moral Understanding." In a letter of September 1952, well before he was invited to give the Carus lectures, he said, "I got back to Ithaca yesterday after a
fine summer in Santa Monica. My work has gone remarkably well and *I think*
I'm near the finish of the 'Theory of Practical Reason.' How does that sound
as a title for my book? Maybe I'll send you a copy of the chapter on the 'universality' of ethical judgments before long for your discerning criticism." He
didn't, and as it turned out he was not near the finish. In a letter of June 1954,
he told me that he had been invited to give the next series of Carus lectures and
had "agreed to do so on 'The Theory of Practical Reason'. So I'll now have to
put up or shut up on that subject. The lectures will be given at the meeting of
the Pacific Division next year and the book, I hope, will follow shortly thereafter. I wish you were near enough to be available for discussion of some difficult points." From a letter of January 1956: "The lectures are over. . . . What
I need now is some criticism. I have a second copy of the lectures (which, thank

God, were written before my other troubles began) and want to send them around to a select group of readers who will be willing . . . to tell me what is wrong with them before I finally commit myself in print. Would you be willing to serve? . . . [There are] some 90 typewritten pages. . . . There's a lot more written but not typed but I won't inflict that on anyone and the three lectures give the outline of my 'position'—such as it is." From a letter of April 1957: "The reason I didn't send you the manuscript of the Carus lectures was that I found so much in it that I wanted to change that it didn't seem worthwhile to bother you with a version that was already out of date. If this goes on the book will never appear. But I'm determined that it won't go on. This coming summer will be really free for work and the draft I then prepare will be, so far as I'm concerned, the final one. . . . You were quite right to surmise that the shift in titles from 'Practical Reason' to 'Moral Understanding' reflects a change in my way of handling the subject. My distaste for Kant has grown. . . . And while Hume gave all the wrong answers in moral philosophy he did ask the right questions. I'd like to think of what I'm doing as an answer to some of those questions. But the main emphasis is on 'Understanding', and here I'm more indebted to Wittgenstein's *Investigations* than anything else. . . . Your current disenchantment with your work has my sympathy—I've had the same experience often. I guess C. I. Lewis was right when he said that the thing to do is go ahead and write the stuff anyway, even if it doesn't seem inspiring. And when you get enough of it written you have a book. Then other people can refute you and you become an authority." From a note of January 1960: "My book . . . is almost done." From a letter of October 1961, typed this time: "I did get a copy of *Generalization in Ethics* and thank you for it. I haven't read it yet. I'm just finishing my own book—and really finishing it this time—and am postponing all reading that might get me to change my mind until I get what is now on my mind in print. Meanwhile your smiling countenance on the cover gives cheerful prospect of good things to come."

I referred earlier to a dramatic shift in Murphy's philosophical interests in 1941 or so. This is brought out, also dramatically, in his contribution to the symposium, "Can Speculative Philosophy Be Defended?" (1943), in which he said, "Nothing is today more important than the development of a sound moral philosophy," and he suggested the need for discussion of "the positive tasks that a constructive philosophy is today prepared to undertake to help in the organization of the harried but still hopeful world of our contemporary experience. It is imperative not only for the future of philosophy, but for that of our culture, that this constructive task be clearly defined and resolutely undertaken" (pp. 141, 143). This might have been merely the expression of a transient mood, stimulated perhaps by the fact that at the time of writing, 1942, the war was not going too well for the Allied cause. After all, in later work he argued against shelving the traditional tasks and problems of philosophy in favor of dealing with the contemporary problems of human beings in civilized society (cf. "Problems of Men," 1947, and "Pronouncements, Propaganda, and Philosophy," 1960). However, there seems some reason to think that Murphy's shining optimism of the 1930s and mid- to late 1940s receded in the last few years of his life into a sporadic pessimism, as his hopes, which he had expressed many times before, for a constructive philosophy which would not "become just another one of the 'isms' " were correspondingly diminished. "One part at least," he said in that paper of 1943, "of a sound philosophy is the capacity to see the several phases of our experience in their distinctive characters and categories, and to apply to each the methods and principles best suited to the articulation of its distinctive nature."

Some time in the early 1930s he started a book, to which he gave the title "Philosophy and Life," which he never finished. I have not come across any typed pages, but have at hand a considerable number of pages of handwritten manuscript. It is interesting for what it shows about his early interests in philosophy that early on he was interested in philosophy as a guide to life and as relevant to life. Thus, chapter 1 begins this way:

> If a realistic observer from some remote region of space or time were set down in America today and asked to give an account of what he found here under the title of philosophy his report, I suspect, would be something like the following. Philosophy in the first place is a subject taught in universities through the exposition, direct or second hand, of certain standard texts of great dignity and, in most cases, of considerable antiquity. A sympathetic acquaintance with these works, as with the Bible and Greek mythology, is regarded as an important part of a "humanistic" education and no one who is unable to appreciate polite references to them can be at home in really cultivated society. Again, philosophy is a subject pursued by professors in their professorial capacity under the guise of "research." The problems with which such research is concerned are abstruse and technical, with special assumptions and a peculiar language, which only the initiated can understand. This adds to the prestige of the researcher in university circles and qualifies the philosopher as a specialist who can speak with his colleagues in physics or biology on terms of real equality, since neither has one chance in ten of understanding what the other is saying. Finally, philosophy is a type of vague but edifying discourse on the "meaning of life" offered with considerable popular success by the liberal clergy, by the more forensic scientists in their mellow moments, by evangelical psychoanalysts, and, more awkwardly as a rule, by professional philosophers themselves when the exigencies of the educational system require it. Such, our observer might conclude, is philosophy in America, and in large measure he would be right.

But not altogether right. For the realistic observer has a way of missing something essential in human activities though often hard to discern in their external manifestations, the spirit that is in them and by means of which they live. And he would see, if he looked more closely, that these secondary activities borrow such worth as they possess from a genuine urgency in human nature itself, an interest baffled today by the complexities of a world to which its own demands seem strangely incongruous but vital enough to maintain itself though precariously and in reduced circumstance, even in such meager habitations as Dr. Will Durant has ironically offered as "The Mansions of Philosophy." Is it possible to work back from these externals of philosophy which today come so dangerously near to being the whole of it to the interest that supports them and to discern the conditions of its adequate expression? I believe that it is, and this book is an attempt to justify that belief. . . .

There are several chapters, some of them possibly finished though unrevised, others in outline form. One chapter, which sounds like the last, begins this way:

The question of our own connection with reality, and of the way in which philosophy intersects "life," has been of great concern for this generation. The few who have achieved the mountaintop of vision have been curiously inarticulate, while those who have not have had precious little to offer as a substitute. We have seen enough of these officious and bungling "philosophers" in the arts and sciences to realize that if philosophy has anything to contribute to life it will be just philosophy itself, and that is what the bunglers have never achieved. And hence the question recurs—how can philosophy be relevant to life, and where shall we stand to see reality?

But we know the answer, we had it all the time and gave it away in the first chapter, if only those who were inquiring had wit enough to read. We must survey reality from the inside, we said, and we must do so because our own standpoint is inside the world. It is a part because it is partial, and relativity is itself relatedness. We are connected to the world by all the forces of earth and air and light, and by the social and material conditions of our being. These are the connections with which philosophy is concerned—the very ones that generated its problem and the ones about which information is sought. Where shall we stand to see reality? Stand where you are—and open your eyes.

The remainder of the chapter, if there is a remainder, consists of notes, and there may be some unworked-out incompatibility between what was to be said at the end and what was said at the beginning. Nonetheless, these incomplete chapters, apparently put aside some time ago for reasons that are not evident, demonstrate quite graphically Murphy's main concerns and the sort of problem he grappled with all his life, that of constructing a sound and adequate philosophy that would be relevant to meeting the problems "to meet which philosophy itself arose."

He tried later to construct such a philosophy in *The Uses of Reason* (1943), a book that, though it was well received early on, was later derided by certain influential philosophers who felt that it was too much enmeshed in events no longer contemporary and dealt with and disposed of only some minor figures no longer of consequence. That is not my reading of a book that, in my considered judgment of long standing, is not just excellent but marvelous, though the references to contemporary figures and books of recent vintage may well bog it down by distracting from its philosophical points, which are now as they were then eminently sensible. It may be well to recall here the opening words of the preface of that book:

> To write philosophy in the present tense and with explicit reference to contemporary issues and doctrines is a hazardous enterprise. For the present of the writer will inevitably, even under the most fortunate conditions of publication, have become the past of the reader and will have lost something of its urgency and altered somewhat with this change in temporal status. This book was written in the summer and autumn of 1942, in the first year of America's participation in the Second World War. . . . One or two of the theories it criticizes have already begun to fade in popular esteem and it seems more necessary now than it did some months ago to remind the reader that they are here considered not chiefly for their individual importance but as symptoms of a state of mind which has a variety of spokesmen but does not alter in its animus or in its potency to confuse the issues of social policy. It would have been safer, surely, to discourse more largely on the eternal verities and maintain a cautious distance from the shifting particularities of the sequence of events.
>
> It is, however, of the essence of the philosophy presented in this book that it can practice no such aloofness and claim no such immunity from the hazards and lessons of history. The philosophic reason it is concerned to exemplify is inescapably involved in the process in which events, losing their immediate urgency as occasions for action, become the subject-matter for reflection and critical evaluation—the process through which we learn from and by experience and apply what is learned to the intellectual mastery of a new present, thus gathering the fruits of temporal experience in a practical wisdom that will stand the test of time.

And he tried again, still later, with *The Theory of Practical Reason,* which he may have worn himself out trying to make better than he could. Still, the temper of that work is on the whole optimistic, as is, on the whole, the philosophy of Arthur E. Murphy. He might have accomplished more philosophically, and perhaps come closer to living up to the high expectations some had of him, if he had not persisted in taking on additional administrative and committee responsibilities. But, if he had not done what he did, he would not have been the person he was.

Murphy died of cirrhosis of the liver. He had had on the whole a pleasant life—he was always cheerful, at least in public—but that was not a pleasant death. Yet not long before he died he said to me, "And I never drank very much, except to be sociable." He was very sociable indeed. And he was almost invariably sensible, exercising and manifesting the virtues he prized most—good will, good sense, and good judgment.[9]

---

9. In this memoir and the other prefatory matter I have drawn on occasion from other accounts I have given of Murphy in the past: the preface and introduction to *Reason and the Common Good*, with W. H. Hay (1963); "Two American Philosophers: Morris Cohen and Arthur Murphy," in *American Philosophy*, edited by M. G. Singer (Cambridge: University Press, 1985), pp. 295–329; the Introduction to "Pragmatism and the Context of Rationality," *Peirce Society Transactions*, 1993, pp. 123–41; and my article "Arthur E. Murphy," forthcoming in the *Biographical Dictionary of Twentieth Century Philosophers* (London: Routledge).

Introduction
Contextual Analysis, Objective Relativism, and Speculative Philosophy

As I said in "Arthur Murphy and American Pragmatism," the introduction to "Pragmatism and the Context of Rationality" (1993), during his lifetime Arthur Murphy was one of the most well known and highly regarded American philosophers, and since his death his reputation diminished to the point of being nearly unknown today in this country and altogether unknown abroad. Hence this work, unpublished and unknown for over half a century, needs an introduction. I will first say something about what this book is about and about the author's conception of philosophy,[1] and in the process will quote liberally from some unpublished portions of the manuscript (designated by *CP*, short for *Contemporary Philosophy*). I will then go on to give some account of contextual analysis, objective relativism, and the distinction the author operates with between critical and speculative philosophy.

This book is about what an adequate philosophy should do and how it can be tested, and about the role of reason in organizing and making sense of experience and in arriving at an adequate conception of reality. "The primary interest of this inquiry," the author insists, "is not historical" (p. 1). It is not merely a commentary on the work of others, though there is considerable commentary on others. Rather, the commentary is the vehicle for supporting the author's vision of what philosophy at its best can be, by contrast with what in the hands of a number of outstanding thinkers it has been.

1. As we might also say, his "philosophy of philosophy," nowadays often called "metaphilosophy." As the latter is a term of philosophical analysis, however, like "metaethics," it might be thought to be that of a contending party, and is thus not fitting in this context. The suit alluded to is *Pluralists v. Analysts,* to use the names coined by the plaintiffs, the contention between those who recognize the claims of speculative philosophy to philosophical legitimacy and/or even engage in the activity (pluralists), and those who do not (analysts). In the 1930s through the 1950s the current defendants were the plaintiffs, and the case would have had a somewhat different name.

The last chapter of the original manuscript begins this way:

> The standpoint of philosophy is that of the reasonable organization of experience, in which nothing humanly significant is needlessly omitted, nothing is seen out of focus or blurred by a biased or one-sided interpretation, and nothing included as true or valid which . . . is found . . . to produce such distortion and thus to impede the development of that comprehensive sanity which is the final fruit and justification of philosophical enlightenment. . . .
>
> The discipline required . . . is that demanded by a matter of fact world which is larger and more varied in its structure than any or all of our ideas, that can be understood only on its own terms and not on ours. . . . There are no short cuts in philosophy, and there is no standpoint so authoritative or congenial as to warrant its selection as the basis for a philosophy until its adequacy has been made out . . . over the whole area of experience in which it claims jurisdiction. A philosophy which can meet these requirements . . . must be just and subtle and broadly wise, and its wisdom . . . must be based on knowledge of the varieties of experience, the categoreal structure of its major aspects and undertakings, the possibilities of the integration of these and of the ideas and beliefs that accompany them in an harmoniously ordered whole, and an adequate valuation of the activities and interests which in this integration should have a primary place. . . .
> (*CP*, ch. 9, pp. 2–3)

It is in the light of this ideal of what philosophy at its best can be that the discussions in this work are to be understood. The author was unqualifiedly optimistic in thinking that this order could be fulfilled. But even if unfulfilled, its credentials as an ideal are not thereby discredited. For the author has been arguing that the dominant philosophies of the immediate past have not only failed to fulfill these aims, but have become so entrapped in the preconceptions from which they started as to have forgotten what they were about. Murphy was fond of repeating Santayana's conception of the fanatic as one who redoubles his efforts when he has forgotten his aim, and he comes close to saying this about the competing philosophies he is examining. His view of the great speculative philosophers—whom he never tired of studying—is that they at least were aiming at attaining an overall vision, a comprehensive outlook, and in this they were superior to the analytic or linguistic philosophers, in whom the love of argument has supplanted the love of wisdom[2] (*TPR,* 368), and who

2. This last remark, of course, quite apart from the fact that they hardly ever argue but are attempting to articulate a vision, is in no way applicable to either Whitehead or Alexander. *TPR* abbreviates *The Theory of Practical Reason; RCG, Reason and the Common Good.* Murphy on the whole had little patience with linguistic analysis, especially that practiced by the logical positivists, which he regarded as bad philosophy just insofar as it was good linguistic analysis. "One

continued "expertly sharpening their linguistic tools" without any conception of what they were to be used for (*RCG*, 245). The author was not disparaging technique. As he further says in the unpublished section from which I have just quoted:

> Philosophy . . . is an arduous and subtle investigation in which it is uncommonly difficult to avoid certain typical short cuts and consequent mistakes. It is . . . so precarious an undertaking that we should be tempted to abandon it altogether, if it were not for the fact that we are committed to it by the need for a reasonable ordering of our experience, and . . . we cannot surrender this, with the discrimination and adjustments intrinsic to it, without surrendering what is best in ourselves. We have, however, no special faculty of "reason" competent to impose its own order on the facts. . . . Reason in operation is a makeshift and precarious affair, borrowing its content from limited areas of experience and guided by interests and preferences of dubious adequacy. It can maintain itself, therefore, only insofar as it is able to achieve a standpoint from which the local and ephemeral can be discriminated from the relatively permanent and inclusive and the scope and interrelation of its various categories and usages adequately estimated. (*CP*, ch. 9, p. 8)

The book as a whole is an argument for the hypothesis formulated in the first chapter that, as A. I. Melden has stated it, "reason when intellectually responsible to the quite particular subject matters to which it addresses itself can serve to provide us with philosophical insight about the way things really are, this in contrast to the intellectual misadventures to which speculative philosophers are led who, because of their zealous preoccupation with certain ideas, give them an unlimited application to every conceivable subject-matter, thereby depriving them of whatever explanatory function they have in the quite particular circumstances in which alone they have any intelligible application." Murphy tells us that "a philosophy that takes itself seriously . . . is a way of dealing with problems and difficulties that arise in the course of men's attempts to set the various aspects of the experienced world in some sort of order, and the measure of its worth is its adequacy for that purpose" (p. 4).

A number of the philosophers discussed in this book are now little known and rarely referred to, even though earlier in the century they were in the forefront of philosophical discussion. This is a phenomenon of every generation and era; a number of philosophical writers now in the forefront of philosophical discussion will be little known half a century from now, though of course

---

is hard put to it to distinguish linguistic sophistication from philosophical naivete in such cases" (*CP*, ch. 8, p. 125). However, he was much impressed with the work of the later Wittgenstein, and that influence can be seen working in *TPR*.

we cannot now say with any assurance who they are. However, let the philosophers discussed herein be taken as representative of certain tendencies in then contemporary philosophy—even though they themselves did not regard themselves as thinking and writing in any representative capacity. Many of the preconceptions they operated with are not now accepted and may seem the vestiges of a distant era. Still, it is not hard to understand what the author of this book is saying about them.

The philosophers not now discussed are Alexander, Roy Wood Sellars, and McTaggart. Others, such as Bradley and Bosanquet, are not now much discussed, Bosanquet hardly at all. Still others—such as Whitehead, Peirce, and Russell—are currently well known and will be so for as far ahead as we can see, for they have entered the philosophical pantheon. However, although Whitehead's philosophy is paradigmatic of speculative philosophy, the excursions of Peirce and Russell into speculative philosophy may not be well known, and that is the aspect of their views that comes in for discussion here. Others not now discussed are the New Realists of 1912 and the Critical Realists of 1920, though some of the members of those two philosophical parties, such as Santayana, are still known and discussed.[3]

It is my considered judgment that the discussions contained in this work are sufficient to explain what the philosophers being discussed are attempting and to appreciate what the author is saying, and that any further explanation in this introduction would be otiose. Although philosophers currently say little if anything about the problem of "ultimate reality," this sort of question has been constant and persistent in the history of philosophy from Plato through Kant. Though the question of what is *real* is not now at the forefront, ontological questions of what there is and what it is to exist are still with us, and the appropriate translations are easily made.[4] The speculative philosophers discussed in this work were, most of them, endeavoring to find an organizing scheme of ideas (often now called a conceptual scheme) and principles for interpreting and explaining everything there is.

3. *The New Realism: Cooperative Studies in Philosophy,* by Edwin B. Holt, Walter T. Marvin, William Pepperell Montague, Ralph Barton Perry, Walter B. Pitkin, and Edward Gleason Spaulding (New York: Macmillan, 1912); *Essays in Critical Realism: A Co-Operative Study of the Problem of Knowledge,* by Durant Drake, Arthur O. Lovejoy, James Bissett Pratt, Arthur K. Rogers, George Santayana, Roy Wood Sellars, and C. A. Strong (London: Macmillan, 1920). The particular dispute between the new realists and the critical realists may now be dead, but the issue between realists and anti-realists, though it has now taken on a different form, is not, may never be.

4. Every one of the philosophers discussed in this work is also discussed, though with greater brevity, along with many others, in John Passmore's superb tour-de-force *A Hundred Years of Philosophy* (London: Duckworth, 1957).

Contextual Analysis

The critical method that the author judges essential for philosophical clarity he calls contextual analysis. Ernest Nagel observed that in *The Uses of Reason* of three years later Murphy's "chief instrument of clarification is the method of contextual analysis which pragmatists have brought into contemporary prominence." [5] Murphy would not be likely to deny this. He said in that work that pragmatism's "emphasis on the plurality of contexts in which ideas can function significantly, and on the importance . . . of interpreting them specifically by reference to their use and function in such contexts, is . . . the greatest single contribution to critical philosophy of our time." [6]

Murphy arrived at the name "contextual analysis" after first employing (after P. W. Bridgman) the expression "operational analysis" and then giving it up after seeing how Bridgman generalized the philosophy of "operationalism" into a speculative metaphysics out of his operational analysis of fundamental physical terms. Operational analysis, Murphy would say, has lost its operational bearings. In chapter 8 of the original manuscript he explained the reason for this shift from "operational" to "contextual analysis." The reason is instructive:

> If "operational" is, as I once took it to be, a synonym for "contextual," then an *operational* theory of meaning does seem in fact to provide the essential basis for any *philosophical* analysis of meaning. If, on the other hand, "operationalism" is a method of *identifying* the meaningful with what some particular set of operations enables us to test or even to *point to* in a particularly obvious manner, then it bears upon it the marks of "analysis" not at its best, but at its worst. . . . It is precisely when we want to indicate relations and uniformities that are not fully exemplified in any particular . . . instance that we resort to general ideas. . . . The instances derive their "meaning" from the fact that they are instances of a structure which . . . no "agglomeration of actual happenings" ever completely embodies. . . . The use of general terms is different from that of terms that can be used denotatively . . . and . . . their sense is to be determined by their role in the theoretical activities which could not stir a step without

5. Review of *The Uses of Reason, The Journal of Philosophy* 42 (1944): 665.

6. Murphy, *The Uses of Reason,* 1943, p. 86. Cf. ch. 3 below. In the same year, Murphy said of "Moore's Defence of Common Sense" (1925) that it is "one of the few really decisive contributions to philosophical enlightenment which this century has given us" (*The Philosophy of G. E. Moore,* 1943), p. 301; *RCG,* p. 108). Murphy obviously regarded these two critical procedures as closely allied, though he never wrote anything about them taken together. In Murphy's view these two accounts—Moore's and Peirce's in "How to Make Our Ideas Clear"—were transcendently important contributions to critical philosophy.

> them. . . . Since the term "operation" . . . suggests such a limited and
> misleading reference it had better be abandoned. . . .
>
> No general theory about the way in which words "refer" to . . . objects
> can take the place . . . of . . . contextual inquiry into the manner of their
> use in the specific activities in which they have a primary meaning. . . .
> (*CP*, ch. 8, pp. 121–122, 124)[7]

In a key 1939 paper Murphy described contextual analysis as "the interpretation and criticism of statements made in terms of their use and testable validity in the contexts in which, *prior* to either epistemological or metaphysical
analysis, they have a discoverable use and meaning," and he claimed that "a
contextual analysis and testing of ideas used in philosophical discussion is
the indispensable basis for any adequate theory of either knowledge or nature" ("Dewey's Epistemology and Metaphysics," 1939, pp. 195–96, emphasis added).

Murphy hoped to avoid christening contextual analysis as an "ism," though
that construal of it did occur and there are philosophers who have been happy
to call themselves contextualists. Murphy was not one of them.[8] He meant this
method of analysis to be neutral among competing substantive views. Whether
it is or not is, like all philosophical points, disputable, though it will not be
disputed here. But contextual analysis is best seen, in accordance with its own
precepts, in operation, in its appropriate context, rather than in abstract descriptions of it, and it is applied throughout the book.

Objective Relativism

Murphy advanced the idea of objective relativism in his first philosophical paper,
"Ideas and Nature." Objective relativism, which was stimulated by Einstein's
theory of relativity and by metaphysical theories, such as those of Alexander
and Whitehead, that arose from it, is the view that events rather than objects
are the primary ontological category, and that the relations things and events
have to one another are essential to their nature. In one relation something has

---

7. In a note to "Two Versions of Critical Philosophy" (1938), Murphy said: "I am using 'operational' here in a wider sense than that of Professor P. W. Bridgman in his *Logic of Modern
Physics* (New York: Macmillan, 1927). Its closest kinship, as I employ it, is with C. S. Peirce's
theory of the meaning of signs and particularly of the 'logical interpretant.' If Peirce's original
article on 'How to Make Our Ideas Clear' had been used as the basis not for a theory of truth
but for a clarification of ideas which are philosophically ambiguous until operationally interpreted, it would have eventuated, I believe, in the sort of critical philosophy here recommended"
(*RCG*, p. 96n). Cf. *The Uses of Reason*, pp. 145–52, on Bridgman, and pp. 296–98, on contextual
analysis.

8. In "A Program for a Philosophy," 1935, Murphy referred to "the 'contextualism' which [he]
imbibed from [his] Chicago colleagues" (p. 362). At that time it was, clearly, still evolving.

one set of characteristics, in another relation a different set. This relativity, which extends to the relations between events and observers (hence the alternate name, perspective realism), is not subjective but objectively real. Hence events and things are objectively real only in their relations to one another, that is, only relative to one another; this relativity is objective; hence objective relativism. "The cat," Murphy said, letting it out of the bag,

> has many characters under many conditions. Each belongs to it in that context, and the cat would be a poor thing apart from its characters. They are relative to it, and it to them, and this objective relativity is the ultimate fact about nature, and about the cat. (1926, p. 211)

In "Objective Relativism in Dewey and Whitehead," he said that objective relativism

> attempts to unite two propositions which have uniformly been taken to be incompatible. (a) The objective facts of the world of nature and of reality are the very "apparent" and relative happenings disclosed to us in perception. (b) In spite (or because) of such objectivity such happenings remain ultimately and inescapably relative. Such relativity is hence an ultimate fact about the objective world. . . . (1927; *RCG*, 50)

On objective relativism events are fundamental, "the stuff of nature" (*RCG*, 56), and to "events time does make a difference." Objects are not basic but are "characters of events"; the "relations of an event are internal, and it is precisely that fact that distinguishes it from an object" (*RCG*, 53).

Murphy did not advance objective relativism as "a complete and coherent philosophy as it stands," but as the basis of a research program that would have to "justify itself in many fields" while "the work in most of them has yet to be done" (*RCG*, p. 66). And he continued to develop the view in a series of papers and reviews in the period 1927–33. Then, in less than ten years, Murphy arrived at the conclusion that objective relativism had to be rejected.

So "what happened to objective relativism?" At one level, Murphy observed in the section of this book published in 1963, objective relativism is enlightening in stressing "the essentially contextual meaning or reference of statements" (*RCG*, 68). Thus the development of contextual analysis was coterminous with the realization that objective relativism had to be rejected. But then, as he says about so many of the views scrutinized in this book, objective relativism was generalized beyond the significant limits of its meaning and application:

> The "objective relativist" holds that "the object" really owns all its appearances and that railroad tracks are *really* convergent when they appear to be. . . . [But] the convergent tracks are not "real" as the "real" tracks

are, for a physical train will not run on converging tracks. Either therefore the physical system in which the tracks are *really* parallel and not convergent . . . has a definite pre-eminence, or else we have simply identified the real object with its appearances and are back . . . in the extravagances of "new" realism.

   If the first alternative is chosen . . . the merely relative appearance does not disclose the physical object as it really is. If the second is accepted, a chaotic phenomenalism in which everything truly is what it appears to be will be the outcome. . . .

Murphy's later diagnosis, which he dubbed a melancholy one, was that the failure of objective relativism "lay in its neglect of the consistent application of *contextual* principles" (*RCG*, 72–73). Objective relativism

   was right in insisting that the perspective relativity of the observable aspects of perceived objects to the conditions of observation . . . is not a barrier to our finding out by observation what such objects are. . . . But it was wrong in neglecting to make clear that this claim is made not in the interest of a theory of the essentially "perspective" character of "reality" . . . but rather in order to specify contextually what the sources of our information are and how and in what degree they function as ways of knowing. . . . (p. 75).

Murphy's general conclusion was that

   The development of objective relativism . . . confirms in a striking . . . way the hypothesis with which we have throughout [this book] been working. *What* "real" object, *what* datum, *what* cognitive relation are we here concerned with? Objective relativism was too faithful to its epistemological antecedents to answer these questions precisely. It is therefore right and appropriate that it should eventuate in speculative philosophy and bequeath to that inquiry the equivocal harvest of its terminological ambiguities. (78)

Thus, owing to its neglect of contextual principles, objective relativism "became just one of the 'isms' and has shared their fate" (*RCG*, p. 74).[9]

---

9. Murphy gave a somewhat different account, in entertaining and lucid fashion, of objective relativism and what led him to give it up, in "A Program for a Philosophy," 1935, pp. 359–60. The view, regarded as a contender in the epistemological championships then at stake, was discussed in a number of places in the 1920s through the 1940s, most prominently in chapters 3 and 4 of A. O. Lovejoy's *Revolt Against Dualism* (1930), though Murphy accepted neither Lovejoy's interpretation nor prognosis. A somewhat more recent discussion of interest is Thomas Robischon, "What is Objective Relativism?" *Journal of Philosophy* 55 (1958): 1117–32. I cite it for those if any who are still curious to know the answer. On Robischon's analysis, there are several answers.

Some elements in his 1935 account are especially illuminating in this context. There Murphy said:

> As a critical weapon my theory worked well. But . . . when Whitehead, in whose earlier works the principles of objective relativism seemed clearly implied, turned speculative metaphysician in *Process and Reality,* my disappointment was deep. Surely, so pervasive and deep-rooted an error must have its origin in something fundamental to current philosophy itself. . . .
> The fault I found in contemporary philosophy came not from a violation of the rules on the part of some competitors, but from the very nature of the rules which all were following. "Objective relativism", if it was to do its business, could not be one among these systems; its whole notion of the function of philosophy must be different. With this realization, my "objective relativism" . . . passed beyond itself in Hegelian fashion and ceased, as an "ism", to exist. (1935, p. 360)

Critical and Speculative Philosophy

What is this speculative philosophy that is here under review, and which objective relativism, by the neglect of contextual principles, eventuated in? Murphy is not, as I interpret him, disparaging speculative philosophy in toto and in every respect. This book is not a wholesale attack on views that do not satisfy some version or other of a verifiability principle and therefore are to be accounted meaningless. Murphy does not claim that the philosophies he criticizes are meaningless. He claims that they have not made out their claims to be believed and that they cannot do so, and that they are involved in what is essentially an intramural conflict when what they should have been doing is redefining the game by revising the rules—for, on the view he advances, given the operative rules, it is a game that no one can win.

Still, it is a game that can be played well or badly, and what Murphy does disparage is "the speculative philosopher in a hurry," whose "ruling passion" is the "passion for the identification of things which, though essentially related, are nonetheless essentially distinct" (1947, *RCG,* p. 125). And his greatest scorn is reserved for such egocentric subjectivists as Kierkegaard:

> Kierkegaard was an original and penetrating thinker, and a singularly honest one. What he lacked was wisdom. He was not even a lover of wisdom. On the contrary, the passionate one-sidedness and egocentricity of his thought are of its essence. . . . An "existentialism" thus limited in its conception of "reality" is simply, in its philosophical pretensions, an attempt to raise egocentricity to the level of a metaphysical principle. . . . If Spinoza is properly described as a "God-intoxicated man," Kierkegaard is, in the same idiom, a self-intoxicated one. It is a significant commentary

on the tortured sensibility of our own time that it has found in the latter, rather than in the former, the appropriate expression of its own religious experience. (Review of *A Kierkegaard Anthology,* 1947, pp. 703–4)

What Murphy says about speculative philosophy, both in general and in application to the varieties of it he examines, is respectful and more restrained than this. He regards every one of the writers with whom he deals as a genuine philosopher, a lover of wisdom, if not a successful one.

We are not really looking for a definition of "speculative philosophy." That is provided by the context and by the book, especially though not solely in chapter 5, in the sections on "What 'Speculative Philosophy' Is" and "Speculation and Speculative Philosophy." And the book supplies enough examples of speculative philosophy to provide a definition by example. What we are looking for is an explanation of the usage.

"Speculative philosophy" has to be understood as correlative to what it is contrasted with, "critical philosophy." Claiming that philosophy is divided into these two types, Broad defined critical philosophy as involving "the analysis and definition of our fundamental concepts, and the clear statement and resolute criticism of our fundamental beliefs." Speculative philosophy, on the other hand, aims "to take over the results of the various sciences, to add to them the results of the religious and ethical experiences of mankind, and then to reflect upon the whole. The hope is that, by this means, we may be able to reach some general conclusions as to the nature of the Universe, and as to our positions and prospects in it." Broad claimed that speculative philosophy presupposes critical philosophy, and thought that "in the first we tacitly assume some things that belong to the second." [10]

Although Murphy accepted this distinction pretty much as Broad drew it, he did not accept Broad's account of critical philosophy, which he labelled "epistemological," and in "Two Versions of Critical Philosophy" (1938) he presented an alternative version of critical philosophy, which he then called "op-

---

10. C. D. Broad, *Scientific Thought* (London: Routledge and Kegan Paul, 1923), pp. 18, 20, and "Critical and Speculative Philosophy," in *Contemporary British Philosophy,* edited by J. H. Muirhead (London: George Allen and Unwin, 1924), vol. 1, pp. 82–100. Broad returned to this topic in "Some Methods of Speculative Philosophy," *Proceedings of the Aristotelian Society,* supp. vol. 21 (1947): 1–32. In the latter piece, Broad replaced critical philosophy with the notion of philosophical analysis, defined speculative philosophy as a combination of synopsis and synthesis, defined *synopsis* as "the deliberate viewing together of aspects of human experience which are generally viewed apart" (p. 4), and defined *synthesis* as aiming to "supply a set of concepts and principles which shall cover satisfactorily all the various regions of fact which are being viewed synoptically" (p. 16). W. H. Walsh has an interesting criticism of Broad's "antithesis" in his *Metaphysics* (London: Hutchinson University Library, 1963), pp. 189–95.

erational" and then later, as we have seen, "contextual." Critical philosophy, on Murphy's view, is, or ought to be, contextual analysis.

The adjective "critical" has had an interesting career, still far from over. Throughout the nineteenth century "critical philosophy" was the name for "the critical philosophy" of Immanuel Kant, and no doubt it still is in certain quarters. In this century "critical" has served as the adjective for a number of different labels, naming a number of different views: first "critical monism" and then the "Critical Realism" of 1920; today we hear of the "Critical Theory" of the Frankfurt School, and also of (the unrelated) "Critical Legal Studies," one of the contemporary schools of jurisprudence. Ideological labels often have interesting careers: "legal realism," a forerunner of "critical legal studies," had a number of adherents from the 1930s on; however, it has absolutely nothing to do with any form of "realism" that has ever been advanced in philosophy, whether epistemological, ethical, logical, aesthetic, or metaphysical. Perhaps it is just as well that Broad replaced "critical philosophy" with "philosophical analysis"—itself not easy to define and standing for a number of different views and methods—and that Murphy moved to contextual analysis, though he often spoke of the latter as the key method of critical philosophy.

The expression "speculative philosophy" is not common currency at this time, has not been since the 1950s. There is no entry under that name in Edwards' *Encyclopedia of Philosophy* (1967), not even an index entry, a fact that I found surprising. In 1867, W, T. Harris started *The Journal of Speculative Philosophy,* the first distinctively philosophical journal started in North America—actually the first journal devoted to philosophy in the English-speaking world. Harris's *Journal of Speculative Philosophy* ceased publication in 1893, but was revived—at least the name was revived—in 1987 at the Pennsylvania State University, a sign that speculative philosophy had already undergone something of a revival since the 1940s and 1950s, the heyday of analytic and anti-metaphysical philosophy.

Metaphysics and speculative philosophy certainly overlap, yet they are not identical; there are examples of non-speculative as well as analytical or critical metaphysics. Strawson distinguished descriptive from revisionary metaphysics on the ground that while "descriptive metaphysics is content to describe the actual structure of our thought about the world, revisionary metaphysics is concerned to produce a better structure." [11] Revisionary metaphysics, as described, is a form of speculative philosophy, and "revisionary" here seems a synonym

11. P. F. Strawson, *Individuals* (London: Methuen, 1959), p. 9. An interesting critique of Strawson's distinction is given by D. W. Hamlyn in *Metaphysics* (Cambridge: University Press, 1984), pp. 4–8, esp. p. 8.

for "normative." But descriptive metaphysics is not speculative philosophy; given that it is metaphysics, it is clear that not all metaphysics is speculative philosophy.

Starting in about the sixteenth or seventeenth centuries in Britain, "speculative philosophy" was used to distinguish distinctively philosophical studies from "natural philosophy," later called science or natural science. This conforms to the history of philosophical speculation and is in part the explanation for the name Harris chose for his journal. The first speculative philosopher was Thales, or else Anaximander, a pupil of Thales'. Philosophers now lumped together as pre-Socratic speculated about the nature and origin of the universe and life on earth and the nature of that from which all things derive. So the pre-Socratic philosophers were speculative philosophers in that sense. Socrates redirected inquiry onto ethical subjects, yet there is certainly speculation in Plato and Aristotle. Some of the early speculations, such as Democritus's about atoms, were early versions of what were later treated as scientific hypotheses. However, the speculative philosophy Murphy is examining, that Broad defined, and that Whitehead, Alexander, and McTaggart engaged in, is not speculative philosophy in that sense.

Whitehead defined speculative philosophy as "the endeavor to frame a coherent, logical, necessary system of general ideas in terms of which every element of our experience can be interpreted." "Can be interpreted" means "that everything of which we are conscious . . . shall have the character of a particular instance of the general scheme. . . ." Whitehead adds that "[p]hilosophers can never hope finally to formulate these metaphysical first principles," [12] which implies that the first principles of speculative philosophy are metaphysical principles, so again we have overlapping. Whitehead speaks of the "fallacy of the perfect dictionary," defined as the belief "that mankind has consciously entertained all the fundamental ideas which are applicable to its existence," and divides philosophers into two schools:

> the "Critical School" which repudiates speculative philosophy, and the "Speculative School" which includes it. The critical school confines itself to verbal analysis within the limits of the dictionary. The speculative school appeals to direct insight, and endeavors to indicate its meanings by further appeal to situations which promote such specific insights. It then enlarges the dictionary.[13]

There is then some resemblance between descriptive metaphysics and "the critical school," and between revisionary metaphysics and speculative philoso-

---

12. A. N. Whitehead, *Process and Reality* (New York: Macmillan, 1929), pp. 4–6.
13. A. N. Whitehead, *Modes of Thought* (Cambridge: University Press, 1938), pp. 235–36.

phy. But why did Murphy (and Broad and Whitehead before him) talk about "speculative philosophy" rather than metaphysics?

Let us go back a hundred years to Calderwood's *Vocabulary of Philosophy*, where we find the following definitions: "Speculative philosophy is metaphysics, concerned with the problems of Being, as these transcend observation and experience"; and metaphysics is "speculative philosophy, transcending questions as to the nature of mind, and including the general problems of Being—ontology. This department of philosophy is concerned with the whole range of speculative problems." [14] Though this gives every appearance of going in a circle, it does tell us something: speculative philosophy is metaphysics, concerned with ontological problems, and metaphysics and speculative philosophy are essentially related.

In his 1930 review of *Process and Reality* Murphy characterized it as "Whitehead's systematic and exhaustive answer to the metaphysical problems raised in . . . his earlier works . . . [and] designedly an excursion into speculative philosophy in the grand and traditional manner . . ." (*Journal of Philosophy*, 1930, p. 433). But the shift between these two terms is not just a form of elegant variation.

Kant's *Critique of Pure Reason* is a critical examination of pure speculative reason, and actually of speculative reason, hence of (pure, that is, solely a priori) speculative philosophy. So the Critical Philosophy, Kant's, is set off against the Speculative Philosophy. The speculative then came to be thought of as any claim that went beyond, transcended, the bounds of any possible sense experience. And in the nineteenth century speculative philosophy came to be identified with the philosophy of Hegel.[15] Since "critical philosophy" is the philosophy of Kant, given that critical and speculative philosophy are conceptually polar—a not too implausible assumption—speculative philosophy is dialectically the philosophy of Hegel, as well as of its descendants, which would include Bradley, T. H. Green, and McTaggart, and so to the other philosophies discussed herein. The idea stems from Hegel, who maintained that what Kant labelled transcendent and beyond human reason, hence specula-

14. Henry Calderwood, *Vocabulary of Philosophy* (London: Charles Griffin, 1894), pp. 318–19, 233.

15. See Hegel's *Logic*, sec. 82: "The Speculative stage . . . apprehends the unity of terms in their opposition. . . . The speculative in its true signification [does not] say something merely subjective. . . . [O]n the contrary, it expressly rises above such oppositions. . . ." And sec. 9: "Speculative logic contains all previous logic and metaphysics . . ." (*The Logic of Hegel*, translated by William Wallace [Oxford: Clarendon Press, 1892], pp. 152–53, 16). In Baldwin's *Dictionary of Psychology and Philosophy* (1901), Dewey has a nice account of "speculation" in the relevant sense: "the conclusion and completion of the movement of thought which apprehends the unity of categories in and through their opposition. It has this . . . technical sense in the Hegelian philosophy."

tive metaphysics involving speculative reason, is philosophy in its speculative mode or "moment."

This then, post Kant and post Hegel, is the origin of the idea and the expression. Those who championed speculative philosophy were transcending Kant. If Murphy, and Broad before him, had spoken of metaphysics instead of speculative philosophy, it would have been misleading, since their characterizations and criticisms, whether or not they validly apply to speculative philosophy, clearly do not apply to all metaphysics, and to make the point clearer they would have had to speak of speculative metaphysics. Speculative philosophy is metaphysics, that is, speculative metaphysics. But it is more than just that. As should be apparent from the specimens here examined, speculative philosophy embraces more than just metaphysics, it embraces the whole of philosophy; and "speculative," I venture, provides the needed emphasis. Hence the language should be no more mysterious than metaphysics—and indeed, philosophy—itself.[16]

16. In relation to this brief study of the nature of speculative philosophy—or rather, into the history and uses of the expression—I have learned much from two works: *Speculative Philosophy,* by A. J. Reck (1972); and Manley Thompson's study of "Metaphysics as Speculative Philosophy," in *Philosophy,* by R. Chisholm, H. Feigl, W. K. Frankena, J. Passmore, and M. Thompson (1964), pp. 133–60. Another work of interest is J. E. Creighton, *Studies in Speculative Philosophy,* edited by H. R. Smart (New York: Macmillan, 1925), by a Hegelian who developed a view he called objective (opposed to Berkeleyian) and speculative idealism, which is "genuinely speculative philosophy" (p. 257); see in particular ch. 14, "Two Types of Idealism," pp. 256–83. The just published *Cambridge Dictionary of Philosophy,* edited by Robert Audi (Cambridge: Cambridge University Press, 1995), contains (page 758) a brief entry on speculative philosophy by Calvin Schrag, as nice, accurate, and informative an account as could be wanted.

Reason, Reality, and

Speculative Philosophy

1 Philosophy in the Contemporary World

Method and Intent of the Work

What is the present situation in Anglo-American philosophy? Where do we stand with respect to the issues and problems which, during the past half century, have engaged the attention of philosophers and to whose solution so much effort and genuine wisdom have been devoted? The question has an historical reference and in answering it we shall be concerned with one phase of the history of philosophy, that of the past still sufficiently present in its influence to determine the subject-matter and direction of current investigation. The primary interest of this inquiry, however, is not historical. This is a period in philosophy of hesitation and confusion of purpose. Sporadic crusades for new and ephemeral doctrines, ingenious apologies for old beliefs, retreat into special investigations, logical or historical, which enable one to be philosophically occupied without having a philosophy, and a troubled desire to be socially useful without any just notion of what philosophy could usefully do for society are features of the present situation of an activity that does not know where it is going or what essentially it is about.

It is time for us to get our bearings, to see where in fact we are, and what, in the light of past experience, we can reasonably hope to accomplish. This book is an attempt to provide such a survey.

From what standpoint, however, is this survey to be made? Each of the major philosophic undertakings of recent times offers its own version of the truth about the world and of the success or failure of various philosophies in their attempt to attain it. In estimating the validity of its claims it might seem that one must be either an ally or an opponent. In either case [one's] survey of the situation will be but another version of the proof that Idealism (say) though crushed to earth will rise again, that those who knew not logical analysis in its latest developments walked in darkness and confusion.

If attempting to find out the results and value of the prolonged debate in which philosophic investigation has come so largely to consist, [such a survey]

3

will be just another contribution to that debate. Or, if impartiality is wanted, one can simply list the positions taken and points made on each side, balancing what each doctrine offers in its own favor with the charges that other claimants to ultimate truth or critical finality bring against it, leaving the reader to choose for himself which on the whole he finds most plausible.

Is there any other way than this of understanding a philosophy? It seems to me that there is. For a philosophy that takes itself seriously is not just what somebody thought and what somebody else said about it. It is a way of dealing with problems and difficulties that arise in the course of men's attempts to set the various aspects of the experienced world in some sort of order, and the measure of its worth is its adequacy for that purpose. However special and technical its analyses may become, they arise out of the need to find an understandable "reality" for things that we know in non-philosophic experience to be genuine and essential but which current doctrines and preconceptions underestimate or exclude, and they mean to eventuate in a view of the world that enables us to see its aspects in their appropriate order and relations and to respond to them in their fullest discoverable significance. Somewhere between this beginning and this ending it is all too likely to become confused, frustrated in its purpose, and finally led off into controversies that are interminable because there is now no way back to facts by reference to which they could be settled. This is not something that adherents of a rival philosophy say about it when they wish to push their own wares at its expense. It is something which we can see happening to it, and that has happened too many times in the recent past to be any longer a surprise except to those who are peculiarly immune to the lessons of experience. Imposing systems of great initial promise arise, each [the] spokesman of some essential interest to which commonly tried doctrines have done less than justice. Each would bring philosophy back to earth by relating it to facts which the plain man knows, or the good man knows in his heart, or the experimental scientist can demonstrate in his laboratory, and which have been culpably neglected in past philosophy. Taking its stand on these facts it develops a method of its own and is able, by relating the "abstractions" of merely special interests and limited views to the truth it takes as central, to tell us something fruitful and important about them. We enjoy a new freedom in dealing with facts and see a heightened significance in their connections. This is philosophy as we had hoped to see it. Anyone who has read Bradley's *Ethical Studies* or *Principles of Logic,* or Dewey's *Experience and Nature* or Whitehead's *Adventures of Ideas,* will recognize what this sense of a new philosophic insight can be. These are men whose understanding cuts across conventional divisions and gets us at things that really are essential but which, in terms of current and limiting ideas, we had been unable adequately to see.

And then something happens. The doctrine which began as a correction of a too-narrow system becomes an apologist for special interests of its own. There are facts that we did not clearly see before that it can teach us to see better. But there are other facts to which its methods are not so evidently appropriate and its effort to deal with these lead to ingenious but finally futile constructions in which ideas meaningful in a special context must be stretched beyond recognition and categories systematically misapplied to give a specious generality to a theory whose claims have actually been unwarrantably extended. The result is a system that is vast in its pretension but dubious in its application, into which all facts will fit when they have been transmuted by the questionable alchemy of an ambiguous terminology and which can include all that is "real" or significant within its scope only when the nature of the "real" or the "significant" has first by dialectical maneuvering been limited to that which it can include. Its claim will then be questioned by the spokesman of a different interest, equally genuine, equally limited, and, in its philosophical elaboration, equally unable to make good its claims. Since each can prove the other wrong, the debate between them is a lively affair, calculated to convince those already persuaded, to make effective replies [to] opponents, and to divert the attention of all concerned from their failure to discern those principles of discrimination and relevant connection which will urgently require [us] to make our response to a complex environment as adequate as it ought to be and as applied intelligence can make it. Considered in this light the philosophies of the period take on a somewhat different aspect than that which they wear in their disputes with their major rivals. In these disputes it is what divides them that receives primary attention. It cannot be *matter* that is the essential reality of things; it must be *feeling*. We cannot understand the validity of ideas by treating them as referring to "antecedent existence"; their *ultimate* reference is always to "experience." What "metaphysicians" (the philosophers with whom one disagrees) allege must be nonsense, since *the* criterion of significance is provided by a "language" which they do not ever profess to follow. In their working application, however, it is the similarity between all these theories that is most impressive. There is a pattern that they follow not revealed in the claims and counter claims of the debate. It is the pattern of theories stretched to cover situations to which they are really inapplicable, in the mistaken belief that only through such extension can we secure a criterion of properly philosophic ultimacy and scope, of theories whose inadequacy is demonstrated by their final disconnection from any other experiance. The standpoint for our inquiry into the present philosophical situation, as the outcome of recent developments, will be that of the history of their rise and decline, of what happens to them when they attempt fully to meet the demands of the situation to which they claim, at least in principle, to be adequate.

But is this really a fair alternative? It will be obvious from remarks already made that I have my own ideas as to what philosophers ought to be doing, and that my analysis of their success or failure may be "biased" by the standpoint from which I interpret them, which is not, certainly, that from which they have been inclined to interpret themselves. And what will that be but *my* philosophy set over against the others, and claiming the right to judge them all in terms of selected criteria of adequacy? We shall not then have got outside the argument, but simply have added another voice to swell the volume of the dispute.

The question is a fair one. And it can be fairly answered. The analysis I propose has in fact its own standpoint and criteria, as it must have if it is to reach determinate results. But I do not ask that this be accepted in advance as the basis of truth by approximation to which the claims of other theories are to be judged. It is offered simply as an hypothesis, and one that can be tested by its factual application. Suppose these philosophies actually developed out. The circumstances under which these philosophies developed are known: the primary sources of their inspiration, the fields in which their ideas found persuasive and fruitful application, the points at which they seemed to their contemporaries peculiarly unconvincing, the devices by which they attempted to meet objections and to fortify their primary claims, the extent to which their final results have remained entangled in the special preconceptions which qualify their selected objects "as real" in the eminent sense but cut them off from connection with what we regard as really genuine and reliable in non-philosophic investigations. If the account here given enables the reader to understand how all this could happen, how philosophy as an investigation carried on by men in a known social situation has come to be what it is, then it will be so far justified. For it is not a stipulation of what philosophy ought to be or would have been if only men had seen the light of some special truth now hopefully advanced, but an analysis of what it has been in fact.

I propose in the remainder of this chapter to outline the hypothesis in question. It is not one which is especially plausible as it stands, and no claims are made for it on its own account. It is an instrument to be used, a way of classifying and relating the facts so as to reveal a structure or pattern that makes them more intelligible. It can be justified only in the whole course of the discussion. But it had best be as explicit as possible at the start. There will be enough to puzzle us in the subsequent inquiry without the complication of doubt as to what we are looking for and what, if we could find it, would settle the questions that confront us.

The Rational Use of Ideas

Suppose then, that the nature of the philosophical enterprise were as follows: Our ordinary cognitive use of ideas is to get us in touch with the world we live in, especially those parts of it that have important bearing on the realization of our desires, in such fashion that we shall know reliably what to expect of it and how to use it for our purposes. In this process of finding out what to expect and what to do, in order to realize our ends, we represent the things around us by means of what, for our primary purposes, we can safely take them to be. One factor in the situation is called a horse, another a thunderstorm, another a hero and leader. In each of these identifications we are, as Santayana has said, "calling names with provocation"—we are recognizing the objects in question or pointing them out to others, in terms of what we like or dislike about them, or what we intend to do to or with them or what we expect them to do for or to us. And there is no doubt that in this manner we often understand each other reasonably well.

Yet this use of ideas is not always reliable, even on the most elementary levels. We may be drunk or dreaming; the light falls oddly on a distant object and we mistake its nature. Our leader proves when tested to be all too human. We require from the start a working distinction between the specious and [the] genuine, between what things look to be and what they are in fact. And this we have in the working tests or criteria in use in our various activities. What purports to be a horse, or a thunderstorm, or a hero, must meet anticipated tests if it is to prove its claim. Up to a certain point its status may be dubious, beyond that point a decision can be reached. These tests are not formulated and argued, as a rule, and it would not be easy for a person who uses them intelligently to say what in detail they are. They function in communication and investigation as the means of settling an argument or inquiry, they determine what we shall look for and what will satisfy us within the limits of our various interests. A real horse is one that is really a horse, that meets our expectations and requirements, such that, given doubt on these points we are inclined to withhold the term in question and when we are satisfied as to them our hesitation ends. To find out what these criteria are in any case, it is best not to *ask* those who use them what they "mean" by the term in question—an inquiry in which philosophers have sometimes and not very fruitfully engaged—but to observe them at work, to see in the kind of situation in which serious questions arise what those concerned with them look for as a relevant answer to the question, and what, after investigation, they are prepared to accept as being in fact the solution of their problem.

These criteria, more or less explicit, have an all-important place in the development of knowledge, for they determine both the direction in which inquiry proceeds and the point at which it will cease—they mark the beginning and end of argument and hence the boundaries of reflection or critical procedure. They may be called our preconceptions, but the use of the term should not suggest that there is anything irrational about them. They represent, rather, the means by which reason works, when it appears as practical sagacity,* and without the organization which they provide we should not be able to stir a step in the effective use of our experience.

It has sometimes been said that a man's ultimate preconceptions constitute his philosophy, his "outlook on life," the standpoint from which he orders and organizes the world as he know its. But "philosophy" in this sense is something quite different from the reflective inquiry which usually goes by that name. It provides the material upon which philosophy works, but, as it stands, it does not generate inquiry at all. It simply sets its limits.[1]

Such elementary wisdom, however, is always in the end the prey of sophistication. Men come to doubt not only the claims of specific beliefs to satisfy accepted criteria but the authority of accepted criteria to serve as standards for the validity of belief. Some actions are good, others bad, by the principles which normally find expression in approval or disapproval. But is the "good" thus certified *really* good? What one nation approves in this fashion, another condemns, and nature seems indifferent enough to all such classifications. The "real" motion of the planets, as observed from the earth, is not their *real* and intelligible motion, as the scientist would describe it. The ordinary perceptual tests do not apply here and would not actually be appropriate. And so for a multitude of conflicts in jurisdiction between the very notions which, on a more elementary level, were themselves the criteria of the real.

Out of such conflicts arises the need for reflective philosophy. Reason is now to be applied to the work of reason itself, and we are to find a justification for that which was itself the justification of our beliefs and valuations. "Justice" needs some better grounding than the verdict of just men, and a Socrates is required to establish the claims of morality, not on the basis of use and acknowledged authority, since these have now been questioned, but by a deeper searching of the real purposes of men who know themselves and what their good consists in. The claims of knowledge are to be maintained against the sceptic who would make man the "measure," but for this purpose Plato must go beyond the ordinary tests of sensible reality to a real existence of which the commonly accepted world is only a reflection. And so on. It is not the conflict

---

1. See Thorstein Veblen's penetrating discussion of the way in which the notion of "reality" as "a preconception, accepted uncritically, but applied in criticism and demonstration of all else with which science is concerned," has functioned in economics to determine the nature and tests of ideas employed (Thorstein Veblen, *The Place of Science in Modern Civilization* [New York: Viking, 1919], pp. 149ff).

* Between "sagacity" and "and without," and within commas, the original has "and mad sense," obviously an uncorrected typist's error, possibly for "and makes sense" or "and made sense." In neither case does it fit very well, and in the absence of convincing evidence I omitted it altogether. Ed.

as such that constitutes philosophy in the sense in which we ordinarily know it, but the attempt to find a standpoint from which these claims can be rationally adjudicated.

The development so far is quite inescapable if the rational organization of experience is to proceed. What has been attacked, and what a growing and complex experience will lead men to attack again and again, is the ultimacy and inclusiveness of preconceptions which in their ordinary use *are* the measures of relevance and finality in our thinking. If a real thing like a tree or a house is not what it shows itself to be in our reliable perceptual commerce with it, then what is it? Well, perhaps it is a pattern of electrical charges, all behaving very oddly. Or, if we take another and no less respected line of reflection, it may be an idea in the mind of God, a transitory but meaningful expression of the eternal purpose. The plain man may dislike such speculation: a primrose by the river's brim is still just a primrose, so far as he is concerned. And there is much good sense in his insistence on this elementary fact. But unless he is plainer than he has any right to be, unless his innocence has become a dogmatic and sophisticated refusal to pay attention to facts which he suspects would lead him into difficulties, he will know that there are other ways of regarding this modest flower than his own, and he may even be duped into supposing that, since eminent scientists say so, the primrose just is his own idea of something which is not a primrose but a set of pointer readings, and that so to regard it is to see more clearly how, in spite of appearances to the contrary, this may be God's world after all. At this point, he, like many who have reflected more extensively on the subject, will be in a state of utter confusion as to the status of the competing "realities" presented for his attention, and while he will, if he is wise, go on dealing with primroses in the usual fashion he will no longer know with any assurance what confidence he ought "really" to put in the judgments which, as a matter of fact, must remain the basis of his ordinary commerce with the world.

There is no use in blaming philosophers for this situation. They did not invent it, and the difficulty would still remain if they all stopped talking about it forthwith. In fact, they are usually people who are particularly troubled by it, and want, if they can, to clear it up. It is an accident of exposition that before they can get people out of the difficulty they must first make them more precisely aware of it, and that this first part of their work is the one that commands most general attention. The real difficulty lies with a world which is broader and more complex than any of our ideas, and yet can only be apprehended in terms of them. It proves docile and amenable to our categories over a considerable area, getting us accustomed to seeing it in some neat pattern or another to which we are comfortably habituated. And then it presents itself in a new guise to which accustomed ideas are inappropriate and challenges us again to match our wits against its surprises. The tactics of human reason in meeting this challenge, in devising new and subtler means of tracing out reliable patterns in a world not made to its measure, constitute an impressive achievement, one of the few, perhaps, in which we have unqualified reason to take pride. But it has as its inevitable accompaniment this disturbing problem of testing the scope and finality of tests which, in their appropriate context, simply *are* the means through which we know the world. We are to decide, if we are to act intelligently, how we are to use such ideas, where they are appropriate, and how we are to understand their relation to that which is beyond their scope, but which is somehow "real" on its own account nonetheless.

The Standpoint of Philosophy

How is this decision to be made? The philosopher is to adjudicate conflicting jurisdictional claims among ideas and, by putting each in its place, allow us to make our total response to the world as inclusive, as discriminating and as harmonious as possible. This, as it stands, is a great task and an essential one. How is the philosopher to accomplish it? The usual answer to this question, the one which philosophers, in one way or another, have usually given, is this. The trouble with our ordinary ideas is that, while they work well enough *for certain purposes,* they are neither ultimate nor inclusive. If we try to [make] special tests of perception, say, the measure of reality we shall find that there is much in its own fashion real to which they do not apply and hence that the "reality" they specify is inadequate and incomplete. There are more things in heaven and earth than such criteria can comprehend. And what such tests take as real is in fact, *for other purposes,* unreliable enough. If we want something to satisfy our souls, or to meet the precise requirements of physical measurement, or to provide a permanent basis for all that changes and passes away, we shall find the things perceived to be but shadows after all. They are not the answer to the questions we want to ask at this stage, and, for these purposes, are to be regarded as not ultimate but provisional.

What we appear to require, then, is something that will be ultimate not in this limited and provisional sense, but finally and inclusively. This would provide the criterion which as philosophers we seek, and, when we got it, we should be able to order the various aspects of experience by their relation to it. This "Reality," at once final in its authority and inclusive in its scope, would provide the standpoint for a philosophy, and by reference to it the work of reason in the organization of experience could be completed, not in any absolute way perhaps, but at least in principle and on the whole.

With the more traditional identifications of such an ultimate standpoint of reference we are all familiar. It may be that all things are ordered by final reference to the good, or that they are modifications of an Eternal Substance whose essential nature is known under the infinite attributes of thought and extension. It may be that in the primary sense all is matter, and human thought and reason are accidents of material configurations or phases in the dialectical development of an historical process in which the necessary next step is the revolutionary dictatorship of the proletariat. We shall in this book be concerned in the main with subtler and more sophisticated products of the philosophical imagination. A pragmatist who scorns all such "metaphysical" excursions will nonetheless insist that "experience" is the ultimate and exclusive referent of all ideas and that the effectiveness of such ideas as instruments for the resolution of doubtful situations is the final test of both significance and truth. We shall find at work in this claim the very same philosophical interest that inspires the Platonist and ultimately confuses his results. What is important here is the recognition that a construction of this sort is the natural answer to an imperative question, and that if it would work it would be a very good answer. We do really need to know what credence we ought to give to ideas which are admittedly useful for some purposes, but plainly irrelevant to others. And our difficulty is that these ideas to be criticized are themselves the criteria of reality and genuineness where they do apply at all. It is natural to say that [the] "reality" they define is *provisionally* real; it suffices for some purposes and in some circumstances. But, taken as ultimate, on its own account it is misleading, unreliable, a mere appearance. It presents an aspect only of the world with which we are dealing but is no reliable guide to its intrinsic nature. Or, if we come at this matter from a more sceptical standpoint, it is an abstraction, useful for certain purposes, but needing a reference to some further fact, the "concrete" experience from which it was derived, or the social organization in which the activity that defines it is carried on, if it is adequately to be understood. An electron is not really a charged particle moving in its own peculiar fashion, in a curious sort of space; it is a construction which the scientist finds it useful to make in order to arrive at equations which will find their ultimate validation in the improved use to which society can put the natural resources at its disposal.

Not only does this enable us to discount the misleading appearance of ultimacy which such ideas have, to distinguish the real from its mere appearances or, to vary direction, to understand ideas in their context in ordinary human experience, to refuse to "misplace concreteness," * but also to see these working ideas in a much wider setting, and thus to find a meaning in them which in their isolated independence they did not possess. It is comforting to know that

---

* The phrase "misplaced concreteness" is an expression coined by Whitehead to mark the "error of mistaking the abstract for the concrete" (*Science and the Modern World* [Cambridge: University Press, 1926], ch. 3; 1932 edition, p. 64; also *Process and Reality* (New York: Macmillan, 1929), p. 11). Ed.

"the things that pass are only shadows" and that the eternal purpose works in all things, however incoherent they may appear. It is no less heartening for a different type of mind to see that one substance underlies and conditions all the changes in nature, or that one method—that of "research science"—is adequate in principle to answer all questions that can intelligibly be asked. If we can see that cultural phenomena are all basically functions of the relation between the forces of production and their social and legal organization we shall have a principle of literary criticism, moral exhortation and economic analysis all at once. We want, then, some standard of reference not relative and provisional in its own turn, and we want some underlying pattern in which all that we know can be significantly related. And since we do find that much which, considered in itself or as the object of a merely special and limited interest, seems arbitrary and unintelligible, can take on a new and helpful meaning when placed in a wider context and considered with respect to relations which, for its own purpose, it neglects, there seems every reason to suppose that the work of philosophy, thus understood, is the adequate answer to an inescapable and fundamental problem.

Such is the seeming, and it has been potent enough to inspire some of the greatest minds the human race has yet developed. Yet I believe we now know enough from hard experience to see that it is essentially misleading and that philosophy is unable in fact to perform the task it has traditionally undertaken. And this is not because philosophers have not done their work skillfully; on the contrary their achievement has been a triumph of ingenuity, imagination, and wisdom of the highest order. It is simply because the undertaking rests on an assumption about the structure of the knowable world which we now have good reason to believe is false, and this falsity displays itself precisely in the discrepancy between the intentions and methods of these philosophies and their actual results.

The assumption is that there is some set of categories so ultimate and inclusive that in its terms the whole of the experienced world, in our various dealings with it, can be intelligibly organized. Interpreted speculatively this would mean that we can find an aspect of the world at once ultimate and sufficient so that to understand it we need refer to nothing but what in its own nature it contains, while to understand anything else we must discern its status as an aspect or derivative of the ultimate reality in question. Interpreted critically, it would mean that there is some context of "experience" or some method of inquiry so fundamental that all ideas are significant and valid only in their reference to it, while it itself needs no further validation than that which [within] its own limits it can secure.

So far as I can see this might have been the truth about the world, and if it had been the rational organization of experience would have been a much simpler affair than it has proved to be in fact. Philosophers were fully justified in looking for it long and earnestly, and in refusing to be discouraged when many efforts in this kind ended in failure. The goal, after all, is far and high, and we should not expect that the first attempts to attain it would be wholly successful. There are many reasonable men today who would say that our failure so far to find this ultimate standard of reference was no real reason for supposing that it was not there to be found. And so long as we consider philosophy simply as the set of problems with which philosophers find themselves concerned, this might seem a satisfactory attitude. Devotion to principle may amount to a lofty idealism, and one may reasonably admire the intellectual [courage] of the metaphysician who refuses to abandon his quest for "reality" even after such continuously discouraging results. But devotion to principle may actually mean a tenacity in the maintenance of congenial preconceptions and a stubborn refusal to learn from hard experience the inapplicability of one's ideas to the world in which they are supposed to apply. Such tenacity has something magnificent about it, but its consequences are less admirable. For it leads to the analysis of facts in terms of categories inappropriate to their nature, and it cuts the philosopher off from aspects of experience which, falling outside the limits of his favored "reality," are out of place in his philosophy. And when that philosophy is offered, not as an ingenious imaginative construction, but as a reasoned integration of experience in all its humanly reliable aspects, the result is an unhappy one. We simply cannot make the discriminations that are required for clear thinking, or grasp the connections essential to a comprehensive understanding, in the terms provided. The failure to do so narrows experience and confuses conduct, for it leaves us without any reasonable notion, except in special and relatively routine procedures, of what we are about and what would really satisfy us in the undertakings in which, as rational beings, we are engaged. The actual dissociation between philosophical canons of "reality" and "authenticity," and the criteria required to make comprehensive sense of our non-philosophical experience and activities should, by this time, be sufficiently apparent. It is time, I believe, to ask ourselves seriously, and with specific regard to the working of actual philosophical systems, whether this dissociation is not reasonable evidence of the inapplicability of current philosophical assumptions and procedures and whether the failure to revise those assumptions, in the light of knowledge now available, is not a mark rather of intellectual irresponsibility than of metaphysical profundity.

The Way Philosophies Work

It is when we introduce into this context the notion of "ultimate reality," or of the meaning of ideas and *the* standard of truth by which in all our rational dealings with the world we must be guided, that its inadequacy becomes manifest. In itself a beautifully simple idea, it does not serve to simplify or enlighten this undertaking; on the contrary it complicates it hopelessly and prevents its satisfactory eventuation. For if we suppose that the way to understand a provisional criterion of limited range of application is to judge it as revealing an aspect of a "reality," or fulfilling a purpose other than those defined by its own specific case and contextual meaning, we misrepresent it. Perceptual knowing becomes a method not of finding out how things look and feel under ordinary conditions of observation, but a bad* guess at the ultimate nature of matter or a way of trying to be certain about the relations of sense data and material objects, which, from its nature, it cannot be. And if we treat any standpoint whatever which human ideas can specify and human use justify, as ultimate not provisionally and for its own purpose but as the adequate basis for an answer to all significant questions, we distort it beyond recognition. "Experience" or "feeling" or "matter" or "love" must then be extended to include their own opposites and a set of non-discriminating words, which seem to provide a means of talking about everything while in fact they borrow what significance they have from special contexts whose limits they must in principle refuse to acknowledge, are the necessary counters of such philosophies. And their outcome for all [the] ingenuity of their authors is the confusion which we should expect from a systematic misapplication of categories.

It is sometimes supposed (particularly by Wittgenstein and his followers)† that this extension is a sort of unaccountable perversity, an original sin of the intellect, which tempts us to ask pseudo-questions which in fact are without sense. We shall see that this is not the case. It is a normal incident in the attempt to discover *the* criterion of reality or of significance. For if knowledge (say) is actually of many sorts, and if we try to judge them all by a single standard, then we shall *have* to say that what passes as knowledge in its own field is not *really* knowledge by our standard. The relevance of the standard is assumed, since *as philosophers* we must have some ultimate reference for all our truth-claims. What we get is at once knowledge and not knowledge, but it is what knowledge of the more dubious sort *meant* to be and in failing to be this it appears to be falling short of its critical alternative. The alternative to this, and the only adequate critical alternative to any variety of philosophical reduction, is a contextual analysis of the use of the ideas in question. What we have so far failed altogether to realize is that this means a refusal to judge these ideas, in

---

* The original has "gad," which could be a misprint for either "bad" or "good." In general, better "good" than "bad," but it is my judgment that by a slim margin "bad" better fits the context. Ed.

† This was written in 1938–40, before the publication of Wittgenstein's *Philosophical Investigations*. Chapter 8 of the original, "Philosophical Analysis," contains a discussion of Wittgenstein. Ed.

their primary meaning, by other criteria, or in a different context than that of their specific use, and hence, since such contexts are many, the surrender of the attempt to find an ultimately significant context to which all elucidations of meaning are to be referred. If there were such irreducibly distinct contexts, and if we operated on the assumption that there could finally be but one, *then* we should find in every variety of philosophy considered a critical confusion of categories of the sort described. We should find, for instance, that [the] "experience" which is actually rendered specific by the *sort* of activity in which it functions, [the experience] categorized as [the] experience * which confirms or confutes a theory, the aesthetic experience which verifies nothing but may supersede thinking in an immediately satisfying intuition, [and] the "experience" of the psychologist which is merely "had" or enjoyed *before* any interpretation is placed upon it—[that] all these would be "experience" but none would do duty for any of the others, and to treat "experience" without qualification as the referent of ideas would be to rob it of any specific meaning. If this were the case, again, we should find the most analytic of logicians tempted to lay down general specifications for meaning, specifications which applied in fact to the operations which they regarded as particularly reliable or important, and then ponderously proving that what had not *this* meaning—ideas involved in a different inquiry, for example—was simply meaningless. What would have happened would be that a *special* set of criteria had been made the basis for a general standard and thus that experience, verification, etc., had to take the special form they assume in this inquiry without surrendering their claim to generality. If this were the case then we might expect something like "physicalism," and [we could] understand it.

It is equally evident that each such identification would be at once irrefutable and inexcusable. It could always interpret the most recalcitrant material, since this would have neither "meaning" nor "reality" until it *was* interpreted in just these terms. If statements are meaningless unless capable of physical verification, then it must be evident that the language not only of science but [of] all intelligible discourse must be the physical language, since only this will have a meaning. If all our statements refer to future experience and [what] we can expect to be, then statements about the past refer to it no less, otherwise they would have no object and no sense. And those who deny this must surely be trying to create an "antecedent reality" out of all relation to human experience. So the "translation" into the terms of the accredited theory goes on, and in principle there is no limit to its success. The technical virtuosity of the philosopher in making the construction may be great, and the result, as in Whitehead's *Process and Reality,* a remarkable feat of constructive imagination.

* In the original, "experiment," replaced here by "experience." Ed.

Yet the essential inadequacy will remain. What has been interpreted is not the facts of non-philosophical experience, as these are encountered on their own level and in the context in which they have a reliable meaning, but only the version of them which remains when they have been reduced to what *another* standpoint can say about them. Nothing is easier than to show that the results of physical inquiry cannot stand in the way of our most hopeful religious convictions. It has been done many times, first by philosophers and more recently by scientists who have some theological leanings. All that is required is to interpret the results of science not *as science,* in the field of their tested meaning, but as attempts at philosophy. Thus judged they are seen to be inadequate, mere appearances, an abstract "aspect" of the world, incomplete in themselves, and ripe for reconciliation in a higher truth. With such an "aspect" theologizing philosophers have no difficulty in dealing. The reconciliation of science (properly interpreted) with religion (adequately understood) is an ironic achievement of the simplest sort. That the reverse process is equally easy, that any instructed psychologist bent on indicating the universal applicability of the scientific method can reduce religious experience to a neurotic symptom by simply specifying that as a sober man, he will acknowledge no more in it than what as a psychologist he can test and verify by processes eminently branches of abnormal psychology, is equally obvious. And it has been done. Each side can dispose of the other, and hence the method, being so catholic in its application, can hardly be as satisfying as we should in advance have supposed.

And each side will be successful not only in its reduction of hard cases to its own measure but also in its proof that the theories that reject this reduction as inadequate are plainly wrong. For the idealist is attacking, e.g., not "science" itself, with which, on its own level, he has of course no quarrel, but only a *special interpretation of science,* called materialism, or what not, which some misguided scientists, publicists, and left-wing agitators have seen fit to adopt. *Other* scientists, Nobel prize winners and sound men will be found as firm as ever in their belief in spiritual values. Now materialism, if we are right, like every other "ism" which finds a single type of object as the referent of all significant predication, really is inadequate. When this has been pointed out, in a sufficient number of chapters, a Gifford Lecturer has only to lower his tone from the controversial to the confidential, to recall to our mind those aspirations of man which "mere" naturalism has never been able to satisfy and to lead us gently to the conclusion, darkly discerned even at the outset, that it is wisdom to believe the heart. If he is not met by the critic who insists that with religious experience *as such* he has no quarrel, but [only] with the interpretation put upon such experience by idealistic philosophers intent on justifying their antecedent bias and belief and escaping into the imaginary security of theologically supported values from a world where they ought to be facing the reality of experimental fact and social need, it is only because critics of that sort are not so frequently asked to give Gifford Lectures.

It is not the damage that each side inflicts on the other in this debate that is serious. For that can always be shown to be due to misinterpretation or to sheer inability to see the fundamental facts on which the theory is based. [What] is [serious is] the damage that it inflicts on itself in the course of its own development. And here the wound is mortal. Each genuine philosophy, we have said, had its inception and inspiration in its contact with an aspect of fact which was genuine and important, but neglected and misrepresented by opposing theories. Here is material for ideas to work on, there are leads to be followed and discoveries to be made. The philosopher who takes his stand on the experience of common men can find in such experience something that any reasonable man ought to know, something without which his adjustment to the world would be abstract and incomplete, since it would be made in neglect of facts which are humanly relevant. When Dewey brings us back from the rarified atmosphere of Absolute Idealism to the homely, practical relations in which refined ideas can make connection with the hopes and fears of ordinary men he does a great service. Its implications for education, for social reform, and for the valuation of intelligence itself are of the first importance. But what is this "experience" on which we take our absolute stand? Is it not itself a relative and contextual affair, the experience of objects, and of a world we never made, but of which our ideas claim nonetheless to afford true knowledge? How does experience occur within nature, and [within] "antecedent existence" if ever there was one, and how does it afford knowledge of it? We can profitably take the human standpoint and see all things as they appear in experience. If we are to retain our sanity we must also be able to assume a different standpoint and see human experience as an event in a natural world in which it occupies a late and precarious position, and yet of which it affords us knowledge. We need to do this, not because Santayana is around the corner waiting to denounce as "half-hearted" a naturalism that takes experience as its ultimate basis of reference, but rather because we need this reference to context and conditions to make "experience" itself a specific and fruitful notion. Experience is "real" to be sure, and its critically fundamental position must not be neglected. But it is real when and insofar as it is specified by the transactions—the commerce—with an independent world in which it is a factor. The idea of "experience" needs the criticism which this operational specification provides to have a fruitful reference. When the reference fails, we begin to deal with non-discriminating words, with an "experience" which must be all things to all men and which to have at once specific content and philosophic scope must be both experience of some special brand, which is definite but inadequate as the referent for all ideas, and "experience" without specification, which can plausibly claim to be adequate to all human interests, since all in *some* sense refer to experience, but which as it stands is useful only for refuting a philosophical opponent and giving the appearance of finality to equivocal statements. The disciple of experience then by turns makes himself the spokesman of some particular interest in which the appeal to experience means, for instance, the control of social conditions, and appears to hold that only in *this* context have ideas a meaning and possible validation or else, disclaiming such narrow criterion, he includes in experience the reference to non-experienced objects and to the past which he appeared at the start to be excluding. And in that sense it is hard to see that he is asserting anything definite or significant at all. This ambiguity and this generation of equivocal referents are essential to the position defended. And not merely to Dewey's position but, as we shall see, to that of his critics as well.* It is only in this fashion that one can reconcile the contextual specification of the content of an idea with its pretension to philosophical generality. The ultimate newness † of this procedure—and it is often most unhappy in its result precisely where the initial standpoint promised most—is that the philosopher ceases to deal with the subject-matter with which he began and finds himself instead in a world of categories that apply in fact to nothing identifiable outside the circle of his own debate. That is why the idealistic justification of religion always seems so thin, why the realist's attempt to defend the common man's belief in knowledge lands him finally in paradox and sophistication, why the logical positivist's insistence that only the language of science is intelligible leaves him with a calculus of languages in which any choice of a "language" is conventional, and [why] that [language] which scientists of our "culture circle" have decided to use [is] as groundless as any other.‡ *We have seen this happen,* not to one philosophy but to many. Why is it that the splendid promise of Whitehead's *Concept of Nature* had as its complement the sterile constructions of *Process and Reality?* Why is it that this great philosopher, interested in talking about the *concrete* fact as we know it, should have ended by identifying this fact with feeling, and provided for "feeling" a general reference and structure like nothing that ever was on land or sea? This is the major tragedy of recent philosophy. Each philosopher in order to say what was true and important, what needed to be said if reasonable men were to see their world for all it is worth and each part of it in its connection with the rest, was compelled

* Murphy's discussion of Dewey appears in chapter 3 of the original, "Pragmatism," not published here. It was published in Part 2 of the three-part article "Pragmatism and the Context of Rationality" (1993), at pp. 346–68. Ed.

† Although "newness" is the word that appears in the typescript, it seems clearly a misprint for something else. Ed.

‡ Positivism is discussed in original chapter 8, "Philosophical Analysis." Ed.

to say along with it what was not true nor defensible. And in the hopeless defense of his position he was forced to generalize his theory not by actually broadening its application but by confusing its reference in such fashion that it has ended by treating of entities and a world which, so far as can be seen, has no relevance outside its own controversial interests, and appears to have it only through this persistent ambiguity. This is the fatality which overtakes our theories. And if our hypothesis is right we know why it should be so. It is because what was ultimate in its own context and essential as one of the factors without which the experienced world could not be "concretely" understood, has been made ultimate unconditionally and "concrete" as it stands. This spurious "concreteness" is the property of a concept that refuses to recognize its contextual limits and pretends to a range of application which is general only so long as it remains equivocal and gains specification only by reference to a usage which contradicts the generality of its pretensions. And of such are the mansions of philosophy. It is to this pass that the search for "ultimate" reality and "ultimate" significance has brought us in a world where no such ultimacy is attainable and where the claim to it dislocates and confuses our use of the criteria by means of which we understand what happens and what we can and ought to do.

The Contemporary Problem

There is one final phase in this development, and it, also, is familiar enough. Any philosophy, we have said, can justify itself if its preconceptions are accepted. Each is evidently false if a different doctrine has the floor. How then is the choice to be made between them? It will be determined by taste, or temperament, or perhaps by the drift of current opinion. In any cultural epoch there will be certain undertakings that enjoy especial prestige. Evidently successful in their own territory, the ideas used, say in religion, or physical science, or economics, or political debate will tend to spread into the adjoining country. We need *some* standpoint after all for interpreting this confusion of tongues with which our special interests leave us. And what should it be but that which we know to be appropriate and reasonable in the activities which, by common consent, are doing their business well? If evolution is the watch-word, we shall see the world as in flux and growth; nothing "static" must be permitted even in such apparently static regions as that of logical analysis. If the age is one of democracy, we shall want a democratic science and a democratic God. Where psychoanalysis has proved its utility in the treatment of nervous disorders, it should be possible to show that everything from the love of mathematics to the love of money is an expression of a love at once embarrassingly specific in its derivation and hopelessly equivocal in its manifestation. If the period is one of economic crisis, nothing will be "real" but what bears directly on this issue or arises directly out of it, and we shall have left-wing mathematics and crossword puzzles to express fully our awareness of the social struggle. *We have seen this happen,* not once but many times in the past few years, as the notions appropriate to a special discipline gain popular prestige, become for the time the idols of the cultural market place and are honored in their turn as sources of philosophic wisdom.

What we should have expected from philosophy in all this, what we had a right to expect, was some sort of leadership. What was wanted was a criticism of the relevance of these ambiguous notions, a discrimination of the context of their significant application from that to which they are ludicrously inappropriate, a sense of proportion, solidly based on knowledge of the breadth of experience and variety of the significant contexts and of the contribution each can make to a rational life, that would enable men to keep their heads and use their reason. This was by no means unattainable in principle. One did not need a knowledge of absolute reality to understand that the "reality" to which popular psychologists referred when they urged us to "face reality" was defined by nothing more ultimate than the range of their own commonplace interests and that to "escape" from such a reality might well be the mark not of mental maladjustments but of some measure at least of cultural discrimination. Philosophers, perhaps, should have cared for none of these things. Their concern was with a more subtle and laborious extension of categories of limited meaning by generalizations of dubious significance. But at least they need not have been imposed on by them. Yet what, but this, in the long run, decided the rise and decline of the reigning philosophies? Idealism was the philosophy of a period of cultural expansion, when spiritual significance was spread abroad and when men found in the world around them the path to that realization of purpose which in spite of scientific developments of a disquieting kind, they could still regard as God's will no less than their own. Logical analysis in its technical developments reflects quite clearly the academic environment of "research" in which it developed. Where all experts are specialists the philosopher must be a specialist, too, with a language and professional manner of his own. And when today at philosophical congresses the one flock or the other congregates to consider the present situation in philosophy is it not largely in these terms that a state of mutual satisfaction is finally attained? What nonsense the idealists talk, after all, and how little they know of that precise and laborious logical discipline, acquaintance with which is the first condition for recognition in analytic circles. In comparison with their wordy and dubious efforts, how admirably neat, how almost mathematical, are the achievements of the analysts. But on the other side, what a poverty of spiritual perception these analysts show. What do they know of the great tradition in philosophy, and, in general, of the great cultural achievements of Western civilization, especially its religion? These conflicting claims are not adjudicated within the area of rational discussion. Why *should* a philosopher be a specialist and by what title does the appearance of mathematical lucidity stand as the hall mark of intelligibility? Because those who do not use it talk nonsense, their statements mean nothing in its terms. What authority have spiritual insights, notably connected with membership in a limited culture circle, to stand as the measure of philosophic truth? They represent a *deeper* meaning which any good man will see, and those who do not see it are classified therewith. Can it seriously be questioned that considerations of this sort are in fact decisive in the choice of a philosophy and the measure of agreement that obtains among its defenders? The argument is there, of course, endlessly ingenious and coupled in many instances with substantial wisdom. But the ultimate issues are just the ones which never get into the debate at all, and just the ones that most need criticism and analysis. Philosophical reason is grounded on an irrational basis—not one that is simply non-rational, but one that ought to be criticized—that can be criticized shrewdly enough by those who refuse to take the standpoint in question as ultimate, but whose obvious limitations must be ignored by those who take it as the measure of *philosophic* truth and hence as final as it stands and not subject to qualification from any other standpoint than its own. The worst fault in the search for the ultimate is that it encourages philosophers to refuse to examine their own preconceptions, and thus, leads them to decide on non-rational grounds the criteria which within the sphere of their application are to constitute the meaning of rationality. The result is a situation in which each philosophy can be shown to be arbitrary by those who reject it, and must be regarded as ultimate by those who accept it. Generalize the awareness of the situation and you have scepticism; deny it and you have a dogmatism which is unable to stand critical inspection and thus demands of its adherents the adoption of a state of mind in which such inspection is not allowed. And are not these the tendencies which actually assert themselves when we grow tired of the debate? A "liberalism" that is prepared to admit in principle the legitimacy of *any* philosophical position, since all are alike unwarranted, while it adopts in practice the one to which non-rational preference inclines it or, when this indifferentism becomes intolerable, a return to belief which is absolute and unqualified, but which requires for its maintenance a surrender of those critical faculties which, if exercised, would expose its inadequacy. For men need to believe in something; they cannot continue indefinitely to use notions which justify themselves in practical experience and at the same time acknowledge these notions to be theoretically indefensible. If wider inquiry leads only to controversy and doubt, they will resort to an attitude which cuts off doubt by a deliberate limitation of areas within which reason is to be applied. We shall have assurance again, and the simple mind, but it will be that cynical simplicity which is the final outcome of the failure to understand. Scepticism, and animal *faith*.

We have seen this happen, and we are seeing it happen today, in the culture of which our philosophy forms a part. There are other and more urgent causes for it than the failure of reason, in philosophy, to justify its use of its own essential categories, to show where and how they are in fact the means through which we know the world. But this is an essential factor. And it is one that must be dealt with before a substantial revival of the faith in reason is to be expected. If the hypothesis here offered is correct, the primary task of philosophy is to show how the several types of categories and criteria which, in their primary application, are the means by which we reasonably apprehend and evaluate the world, can be integrated in a working adjustment in terms of which we might say, with Aristotle and Santayana, that life at its human and attainable best, is reason in operation. We are very far, either in philosophy or in social relations, from that state today. It may be that to see clearly where we are and how we have come, will be of some help in furthering the long, hard, but indispensable work that has still to be done if man is to actualize the possibilities of his humanity. But our present concern is not with a prospectus of philosophical salvation. There have been enough of those. It is with a diagnosis of the present situation as precise and just as we can make it.

2 Idealism

The term "idealism" has many meanings. I use it here to designate the doctrine which played the leading part in British and American philosophy at the end of the last and the beginning of the present century. This doctrine had as its central tenet the claim that the "values" which embody what is most central and most genuinely spiritual in human experience are somehow guaranteed, validated, or sustained by the nature of reality. Its prevailing method of proof, instanced most characteristically in the writings of Bradley, Bosanquet, and Royce, was an appeal from what is provisional and abstract in experience, as this is formulated, for example, in the hypotheses of the physical sciences or the individualism of current political thought, to what is found to be ultimate, concrete and inclusive when these ideas, or any others, are fully and philosophically thought out and coordinated with what, on the whole, both thought and experience compel us reasonably to affirm. The clue to what is basic or foundational to reality thus grasped in its wholeness is held to be "mind," where "mind" denotes that function of self-transcendence in virtue of which an individual's experience moves, through the development of its own purpose, to those even larger and more "meaningful" wholes in which its fullest satisfaction is to be found. That "mind," following consistently the laws of its own nature, does affirm a total and "spiritual" reality in which its demands are fully satisfied, that to this affirmation there is no meaningful alternative and from it no escape save in nonsense, confusion, or willful failure to follow the plain implications of thought and practice to their appropriate conclusion, and finally that all this is philosophically demonstrable, is the doctrine of speculative idealism as the term is here employed.

It will be evident, as the analysis proceeds, that not all who for one reason or another were called idealists in this period subscribed to this doctrine in the same form or to the same degree. With these divergences, so far as they are pertinent to the main case for "idealism," we shall later be concerned. For the present, it is enough that this was the main or prevailing doctrine, variously specified in terms of the particular interests of individual philosophers, and that at a period not remote in time from our own, however remote it may appear in its verbal habits and emotional temper, this was the normal way in which serious and reasonable men intent on thinking through and making sense of the ideas and preconceptions of their time, actually reasoned. If we are to understand what philosophy is in operation and use, not what the defenders of a particular theory tell us that it ought to be, we shall have to take idealism very seriously indeed, not, perhaps, as the disclosure of ultimate reality which its disciples take it to be, but as a specific and instructive instance of how a philosophy comes into being, how it develops, and what, finally, happens to it when the synthesis it has evoked ideally is called upon to justify itself in the situations to which it claims to apply. Our purpose here is to understand idealism thus in terms of its motives, development and consequences and, through it, to see something of how philosophy works.

The Standpoint of Idealism

The Guarantee of Values

"Higher, truer, more beautiful, better, and more real—these, on the whole, count in the universe as they count for us. And existence, on the whole, must correspond with our ideas." [1] This, in Bradley's striking statement, is the conclusion to which speculative idealism leads, and it is chiefly because it does lead to it by a rationally persuasive route that it commended itself in this period to many good and learned men. Bosanquet, characteristically, states the same conclusion more clumsily but with equal fervor. As a result of philosophical reflection we find that "we are sure that the things which we care for are valued in the universe on the whole as they are for us, and are by the very nature of the universe guaranteed as characters of the Reality throughout its appearances." [2] Other statements to the same effect, though with varying degrees of emphasis on "the Universe" as the cosmic guarantor of our "highest" value judgments could, of course, be cited from [Josiah] Royce, [James] Ward,

---

1. F. H. Bradley, *Appearance and Reality: A Metaphysical Essay* (2d ed., 1897; Oxford: Clarendon Press, 1930), 9th impression, p. 488. [This book was first published in London by Swan Sonnenschein in 1893. The Swan Sonnenschein edition appears to have retained uniform pagination, judging at least from the July 1902 printing and the "fifth impression" of November 1908, the only two I was able to examine. The Clarendon Press apparently reset its edition with each new printing. I do not know which edition Murphy was quoting from, but it was not the ninth impression and the citations here and on the following pages have been changed to bring them into line with that one. Ed.]

2. Bernard Bosanquet, *The Value and Destiny of the Individual* (London: Macmillan, 1913), p. 260.

[A. Seth] Pringle-Pattison, [George Holmes] Howison, and [Norman] Kemp Smith. What is common to them all is the assurance that the claims we make to truth and to the validity of value judgments, in our philosophical thought and practice, require, and happily can secure, a guarantee or support from the primary or essential nature of "reality" itself, and that philosophy, by demonstrating this, helps us to estimate the worth and "significance" of such claims more wisely than we should otherwise be able to do.*

What sense are we to make of such statements? It will not do to say that this is the way in which philosophers talk and that they and some who hear them find their statements comforting. Our aim is to understand these philosophies in terms of the problems and needs in response to which they developed, and it is not difficult to see that there was a quite genuine problem of the period to which these statements could with reason be supposed to provide a solution.

In one sense, of course, it does seem paradoxical to the uninitiated to invoke "reality" or the "universe" to guarantee the truth of true judgments or the value of worthwhile experiences and actions. The guarantee that an idea or belief corresponds to reality is, surely, simply the evidence that it is true, and this, in the ordinary case, is supplied not by speculative philosophy but by the particular inquiry through which such evidence is obtained. It is not "Reality" as idealistically identified but theoretical physics that guarantees the truth of my belief that light travels with a finite velocity. Nor is it at all obvious that what by moral criteria is certified as a right action needs any further speculative "implementation" to warrant its claims to validity. To say that "Reality" guarantees the validity of value judgments is either to say that they are in fact valid and can be found to be so by the application of tests appropriate to the situations to which they refer, *or else* to introduce a further sanction which seems *prima facie* neither necessary nor even pertinent.†

Yet here, as Bosanquet has so often warned us, the "first look" is philosophically deceptive, for there *is* a sense in which an idea can be "true," or a value judgment warranted, insofar as it satisfies the criteria by which in practice such ideas and judgments are tested, and yet not 'really' true or warranted in reference to a further standard believed somehow to be relevant to the claim in question. A man may be guilty according to the law and rightly convicted of a crime, yet at the same time not guilty according to a moral standard by which

* This sentence has been restructured from "What is common to them all is the assurance that the claims we make to truth, and to the validity of value judgments, in our philosophical thought and practice require, and happily can secure, a guarantee. . . ." Ed.

† This sentence has been recast. It originally read: "*Either* to say that "Reality" guarantees the validity of value judgments is to say that they are in fact valid and can be found to be so by the application of tests appropriate to the situations to which they refer *or else* it introduces a further sanction which seems *prima facie* neither necessary nor even pertinent." Ed.

we think his actions ought in some further sense to be judged. And unless the legal tests of guilt bore some satisfactory relation to moral estimates of right and wrong we should be inclined, I think, to say that a man who was merely legally guilty was not "really" guilty at all, and to feel a sense of dissatisfaction and distrust of legally correct verdicts until their warrant with reference to ends we took to be not merely legally but morally valid had been made out. One need not be an idealistic philosopher, or even a wishful thinker, to understand this.

An analogous situation can cause disquiet and confusion in somewhat more complicated cases, and whenever it does so, characteristically philosophical reflection, in the sense in which the preceding chapter defined it, will normally arise. The language in which we find it natural and appropriate to refer to moral behavior, for example, makes use of such terms as "right" and "wrong," "ought," and "ought not," with a quite special normative significance which nearly anyone who is not already sophisticated by ethical relativism can understand. They are terms of praise and blame applied to actions judged to be just or unjust, actions which a morally responsible person could have performed and ought in some cases at least to have carried out. The question of what is right or wrong in terms of the standards of moral behavior currently acknowledged is a perfectly meaningful one and can frequently be answered with reliable accuracy. Men by such standards wise and good will set great store by such judgments and will serve as guides and monitors for those less securely grounded in moral realities.

Suppose, however, that doubt arises as to whether what is right and reasonable in this sense has any "real" meaning or corresponds to anything that is really the case. This may mean that new moral standards are being offered and that what is right by the old standards is wrong by the new. It is in this sense that a moral prophet like Nietzsche asks us to look beyond good and evil as currently understood and to revalue our values. But it may mean that reference is being made to a description of "facts" in which the terms "right" and "wrong" in their ordinary moral application have no standing at all, and that this description is felt to be more accurate, more fundamental, or in some other sense more ultimate than the one in which moral predicates are employed. In that case the whole scheme of moral valuation would have a certain insecurity or dubiety, and those who felt it important to go on believing that what they could see to be right by moral standards was *really* so would look for some further warrant of validity than that which these standards themselves could supply.

We all know that such a situation had arisen in the later years of the nineteenth century, and that the extension of the methods of the more exact sciences into fields of organic behavior and even of mind in its "higher" or more "spiritual" manifestations had tended seriously to unsettle established beliefs, not only about matters of fact but about the valuations placed on conduct. What concerns us here is not the more obvious manifestations of this disquiet—"the age of the rocks versus the Rock of Ages" as one earnest tract of the times expressed it—but the felt discrepancy between the interpretations offered by scientists and popularizers of science of "the nature of the world and man" as science sees them, and the pictures both of man and of the world with which the whole cultural and moral outlook of western Europe was closely bound up. It is easy today to be amused at the characteristically Anglo-Saxon attitudes of a generation alarmed at the interstellar spaces and resolved to be either proudly defiant or still wishfully hopeful in the face of an alien world. Actually, the matter goes much deeper than that. The sciences that set the style for the exact description of discoverable facts have no concern with "values", that is to say, with the factors which are regarded as of primary significance for the understanding of men's "higher" activities. Nature, as thus described, knows nothing of right and wrong, and man is a part of nature. What has been held to be central to the one description is irrelevant to the other. Nor are the two simply independent of each other. For moral predicates attach to man as he actually is, or as he is believed to be, and to the sort of action that is right and reasonable in the world in which he finds himself. But the sciences also deal with man as he is, and their descriptions are beyond comparison more exact and reliable than those with which our moral judgments are associated. If man as he is, that is, as the sciences describe him, is not an appropriate subject for moral predicates, and if the environment to which he responds is not at all describable in terms of the kingdom of ends toward which his moral effort is supposed to be directed, then moral judgment in the sense in which we have previously understood it appears to lose all essential contact with the situation to which it ought to apply, and this is naturally expressed by the statement that its valuations are so far not warranted or guaranteed by the nature of the real world.

It must be recalled, of course, that this exposition is not intended to represent the essential merits of the case, but only the way in which it presented itself to those who, in this period, found their conviction of the essential worth of what they regarded as man's higher nature in collision with an account of what human nature and its natural environment actually are, and with the claim that what they are thus disclosed as being is all that, in intellectual honesty, we can take them to be. The sciences, it was plausibly maintained, are our sole reliable instruments of knowledge; what cannot be certified by their tests and in the terms appropriate to the "grammar of science" cannot be matter of reasonable belief, perhaps not even of significant discourse. The result of this collision is what the disciple of Wittgenstein would describe as a "language cramp," a basic dissatisfaction with the language offered as the only one appropriate for rational discourse, because one cannot in its terms make the discriminations or justify the conclusions which are still felt, on other grounds, to be essential.

In terms more appropriate to the thought of the period, this dissatisfaction with the "naturalistic" (or generalized scientific) account of human behavior has been admirably expressed by Kemp Smith. "Many opponents of idealism, to judge from their frequent practice, seem to believe that the more they keep their eyes off the human values, or at least away from the great traditions in which they have found expression, the less they will be biased in passing philosophical judgments upon them. They approach them only through the study of our natural and economic setting, or through analogies derived from the study of animal behavior. Virtually, the result is that they do not study them at all. In effect, though not in intention, they depict them from hearsay and condemn them *in absentia.* The outcome is not science but pseudo-science and a violation of all those principles of sound reasoning to which they give their adherence in the fields in which they are more familiarly at home. The more intimate aspects of human existence must be appreciated from the inside; otherwise the distorting preconceptions that are inevitable to an outsider will never be detected." [3]

It is fashionable among the syntactically enlightened to dismiss this difficulty as wishful thinking—a desire to continue to believe what an emotionally congenial view of the world has in the past comfortably sanctioned. But that is the criticism of an opponent already persuaded that whatever is not statable in the terms he has selected as scientifically, empirically and hence syntactically respectable, is nonsense, and [that] its acceptance by otherwise reasonable men [is] to be explained wholly on "emotive" grounds. The previous question, and the one that the idealists very rightly determined to investigate, was the title of the scientific language to this sort of exclusive validity and, more particularly, its right to describe *Reality* in the terms admittedly appropriate to its more special scientific concerns. Not "wishful thinking" but critique of language or, as it was then called, of categories, is the device to which a philosopher will turn when he wants to justify the continued use of standards whose authority and primary meaning have been compromised by a rival description which claims, or whose expositors claim for it, jurisdiction in matters to which its methods and categories are not appropriate. Granted that the sciences are, in their own territory, sovereign, does it follow that they are competent to reveal all that a reasonable man needs to take account of in his moral or religious behavior?

3. Norman Kemp Smith, "The Present Situation in Philosophy," *The Philosophical Review* 29.1 (Jan. 1920): 1–26, at p. 24.

The clash of standards and confusion of tongues here give rise inevitably to the question of jurisdiction, that is, to a question of critical philosophy.

The Limitations of Science

It was natural—though, as will later be seen, in some respects unfortunate—that the attempt to ascertain the relevance of the findings of the special sciences to prevailing views of what was valuable and significant should thus have taken the form of an inquiry into the limits of scientific knowledge. The motives for such an inquiry are many, and not all, by any means, are directly traceable to a concern over the precarious status of values in a world of which the language of physics or of Darwinian biology is believed to supply the most accurate description available. But this concern does serve to give the inquiry a peculiar urgency, to link it with the special interests and standpoint of idealistic philosophy, and to stress its predominant conclusion—that scientific description does not supply us with knowledge of "Reality" in its concrete and ultimate being and hence that, with reference to such Reality, the conclusions which on non-scientific grounds we should like to reach may, after all, be true.

Some reliable means of finding out what, in the light of "modern science," it is reasonable to think about the world and man's place and duties in it was evidently essential. Even those who had little concern for a guarantee of values could see that there was something seriously misleading in such slogans as "the survival of the fittest, the triumph of the best." A more sophisticated public was bound to be dissatisfied with Spencer's slipshod use of "force" to designate a physical constant, an Unknowable Reality, and a concept of "Social Statics." And even admirers of Huxley's remarkable prowess as the expositor and defender of the biological sciences might well be inclined to wonder whether the "Lay Sermons" to which the great controversialist was addicted were not as much out of place as the pious incursions into biology against which he so properly protested. In general the conviction was growing, that what a scientific hypothesis can be understood to mean when put to its own proper use in the classification and coordination of experiences in terms of general laws and the reliable prediction of further experiences on the basis of such laws, is one thing, and the use of the concepts employed in such hypotheses to lay down the moral law, solve "the riddle of the universe," or even provide the basis for an agnostic "faith"—which, as Huxley said, "if a man keep whole and undefiled, he shall not be ashamed to look the universe in the face, whatever the future may have in store for him" [4]—is quite another. The proper technique for "looking the universe in the face" is not obviously the same as that of framing

---

4. T. H. Huxley, *Science and Christian Tradition,* Collected Essays, vol. 5 (New York: D. Appleton and Company, 1897), p. 246.

and testing scientific theories, and the excursions of eminent scientists into this field were frequently remarkable not so much for hard-headedness as for intellectual irresponsibility. To assume the authority of philosophy, to attempt to speak for experience as a whole, on the basis of concepts warranted only by their utility in furthering special and limited inquiries which specifically abstract from much that in experience as a whole we find to be concrete, genuine and important, is just such an irresponsible proceeding, and it is no wonder that it called out in reply the merited, though equally one-sided response of the idealist, a response of which James Ward's *Naturalism and Agnosticism** is perhaps the most impressive instance.

Not only were critical philosophers incited by the illegitimate pretensions of specialists to set down firmly the limitations of science, but they were also provided by current positivism, itself largely the work of critically minded scientists, with the principles according to which this could be done. The work of [Ernst] Mach, of [Karl] Pearson, and, above all, of [Henri] Poincaré, cannot here be given that consideration on its own account that it deserves. We are concerned with the standpoint of idealistic philosophy in this period and the reason why it should have seemed reasonable to philosophers of this school to insist that the sciences apply not to reality, but only to phenomena, that their principles are abstract, conventional and provisional, justified not by their conformity either to "objective reality" or to experience as a whole but by their special usefulness for the work of description, classification and prediction in which they are properly employed. Such statements as these, made by philosophers of science, were intended primarily to emancipate science from metaphysics, to guarantee to the investigator the right to make use of such notions as he required and to press his inquiry as far as and no farther than seemed necessary for his own purpose, without regard to what, on non-scientific grounds, the "true" nature of the world was supposed to be, whether or not it was knowable, or whether or not his conclusions were such as our higher natures demand. Not being in *this* sense concerned with "reality" he was content, on the whole, to concur in the then current epistemological view that experience consists "ultimately" in "states of consciousness" and hence that statements with an empirical reference, even when they ostensibly deal with material objects, are really concerned with such states of consciousness and nothing else. Insistence on the right to ignore metaphysical questions, acquiescence in the epistemology of mental states which was the unhappy heritage of British empiricism, and a growing critical awareness of the "conventional" nature of the principles of science, here conspired to support the conclusion that the sciences do not deal with "reality" as such or as a whole and hence are not in a position

* James Ward, *Naturalism and Agnosticism* (New York: Macmillan, 1899). Ed.

to lay down rules for it. And this, in turn, fits in neatly with the idealistic interest in somehow grounding values in "reality" and in making sure, meanwhile, that the scientific theories which have made such grounding necessary by emphasizing the irrelevance of "values" to fact as scientifically ascertainable, do not preempt the field of "reality" for themselves. The limitations of science provide the opportunity for speculative idealism.

The Criterion of Truth and Reality

How then is reality itself to be discovered, the "real" reality which is to be sufficient to guarantee the worth of our values, and to which the sciences, for all their exactness and verifiability, cannot lead us? The answer, in terms of the state of opinion of the time and the requirements of this philosophy, is obvious enough. The trouble with limited inquiries of the sort just criticized is that their principles are provisional and partial; useful for special purposes, they have not been thought through with respect to their ultimate consistency and capacity to include all that, in experience as a whole, we find to be genuine. Metaphysics must redress the balance. As Bradley says, "We may agree, perhaps, to understand by metaphysics an attempt to know reality as against mere appearance, or the study of first principles or ultimate truths, or again the effort to comprehend the universe, not simply piecemeal or by fragments, but somehow as a whole." [5]

The juxtaposition of terms here is enlightening. It is "reality" and not mere appearance that we are seeking. But this reality is simply what experience itself compels us to affirm when we interpret it under the guidance of first or ultimate principles, those in which an intelligence intent on thinking its problems through and seeing its world consistently and as a whole, can acquiesce. There must be such an ultimate criterion, if we are at all to distinguish what is finally actual from makeshift and provisional notions which cannot, on the whole, maintain themselves.

It will not do to say, as some sceptics have done, that "reality" thus used is a meaningless term. Actually, if we take any pains at all to understand the problem to which it is to supply an answer, we can see quite clearly what it means. A guarantee of *ultimate* validity is wanted in reference to which the doubts felt about the place of values in a world of facts can be set at rest. The standard of current morality will not do, since it is this that is being called in question, and it is its relation to something more ultimate or final that is to be certified. The tests applied in the sciences will not do, since these, for their own purposes, abstract from the very considerations of value with which we are here concerned. Confusion arises when such partial and limited views are taken

5. Bradley, *Appearance and Reality*, p. 1.

to be absolute and thus applied in situations to which they are not relevant. How else could we clear up this difficulty, which arises from a failure to distinguish the partial and provisional from the inclusive and ultimate, than by the use of a criterion which makes such inclusiveness and ultimacy the tests of Reality? By the use of such a criterion, and by it alone, could an experience unbalanced and confused by the failure to make just this distinction, be set in order once more. Ultimate reality is simply what thought, consistently and comprehensively applied to the data of experience, plainly shows the world to be, and its "meaning" for non-philosophical beliefs is to be found in its ability to resolve the conflicts that arise when these are given a false absoluteness, through a misunderstanding of their partial and limited validity, and to support those that merit support by an indication that in reality as a whole, their place is a high one. "Everything is justified as being real in its own sphere and degree, but not so as to entitle it to invade other spheres, and, whether positively or negatively, to usurp other powers. The absolute right owned by every side of life is, in other words, conditional on its service, and on its acceptance of limited value and reality. And it is the true Absolute alone that gives its due to every interest just because it refuses to everything more than its own due." [6]

The Place of Mind in Reality

If this were the whole story, we might well say that Bradley's philosophical criterion represents a demand not for a particular sort of philosophy, but for philosophy itself. But it is not the whole story. For it was not Reality as a whole, nor what in the whole course of our commerce with the world we can reasonably take it to be, but rather the specially favored status of one aspect of the experienced world as a clue to what Reality as a whole or in its absolute nature is, that was the primary concern of the Idealists. It is not, we shall find, the whole of Reality, but the other half, the half that the scientific account had omitted, regarded as a peculiarly "concrete," "ultimate", and satisfying manifestation of the whole—the "world of appreciation" as contrasted with "the world of description"—that provides the basis of the world view of Idealism. Thus the lack of balance and proportion incident to the over-eager extension of scientific concepts without regard to their contextual meaning is carried over into the philosophical attempt to compensate for it. If the sciences do not give the whole truth, then they do not give the truth about "reality." Taken as aspirants to such total truth they are pretenders whose claims cannot be philosophically sanctioned. Where then are we to look for the "deepest" manifestations of "the real" if not in that which is ultimate where the sciences are provisional, concrete where they are abstract, inclusive of the values and meanings to which

---

6. Bradley, *Essays on Truth and Reality* (Oxford: Clarendon Press, 1914), p. 470.

their descriptions do not apply? And what is this but "mind" considered not merely in its ordinary manifestations, biological and social, but as the locus of immediacy and value and thus as the most concrete available revelation of reality? In the fashion suggested by this query the stage is set for the conclusion that philosophy as the representative of balance and inclusive consistency in the attempt to coordinate special ideas in a rational harmony is the spokesman for "mind" as a metaphysical pretender to ultimate reality or at least as the most eligible among contenders already in the field. There are degrees in the completeness of this transition, and, as will be seen, the inner tension within idealism is precisely between those who are relatively more interested in the world as an absolute whole and those who are more concerned with the special claims of mind, whether as knower, moral agent or feeler of feelings, to serve as a clue to its nature. But even in Bradley and Bosanquet at the one extreme the "nisus" toward "totality" has thought as its highest expression and the universe echoes "somehow" the judgments of importance that a really wise man would make, while, at the other extreme, even the "personalists", who wish reality to preserve the social relations they cherish in a much more literal fashion, are concerned to show that this cosmic companionableness is what we are compelled to accept when the concreteness and ultimacy of mind and its ubiquity in the world we know are understood. Thus philosophy is *at once* authority for the claim that every aspect of "reality" shall have its due *and also* the advocate of the quite special claims of that aspect which is held to be the unique locus of meaning, value and metaphysical significance.

The consequences of this philosophy will concern us later. What is pertinent here is its understandableness under the circumstances and the philosophical resources on which it could draw. British and American idealism of this period are usually treated in the textbooks as revivals and adaptations of the German idealism of Fichte, Schelling, and Hegel. Such an account does less than justice to the factors that made this philosophy an important answer to contemporary difficulties, and not merely an academic revival of an impressive speculative doctrine. But it does help to explain the particular way in which the later idealists developed their theory. The primacy of "mind," at least in the "phenomenal" world, is guaranteed by Kant's demonstration that the mind gives laws to nature, and thus that the world of external events to which the overzealous naturalist would reduce man's higher nature is "ultimately" the creation of his own thought or at least of a thought which his own thinking reflects. The Kantian "critical philosophy" had been searchingly criticized in the course of the century, and its machinery of categories and forms of intuition in considerable part discredited. But for all that the slogan "back to Kant" kept recurring, and for the sound reason that, in the theory of knowledge, philosophy had never really got away from him. That the ultimate empirical elements to which a critical analysis of knowledge leads are "states of consciousness," that the world of nature is *for knowledge* a "construction" not warranted by such data themselves but imposed by mind for its own purposes and according to its own laws, and that to refer to nature except as it is for knowledge and experience is to refer to the unknowable or—if the later and more radical Kantians are to be believed—the unmeaning, was pretty much common doctrine in the enlightened circles of the period. *For knowledge,* at least, mind thus has a preferential ultimacy which the critical [thinker] can hardly fail to acknowledge. And while the stricter Kantians follow the master in refusing to use this primacy as the basis for a theoretical speculative construction, those more ambitious have in it a lethal weapon against all forms of "realism" and "naturalism" and a permanent incitement to find in "mind" the ultimate nature of the "real."

Again, the legacy of the Hegelian philosophy, in spite of its dialectical flaws, is a peculiarly useful one. In the Hegelian interpretation "mind" is to be understood in terms of its objective achievements in social organization, in the arts, and in religion. It here shows itself as an expansive and coordinating principle assimilating apparently alien materials to its rational purposes and thus resolving the "contradiction" which such separateness involved in a systematic unity which is both rational, as the full satisfaction of its own highest purposes, and real, as the realized nature of the world when this is comprehensively understood. There is no doubt that the pattern of "objective mind"—purpose and intent actualized in institutions which lend meaning to and express the meaning of conscious behavior—is a useful "leading principle" for the social and cultural sciences at an early stage in their development. It enables investigators to describe political behavior, for example, with reference to the common purposes and ideas involved in it, and to see in it more than the balance of pleasures and pains that an over-simple psychology and economics had made the basis for social theory. It is no wonder that men like T. H. Green, Royce, and Bosanquet, who discovered in their own social experience the "reality" of over-individual purposes and ideas, were tempted to adopt the notions of "objective mind," and of the tendency of individual interests and ideas to complete themselves in larger and more organized wholes in which their inadequacies are overcome and their original intent at once "negated" and preserved, as basic for social philosophy. The revival of "idealism" in the interpretation of "cultural" phenomena is primarily to be accounted for by the fact that the categories of this philosophy did allow men to say what they saw needed to be said and what could not be said in the language of the sciences as then developed.

That this same idealism was also fatally ambiguous, that it tempted its followers to test their statements about "objective mind" not so much by reference to verifiable facts of social behavior as by appeals to the "higher reality" of group interests and the ultimate coincidence of reality and value in a unity of which the political state is perhaps the highest earthly manifestation, was not so likely to be discerned at that time, though it has since become all too obvious. There was, then, a remarkable body of learned doctrine, quite as technical and professional in its language as that of the sciences, available for those who were interested in taking "mind" as the clue to the nature of the real, and this doctrine did serve in fact to provide an unanswerable "critical" argument against rival doctrines, and, in its Hegelian application, to open up new possibilities of interpretation in just those subjects, society, "culture," the arts, to which the methods of the abstract sciences had so far proved least adequate. Attempts to elucidate "The Secret of Hegel," to make available to British audiences "The Critical Philosophy of Kant," * and to reconcile in the higher unity of mind objective and absolute the partial and conflicting theories of the intellectual market-place fitted normally into the dominant philosophical interest of the times.[7] Kant and Hegel were thinkers who could be used in the work of philosophical coordination, and what is called "neo-Hegelian" idealism is actually the process of this use and assimilation.

"Mind" thus serves as a principle of critical primacy and of social and cultural synthesis. It is also, and obviously, the locus of those values whose insecurity had previously concerned us. If, then, we are to find in experience a clue to reality, it is to "mind" not in its empirical manifestations but in its higher philosophical functions that we naturally look. "Reality" is essentially continuous with "mind," it is the world in which the mind finds its spiritual fulfilment, and surely, in the end we cannot but believe that somehow it is what, in our best moments, we would wish it to be.

The Romantic and Religious Background

The *argument* for this absolute spiritual reality will concern us in the next section. Here the point is to see how and why it did function to satisfy or appease the speculative demand for an ultimate reality and to provide a solution in which the thought of the period could rest. Thorstein Veblen, in his brilliant essays on "The Preconceptions of Economic Science," [8] has made some illuminating observations on the way in which the notion of "reality" actually

7. See the admirable account of this period in J. H. Muirhead, *The Platonic Tradition in Anglo-Saxon Philosophy* (London: George Allen and Unwin, 1931), Part 2, chs. 2–4.

8. Thorstein Veblen, *The Place of Science in Modern Civilization* (New York: Viking, 1919), chs. 4–6, pp. 82–179.

* J. H. Stirling, *The Secret of Hegel* (London: Longman, Green, Longman, Robert, & Green, 1865, rev. ed.; Edinburgh: Oliver and Boyd, 1898), was one of the first competent attempts to explain Hegel to English readers; Edward Caird, *The Critical Philosophy of Kant* (Glasgow: J. Maclehose and Sons, 1889), helped bring Kant's work to notice in Britain. Ed.

functions in our thinking. It serves, as he says, to mark the spot at which criticism and analysis stop, where inquiry can rest in that which is so currently final and acceptable as to require no further justification. This finality, in the cultural history of western Europe, has traditionally attached to the Christian view of a world in which man has a spiritual destiny and in which the order of events in time is, in its main outlines at least, subordinate to a morally intelligible drama of sin, redemption and eventual salvation. Such a world is "spiritual", not in the vague sense that "somehow", or "in the end," it can reassure us about the cosmic respectability of our preferences, but in the quite special sense that the knowledge and love of God constitute the true end of man and that the sequence of events in this world and the next is so ordered that destiny and desert with respect to ultimate happiness will coincide. There was a time when that notion, embodied with wonderful richness and subtlety in theology and art, supplying first principles for the sciences, claiming, not always ineffectively, to guide and order the world of political affairs, offering inspiration for the devout and admonition to the erring, did provide the most nearly complete philosophy of life that we have known. Today in many quarters it has lost its authority and does not directly influence our thinking. But it remains nonetheless in the background of our thought as supplying the model of what a view of the world which did satisfy us "concretely" and on the whole would be like, and there is no doubt, I think, that a philosophy which manages to evoke the emotional associations and to sound the "spiritual" overtones of that doctrine without explicitly committing itself to the theological views which have rendered it for many of us unacceptable, does thereby acquire a plausibility and "reasonableness" which are very persuasive. I do not at all suggest that the idealists were deliberately trying to take advantage of the emotional satisfactions of this view without accepting its intellectual content. What I do maintain is that with them as with most men of their generation, and many of ours, there is a spiritual homesickness for the unity and "meaning" of a world view which we have inherited not only through organized religion but through all those cultural channels which we should be inclined to regard as "best," and that any theory that is able, without offending our beliefs in matters of fact, to revive some elements of that "meaningful" world has a "reality" about it, in Veblen's sense of "reality," that goes a long way toward explaining its acceptance. It is precisely what "in the end" we "cannot but believe," though we should not be able to accept it unless it were buttressed and subtletized by just such critical and metaphysical reasonings.

Among the idealists, this religious background is supplemented by the literary and emotional legacy of romanticism. Romanticism, as T. E. Hulme has elegantly and precisely identified it, is "spilt religion," a sense of something if not far more deeply interfused at least more generously diffused than the "meanings" of ordinary practice or even of orthodox religion, which lends an unapparent and cosmic significance to objects which, in their ascertainable relations, will hardly sustain it. When the beauty of nature, or the importance of world peace, or the epistemological significance of Kant's "synthetic unity of apperception" is apprehended with a religious fervor and awe which only an indwelling spiritual reality could warrant, and to which an indwelling spiritual reality is thereupon imputed, romanticism is on the way to becoming a philosophy, though not, I think, a sound or adequate one.

Here, again, the overt influence on idealistic philosophy of the emotional attitude referred to is not great. Within the limits of his preconceptions, no harder or clearer thinker than Bradley ever philosophized, and a portrayal of his view of the spiritual nature of the universe as mere romanticism would, of course, be a caricature. Nonetheless, the acceptance of the view in many circles, its philosophical *plausibility* for many who never tried to understand Bradley's arguments, does depend in considerable part on its harmony with just this attitude. A very instructive study could, and should, be made of the influence of the poetry of Goethe and Schiller, and of the English romantics, on philosophical idealism. It would indicate, I think, that the philosophical function of this poetry is to remind well brought up and sensitive spirits of what in their *best* moments they do actually take the world to be, and that Bosanquet, for example, has crossed many a dialectical chasm on the somewhat airy bridge which a well-chosen literary allusion has supplied. And in Pringle-Pattison's *The Idea of God* good poetry put to bad uses plays a truly alarming part.

This does not mean that idealism is mere wishful thinking. This motive, by itself, would have persuaded no important thinker of the truth of this philosophy, and there were first rate philosophers among the idealists. If the argument of this section has shown anything it is that idealism was the product of a remarkable *convergence* of interests, all of which seemed to point in the same direction and which, in this philosophic coordination, provided a standpoint for criticizing the categories of the sciences, for "conserving" and clarifying "values," for harmonizing the conflicting claims of partial interests in a synthesis of philosophic scope, and for bringing the mind to rest in a world view in which its culturally best hopes were realized. Such a philosophy is certainly not "nonsense" in any usual sense, nor is it a shallow or obviously fallacious doctrine to be explained and dismissed by facile refutation. It is the best that a generation of acute and able thinkers could make of the task of rational coordination of a remarkably full and complex experience. As such it is understandable and important. Whether it "proves" all or any of its contentions, and whether it has been able to maintain its precarious synthesis in the face of subsequent developments and, more particularly, of the consequences of its own consistent application, are further questions, to which we now must turn.

The Dialectic of Idealism
Appearance and Reality

The attempt to develop the standpoint of Idealism into a reasoned and systematic demonstration that "reality" in its ultimate nature is such as to warrant and sustain what, in our best moments, we are impelled to believe, has its clearest and most rigorous development in Bradley's philosophy. And it is with it that I propose to deal in this section, reserving for later comment the manner in which this philosophy is modified and attenuated in its application by more accommodating and less dialectically relentless thinkers.

It is, in Bradley's view, the business of metaphysics to discover "reality" as contrasted with mere "appearance," and to elucidate the manner in which the real is at once manifested in its appearances, so that we understand them adequately only when we see them as its aspects, and at the same time not completely or fully manifested in any of them, so that they are *only* appearances and not, under penalty of philosophical confusion, to be regarded as possessing that absolute or self-contained being which belongs, in fact, not to them but only to the Reality whose nature, with various degrees of adequacy, they disclose. How is this doctrine to be understood? It can be adequately understood, I think, only when we interpret the appearance-reality contrast on two different levels and at the same time regard the one of these as ultimately or "in the end" reducible to the other.

In ordinary usage what a thing "really" is is simply what it shows itself to be in terms of such tests as are conventionally regarded as adequate to disclose its nature. The "real" color of an object is the one it is found to have under relatively normal conditions. Yet objects are, in another sense, not "really" colored at all, since a physical description of them would not be in terms of colors, but of measurable physical properties. A man is apparently honest when he acts under some conditions as an honest man would, but he is not really honest if, under other conditions, his conduct fails to measure up to the approved criteria. And so on. Such tests are various, and the attribution of "reality" is ambiguous until we know what sort of test or criterion is understood. To say that anything really *is* what it appears to be is, then, to say that it is so or can be found to be so with respect to criteria definitely or vaguely presupposed. In many cases the term is used confusedly, as when the inquirer wants to know what electricity is "really," or, as in "Juno and the Paycock," what *are* the stars. In such cases, what is expressed, as a rule, is a half-thought-out dissatisfaction with the criteria currently employed and a desire for some further intellectual appeasement of a sort not specified.

When this dissatisfaction comes to coherent and reflective expression, we get a second-level question about "reality." The ordinary tests are then themselves to be tested by reference to some further standard. We ask not whether a scientific statement is valid by scientific tests, but how far science is competent to reveal the true, ultimate, or concrete nature of the real, not whether we do perceive what we seem at first sight to perceive, when this would be answered by the further application of perceptual tests—seeing, touching, etc.—but whether perception is competent to disclose real objects as they really are, and so on. What is wanted, then, is an ultimate criterion, by whose use we shall be able to decide how far the sciences, or religious experience, or our deepest convictions, are to be trusted as disclosures of the real.

Is this a sensible demand? It is certainly an understandable one, as has already been seen. For if we are at all to set our experience *as a whole* in order we must have some reasonable method of resolving the jurisdictional conflicts that arise when the results reached by diverse and limited methods of inquiry are to be correlated with each other, and of testing their relevance to what *on the whole* we must take the world to be if we are to respond to it adequately and intelligently. The report that ordinary perception gives us of material objects is widely different, in the nature of the predicates employed and the statements made, from a scientific theory as to the ultimate constitution of matter. Solid objects, as the popularizations of physics always tell us, are not "really" solid. Does that mean that we were mistaken when we thought that they were and that our tactual experiences are after all not to be trusted? But if they are not trustworthy what becomes of the appeals of physical sciences to *experience* for its own validation? Perhaps science is not *really* true at all, but just mind spinning, and it is wisdom, after all, to believe the heart. This is a matchless mess, but not by any means an unfamiliar one. Evidently what is required is some method of determining what and how much perception, or science, or "the heart" could reasonably be expected to tell us, where we ought to trust them and where we should look for further information on the matters with which we are all humanly concerned and about which we should like to be as intelligent as possible.

It seems natural to treat questions of this sort as simply carrying the inquiry as to what is *really* the case a step further. Just as the view of a man from a distance gives us only an "aspect" of his perceptible figure, size, and the like, an aspect which must be correlated and synthesized with others if we are to discover what he *really* looks like, so his total perceptible appearance is just an "aspect" of the man and must be coordinated with what science and religion, with their different methods, disclose him to be if we are to see what, in his total nature, he really is. And just as it would be a mistake to take any one of his perceptible appearances as *in itself* the *real* man, since each is incomplete and relative, distorted in part by the standpoint of the percipient, so it would be wrong to take the *aspect* of truth which science, or religion or art, discloses as in itself the whole truth. The real transcends all its appearances, and only when our various sources of information have been criticized with respect to their consistency with the more inclusive truth, and their contribution to it, can we see the measure of "reality" that is in them.

This, I take it, is the empirical basis for the philosophical doctrine of "appearance" and "reality." As it stands it is at once highly plausible and fatally ambiguous. This combination of plausibility and ambiguity will account, I believe, for both the initial success and final breakdown of the theory.

The ambiguity consists in this. It is one thing to ask of any alleged source of information about the world, or its meaning, or man's place in it, what, by the methods it employs, we could reasonably expect to find out and how far its reports are consistent with what, on other grounds, we have reason to believe. But it is quite another thing to suppose that the way to find out what it can tell us is to treat it as an attempt to characterize or describe Reality as a whole, in its absolute nature, or that its consistency with the rest of what we know is measured by its capacity to serve, without contradiction, as in its own person a substitute for "ultimate reality." Suppose the cognitive adequacy of perceptual observation is in question. It is clear that perception alone, without the aid of scientific hypotheses, cannot tell us what the constitution of matter on a microscopic level is and hence that to object to the "world of physics" on the ground that it is very unlike what we perceive with our unaided senses would be merely silly. Our sense organs being what they are, we would not reasonably expect the picture of the world they supply to carry us beyond the human scale. A recognition of this fact would resolve many spurious problems. Equally, if the reliability of perception, within its own appropriate limits, were questioned, we should have to meet any reasonable charges brought against it by showing that perceptual judgments, in their contextual use and meaning, are perfectly compatible both with what the sciences tell us and with anything else that there is good reason to believe, and by insisting that we cannot reasonably or practically get along without trusting in perception as a reliable, though limited, source of information about the external world. Thus *on the whole* it is sensible to credit perception with having "really" or in fact the degree of reliability which in use it shows itself to have. When Bradley's philosophy seems plausible or persuasive it is because we think of it as dealing with problems of this sort and thus actually attempting to provide within experience the balance, inclusiveness and sanity which it is the function of philosophy, in contrast with any partial or one-sided interest, to supply.

This, however, is not what Bradley has done. The criterion of philosophical adequacy which is actually secondary and derivative, a correlation of results derived from other sources, he has taken to be primary. Each "aspect" of experience is to be judged philosophically, not by what it is found to be when we apply the tests appropriate to the special context in question, but by what it would be if [it] were taken as in itself the whole truth about the world. Its essential meaning, insofar as we claim "reality" for it, is to qualify and manifest "the Real." Since every judgment that claims truth claims to be "really" true, "Reality" is the subject of every judgment, and since Reality is an ultimate or inclusive whole it is the degree of adequacy of any statement in disclosing the whole or absolute truth which is the measure of its validity in its own primary meaning and content. All predications of "solidity" are partially false, and false to an unknown degree, not because material objects are not sometimes verifiably solid as they appear to be but because solidity, and all other such material properties, are inadequate characterizations of ultimate reality, and my chair cannot be quite truly or genuinely solid because in reality as a whole solidity has but a subordinate place. Moreover, the predication of solidity is ultimately contradictory because a materialistic philosophy which made the sense of touch the exclusive criterion of "the real" would be involved in inconsistencies. And if "matter" is unreal, perhaps spirit will have the final word after all.

Stated in this fashion the thesis is as unplausible as its equivocal counterpart was persuasive. Yet the transition from the one to the other is not at all difficult to display. My chair is "really" solid by normal perceptual tests. Now perception as it stands is not the whole truth about the world. Hence we must inquire how far perception *is* adequate to reality, that is, how far it furnishes, as it stands, metaphysical information about it. Thus interpreted as a pretender to absolute truth (or truth about the Absolute) any perceptual judgment is largely false and misleading. But it did claim to be *really* true and hence its inadequacy to Reality is the measure of its failure to meet its own claim and fulfil its own intent. As a makeshift it will do for practical purposes, but in a philosophy that claims to be consistent and think its problems through, it can hardly be taken seriously. And what is true of perception is true of the sciences, and, indeed, of all "finite" truth whatever. Reality lies beyond all that, and in failing to reach "Reality" such "finite" truth is always partially false.

Now this theory instead of clarifying philosophical issues serves actually to confuse them. Nothing in Bradley's philosophy can be judged for what it shows it to be when it is about its own business, but only as a pretender to metaphysical honors which do not become it. Hence, when its consistency with and contribution to a wise adjustment of interests and beliefs to what, on the whole, we find the world to be, is assessed, we see it inevitably out of focus. It is not the "nature" in which men are born and die and about which the sciences provide remarkably reliable information that Bradley is concerned with; it is the physical description of nature pretending to constitute in its own quantitative abstraction the sensuous content of experience—an "unearthly ballet of bloodless categories" indeed. One might well wonder why Bradley or anybody else should have expected to get blood out of a category, but after all, if *Reality* is the subject of every judgment, and if our scientific descriptions thus intend to characterize the Real, it is plain that their bloodlessness is a failure to satisfy their own intent, and a sign of their intrinsic inadequacy. The trouble with this is that it tempts us to suppose that since "nature" as an "abstraction" has only a low degree of reality, the natural world and our knowledge of it have relatively little to teach us about what human nature is and what sort of a world we live in. And that would be a very grave mistake indeed, though not without a comforting mission to those for whom the conservation of values is a major interest.

The substance of the account so far given is that the appearance-reality contrast basic to Bradley's metaphysic is the result of a misinterpretation of criteria of relative adequacy and reliability as adumbrations of an ulterior Reality, a Reality which, when substituted for the objects of non-metaphysical inquiry as an "ultimate" subject of judgment, prevents us from estimating on its merits the adequacy or reliability of the very claims which are supposed to refer to and presuppose it. The following sections apply this thesis to the more puzzling aspects of this philosophy.

The Unreality of Time

That time is unreal, and that temporal facts occupy a very subordinate place among "appearances," Bradley emphatically maintained. To some of his critics, G. E. Moore particularly, this has proved a very hard saying. For Moore has insisted on understanding "real" and "unreal" in their ordinary or prephilosophical usage.[9] And in *this* sense, to say that time was unreal would be to say that there were no temporal facts, that, e.g., nothing was ever temporally earlier or later than anything else. Similarly of change. If "change" is actually, as Bradley argues, a contradictory appearance only, it would seem to follow that nothing ever does change, that change is not a fact. Yet Bradley emphatically rejects this implication. "Change is a fact, and, further, this fact, as such, is not reconcilable with the Absolute. And, if we could not in any way perceive how the fact can be unreal, we should be placed, I admit, in a hopeless dilemma. For we should have a view as to reality which we could not give up, and should, on the other hand, have an existence in contradiction with that view. But our real position is very different from this. For time has been shown

9. G. E. Moore, "The Conception of Reality," in *Philosophical Studies* (New York: Harcourt, Brace and Company, 1922), pp. 197–219.

to contradict itself, and so to be appearance. With this its discord, we see at once, may pass as an element into a wider harmony. And, with this, the appeal to fact at once becomes worthless." [10]

This passage is instructive. In the first place it shows that the statement that time or change is unreal is not in the first instance meant to contradict what, as Moore rightly observes, would *ordinarily* be understood by the statement that time is real. It does not mean that things do not change, or precede or succeed other things in the order of occurrence. Change can be a fact, and thus meet the conventional test for "reality," and still be unreal. Clearly, some further test is referred to, with respect to which what is factually and verifiably real may fall short of Reality. Nor is it doubtful what this test is. Facts can be more or less real in that "less or more they actually possess the character and type of absolute truth and reality. They can take the place of the Real to various extents, because containing in themselves less or more of its nature. They are its representatives, worse or better, in proportion as they present us with truth affected by greater or less derangement." [11]

Thus, if we try to think of Reality *as a whole* as in process of change we shall fail since "the Whole," as Bosanquet has lengthily shown, is all there timelessly is, including all that was or is to be, and this, as a whole, can never come to be or pass away. There simply isn't anything more, and no transition to something more, since any such transition would fall within the Whole.[12] This tautological triumph becomes important only when we recall that Reality is the ultimate subject of judgment, and hence that if transition does not ultimately characterize the Whole, the judgment that anything changes is not "finally" true. Again, if we try to *reduce* Reality, including all that is humanly important, to its temporal manifestation, thus "taking time seriously" as the representative of such reality, our total view of life would be impoverished. It was on this point that Bradley felt most strongly. "Our life has value only because and so far as it realizes in fact that which transcends time and existence. Goodness, beauty, and truth are all there is which in the end is real. Their reality, appearing amid chance and change, is beyond these and is eternal." [13]

The "derangement" consequent on treating time as real is not anything contradictory, in the ordinary sense, in the statement that events occur and that such occurrence is a fact, but the contradiction that would result if we held that *only* what is in process of change has any actuality at all, or that everything to

10. Bradley, *Appearance and Reality,* p. 182.

11. Bradley, *Appearance and Reality,* p. 321.

12. Bernard Bosanquet, *The Meeting of Extremes in Contemporary Philosophy* (London: Macmillan, 1921, ch. 9, pp. 176–77. [There is no footnote superscript in the text; this seemed the appropriate place for it. Ed.]

13. Bradley, *Essays on Truth and Reality,* p. 469.

which we attach a meaning must be understood under the form of mutability. Such a view, Bradley holds, would compel us to impute an ultimacy and absoluteness to temporal distinctions, as characterizations of the Absolute, which their own nature does not warrant. Their pretensions would then be in conflict with their finite nature, and a philosophy based on them could not consistently be thought through or applied to all that we need, philosophically, to take account of. By the criteria of consistency and adequacy it would thus have failed to meet the tests for reality, and, in spite of its factual character, have shown itself to be mere appearance. It is in *this* form and under *this* aspect that "the finite" contradicts itself and only an absolute, all-inclusive, supra-relational whole of "sentient experience" will satisfy our intellectual demands.

If exception is made for some very acute comments on the relativity of time, it will be found, I believe, that Bradley's demonstrations of "unreality" proceed uniformly on this model. The attempt to think "Reality" under the form of terms in relation breaks down. Why? Not, apparently, because many things are not, by all non-philosophical tests, actually related as they appear to be. It is when taken as a characterization of *Reality* that the machinery of terms and relations breaks down. "From terms taken as themselves unrelated, and from a relation not taken as itself their relation, there is no logical way to the union present in, and required for, the relational fact." [14] Why should anyone who defended the "reality" of the relational fact have found himself in the preposterous position of defending terms "themselves unrelated" and a relation "not taken as itself their relation" as the elements in a relational fact? Because, presumably, if terms were ultimately real they would be real apart from their relations, or really and essentially unrelated, and a *real* relation would enjoy its relational status independently of the terms it related or the situation in which it applied. It is to this unhappy pass that the attempt to think through "the relational form" has brought us. It is not surprising that similar attempts to understand the meaning of past, present, and future in time, the distinction between primary and secondary qualities, or the unity and continuity attributed to a "self," without regard to the contextual meaning of these notions in the situations in which, in non-philosophical use, they apply, should involve comparable difficulties. And such is the vice of the finite, the proof that only the whole is real.

Why, finally, should this analysis, as applied to time or anything else, appear to have any cogency, except as a one-sided criticism of one-sided attempts to stretch the meaning of ordinarily reliable notions beyond the range of their significant application? Because, if Bradley is right, this is the way in which

14. F. H. Bradley, *Principles of Logic* (2d ed.; London: Oxford University Press, 1922), vol. 2 [p. 643 is the citation in the MS, but I have not been able to locate this passage. Ed.].

"appearances" *ought* to be understood if we are to see the degree of truth and validity which they actually possess and the extent of their philosophical reliability. It is the finite in its own nature or "ideality" which, as soon as we begin to think about it, manifests this nisus toward totality, or as I should prefer to say, this unhappy incapacity of those who talk about it philosophically to respect the meaning in use of the terms they apply. Consequently the failure in this fashion to make consistent sense of the categories of non-philosophical thought is to be taken not as evidence that a wrong method has been used, but at the clue to the self-transcendent and ultimately spiritual nature of the real. The speculative criterion for reality thus interpreted is not only different from those of non-philosophical usages, but it is also more primary or fundamental, the clue to what these really mean and the measure of their validity when they are clearly or philosophically understood.

Degrees of Truth and Reality

We return, then, to the problem with which we began, the method by which the meaning for philosophy of categories employed in limited but factually reliable investigations is to be determined, and the significance of their results for an inclusively rational interpretation of our valuations and hopes is to be disclosed. The solution is now quite explicit. "[E]ach [appearance] really is based on, and is an attempt to realize, the same principle, a principle which is not wholly satisfied by any, and which condemns each because each is an inadequate appearance of itself." [15] Not all, however are condemned equally. Some are truer and more real than others, and it is the discernment of this that supplies us with our fundamental principles of philosophical wisdom in the ordering of appearances. "[T]o be more or less true, and to be more or less real, is to be separated by an interval, smaller or greater, from all-inclusiveness or self-consistency. Of two given appearances the one more wide, or more harmonious, is more real. It approaches nearer to a single, all-containing, individuality. To remedy its imperfections, in other words, we should have to make a smaller alteration. The truth and the fact, which, to be converted into the Absolute, would require less rearrangement and addition, is more real and truer. And this is what we mean by degrees of reality and truth." [16] It follows that for metaphysics there cannot be any "hard and absolute" distinction between truth and falsehood. "With each assertion the question is, how much will be left of that assertion, if we suppose it to have been converted into ultimate truth." [17] When it is recalled that ultimate truth is truth about the Absolute, and that only in its

15. Bradley, *Appearance and Reality,* p. 497.
16. Bradley, *Appearance and Reality,* pp. 322–23.
17. Bradley, *Appearance and Reality,* p. 323.

measure or degree of adequacy to characterize the absolute is any "finite" truth really true at all, the doctrine that no ordinary statement is quite true and none wholly false is easily understood. It is not, and is not meant to be, a report about what truth is as tested by non-metaphysical criteria; it is a statement about what truth comes to when these criteria are judged in their capacity to reveal the whole of what is actual and valuable, and a claim that only in this capacity are such criteria ultimately to be judged. If the critics of the "monistic theory of truth" had realized this, much futile and question-begging argument on both sides would have been avoided.

The consequences of the use of this notion of truth and validity are instructive. The philosopher is confronted by "nature" as an apparently external world, in which human life develops and by which its "values" are in large measure conditioned. How are we to relate the "reality" of nature to the higher claims of "spirit"? This is the paramount problem for idealism. But what is nature "really"? Only when this question is answered can we assess its philosophical significance. Bradley holds that "nature" as the physical sciences describe it is a mere abstraction, very far removed from the ultimate truth. Bring in the relation of "nature" to man and it becomes more concrete, nearer to an adequate representation of all we find in experience, hence more "real." "The Nature that we have lived in, and that we love, is really nature. Its beauty and its terror and its majesty are no illusion, but qualify it essentially. And hence that in which at our best moments we all are forced to believe, is the literal truth." [18] This is a very satisfying conclusion for those who find in romantic poetry the expression of what, in their best moments, they cannot but believe. But it is also the result of a strict intellectual principle, rigidly applied. "Our principle, that the abstract is the unreal, moves us steadily upward. It forces us first to rejection of bare primary qualities, and it compels us in the end to credit Nature with our higher emotions. That process can cease only where Nature is quite absorbed into spirit, and at every stage of the process we find increase in reality." [19]

What does this actually mean? Have we found any independent evidence for the conclusion that "nature" as the world of events in space and time possesses any "spiritual" character which, in our non-philosophical dealings with it, it does not disclose? Or have we simply employed a criterion which enables us to believe that since our knowledge of nature, except in its special relations to sentient organisms, is necessarily abstract, "nature" is ultimately an abstraction, of little moment as compared with our more "concrete" feelings in determining what, as reasonable men, we ought ultimately to believe? It seems to me that the latter is the case.

18. Bradley, *Appearance and Reality,* p. 437.
19. Bradley, *Appearance and Reality,* pp. 438–39.

"That world of fact which we so confidently contrast with the imaginary, and which we set up as real, has turned out, when we take it absolutely, to be false appearance. And in our practice, when we do not sink into convention or worse, we assume our right to deal freely with such reality, to treat it as of secondary moment, or even, it may be, as illusory." [20] It is not difficult in this mood to conclude that "Goodness, beauty and truth are all there is which in the end is real," but it is not clear that this result constitutes a reliable and independently confirmable discovery, calculated to enlighten our practice and render experience as it comes to us in the contexts of scientific, political or moral behavior more intelligible. It appears rather to have for its warrant only an equivocal use of the term "reality" and the sanction of emotions which, in losing their traditional objects, have not lost their urgency or their influence on our beliefs.

Thought and Reality

The moral of the foregoing discussion can now be summed up. It is the business, surely, of a sound philosophy to include the claims of all aspects and activities that are pertinent to a rational organization of experience. It should include them, however, for what they show themselves to be in the contexts in which they have an independently certifiable if "partial" warrant in use. If it does not, but undertakes to transmute them into speculative guesses at "reality" to be shunted about at the demands of our higher natures for "concreteness" in a world which shall be *as* a whole very much what *on the whole* would satisfy our spiritual hopes, it will not have unified *in fact* the aspects of the world with which in fact we have to deal. It will simply have seen them out of focus. This conclusion is substantiated, I believe, by an examination of Bradley's theory of "thought" and its relation to reality.

How should we expect that the relation of thought to "reality" would become a problem? If it was a question of finding out whether by the aid of "thinking" we can sometimes find out what is true and important for us to know, we should have no ready answer *in general* to such a query, but should have to proceed to the various methods used in different types of inquiry and to try to estimate their reliability for the primary purposes in respect to which they function and the extent to which they would be likely to prove helpful or misleading if their use was extended to other and less clearly appropriate applications. "Thought" thus understood is warranted by its knowledge-yielding capacity, and there is no general guarantee of its truthfulness, but only the steady support which, in specific inquiries, its hypotheses find in applicability to experience and ability to clarify the issues of both theory and practice. To suppose that "reality" must in this sense meet the demands of thought in gen-

---

20. Bradley, *Essays on Truth and Reality,* p. 63.

eral would be quite unwarranted. The progress of the sciences has involved too many surprises, too many cases in which we have had to recast the preconceptions of our thinking in order to accommodate them to the subtlety of the structure of a world which neither we, nor our thinking, ever made, to make that sort of claim a plausible one. But to claim, on the other hand, that thinking—the use of general ideas and principles in framing hypotheses, guiding investigation into fruitful channels, and reaching conclusions which on the whole sustain themselves in application to events—is radically defective, and needs, as an instrument for securing knowledge, to be transmuted in a higher synthesis of feeling and will, is most unplausible. So long as we keep *on this level* of investigation, the Bradleyan account of thought will hardly be persuasive.

The essence of Bradley's method, however, is to remove the whole discussion to a different level, and to treat results there obtained as the ultimate truth of the matter. We already know in principle how this is done. Epistemologically and metaphysically considered, "thought" is not the process of framing and using ideas previously described. It is the function of mediation, ideality, or self-transcendence which leads us from an immediate experience "below" our ordinary intellectual destinctions through a process of self-completion beyond self, an attribution of "ideal" content to an ulterior reality which is in fact and progressively shows itself to be ultimate reality, to a final recognition of "thought's" inadequacy and "happy suicide" in a supra-intellectual unity, at once beyond mere thinking and the fulfillment of "thought's" own inherent demand. In terms of Bradley's philosophy this account is comprehensible and remarkably cogent. It is our business to understand it.

"Thought" has its point of departure in feeling or immediate experience. This starting-point is held to be quite inescapable. Every intelligible statement, every meaningful reference brings us back somewhere to experience, and experience in its immediacy is feeling. "To be real is to be indissolubly one thing with sentience. It is to be something which comes as a feature and aspect within one whole of feeling, something which, except as an integral element of such sentience, has no meaning at all." [21] "Nothing in the end is real but what is felt, and for me nothing in the end is real but that which I feel." [22] And feeling "means for me, first the general condition before distinctions and relations have been developed, and where as yet neither any subject nor any object exists. And it means, in the second place, anything that is present at any stage of mental life, insofar as that is only present and simply is." [23] "Feeling," thus defined, functions as the ultimate referent of all meaningful assertions, the da-

21. Bradley, *Appearance and Reality*, pp. 128–29.
22. Bradley, *Essays on Truth and Reality*, p. 190.
23. Bradley, *Appearance and Reality*, pp. 406–7.

tum on which mediation or reference beyond the given is based and the matrix out of which it has developed. As such it has a position of quite peculiar importance in this philosophy. Any development in thought must somehow be warranted by what can be directly had or possessed, that is, by feeling, and yet no thought "ultimately" can be thus warranted. It is not that thinking is a less adequate method of *finding out* about the world than feeling; it is that it is a less satisfying form of experience. What is felt is had, or enjoyed; it is a unity more primitive and ultimate than any that thought as discursive and descriptive can warrant. Thus it is inferior not in its cognitive claims in the ordinary sense, but in the concreteness and freedom from "relational" falsification of what it presents.

Thought must go beyond immediate feeling, for there are felt discrepancies even here which can be alleviated only by reference to a wider whole than that explicitly felt. And thought, for all its abstractness, is our means of transcendence, of reference to the wider whole. But in making this reference, we are losing just that in feeling which made it, as a clue to reality, so satisfying, its inarticulate, sentient concreteness. "The reality that is presented is taken up by thought in a form not adequate to its nature, and beyond which its nature must appear as an Other." [24] That is, thought must try to reproduce the immediacy of feeling in a medium inappropriate to such immediacy, and its inadequacy to this task is the measure of its essential defect as a revelation of Reality. Thus considered, thought has one strike called on it from the start.

We may not unreasonably question the cogency of this demand. Why should anybody suppose that the business of valid thinking is to reproduce discursively the felt unity of such experience as can be directly enjoyed. Because feeling is immediate experience, it is in such experience only that we come at "reality" at first hand, and all our more derivative references to it must find their warrant somehow in the "reality" thus given. This will seem profound or perverse, depending on the reader's degree of addiction to epistemological theory. Feeling as an introspective psychologist would describe it—and Bradley is a brilliant introspective psychologist—is not "the datum" for the sort of inquiries in which we gain our most reliable knowledge of the world around us, nor is the reliability of such knowledge tested by its approximation in vividness or "sentient concreteness" to what we experience when we are knowing not perceptible objects but our own sensations. The interposition of such a datum and such a criterion would be simply impertinent for the inquiry in question. Such data, however, are not *ultimate* data and such objects not *ultimate* reality. Perception always involves some interpretation, therefore some mediation; it does not take us back either to "the general condition before relations

24. Bradley, *Appearance and Reality*, p. 179.

and distinctions have been developed," or to anything experienced insofar as it is *only* present and *merely* felt. It is to this that we must retreat if we are to reach the absolute datum, without any shred of "ideal" reference. And epistemology can, in the end, not stop short of such data. Moreover the ultimate object, as has already been seen, is reality as a whole, in all its aspects. This must include feeling, since it must include everything and so far as "thought" omits this it falls short of its own goal, and is seen to be inherently defective. To try, with such a datum and such an object, to establish the sort of relation that exists between what is taken as datum and what as object of inquiry in non-philosophical inquiries and to show how, by the use of thought or intelligence, we can employ the one as a clue to knowledge of the other would, of course, be quite out of the question.

Given such a task, however, how is thought to proceed? As a speculative introspective psychology provided us with an account of "the datum," so logic, as a curious combination of the principles of traditional formal logic with the speculative requirements for absolute knowledge, gives the basis for an estimate of the distinctive work of thought. "We start from the diversity in unity which is given in feeling, and we develop this internally by the principle of self-completion beyond self, until we reach the idea of an all-inclusive and supra-relational experience." [25] How is thought to complete itself? By avoiding contradiction in the first place. If this means formal contradiction it will not take us far; if it means metaphysical contradiction of the sort already described it will take us as far as the Absolute, but only in a rather negative fashion. Actually it must be both at once, since its metaphysically desirable conclusion needs the sanction of logic in the more usual sense. Yet the gap between the two remains extensive. The demand for formal self-consistency is not enough. We need some justification for inference in which the conclusion carries us beyond the premises: "an object developing itself ideally by virtue of that which is both itself and is also beyond itself." [26] And this is to be an internal development, one which "thought" in its merely discursive capacity is competent to trace. Outside philosophical logic, objects whose necessary or logical self-development can thus be traced are very hard to find. Responsible thinking borrows clues and hints from the nature of its special subject-matter and follows leading principles which, by no means logically necessitated, are nonetheless warranted in their capacity to guide investigation to an empirically certifiable issue. This is an environment in which thought can *move,* not through the dialectical development of its own demands for a world in which its urge to self-transcendence will be fully satisfied, but as a partner in an enterprise

25. Bradley, *Appearance and Reality,* p. 494.
26. Bradley, *Principles of Logic,* vol. 2, p. 605.

where its "demands" are constantly modified and reformulated under the guidance of subject-matter and where the subject-matter takes on, in the give and take of inquiry, the order and connection which only "relational thinking" is competent to reveal.

The tragic inadequacy of "thought" as Bradley describes it is not that it is merely discursive, but that it is cut off by its epistemological and metaphysical pretensions from contact with those subject-matters which would give it something to work *on* and some clue as to how in particular to proceed. For all its air of speculative magnificence, there is an unhappy meagerness about it, and its claim that reality as a whole shall provide an object adequate to its own ideal self-development seems but a poor compensation for its failure to see in particular the way in which thought "moves" when it is about its cognitive business and not laying down laws for ultimate reality.[27]

The final evidence that the reality which thought demands is one which its own nature as *mere* thought is unable to grasp is supplied by the consideration that discursive thinking proceeds by means of abstractions, that it leaves out whatever is taken to be irrelevant to the particular inquiry in which it functions. If its object is to discover what *is* relevant and what is not to generalizations and hypotheses which, by their very abstractness, extend our power to deal with a wide variety of instances, this abstractness is a positive advantage. But if it aims at the Reality in which all truth is contained and transmuted, it is a fatal defect. "No abstraction (whatever its origin) is in the end defensible. For they are, none of them, quite true, and with each the amount of possible error must remain unknown. The truth asserted is not, and cannot be, taken as real by itself. The background is ignored because it is assumed to make no difference, and the mass of conditions, abstracted from and left out, is treated as immaterial. The predicate, in other words, is held to belong to the subject essentially, and not because of something else which may be withdrawn or modified. But an assumption of this kind obviously goes beyond our knowledge. Since Reality here is not exhausted, but is limited only by our failure to see more, there is a possibility everywhere of unknown conditions on which our judgment depends. And hence, after all, we may be asserting anywhere what is but accidental." [28]

This argument actually proceeds on the assumption that for knowledge *nothing is irrelevant,* that the scope of an inquiry is limited only by our failure to see more. That in some cases the abstractness of knowledge is the result not of

---

27. For a more explicit emphasis on the *internal* development of "thought" and the necessity that "reality" shall meet its claims, see Royce's theory of the "internal meaning" of ideas, *The World and the Individual* (New York: Macmillan, 1900), 1st series, esp. lectures 1 and 7.

28. Bradley, *Appearance and Reality,* pp. 478–79.

leaving out what we do not know but of knowing what to leave out would not be a convincing reply, though it is obviously the truth about knowledge in the "abstract" sciences. For if anything is left out an explanation is partial, and thus partly false. "But a partial explanation, I may here be reminded, is better than none. That in the present case, I reply, would be a serious error. You take from the whole of experience some element or elements as a principle, and you admit, I presume, that in the whole there remains some aspect unexplained and outstanding. Now such an aspect belongs to the universe, and must, therefore, be predicated of a unity not contained in your elements. But, if so, your elements are at once degraded, for they become adjectives of this unknown unity. Hence the objection is not that your explanation is incomplete, but that its very principle is unsound. You have offered as ultimate what in its working proclaims itself appearance. And the partial explanation has implied in fact a false pretense of knowledge." [29]

This is quite true if we suppose the claim of "abstract" thought to truth in the ordinary sense is really an abortive claim to be the whole truth and hence a "false pretense" to an adequacy which, since it admittedly leaves something out, it cannot actually achieve. And it does serve to indicate that the ideal of thought as here propounded is fundamentally discrepant with the procedure of effective thinking. The remedy is heroic, but hardly helpful. Appeal must be made to other sides of our nature—will and feeling—to supply the concreteness which thought, cut off from its empirical objects and trying by its own dialectical necessity to encompass the universe, can hardly supply. This must be so, if the demand for completeness is to be met, and to deny that demand is to lapse into contradiction and the unmeaning. But how it can be met and what the higher unity is which supplies a pacification of the "unrest" of the intellect without giving a cognitively certifiable answer to its questions, "thought" is hardly competent to say. For "in reaching a whole which can contain every aspect within it, thought must absorb what divides it from feeling and will. But when these all have come together, then, since none of them can perish, they must be merged in a whole in which they are harmonious. But that whole assuredly is not simply *one* of its aspects." [30] And hence, assuredly, not thought.

This acknowledgment of its own ultimate incapacity to understand the way in which its "demand" is satisfied, Bradley describes as a happy suicide. But must we not rather report it as suicide while of unsound mind? Only a "thought" suffering from delusions of grandeur would set itself a goal so vast, a datum so cognitively unpromising and a method of procedure so logically and metaphysically barren as these have proved to be. The final despair of "the intel-

29. Bradley, *Appearance and Reality,* p. 416.
30. Bradley, *Appearance and Reality,* p. 151.

lect" and recourse to other sides of our nature is necessitated only by this assumption, and not at all by what thinking, about its more pedestrian affairs, has
shown itself to be.

Ultimate Doubts

What, finally, are we to say of this philosophy? Given its assumptions and identification of "reality" it is very formidable. When he is laying stress on the
cogency of the dialectical procedure, Bradley makes very high claims for it.
"We hold that our conclusion [that Reality is a single, supra-relational whole
of sentient experience in which all appearances are somehow harmoniously
united] is certain, and that to doubt it logically is impossible. There is no other
view, there is no other idea beyond the view here put forward. It is impossible
rationally even to entertain the question of another possibility. Outside our
main result there is nothing except the wholly unmeaning, or else something
which on scrutiny is seen really not to fall outside." [31] For whatever can be meaningfully referred to must fall within "sentience," and whatever can be thought
must meet the demand of the intellect for consistency. And the Absolute is just
what, starting from sentient experience and following remorselessly the demand of thought, we have been "compelled," on penalty of self-contradiction,
to affirm. Nothing to which the slightest sense can be attached falls outside its
scope.

And yet, just as truly, everything falls outside its scope. The ordinary procedure of thinking, the practical adjustments that are, beyond the limits of this
debate, our contact with what is genuine, reliable and real, do not, in their
own right, appear in it at all. Nothing comes out of its initial assumptions but
what was put into them by the identifications of "Reality," "appearance," and
"thought" with which the theory operates, and which, so far from being evidently correct, are comprehensible only with reference to the standpoint of
idealistic philosophy and the powerful and complicated motives that led, in
this period, to its wide acceptance. And nothing to which we look for independent confirmation confirms or is even compatible with it unless it has been
transformed into a mere appearance by the speculative machinery of the theory
itself.

"What must be and may be, that certainly *is*." This was the rather dreary
formula with which Bradley bolstered up his own doubts about his theory,
doubts to which he returned again and again, with fine intellectual honesty, and
which were never really set at rest. "Must be"—because "thought" (as interpreted by this theory) demands it and "reality" (as so interpreted) will tolerate
nothing less. "May be," since what seems to fall outside it is, *if the theory is*

31. Bradley, *Appearance and Reality,* p. 459.

correct, mere appearance whose factual ultimacy cannot stand against the theory. "Is"—but only in a way we do not really understand, which rather appeases those sides of our nature which were committed in advance to a "spiritual" conclusion, than raises our commerce with the world about us to the clarity, scope, and rational coordination of philosophic wisdom.

We are not, then, compelled to accept this philosophy. What it presents as a logical necessity is actually the result of the choice of a philosophic standpoint, naturally attractive under the circumstances to men of idealistic good will and philosophical learning. Its justification is to be found, not in its equivocal and finally circular dialectic, but in its capacity to provide, in its applications, the philosophical enlightenment to which it lays claim. It is time now to consider these applications and to see what idealism in its use and operations has come to.

Applications and Outcome
The Criterion of Value

The guarantee of 'values'—that is, of what, in our best moments, we take to be true, beautiful and good, by Reality has already been considered. A no less important issue has to do with the extent to which Reality, as metaphysically arrived at, can help us to discern what is valuable, what our best moments *are,* and what it is that in these moments we really desire the universe to conserve for us. It is one of the major virtues of the idealism of Bradley, Bosanquet, and Royce that it did attempt a criticism of value claims, so that in those philosophies it is not what the uninstructed heart desires but only that which in the light of what we know of ultimate reality we should really and in the end desire that the absolute is bound to support and sustain. Insofar as this involves a recognition that the "finite" mind is not in a position to legislate for Reality until it has adjusted its demands to what the world on which its demands are made actually is, it is a distinct advance on the more subjective and wishful forms of idealism. It is highly important, however, that the criterion by which we scrutinize the validity of our valuations be one appropriate to their nature. If it is not, our actual discriminations of better and worse are more likely to be confused than clarified by the criticism offered. Is "Reality," or rather, since *ultimate* Reality is hardly to be reached in its fullness, is *degree* of reality in the sense already indicated, a just measure of the value which we ought reasonably to place on the actions, experiences and ends about whose worth in non-metaphysical matters we have to come to a decision? The result of experience in the use of this criterion has been, I believe, to show that it is not.

In the first place, how could ultimate Reality, or the universe as an Absolute spiritual Unity, serve as a measure of what we take to be valuable? No "finite" truth actually as it stands does justice to this reality, and every finite valuation would require transformation in it to an extent which we can hardly estimate. "Every finite truth or fact to some extent must be unreal and false, and it is impossible in the end certainly to know of any how false it may be." Some alteration is in every case required and "in any case . . . the alteration may amount to unlimited transformation." [32] This applies to moral, aesthetic and religious experience and belief as well as to any others. Religion gives us reality on a higher or more inclusive level than mere science, to be sure, but it is still but an aspect, and the ideas involved in it, while justified practically for religious purposes, are not ultimately true. The Absolute is not God and any attempt to conceive Reality in the terms of religion is partially false. Since morality is a less "concrete" aspect of experience than religion, its valuations and assumptions are even more subject to transformation. In the specific context in which moral duties ordinarily present themselves, "the world of claims and counter-claims" as Bosanquet disparagingly called it, only a relatively low share in ultimate reality can be allowed. Any verdict reached in this lower court is likely to be set aside in the higher. And since "Reality" is the ultimate criterion of value, as of truth, we shall not know how far our moral judgments are valid until we know how far the whole sustains them.

The difficulty is that this, in any ultimate sense, we do not know. Reality as a whole is simply not available as a criterion and there is no use in appealing to it save for such portentous and question-begging verdicts as that somehow, in the end, it must contain all that we demand in a form which, if thought were transformed into something that is not thought, would be seen to satisfy its highest demands. This is, at best, an equivocal assurance and a dubious guide. Those values which the universe conserves, in the form in which it conserves them, are finally warranted. "Higher," "better," and the rest count in the universe as they count for us. But there is a proviso, which, in quoting Bradley earlier, I did not add. Higher and more real count for the universe, "For, on the whole, higher means for us a greater amount of the one Reality, outside of which all appearance is absolutely nothing." [33] And Bosanquet adds that "In general, we know that what we care for, insofar as it is really what we care for, is safe through its continuity with the Eternal." [34] But what we really care for is what is really higher, and that is what the Eternal really preserves. Which is to say that in the end the Eternal does "preserve" whatever it does, and that our judgments of value, if they reflect this status adequately, are guaranteed by the real world. Until we know, as we do not know, what in this final synthesis is

32. Bradley, *Appearance and Reality,* pp. 480, 479.
33. Bradley, *Appearance and Reality,* p. 488.
34. Bosanquet, *Value and Destiny,* p. 261.

preserved, it is very difficult to know what we ought to want or how far what, independently of this metaphysical criterion, we took to be higher and better is actually preserved.

If this were the whole story, it would be hard to see how this criterion was really usable at all. It gains its application only when coupled with another, to which it is somewhat dubiously linked. This is the criterion of *wholeness,* not in the absolute or metaphysical sense, but in a quite relative and all-too-human one. In our own experience, when we try to make the most of it and get the most out of it, some aspects count for more than others. We should miss them more if they were absent, we feel most strongly about them, and we can best organize the remainder of our life by taking these factors as essential and others, that matter less, as peripheral. Bosanquet describes such factors as central, and the measure of their centrality is the extent to which they lend wholeness to experience, and to which our total adjustment to the world would be disturbed without them. When use is made of the metaphysical criterion of value it will be found I think that we have passed from "wholeness" as absolute inclusiveness in the universe to centrality as that which lends wholeness and "meaning" to experience. Bradley makes this sort of appeal only on occasion, as in the case, already noticed, in which the greater "concreteness" or wholeness of an emotional and poetic reading of nature as contrasted with a scientific description of it is taken as proof that it is truer and more adequate to Reality as a whole. Bosanquet, however, uses it consistently and with enthusiasm, and it is in his version of the theory that its implications are most clearly seen.

We are, on Bosanquet's view, "to take for our standard what man recognises as value when his life is fullest and his soul at its highest stretch." [35] We find "centrality," which is to be our guide to wholeness and hence to Reality, in a "strong" and "profound" impression of life such as a great poet—Dante or Wordsworth or Tennyson—can give us. In ordinary moral behavior, with the valuations that accompany it, there appears to be a sharp contrast between good and evil. But this "does not represent our central impression," it does not "confront the more complete and sane and courageous experience." [36] The achievement of this higher sanity is no easy task, but it is essential. "[T]o be right in one's birds-eye view of centrality and the scheme of values, demands a higher intellectual character and even a more toilsome intellectual achievement than to formulate whole volumes of ingenious ratiocination. . . . no skill in [logical] development will compensate for a defective attitude toward life." [37]

There is evidently much sound sense in this, and it would be merely flippant to treat it lightly. But does it mean quite what Bosanquet takes it to mean?

35. Bosanquet, *The Principle of Individuality and Value* (London: Macmillan, 1912), p. 3.
36. Bosanquet, *Principle of Individuality and Value,* p. 5.
37. Bosanquet, *Principle of Individuality and Value,* p. 6.

"Sanity" and "centrality" in the organization of values are the result of life in particular and quite local communities in which activities, ideas, and purposes are well adjusted to each other and to the demands of the environment. Practical wisdom and good sense are the fruit of such wholeness and adequacy of adjustment, and anyone who shares fully in the way of life in question will rightly feel such values as for him "central" and will regard an attack upon them as a disruption of what, in the whole course of experience, he has found to be good. The emotions surrounding these practices and beliefs in which his "values" center will be strong ones and when these are evoked in poetry or ritual he will naturally feel that they express more of what is "really" good than he can say and more than any discursive analysis of "values" could do justice to. If the community life in question is that of a cultivated Englishman at the end of the nineteenth century, those values will, I think, be very like those that Bosanquet found to be central, sane, and strong.

A theory of value which neglects this situation is likely to be quite thin and to merit some at least of Bosanquet's strictures. But does it help here at all to identify what is thus found to be central with what the Universe with all its stars and milky ways requires? Has not the transition from "Wholeness" in a particular sort of practical adjustment to wholeness as a measure of Reality confused both value and Reality? I think that it has. For if the "Reality" side of the identification is insisted on, we are likely to want to transform the local and quite genuine goodness which sanity and practical wisdom discern into a higher good which, if pressed, becomes inhuman and morally misleading.

The necessary structure of the universe is the final criterion of value, after all, and if the Universe not only tolerates evil but reconciles it in a higher good who are we to say that in the deepest sense it should not be there? The Absolute, as Royce remarked in a rather unhappy passage, is no respecter of persons. "It would tear down these individual barriers of our petty lives, as the corporation of a great city may tear down wretched old rookeries." [38] This is quite consistent as applied to the Absolute in which speculative idealism asks us to believe. But it is, I think, neither "sane" nor "central" in any sense in which those terms have an independently certifiable meaning. If we are really serious with the Absolute, it is the part of wisdom to keep clearly in mind the difference of its good, which is metaphysical perfection, with its accompanying absorption of the "finite" distinctions which in practical wisdom we maintain, though with some shrewd sense of their local application and limits, from the "centrality" to which Bosanquet refers. Otherwise we shall be rather heartless when we deal with relative human suffering from the higher standpoint in which all evil is a metaphysically welcome contribution to an ultimate per-

38. Josiah Royce, *The Religious Aspect of Philosophy* (Boston and New York: Houghton Mifflin, 1885), p. 201.

fection, and priggish when we identify our own estimate of importance as nice Englishmen or good Americans with a disclosure of ultimate reality. Such heartlessness is to be found, I think, in Bosanquet's account[39] of the meaning and value of pain in "Reality," and such priggishness in his estimate of the worth of the feelings expressed by Tennyson as a clue to Reality. And it is these two characteristics which keep us from accepting the idealists, in spite of their quite genuine wisdom, as really reliable guides to the nature of what we are to accept as good. Actually the standard of metaphysical wholeness or perfection and that of human importance and "centrality" are quite distinct. They might be identified in a mystical experience or a pantheistic religion in which the "finite" is in fact absorbed in the infinite. Short of that, however, the attempt to make the latter the "clue" to the former and the former the sanction of the latter is bound to end in the attribution of absolute status to relative values and the distortion of those values in the attempt to make them conform to an absolute metaphysical standard.

The Philosophy of the State

A specific issue, much debated in the last thirty years, will illustrate the consequences of this confusion. That the political state is an embodiment of objective mind or purpose, that the "mere" individual, considered as real in himself and apart from his social relations, is a "mere" abstraction and that, relative to this mere individual, the state represents a higher measure of reality and of value, since it is more concrete and since it is only in the community that the individual realizes his own higher good, are among the most important and widely discussed deliverances of philosophical idealism. They represent as they stand a curiously intricate mixture of social psychology, ethics, and metaphysics, and the nature of that combination must be grasped if we are to understand its importance and wide influence and its unhappy consequences.

If we are to explain the social behavior of individuals we must have recourse to the context in which their social behavior is manifest—that is, as members of groups and communities of various sorts—and must be prepared to attribute to them the character which, in that context, they are found to have. This, as it stands, is merely a truism of method. But in relation to the evolution of the social sciences it is a doctrine of some importance. In the development of these sciences the tendency has been to carry over from a psychology of "mental states" and a hedonistic ethics assumptions about human nature which do not do justice to its complexity and to the specific motives that the behavior of men in groups manifests. The tendency to think of "ideas" as private possessions and interests as drives for units of pleasure is, it appears, too simple to do justice to the subject. A *social* behaviorism at least is required if we are to

---

39. Bosanquet, *Value and Destiny of the Individual,* lecture 6.

understand social behavior, and social behavior is manifest in such "objective" achievements as science, art, and religion, the "higher" activities of man, as well as in his reception of impressions and [in his] desire to avoid pain.

One major reason for the initial plausibility of the idealistic philosophy of the state is that it did stress these social activities and thus allow factors which actually count in human behavior to have a respectable place in the descriptions we apply to it. "Objective mind" is a convenient alias for those types of activity in which ideas are communicated and purposes shared. Man is a political animal in this sense, at least, that he does frequently care greatly for causes—the advancement of learning, the relief of suffering, the creation of socially valued and useful objects—which are of more importance to him than his "individual" interests, as the current individualism would have computed them, so that the best of him is in them and without them he would not be himself. I do not suggest that this aspect of social behavior requires recourse to idealistic metaphysics for its adequate description. But I do suggest that idealistic metaphysics provided men with a terminology, warranted as philosophically respectable, with which they could describe such behavior more "concretely" than the current attempts at social science had, on the whole, been able to do. It is not unnatural to express the conclusion to which a preference for this terminology leads in the statement that man is himself only as a member of a group and that the "mere" individual is an unreal abstraction.

This same emphasis on the social context has important ethical implications. Among the morally admirable qualities of an individual are those he manifests when he devotes himself to such causes, losing his individual life if need be for the sake of a good which, if it requires his own extinction, he nonetheless acknowledges as his own. The process in which a man learns to subordinate those of his interests and appetites which are immediately satisfying to those which are socially acceptable is, in part at least, a moral progress, and one not unplausibly described as a process of self-transcendence, at once the fulfilment of his original nature and its transformation, the process in fact in which, by becoming fully a member of a community he comes, in a eulogistic sense, to be himself. Self-realization and social significance are thus happily blended, and the urge toward social service and moral expansion which, in the [1880s and 1890s] fostered Christian socialism and ethical culture, is sanctioned as well in moral philosophy. An ethical liberalism which sought to correct the traditional Utilitarianism without surrendering the ultimate claims of the *moral* individual could hardly have found a more convenient vehicle. T. H. Green's *Lectures on the Principles of Political Obligation* represents this philosophical standpoint at a very high level.

There is, finally, the metaphysical strand in the fabric, and this receives full expression in Bradley's *Ethical Studies* and Bosanquet's *Philosophical Theory of the State*. The community in which minds meet and purposes are shared has, as we should expect, a higher degree of *reality* than the mere individual. It is a "greater" thing, and the purpose embodied in it a higher purpose than any the individual as such can possess. Moreover, the process by which the individual identifies himself with this greater purpose or realizes his own will in a will that is above himself is that very process of self-transcendence in virtue of which all appearance strives to complete itself in a wider whole in which its own imperfections are overcome and its own nature at once absorbed and, on a higher level, preserved. Even as an individual a person is only a provisional unity, and "When you have admitted the unity of the person with himself, it is impossible to stop short of his unity with others, with the world, and with the universe; and the perfection by which he is to be valued is his place in the perfection of these greater wholes."[40] Thus the relative abstractness of an incomplete description of individual behavior *apart from* society becomes the evidence that *the individual* as such is a mere appearance and the social group a higher or more concrete one, and the value judgment that individuals find their good as members of communities becomes the metaphysical truth that the "nisus toward totality," as manifested in their unity within more and more inclusive wholes, in terms of whose "perfections" their own perfection is to be judged, is the true expression at once of their reality and their value.

What is wrong with this picture? Surely, in the first place, this. The "individual" that is shown to be an "abstraction" is not the individual human being who is a member of various social organizations, but only an incomplete description of such an individual. And the community in whose "perfection" his value is to be found is not a higher revelation of "reality" but an organization of individuals in which their wants are satisfied and, it may be, their better natures given an opportunity for expression. The contrast *in value* which is important for political theory or moral philosophy is not that [one] between the individual as such and the state, but [that] between the individual in his "concrete" social nature and capacities and the various organizations and groups in which these capacities are exercised. The political state is one among these and, as including various group interests and adjusting their conflicting claims, it is in one sense the most inclusive. If we are tempted to carry over into our thinking about men as members of groups the value distinction which the metaphysical theory suggests between "the individual" and "the state" we shall be badly misled. For, by every humanly justifiable standard, the values most worth preserving are those which attach to individuals and not to the groups to which they belong. Integrity, magnanimity, moral responsibility, and personal kindliness belong to individuals, not to groups, though, to be sure, they belong to individuals only as members of groups. The perfection of a political commu-

40. Bosanquet, *Principle of Individuality and Value,* p. 315.

nity—power, efficiency, just administration or racial solidarity—is not a more valuable perfection than this, but a more dubious one. In fact the best thing that can be said about such a "greater" whole is that it sometimes serves as the instrument and medium through which the goods of personal life can be more securely and fully enjoyed. To talk of the perfection of a social group or organization as a greater perfection than that of an individual person, if this is supposed to mean that morally or socially the group enjoys in its communal aspect a higher good than that which belongs to individual persons, is to provide the excuse for a really serious perversion of values. The language of idealism does suggest that reading of the situation, and has therefore lent itself to the uses of those who find in the destiny of state, race, or the like a "greater" good in which the moral values belonging uniquely to persons have at best a subordinate place, and who are glad to borrow an edifying terminology in which to recommend that otherwise unpalatable doctrine. I do not think that the philosophical idealists themselves were committed to this position, but I do think that they were confused about it and were led by their metaphysics into statements which seem to support it. Consequently, in the long and fruitless debate about the ultimate priority of "state" and "individual" their attitude was equivocal and misleading, and the initial promise of their approach to social situations in the concrete was dissipated in an unhelpful glorification of the state as against the individual, [a position] which is, at best, unenlightening.

Nor has the fate of the doctrine that communities are the embodiment of ethical ideals and objective purposes been happy. Viewed morally, the state or any other social organization is justified in the degree to which it does realize purposes which reasonable men find good. And only insofar as an existing institution can be seen to serve good ends is our allegiance to it a rational loyalty and not the result of habit, fear, or selfish interest. This is a consideration definitely pertinent to an inquiry into the *ground* (as distinct from the cause or origin) of political obligation. The degree, however, in which such purpose *is* realized and [in which] men are thereby obligated to subordinate their private wills to a rule they think will serve the common good, is only empirically, not metaphysically, ascertainable. No government represents the "ethical" ideal save as it provides in its day-to-day operation means for the security and well-being of its members, and no state is "actual" save through the governmental agencies through which it functions and the command these have on the loyalty of its citizens.

What happens when we call the purpose of "the state" a higher purpose than that of the individual and suggest that in reconciling his will to it he is realizing his own true good? Just this, that we substitute a relation of acquiescence, identification, or absorption of the lesser in the greater for that of free cooperation with an agency judged on the whole to serve good ends. The difference is an important one. When the obedience of the individual to the state, or his service to any "higher" group, is thought of as a nisus toward self-transcendence, it takes on an essentially religious and quasi-mystical aspect. Indeed, as Bosanquet describes religion, it is essentially religious. "Whenever, then, we find a devotion which makes the finite self seem as nothing and some reality to which it attaches itself seem as all, we have the essentially religious attitude." [41] The true social consciousness thus possesses "the essential feature of religion." "It has the value of the self placed in a real whole in which it is absorbed and with which the will is identified." [42]

This seems to me a case of the spilt religion to which allusion was earlier made. Insofar as this metaphysics suggests that we should take an essentially religious attitude—even in this somewhat tenuous sense of "religion"—toward the political state, it is, again, not helpful. Absorption in a higher will is not a wise or reliable attitude for good citizens in their dealings with their government, as recent experiments in Europe have all too obviously displayed. We need not go as far as Hegel's celebrated dictum that the state is the actual march of God in the world. We need only observe that the state possesses its authority ultimately not as an instrument of goods fully actualized only in the lives of individual persons, but rather as a manifestation of ultimate Reality higher in its own right than the mere individual, and that the proper attitude of the individual toward this more inclusive reality is that which, in social life, religion, and metaphysics, involves the ultimate absorption (and preservation) of the lower in the higher. Guard such a doctrine as we will, and Bosanquet was anxious to guard it against misuse, it does suggest and support the conclusion that actual states are spiritual, as manifestations of the real, in ways in which they do not appear to be in their more mundane behavior, and that they are fit objects for religious or quasi-religious devotion. This devotion is to be qualified, of course, by reference to the still higher unities with respect to which even loyalty is not enough, and to the final absorption of all "aspects," the political among the rest, in Ultimate Reality. This gives the doctrine a breadth and freedom from fanaticism to which neither its critics nor its more politically minded disciples have done justice. But so far as it deals with the *relative* value of "the individual" and "the state" its implication is the one suggested. It is a very unfortunate one.

The idealistic theory of the state is today unpopular, and I have not resuscitated it in order to link the idealistic philosophers with a now unfashionable cause. It does serve, however, as a specimen of the specific way in which the attempt to interpret and justify values on the model of a metaphysics of "ab-

41. Bosanquet, *Value and Destiny of the Individual*, p. 235.
42. Bosanquet, *Value and Destiny of the Individual*, p. 240.

stract" appearance and progressively more inclusive and therefore more perfect Reality distorts the issues with which in practice it is called upon to deal. It is only as such a specimen that it is here important.

Value and Existence

The transcendence of the more humanly recognizable and reliable values in the perfection of "the whole" did not, of course, meet with universal, or even general, approval among those whose primary concern was to find a guarantee in Reality for what, in their best moments, they desired. The tendency of the Absolute Idealists to minimize the importance of the "finite" individual or, in less speculative terms, the human person, was especially viewed with alarm, and "personal idealism" emerged to correct this error, and to insist, in Howison's words, that "personality alone is the measure, the sufficing establishment of reality" and "*unconditional* reality alone is sufficient to the being of persons." [43] The varieties of such idealism are many. McTaggart deduced from self-evident principles the necessity of a world whose demands, so far as he could see, only a society of timeless spirits, eternally related by love, could satisfy.[44] Since no spirit in this society occupied a position of metaphysical preeminence, none could properly be called God. The result was thus spiritual pluralism and atheism. James Ward was anxious to have a place left for a God who could unify "the many" and, happily, successful in finding a world that satisfied this requirement, a world of spiritual agents, all active and striving for a unity which would be one of mutual adjustment and not monistic absorption, but with a theistic agent to start things going and guarantee their ultimate harmony. Pringle-Pattison wanted more unity in the world than any sort of limited God could guarantee but less than the Bradleyan Absolute would necessitate. His conclusion is a masterpiece of judicious vagueness.

The varieties of non-Absolutistic idealism cannot here be catalogued. What is relevant is simply the fact that, while retaining the claim that a synoptic or inclusive philosophy will prove the primacy of mind and the ultimate security of value in the world, they all rejected the recourse to "the Whole" as the measure of value and status in the Absolute as the guarantee of its reality. Thus all agreed, at least in considerable measure, with the claim of Henry Sturt, speaking for the "Personal Idealists" of Oxford, that a basic sin of Absolute Idealism was "its way of criticizing human experience, not from the standpoint of human experience, but from the visionary and impracticable standpoint of an absolute experience." [45] Values are to be guaranteed, but the detour by

43. George Holmes Howison, in *The Conception of God* (New York: Macmillan, 1898), p. 93.
44. See the extended discussion of McTaggart, ch. 6, below.
45. Henry Sturt, in *Personal Idealism* (London: Macmillan, 1902), preface, p. viii.

way of the Absolute is held to be not the proper route to the "homeland of the spirit."

The consequence of this is important. If we are to remain Idealists and cease to be Absolutists, we must insist on the right of our assurances about "value" to speak for Reality, not after they have been transformed and purified but as we find them here and now. We take our stand on "the conviction of the essential greatness of man and the infinite nature of the values revealed in his life. Without this absolute judgment of value, how could we argue, how could we *convince ourselves,* that in our estimates, it is not we who judge as finite particulars, but Reality affirming, through us, its inmost nature?" [46] How indeed? An absolute judgment of value that is also a judgment in which Reality affirms through us its inmost nature is a portentous and may be a very dangerous thing. It is only with the support of such a judgment, if the Idealists are correct, that human values can retain their validity, for only thus does "Reality" warrant what, in our own persons, we prefer. This reference of value to Reality for its warrant as valuable, and consequent assurance that, if we are sure of its value we can be sure as well of the Reality on which such value depends, is the essence of the philosophy we are considering. If [this philosophy] is not to lapse into unbridled voluntarism and anthropomorphism, there must be reason offered to show that values, in the sense in which human beings are in a position to discriminate and appreciate them, are in fact an adequate indication of the nature of existence, or what would ordinarily be regarded as matter of fact, as well. The argument, in other words, must be from value to existence, and its basic premise, somehow to be justified, must be that value and existence are essentially connected, so that reality is "a realm in which thought and thing, fact and value, are inseparable." [47] The nature of this argument, and the capacity of the theory it supports to aid in our appreciation of values or understanding of existence have now to be examined.

The argument, which is presented in many forms and with varying degrees of subtlety by its protagonists, proceeds, I think, by three relatively easy stages. First, there is at least *some* genuine connection between value and existence. The two are not *merely* irrelevant to each other, for what we call valuable is what would be valuable if it existed; it is its existence and not its merely "ideal" character which is essential to its value. And equally, we decide by means of "norms", standards and "valuations" what exists. Truth itself is a "value" and yet we confidently believe that what we accept as true by the criteria of validity which our own minds "acknowledge" is a revelation of what

46. A. Seth Pringle-Pattison, *The Idea of God in the Light of Recent Philosophy* (2d ed.; Oxford: Clarendon Press, 1920), p. 236.

47. Wilbur M. Urban, "Metaphysics and Value," in *Contemporary American Philosophy,* edited by George P. Adams and William Pepperell Montague (New York: Macmillan, 1930), vol. 2, p. 375.

actually exists. Considerations of meaning, "validity," and the like are thus bound up with questions of fact, and, unless we are to lapse into scepticism and agnosticism, we must hold that "in some manner meanings and values are integral to existence and to reality." [48] *In some manner,* but more specifically, *what* manner?

Second, if our judgments of validity are not irrelevant to existence, they can supply information about its real or intrinsic nature. We find out about the world in our practical relations with it as well as in mere abstract thinking, and in practice more evidently than in mere theorizing values have a predominant place. "There must be at least as much to learn about the inmost character of the real from the fact that our actual spiritual life is controlled by such-and-such definite conceptions of good and right, such-and-such hopes and fears, as there is to learn from the fact that the laws of motion are what they are, or that the course of biological development on our planet has followed the lines it has followed." [49] That we learn something from a study of our practical attitudes is evident enough. And if that means, as Taylor's argument assumes, that we learn something about "the inmost nature of the real," we are well on the way to a desired conclusion.

Third, if this value reveals Reality, it only remains to say how, in Reality, our values stand. And surely it is not too much to say that in a world with value at the heart of things "every human being has a presumptive meaning in the cosmic order; . . . our judgments of worth must be essentially valid; . . . our most universal standards, including those ethical standards of honor, beauty, loyalty, cannot be indifferent to the nature of things." [50] Nor can it be a matter of "cosmic indifference" whether or not we observe those standards. Which brings us back essentially to the "absolute judgment" cited above, that in our valuations we speak for the inmost nature of Reality.

This sequence of disconnected quotations does less than justice to the subtlety and tortuous course of the argument we are trying to understand. The reader who intends to test our hypothesis in detail must work it out through many volumes of Gifford Lectures. My claim is that it will be found to work in detail and that the sequence [from] "in some manner integral to existence and reality" [through] "the inmost nature of the real" [to] "the cosmic order is not indifferent" does fairly mark the progress from the true and important statements that an adequate philosophy must take account of "values" in their connection with existence in the context of our own experience and striving, to the very different and far more dubious statement that the cosmic order cares about

48. George P. Adams, "Naturalism or Idealism," *Contemporary American Philosophy,* vol. 1, p. 85.

49. A. E. Taylor, *The Faith of a Moralist* (London: Macmillan, 1930), vol. 1, p. 65.

50. W. E. Hocking, *Types of Philosophy* (New York: Charles Scribner's Sons, 1929), p. 320.

us, and that our deepest appreciative moments can supply metaphysically valid information as to its essential constitution.

The trouble with the argument, if it proves less than persuasive, lies precisely in this notion of "Reality" and its "inmost" nature. To be valid is to belong to "the real," to be truly valid is to reveal its inmost nature, to be quite sure of what one values is thus to make a claim of cosmic scope and pretensions. Surely, we should want to make some distinctions here and to begin with some analysis of the *way* in which the human situation belongs to "reality" and hence to the "cosmic order" and thus provides information about it. The argument as stated is a perpetual incitement to neglect such distinctions and qualifications. Professor Hocking, who accepts and defends it, has explained very plainly its essential nature. There is *some* meaning or value in the world: why should we not conclude that there is a metaphysical maximum of it? "We have no reason to assume that there is any limit to the objective value of the world. On the surface, we find it moderately good and moderately bad: but moderation has no metaphysical standing." [51] This, I think, brings us to the heart of the matter, if not to the heart of reality. Moderation *has* no metaphysical standing, and we are therefore presented with the spurious dichotomy of no value at all, irrelevance of value to existence, which surely we cannot accept—or else a world in which the cosmic order somehow cares for what we care for, and for us. Whatever the merits of this way of thinking in its own field, it does not, in its application to non-philosophical problems, help us to think judiciously and accurately of the place and prospects of our value claims in the world with which we have to deal.

Yet there was a genuine problem here, on the level of the rational coordination of our beliefs. It is not difficult to see its character, even in the distorted reflection of it which metaphysical controversy supplies. Many of our valuations do in fact depend, at least in part, on our beliefs about the environment in which we act and the beings with whom we have to deal. The issue as to whether, as Urban puts it, we are high-grade Simians or Sons of God or, as he neglects to add, something between the two, *is* pertinent to the valuation we place on human life, and even to such mundane questions as birth control, the moral legitimacy of suicide, "mercy-killings" and the like. The "sacredness" of life depends on the sort of thing it is, and if religion as well as biology has something to tell us on this score, we ought certainly to take account of it in our judgments of what is right and good. Books like Krutch's *The Modern Temper* and Lippmann's *Preface to Morals* * register the literary echoes of the

51. W. E. Hocking, "What Does Philosophy Say?" *The Philosophical Review* 37.2 (March 1928): 133–55, 152–53.

* Joseph Wood Krutch, *The Modern Temper* (New York: Harcourt, Brace and Company, 1929); Walter Lippmann, *A Preface to Morals* (New York: Macmillan, 1929). Ed.

impact of advancing scientific knowledge on accepted value judgments. Discounting all heroics involved, there is still the fact that a life lived wholly between the period of birth and death in this region of temporality is a different sort of life in many respects from one with an eternal destiny. The question as to whether the valuations placed on action when it was thought to have a supernatural environment are still reasonable if we believe it to have a more restricted scope is a perfectly pertinent and intelligible one.

What, however, will the natural response to this problem be for a man who is very sure of his valuations and genuinely convinced of their validity? If he sees both that these valuations depend on certain beliefs about matters of fact, and that they are valid as they appear to be, will he not be inclined to say that the world must be what it would have to be in order to render his preferences reasonable, that only such a world is from a *valuational* standpoint "intelligible" and "livable," and that any other world is "intolerable"? And if he can find reason for supposing that philosophy must somehow take account of his values, will he not be inclined to say that what his value judgment claims is really true, true of reality, and hence of the very existent world in which on the "first look" it had seemed only dubiously grounded? The "practical" reason, here oriented toward values, will have reasons that mere theory knows nothing of and from a firm assurance of what is really valuable we shall be able to deduce the existence of that environment to which conduct thus valued would, from a teleological or moral standpoint, be "reasonable." This, I believe, has been the procedure of the "practical reason" from Kant to A. E. Taylor, and there is no reason to suppose that it has yet lost its persuasiveness.

The case is much strengthened by the fact that the cultural and especially the moral valuations of the civilization of Western Europe are very closely bound up with the world picture provided by the Christian religion, and that this religion does involve beliefs about a great many "matters of fact." If a moral philosopher starts with traditional ideals of conduct, of what is "noble" and "admirable" and the like, or of what is base and sinful, he will not find great difficulty in tracing them back to a supernatural setting and superhuman hope. We are still deeply attached to these "values," even when we have become uncertain about the beliefs with which they were formerly associated. The necessity of a religious sanction for morals is highly debatable, but the support which the moral codes we actually accept have received from religion is not really doubtful. Hence to reaffirm the unqualified validity of these codes, and to trace them back once more to their source, is a very persuasive way of rehabilitating the beliefs as to matters of fact with which they are associated. And if we could know that our value judgments here were certainly sound, the procedure would be a reasonable one.

This can be done directly, or indirectly. The idealist's method was indirect. To say straight out that God rules the world would, in the atmosphere in which

Bradley and Royce and Creighton worked, have been quite unacceptable. The specific tenets of religious belief were in those circles being painlessly sublimated into a confidence in the general "meaning" of the universe. But to say that all that is manifests a Supreme Reality, and that this Reality which is not indifferent to our values is least inadequately conceived as the God of the great religions, comes "in the end" to something not very different. It strips our belief of merely local accretions and provides an object fit to elicit cosmic emotion. Yet remnants of the older belief remain. Even Bradley is repelled by a theory of value which would not permit us to say that "for the universe" what we value "has any degree of difference or matters at all." What matters for the universe or is an object of Cosmic concern is what "in the end" we would wish to cherish. The synthesis thus provided of an absolute value judgment with an attenuated religion, in a Cosmic consciousness, has not worked well. Nor is this really surprising. To maintain one's belief in the absoluteness of the value in question with no more firm assurance than this of its appropriateness to the existent world is not easy. The question that is bound to arise and to become more pressing is this: granted that some judgments about what is good, right, and admirable would be "intelligible" only if a spiritual environment was presupposed, ought we not rather to question the reliability of the judgments, in the light of what, from other sources, we know about the world, than to insist that, since we are sure of the value judgments, the world must be such as to render them "intelligible"? If we remain absolutely sure about the values, all is well. But if we do not, then the stage is set rather for a revaluation of values than for a metaphysics of the practical reason.

The trouble with idealism as a philosophy was that it presupposed such an assurance, but did not, save provisionally and for those already persuaded, sustain it. If there is independent religious evidence of a spiritual order, nothing could be more important for a theory of what, as wise men, we ought to regard as valuable. This evidence, however, if it is to be persuasive, will come not from metaphysics but from the religions. Insofar as a man is able to identify himself with such a religion, submit to its authority, and, through participation in its rituals and beliefs, assure himself of its validity, his conviction of the "concern" of the cosmic order for his conduct and hopes is likely to remain unshaken. And if the experiences and beliefs guaranteed and sustained by such religious practices are a reliable source of information about the world, what he is thus persuaded of will be in some cases true. The appeal, however, is not to the general connection between value and existence, but to the faith and practice of the religions, and it is here, if at all, that the persuasion of the absoluteness of our value judgments as representatives of ultimate reality is likely to find its sanction.

Nothing is more striking in the intellectual history of the last generation than the swing away from the *general* claim that reality is spiritual and toward the apology for specific religious practices, beliefs, and organizations as sources of information about the world, of which philosophy must take account, not in a higher synthesis, but in the particular forms in which the religions present them. William James' recourse to the varieties of religious experience as a source of information about the "wider consciousness" to which idealists had appealed and his resultant "piecemeal supernaturalism" was a pioneer excursion. Hocking's delineation and defense of "the mystics and their worship" was a far more convincing contribution to "The Meaning of God in Human Experience" than his revival of the ontological argument. A. E. Taylor's *The Faith of a Moralist,* with its detailed defense of institutional religion, with the concrete rites, doctrines and practices appertaining to it, shows very strikingly how far a disciple of Bradley can move in these matters. When Karl Barth was imported to offer Gifford Lectures on "natural theology" * the movement reached what, for the present, may be regarded as its climax. The revival of scholasticism tends obviously in the same direction. When recourse can be had, in an important series of Gifford Lectures, to the steadying influence of the book of Exodus as a guide to the view that Being is prior to Knowing, it becomes clear that we have moved a long way from Idealism as the guarantor of truth in matters of the spirit.[52]

It is not my purpose to evaluate this newer tendency at this point. What is pertinent is the fact that the recourse to absolute value judgments has led men away from the speculative constructions of the idealists and toward much more dogmatic, authoritarian, and practical sources of assurance. The result, whatever it is, is certainly not idealism. The concern of these thinkers is not to do equal justice to all sides of our "nature," but to treat one "side" of it—held to be incomparably the most important—as absolutely authoritative, and to judge the rest in relation and subordination to this. Philosophically, their yoke is not easy, nor their burden light. Nor is it at all obvious that the adoption of this standpoint makes our total outlook on the world broader or more inclusive. A specific religion is likely to have consequences and make claims, in matters of political policy for example, which follow naturally enough from its absolute authority, but which are very hard indeed to reconcile with what, on other grounds, we should regard as just or generous, or even, as to matters of fact, simply true. The synthesis of such spiritual claims with what, on the whole, a reasonable man would on other grounds believe, is a "costing" and bitter one,

---

52. Etienne Gilson, *The Spirit of Medieval Philosophy* (London: Sheed and Ward, 1936).

* W. E. Hocking, *The Meaning of God in Human Experience* (New Haven: Yale University Press, 1912); Karl Barth, *The Knowledge of God and the Service of God According to the Teaching of the Reformation* (London: Hodder and Stoughton, 1938). Ed.

not an expansive transition to wider and wider spheres of meaning. If the reader is interested in studying the problems that confront a mind of deep religious piety and philosophic scope in its attempt to reconcile positive religious belief with what experience "as a whole" inclines it to accept, he will get far more instruction from a study of the life, letters, and doctrine of the Baron von Hügel than from most axiological discussions. To retain the specific content and environment of religion, within which a belief in absolute cosmic values can live, and at the same time to assimilate and appreciate the full value of modern life and learning, was a task which even this wise and good man found profoundly difficult. The result of his spiritual struggle looks, to many of us, more like a defeat than a victory. But at least it was a meeting of issues on the plane where they actually arise and must, in the end, be settled.*

The sum of the discussion is this: the argument from value to existence, when it is more than equivocal and vague, depends on a conviction of absolute values of cosmic significance. This conviction is not at all easy to maintain in what is conventionally described as "the modern world." To insist that the world must be such as to make certain value judgments intelligible, where such intelligibility commits us to beliefs in matters of fact which our experience, in other respects, does not tend to confirm, is a peremptory and pretentious demand. It can for the most part be sustained in practice only with the support of institutions and practices of a rather special character. With their support it takes a dogmatic and authoritarian tone hard to reconcile with the cosmic liberalism of the idealists. Without it, the tendency toward a contextual examination of values in their relative "significance" and human setting is likely to supplant the cosmic theory of values and the appeal to "inmost reality" to lose its meaning.

Meaning

"Take idealism from an idealist, what remains? The answer is that 'meaning' would remain." The elucidation of this possibly cryptic dictum is the task of the following paragraphs.

The speculative backbone of idealism, as previously suggested, was the claim that Reality as a Whole or in its inmost nature is an object metaphysically accessible, and that the information we obtain about it is such as to warrant the cosmic status of values and the general conformity of existence to what our thought demands. The theoretical ground for this claim is a dialectical demonstration that this "Reality" is presupposed in all its appearances and is denied only on pain of willful partiality or nonsense. The results reached by this method were supported, though with some doubts about the "absolutism" involved, by the conviction of cosmic values, inherited from religion and pre-

---

* On von Hügel, see the interesting article by Ninian Smart in volume 4 of *The Encyclopedia of Philosophy* (New York: Macmillan, 1967).

served in romanticism. They were further bulwarked by the epistemological conclusion, carried over from German Philosophy, that Mind in some sense legislates for the world of phenomena and is thus "foundational" to Reality. The resulting philosophy had, in the days of its maximum prestige, many uses. It served as a temporary but helpful shelter from the winds of modern doctrine for beliefs to which religious support was no longer available but which still seemed essential to that "significance" which philosophers have always tried to find. It enabled investigators who wished to stress the "higher" or cultural aspects of human behavior to deal "concretely" with their subject matter and to take account of factors which current scientific theories had, on the whole, neglected. And stressing the importance of "thought" in its constructive operations was a valuable corrective to scepticism and agnosticism. In all these capacities it recommended itself to many who were primarily interested in "meaning"—the "meaningfulness" of a significant or emotionally satisfactory universe—the "meaning" involved in the social sharing of ideas and purposes through intelligible communication—the "meaning" or relatedness which enables mind to transcend the datum in knowledge—and much more.

Even when the central faith of Idealism in the Absolute weakens and the confidence in cosmic values fades, the helpful work involved in the discernment of "meaning" will remain, and it is this that stands today as the residue of Idealism, and that warrants such claim as it has to relevance to contemporary issues.

There is no doubt, I think, that the present generation of idealists is dealing, under this heading of "meaning," "significance," and "norms," with important problems, and that it has much that is true to say about them. It is dealing with them, however, in terms of concepts derived from the older speculative debate which do not precisely fit the subject-matter, and which serve as a perpetual incitement to regard tautologies as epistemological revelations and to use a theory of signs and of communication as a hopeful hint of *ultimate* meanings. This conduces to equivocal utterances of problematic import and leaves both the philosopher and his readers unclear as to what he is doing or where specifically his "meanings" are to be understood to apply.

The epistemological attenuation of idealism has been traced with great acumen by G. W. Cunningham in *The Idealistic Argument in Recent British and American Philosophy*. His critical analysis of the subjectivist and *a priori* arguments for Idealism, and of the speculative claim that experience discloses a "nisus" toward "real" reality are remarkably convincing. The positive conclusion, however, is a rather meager one. We must identify reality "with what intelligence and its relational machinery is in the end forced to accept" [53] and

---

53. G. Watts Cunningham, *The Idealistic Argument in Recent British and American Philosophy* (New York: The Century Company, 1933), p. 402.

"the character of transcendence in the object in knowledge seems to be indispensable to any sound epistemology." [54] In the light of the traditional idealistic argument these statements have a certain importance as indicating the minimum to which the doctrine is reduced when its speculative wings have been ruthlessly clipped. But what do they tell us about "reality" or the object of knowledge? Only, apparently, that the world is what we find it to be when we make use of such intellectual means as we have of finding out about it, and that we can know objects which are not given because given experience provides more or less reliable clues as to their nature. Against an epistemological theory which held "thought" powerless to reach "reality" or maintained that only animal faith and not reasonable belief can take us beyond "the datum," this stands as an eminently sensible doctrine. It holds that "meaning" enters into knowledge and that, in reality, what by the use of such intellectual machinery we take to be so is so. Outside that debate, however, it is of little help. For the "real" is here just what we can find to be the case, and we still need to know, from more special investigations than epistemology, what this is. And transcendence reduces to whatever clues in inquiry help us to extend our knowledge. If "meaning" and transcendence are to help us much they require some further specification than this. In a series of substantial studies,[55] Cunningham has carried his investigation of meaning much further and has stressed the connection of mind, object, perspective, and context in the meaning-situation. This represents the most hopeful attempt to tie down the concepts of idealistic epistemology to a field of reliable application with which I am acquainted. But it is doubtful whether even here the ponderous categories employed are not a hindrance rather than a help. There is need for more of signs and their uses and less of significance, more of inquiry and less of mind, and above all more of things seen and handled and verifiably observed and less of "the object," if we are ever to get in touch with a subject-matter in which "meanings" as they function in knowing are reliably to be described. But this, at least, is the line along which progress may be anticipated, and it leads straight away from the claims of thought on reality and the character of transcendence in the object and toward a contextual analysis of knowledge-claims in the non-epistemological situation in which they can be tested.

Of meaning and "communication" in the social sciences, much might be said. The field is a fruitful one for inquiry and it is doubtful whether the professional scientists have yet done as much to enlighten it as have such philoso-

---

54. Cunningham, *Idealistic Argument*, p. 455.

55. See especially "Meaning, Reference, and Significance," *The Philosophical Review* 47.2 (April 1938): 155–75, and "Perspective and Context in the Meaning Situation," *University of California Publications in Philosophy* 16.2: (1935): 29–52.

phers as Peirce and Mead. The contribution of Royce's theory of interpretation in *The Problem of Christianity* is also worth consideration it has hardly yet received. But here again, it is doubtful whether "meaning" with its idealistic associations is a help to clear thinking. There is still the constant temptation to slide from meaning to purpose and from the relevance of teleological considerations in a description of human behavior to the primacy of norms in all knowledge and hence in all reality. And at that point we are off again on a path which leads to edifying confusion or religious apologetics.

Contextually applied, "meaning" is involved in intelligible discourse, conduct appropriate to a result aimed at, and the like. Coupled with the categories of idealism, however, it at once wants a warrant outside its contextual application. It wants a "guarantee" in reality, and must secure this by spreading the social situation over the entire natural world (animism and panpsychism) and thus showing that everything existent is really of the same mental nature as our own experience, or else by arguing dubiously that if social behavior is "intelligible" only with reference to purposes pursued and ends sought, only a purposive explanation is "really" intelligible and existence and value are inseparable. And when we deal with significance in general the temptation is to substitute for an inquiry into the bearing that, e.g., a religious view of the world would have on our conduct if it were true and the reasons for supposing that it is true, a general use of such expressions as "at the heart of Reality" which, independent of such a religious doctrine, lack any specific sense. Even where conclusions of this sort are not explicitly drawn, the idealist is constantly hovering on the verge of them and hinting at an outcome which he hesitates explicitly to espouse. And this is not a defect in particular thinkers, it is the natural implication of the theory itself. For "meaning" in the context of idealistic philosophy appears always as "more" than opposing theories will allow the world to be, a "more" that could be anchored securely only in ultimate Reality and which, lacking such anchorage, floats uneasily on a sea of equivocal references. There is no safe way out of this situation but [through] an explicit rejection of the view that "meanings" must find their warrant in ultimate reality and that ultimate reality, in its total, inmost or intrinsic nature must therefore be "meaningful" in a fashion which independent investigation will hardly warrant. So long as this reference remains, "values," "meanings," and "ideas" must always be taken to be what they probably are not in order to be reliably what they are, and thus we shall not see clearly what they are or what, philosophically, they mean.

The central elements in the idealistic synthesis have fallen apart, and it is not likely that a philosophical work of the first magnitude will in our time be inspired by it. That does not mean, however, that the idealistic philosophy will not continue or, within academic circles, perform a useful function. While facile generalizations that claim jurisdiction over but fail to do justice to the more complex and humanly important aspects of human behavior are current, it will be useful to insist that there is "more" in experience than this, and of this "more" the idealists are the traditional custodians. And a synthesis, however provisional and equivocal, which includes this "more" will always, in contrast to its rivals, seem sane and broad and "fundamentally" sound. The only really convincing alternative to idealism is a social theory "concrete" enough to take account empirically and reasonably of the factors in experience to which this philosophy appeals, but of which it can give no clear account. It is in the construction of such a theory that the energies of those who now "refute" idealism could most profitably be employed. Meanwhile among seekers of philosophical truth, the idealists will remain as those who seek it with jam and judicious advice * and who find in admonitions to respect the deeper values and epistemologically flavored hints of spiritual satisfaction a working substitute for the philosophic wisdom which has not yet been achieved.

Such is the interpretation which on our hypothesis seems to find empirical warrant in the working of "idealism" as a philosophy.

* Cf. Lewis Carroll's "The Hunting of the Snark, An Agony in Eight Fits," first stanza of "Fit the Third":

> ". . . They roused him with jam and judicious advice—
> They set him conundrums to guess."

I am grateful to Elizabeth Steinberg for drawing my attention to this passage. I had originally thought that "jam" was a misprint for "sage." Clearly it was not. Ed.

3 Peirce's Pragmatic Metaphysics

The Pragmatism of Peirce

Whether or not Peirce was "really" a pragmatist is a question on which much argument might, not very profitably, be expended.* In some respects, certainly, his philosophical interests were widely different from those of James and Dewey. The application of philosophy to questions of "vital importance" in non-philosophical affairs he viewed with considerable scepticism, while his speculative identification of habit with "efficient reasonableness" and his extension of the notion to explain the evolution of order in the Universe carried him considerably beyond the limits which the more empirically-minded pragmatists have set for fruitful philosophical inquiry. There are, however, several respects in which his thinking does follow the pragmatic model, and these are of primary importance for his philosophy as a whole. To see how they operate here, and how, in an environment dissimilar in many ways to their more usual habitat, they produce their characteristic fruits will help us, I believe, to complete our picture of pragmatism in operation.†

In one respect, of course, Peirce is not only one of the pragmatists, but is properly described as the pioneer and first defender of the faith. His analysis of the meaning of concepts is not only the earliest, but in many ways the clearest and most incisive statement of the essential reference of signs both to the conduct which they elicit and to the empirical situations to which this conduct would be pertinent, that we have had. The insight that, to make our ideas clear philosophically, we must get back to the situations in which general signs are

---

* The title of this chapter has been supplied. Ed.

† As mentioned in the preface, the first one hundred pages of the original chapter are omitted here; the whole has been published elsewhere, under the title "Pragmatism and the Context of Rationality" (1993). The reference to the purpose of an omitted chapter must be understood accordingly. The present chapter may be read as a preface to the section in chapter 6, below, entitled "C. S. Peirce on 'The Logic of the Universe,'" which may in turn be regarded as continuing the discussion of Peirce begun here. Ed.

---

used and the referents to which, in these situations, they apply, and specify meaning in terms of such use and reference, is of decisive importance, not only for pragmatism but for all subsequent critical philosophy. If Peirce had contributed no more than this, his place among the notable few who, in philosophy, have helped to change our primary ways of thinking and direct them to a more fruitful issue, would still be secure.

The theory of signs with which this insight is associated has not as yet been adequately explored. Its usability for a wide variety of purposes has been evidenced, but it is so bound up with a dubious idealistic metaphysic and so complicated by the terminological vagaries and personal crotchets of a great but wayward genius that it remains extraordinarily difficult to say what, precisely, its reliable import is. Here, as in some types of psychoanalytic investigation, an eminently usable insight has been announced in a mythological terminology. The *triadic* character of a sign situation, as involving the response of the interpreter to the object signified through the stimulus provided by the sign, and the primary role of generality in sign (the generality of a word) in response (the generality of a habit) and in referent (the generality of a uniformity as exemplified in the long run of its instances) very much needs emphasis. Their identification with "thirdness" as a mode of real being other than existence, the identification of "thirdness" with efficient reasonableness or the tendency of the ideal to actualize itself, and finally the identification of reason as an agency with evolutionary love or the becoming of order in the Universe, are less reliably informative. But the separation of myth from fact in this theory has yet to be accomplished.

Our present concern, however, is not with the theory of signs as such, or with the science that may some day develop out of it, but rather with its bearing on a contextual analysis of concepts which philosophers employ but which, in such usage, are of equivocal import and questionable authenticity. Here Peirce's procedure agrees essentially with that of the other pragmatists. He specifies the primary context in reference to which the meaning and use of concepts is to be determined. If the contextual specification were adequate it would provide a standpoint for the clarification of meaning and estimate of validity of a quite fundamental sort. If, on the other hand, it proves inadequate, being dictated by ulterior considerations of philosophical "ultimacy," the attempt to understand the meaning of concepts in terms of their use in this context will result in confusion, an insufficient factual basis for the philosophical synthesis based on it, and a final failure of the theory to apply to the very situations which were to have been its primary concern. The context to which Peirce appeals, though characterizable as "practical" and "empirical," is quite distinct from those which James, Dewey, and Mead took to be fundamental. But the consequences of accepting it as the primary locus of all meaning and thus substituting a philosophical reduction of concepts to their role in the operations in which the philosophical interests and preferences of the theorist are most immediately satisfied, for an analysis of their meaning in use, are of the same sort in all these cases. Hence, in tracing out these consequences we shall still be investigating the primary topic of this section—the fruits of pragmatism.*

The Fixation of Belief

Peirce's early statement of the pragmatic theory of meaning is clear and uncompromising. The meaning of concepts will be clear when we have indicated their role in thinking. Now what is the aim of thinking? "Thought in action has for its only possible motive the attainment of thought at rest; and whatever does not refer to belief is no part of the thought itself." [1] But belief is a habit of action. Therefore, nothing that does not affect belief, or have bearing on the readiness to act in which believing consists, can have any bearing on the aim of thought. "The whole function of thought is to produce habits of action; and ... whatever there is connected with a thought, but irrelevant to its purpose, is an accretion to it, but no part of it." [2] Now the only thing that can have any bearing on action is sensible experience. One does not act on things in themselves, but on things as they present themselves in our empirical commerce with them, in their sensible effects. There can, then, be no difference in thought that does not correspond and refer to a difference in practice, in the habit of response which constitutes belief. And only in their sensible effects have objects a bearing on practice. Consequently the whole meaning of a concept is contained in the habit which it helps to determine and in the sensible effects in reference to which that habit operates. Therefore: "Consider what effects, that might conceivably have practical bearings, we conceive the object of our conception to have. Then, our conception of these effects is the whole of our conception of the object." [3] Such is the pragmatic maxim. It is apparent here that the limitation of primary meaning to bearing on what is assumed in advance to be the essential goal of thought is quite relentlessly carried through, and that the philosophical validity of the conclusion depends on the correctness of this limitation.

But has the goal of inquiry here been correctly specified? It would ordinarily

1. C. S. Peirce, *Collected Papers* (hereafter cited as CP), edited by Charles Hartshorne and Paul Weiss (Cambridge: Harvard University Press, 1932–35) [cited henceforth in the standard way by volume and paragraph number, thus], 5.396. [Murphy had originally cited *Chance, Love, and Logic,* the first collection of Peirce's essays, edited by Morris R. Cohen (New York: Harcourt, Brace and Company, 1923), often also supplying the volume and page number in the *Collected Papers* as well. There are some differences in language and form between the two sources; it is the latter that is followed here. Ed.]

2. CP, 5.400.

3. CP, 5.402.

* Murphy is here again referring to material omitted in the present work. Ed.

be said that we inquire, sometimes at least, in order to get at the truth. Is not a true belief, and not just a stable habit of action, the thing at which we aim, and should not the meaning of "hard words" and "concepts" be understood at least in part by reference to this aspect of inquiry? Peirce's answer is of crucial significance in his philosophy. What *actually* terminates inquiry and brings argument to a conclusion is simply what *in fact* we cannot doubt, not what is known to be true. "As soon as a firm belief is reached we are entirely satisfied, whether the belief be true or false." [4] At some point or other short of infallible certification, we reach something which we cannot help believing. And there is simply no sense in criticizing the acceptance of a belief when it is really not within our power seriously to question it. Nor can we reasonably ask for more than this. "If you absolutely cannot doubt a proposition—cannot bring yourself, upon deliberation, to entertain the least suspicion of the truth of it, it is plain that there is no room to desire anything more. . . . For what one does not doubt cannot be rendered more satisfactory than it already is." [5] The recognition of this *de facto* determination of belief, without ultimate theoretical warrant in certainty, as final for logic and criticism is the "common sensism" which Peirce cogently defended. Insofar as it accepts beliefs as *de facto* authoritative only after examining and trying to doubt them, it is critical common sensism, but the ultimate limitation of criticism to the sphere within which rational control of belief is possible, and insistence on our inability to criticize what, in the long run, we can't help believing, are recognized throughout. We cannot get behind firm belief. All we can do is to see to it that where belief has not yet been settled we proceed by means of a method as reliable and rational as possible. "The sum of it all is that our logically controlled thoughts compose a small part of the mind, the mere blossom of a vast complexus, which we may call the instinctive mind, in which [a] man will not say he has *faith,* because that implies the conceivability of distrust, but upon which he builds as the very fact to which it is the whole business of his logic to be true." [6]

The bearing of this on the pragmatic maxim should be evident. We cannot finally distinguish between what is true and what is firmly believed, since a firm belief, so long as it remains in that status, is, for the believer, absolutely true, and he cannot seriously criticize it himself, nor can he properly be criticized for holding it. And at some point we all reach such beliefs, to which it is the whole business of our logic to be true. Rational criticism must then be directed not toward the truth of beliefs as such, but rather toward the method by which beliefs are stabilized. And if the meaning of concepts is to be understood with reference to their role in inquiry, it is here that we must look for it.

4. CP, 5.375.
5. CP, 6.498.
6. CP, 5.212.

Peirce sees that this does not include *all* significant reference, but only, as he says, that of "intellectual concepts," on which reasonings may turn.[7] The pragmatic maxim is limited in its application to such concepts.

Now there are important differences between alternative possible methods for bringing thought to rest in firm belief. One may rely on authority, on subjective bias and tenacity, or on allegedly "a priori" evidence. In none of these cases is there any assurance that the belief can actually maintain itself in the long run of experience. The only reliable method for securing such stability is to let the belief be determined by what is independent of the believer, that is, by what in the actual course of empirical investigation is found to be the case. This is the method of science, and while we have no guarantee that at any particular time it will disclose the truth, we can be sure that, if persisted in, its errors and inadequacies will be corrected by further empirical testing, and that the belief to which in the long run it would lead is what experience in the long run will warrant, since it is precisely what this long run is that the method, if persisted in, must finally disclose.

If we accept as the truth the belief to which this endless fidelity to the lessons of experience would finally lead, then "truth is simply the last result of following out the right method of thinking." Such a belief could only actually be achieved in a community of rational inquirers who continued so long and faithfully in their quest that all error and aberration finally cancelled out. Whether such a community can ever exist we do not surely know. But we are entitled to hope that it may be so, and to refer to the judgment of such a community as the truth toward which our own efforts approximate. It is in this sense that Peirce's dictum that "The opinion which is fated to be ultimately agreed to by all who investigate is what we mean by the truth, and the object represented in this opinion is the real," [8] is to be understood.

The meaning of an *intellectual* concept is to be ascertained, then, by reference to its role in advancing those inquiries which would lead to truth in the long run, or which would *finally* fix belief in a community of endlessly laborious and conscientious investigators. What in particular this [final belief] would be we are not now in a position to say. It would be not only premature but irrational to take any belief held at present, and based on the evidence now available, as the adequate representative of that final truth. It would "block the path of inquiry." Short of such finality, however, we are far more sure of our methods than of any results achieved by them. The proper attitude if we would reach firm belief by the surest method is, accordingly, not to believe firmly in any of the provisional conclusions or working hypotheses of inquiry, but to go on following the method which would achieve a final belief only in a commu-

7. CP, 5.8.
8. CP, 5.407.

nity we shall not live to see, and which may never actually exist. Hence, there is a certain opposition between the* fixation of belief which [is] the final aim of thought and the method recommended for its attainment. Thus Peirce is inclined at times to say that belief, as full acceptance of a proposition and readiness to act on it, "has no place in science at all." For "pure science has nothing to do with action. . . . There is thus no proposition at all in science which answers to the conception of belief." [9] If, then, as the pragmatists claim, inquiry aims at an eventual satisfaction, this "cannot be any actual satisfaction, but must be the satisfaction which would ultimately be found if the inquiry were pushed to its ultimate and indefeasible issue." [10] It thus appears that between the goal of thought—the fixation of belief—and the method recommended—that of scientific inquiry—there is a very considerable gap which only the long labor of an ideal community could finally bridge. The *aim* of thought is to bring inquiry to a close in a belief which would, just so far as it did terminate the period of doubt and rational criticism, "block the path of inquiry." The method proposed forbids us, insofar as we pursue it, ever to attain belief in this sense at all.

"Concrete Reasonableness"

How is this apparent disproportion of means to ends to be explained? The truth is, I think, that Peirce is not really interested in belief, as concerned with particular matters of fact, but rather in the formation of rational habits. The preliminary analysis has served simply to delimit sharply the area within which such habits can be seen to operate, and to exclude from consideration anything not directly pertinent to the rational estimate of evidence, in the special aspect in which Peirce wants to consider it. The *true* end of inquiry can then be identified as the formation of rational habits, or the "development of concrete reasonableness." [11] The attainment of such reasonableness is the true end of man, and, indeed, of the universe in which active law or efficient reasonableness is extending its evolutionary sway. The final goodness of argument is to be estimated by its contribution to this aim. "What does right reasoning consist in? It consists in such reasoning as shall be conducive to our ultimate aim." [12] This aim could not have been defined without reference to the capacity of the methods approved as rational to get us to the truth—or final compulsory belief—at last. And in this definition the identification of truth with compulsory belief is

9. CP, 1.635.
10. CP, 6.485.
11. CP, 5.3.
12. CP, 1.611.

* The phrase "method recommended for that," in original at this point, has been deleted; it is almost certainly a typist's error, though it makes a certain kind of sense if interpolated in. Ed.

essential, for we have to exclude any other norms of truth [besides that] belief to which empirical inquiry in the long run would lead. Having served its purpose, however, the emphasis on belief as the goal of thought can be abandoned. For the belief to which a reliable method would lead is known to us only as the far-off goal of rational inquiry, right habits of thinking. The development of such habits and the specification of the criteria of rational validity thus become our primary concern, and the meaning of intellectual concepts is what, in this context, they are found to be.

At this point the pragmatic maxim takes on its most characteristic meaning for Peirce, and its justification becomes a quasi-tautological affair. What we are here concerned with is a rational habit. If we take the meaning of a concept to be the interpretant of the sign-situation in which it applies, then this meaning will simply *be* the habit in question. Taking the meaning of a concept to be the interpretant, Peirce asserts that "the most perfect account of a concept that words can convey will consist in a description of the habit which that concept is calculated to produce. But how otherwise can a habit be described than by a description of the kind of action to which it gives rise, with the specification of the conditions and of the motives?" [13] Hence the essential reference of meaning to action, or practical considerations, is made out. *Practice* is here the behavior in which rational habits are manifest, and if it is rational habits and nothing else that intellectual concepts are concerned with, then it is here, surely, that their meaning is to be found.

There is an equal "generality" in the referents of intellectual concepts, for these concepts "essentially carry some implication concerning the general behavior either of some conscious being or of some inanimate object, and so convey more, not merely than any feeling, but more too than any existential fact, namely the 'would-acts,' 'would-dos' of habitual behavior; and no agglomeration of actual happenings can ever completely fill up the meaning of a 'would-be.' " [14] Since reasoning is concerned not with the particular instance as such but with laws [and] uniformities, [i.e., with] what would be found out in the whole course of inquiry, its referent is something essentially general. But how, again, can that which is general be manifest except in the long run of its empirical instances? And how can these affect our rational habits except as they are observable in experience? What an object is, so far as it has any *rational* bearing on our habits of investigation, is simply what it can be found out to be, or what it is as an experimental phenomenon. Whatever there may be in it more than this has no bearing on the activity in respect to which the meaning of concepts is defined. The past has meaning as a guide to future action. Only such action is controllable, hence criticizable, hence an element in the rational

13. CP, 5.491.
14. CP, 5.467.

purport of our concepts. Therefore: "The entire intellectual purport of any symbol consists in the total of all general modes of rational conduct which, conditionally upon all the possible different circumstances and desires, would ensue from the acceptance of the symbol." [15] This is what Peirce called "pragmaticism," to distinguish it from the versions of pragmatism of which he did not approve. It is, however, simply what pragmatism becomes when the context of meaningful reference is identified with that of rational inquiry and this is narrowed until the formation of good intellectual habits in the description and prediction of what is general in experience is all that it really includes. The method is that of pragmatism; the result is here determined by the specification of context as that peculiarly acceptable to a logician with a special interest in the manner in which the *general,* or rational, is exemplified in instances and especially in those habits of response of which he particularly approved.

The Criticism of Argument

The sphere of rational criticism and hence of the meaning of intellectual concepts, insofar as pragmatism (or pragmaticism) can define it, can now be further circumscribed. All reasoning has its basis in perception and its outcome in some sort of action. But neither of these is ultimately subject to rational criticism. A perceptual judgment involves generalization, it is already an interpretation, a discernment of the element of "thirdness" in phenomena. And it is not theoretically infallible. There is not, however, any way in which we can get behind it, and when we reach the point where we *do not doubt* what, on the basis of perception, has been accepted, reason can go no further. Again, when inquiry and investigation lead over to action, the border-line from the sphere of logic to that of practice has been crossed. Yet thought depends on perception for its data, and on relevance to action for its final justification. "The elements of every concept enter into logical thought at the gate of perception and make their exit at the gate of purposive action, and whatever cannot show its passports at both those two gates is to be arrested as unauthorized by reason." [16]

Even in the sphere of rational criticism, however, where our only concern is with the goodness of argument, a further limitation on the scope of pragmatism is to be noted. What we approve or disapprove in a process of reasoning is not the conclusion as such, but its conformity to a more or less reliable habit or method of reasoning. The goodness of the kind of reasoning and the goodness of the specimen as an instance of its kind are what logic can decide for us. There are three such logical methods, deduction, induction, and abduction or retroduction. The first requires no pragmatic elucidation, its cogency lies simply in the intrinsic necessity of the connections it exhibits. Induction has a

15. CP, 5.438.
16. CP, 5.212.

similarly necessary and finally tautological warrant. For induction simply evaluates an objective probability; it ascertains what proportion of an examined lot actually has the character or property whose presence or absence is the object of inquiry. There is no guarantee that the proportion found in the sample will be the same as that in the whole lot. But induction makes no such claim. It only holds that the continued employment of the same method, if persisted in, would lead us at last to the ratio we want. For what we are looking for is the character present in a whole lot or series of instances, and how could this character be manifest except in the series itself? What the instances show in the long run is therefore the character we are looking for, and this, induction, if persisted in, must surely find. "The validity of an inductive argument consists, then, in the fact that it pursues a method which, if duly persisted in, must, in the very nature of things, lead to a result indefinitely approximating to the truth in the long run." [17]

There is relatively cold comfort in this if we are concerned not with the justification of the method at very long last, but [with] * the reliability of such estimates as we can now make by the use of it. The conclusion of an induction has no definite probability and if it is this [conclusion] that we want good reason for believing or disbelieving, we cannot look to Peirce for help. His preoccupation with the adequacy of his methods to attain a final satisfaction has left him with little concern for the factual adequacy of the conclusions we should like to draw by their means.

The third method is that of "abduction." Here our concern is with hypotheses that may be true, and with the grounds for preferring one such to another. Such hypotheses may very possibly not be true, but if they have considerable explanatory value, and if they are such that their falsity could be found out through empirical testing, then we are warranted in making use of them. For it is through such hypotheses that we gain insight into law, uniformity, or "thirdness" in things, and the success which such hypotheses have had, particularly in the sciences, is sufficient to show that there is a real, though far from complete, harmony between our rational powers and the order in the world which we are trying to discover. Hence it is reasonable to try out such hypotheses and use them to advance our inquiries. The tests of the goodness of abductive hypotheses are (a) their capacity to aid in the discernment of "thirdness" and hence in the development of rational habits of response and (b) their empirical testability. The first is a practical consideration, in Peirce's sense, the second an empirical one. Hence in the criticism of hypotheses the pragmatic maxim is plainly applicable. At times, Peirce appears to hold that this is its *only* appropriate application. Thus he asserts that pragmatism is simply a "rule about the

17. CP, 2.781.

* The preposition "in" of the original is replaced here by "with." Ed.

admissibility of hypotheses." [18] By limiting the meaning of intellectual concepts to their role in the formation of rational habits, and thus to the framing and testing of hypotheses for which no conclusive logical warrant is obtainable but which promise to be useful in inquiry and applicable in experience, it is possible to find a true interpretation for Peirce's pragmatism. But the result is achieved not by showing the validity of the maxim as a general criterion of meaning and truth, but by narrowing the universe of discourse to the field of its reliable application.

What Peirce Has Proved

In this somewhat tortuous line of reasoning there is, as in all Peirce's philosophic thinking, much that is enlightening and important. The criticism of argument by reference to the reliability of the method or habit of reasoning employed, its capacity to arrive at truth always or for the most part, or in the long run, and his remarks on the logic of abduction have been used, and will be used again, as starting points for fruitful logical investigations. And the emphasis on the element of generality in both the referent and the interpretant of the signs used in reasoning is peculiarly relevant to current over-simplifications in logical theory. This is a point to which we shall return later.*

But for all its brilliance and suggestiveness, one cannot help concluding that the standpoint from which Peirce's analysis is made is both arbitrary and unstable. How, and on what basis, are we to stipulate what "the goal of thought" is to be? To describe it as simply the fixation of belief does less than justice to its essentially cognitive intent. To supplement this by appeal to a method in which belief would be sure, in the end, to be fixed in accordance with the conclusions which a cognitive inquiry would warrant is a brilliant expedient for avoiding the consequences of a dubious theory, but it does not really help. The "final" agreement of the community provides a standard of truth not because of its status as secure social agreement but because it is the agreement of a society which Peirce, on logical grounds, holds to be suitable for the purpose. If what we are trying to find out is what the result of endlessly patient and conscientious correction of belief by reference to empirical instances would be, then of course the result of such investigation is the truth. But its authenticity as truth is guaranteed by its agreement with the whole run of experience, and whether or not any actual community will ever be sufficiently objective and patient to fix its beliefs by any such method, and whether beliefs so fixed would be psychologically secure against the emotional appeals of the propoganda devices which civilization in the meantime had developed, are further

18. CP, 5.196.

* In original chapter 8, "Philosophical Analysis," not included herein. Ed.

questions. Of course, *if* belief was fixed in this way and no other, there would be nothing in the empirical instances examined to overturn it, for it would, by definition, be adequate to the whole course of such experience. What we should find out, if we looked long and hard *enough,* would be the truth, to be sure. But its connection with stability of belief in a "community" as the final goal of thought is a tenuous one.

It is, of course, the pragmatic emphasis on the practical use of concepts where the practical is defined with reference to an end other than the discovery of truth, that causes the difficulty. If the aim of thinking is to remove doubt and to lead to firmly held belief, then to show that an idea is true is to show that it somehow contributes to this end, even if only in a community that may never be. The means to this latter goal, however, are so different from those which contribute to stability of belief here and now as to constitute an essentially different subject-matter. The formation of rational habits of *not* believing, in the matters on which inquiry is directed, but of keeping investigation steered on toward its ultimate goal, is, as has been seen, a very different sort of "practice" than that of acting on belief firmly established. In substituting the former for the latter* Peirce has brought the subject back to the logical domain in which he is really at home, but he has also come at it from an odd angle, and one that is very likely to distort a philosophical estimate of its nature.

For how, finally, is the "reasonableness" of habits of inquiry to be judged? The question does not concern merely the *formal* validity of argument, it has to do, as Peirce explicitly insists, with the capacity of the various types of reasoning to lead us to truth. With truth understood in the more usual sense this would mean, in addition to general logical considerations, a consideration of the reliability of methods and principles employed in the special inquiries in which we get at truth. The goodness of "reason" here is discovered by reference to the subject-matter which is ordered and whose structure is more or less adequately disclosed by the use of the methods appropriate to the inquiry in question. There is, in such cases, no general question as to whether inductive reasoning, for example, is of such a nature as certainly to lead at least to stable belief, a question which, as we have seen, has only a tautological answer, but there are many questions as to what, beyond formal consistency, distinguishes good methods of inquiry from bad, how far the methods found in particular inquiries to be adequate can usefully be extended to other fields, and so on. To judge that particular perceptual judgments are trustworthy, though not infallible, because they satisfy the tests which, in a particular empirical inquiry, serve *on the whole* to distinguish what is reliably observable from what is not,

---

* In the original, "the latter for the former"; it makes more sense to me as I have modified it, but it also makes some sense the other way around; hence this note. Ed.

is a reasonable procedure. For a different inquiry more refined observations may be required, and in none that is humanly workable shall we get behind data which are theoretically dubitable, but nonetheless, in the investigation for which they provide an empirical basis, not reasonably to be doubted.

When we think of Peirce's reference to reliable methods rather than ultimate certainties, as providing the criteria of reasonably grounded investigation in this application, it becomes a plausible and helpful suggestion. But this is not the application which he himself normally makes. If "truth" is the verdict which the community of investigators will finally reach, and if the primary rational virtue meanwhile is simply in keeping on investigating, our methods of inquiry are to be valued rather as specimens of that habit-taking in which the growth of reasonableness consists than for their capacity to lead to truth as it is here and now attainable. In reference to this goal, which will finally adjust our "habits" of belief to the "habits" which are uniformities in observable occurrences, reason functions as "insight into thirdness," and a hypothesis which attributes more order or uniformity or "habit-taking" to the world is so far more reasonable than one that does not, and to be preferred above it. The point is that for truth as thus defined, the general criteria of "reason" as uniformity, "habit-taking," and the like are disconnected from the particular applications of reasoning in the fields where its capacity to lead to factually warranted conclusions can be tested. Reason still needs some guarantee of its agreement with "reality," but this is now sought in a metaphysical assurance that there is a real "thirdness," or tendency to habit-taking in things, and that our own rational tendencies are in harmony with this objective reason. For "the saving truth is that there is a Thirdness in experience, an element of reasonableness to which we can train our own reason to conform more and more. If this were not the case, there would be no such thing as logical goodness or badness." [19] The more "thirdness" there is the more rational the world will be, and hence, in his actual use of the logic of abduction, Peirce is led to give very surprising weight to hypotheses that present the world as "spiritual," give "mind" or effective reason a growing place in it, and find in a developing tendency to take habits the explanation of the order in the world.[20] There is little warrant for such hypotheses in the evidence which reliable inquiries elsewhere provide, nor are they the sort of hypotheses which have proved fruitful in such inquiries. But they impute "efficient reasonableness" to things, they *might* be true, and their provisional acceptance meanwhile furthers those rational habits which we ought, on the whole, to approve.

The pragmatic expositors of Peirce's logical theory have looked with little

19. CP, 5.160.
20. See the discussion of Peirce's speculative philosophy, ch. 6 below.

favor on the speculative metaphysics in which hypotheses in this sense "rational" are developed by Peirce, and have tended to treat this phase of his philosophy as an aberration. What they have failed to see is its intimate connection with the theory of reasoning they admire. Peirce's speculative philosophy is really just logic on the loose, cut off from its linkage with the specific inquiries in which its capacity to lead to true conclusions can be tested and related instead to a final belief which, if we keep on investigating and correcting our opinions, must one day be achieved, and to a growth of "reasonableness" in things of which this continued investigation is an impressive instance. A way of thinking [that is] formally, generally and indeterminately related to its subject-matter will find a "reality" suited to its peculiar powers, and such, as will later be seen,[21] is the "universe" to which Peirce's synechism leads him. But the initial dislocation which thus sets "reason" as the critic of those ways of thinking which lead to truth, adrift in a sea of "thirdness," is the fruit of pragmatism itself. For the context in which the criteria of reliable thinking are testable, if Peirce is right, is not that in which the primary meaning of such criteria could be exhibited, but that to which his notion of the goal of thinking and the peculiar status of rational habits as deputies for a truth we shall never attain, had led him. The inaccuracy of this reference is evidenced by the "reason" with which it leaves us. And it is "reason" thus identified that is the appropriate instrument for speculative explorations of the reason in the Universe. That the outcome of pragmatic criticism should in this case have been "new" metaphysics may in some quarters be taken as evidence that we cannot get away from such "perennial" habits of thought. Of that more will be said in a later chapter. It may, however, be evidence that we shall never get an accurate statement of our problems until we are prepared to relate our concepts clearly to the contexts of their primary use, and that in failing to make this reference clear pragmatism has left its subject in that sort of ambiguous dependence on inadequately specified ulterior "realities" which breeds metaphysical solutions for equivocal problems. If this were true, as I believe it is, our first task, as Peirce saw, would once more be to make our ideas clear through contextual analysis. We should thus return to the procedure he recommended, though not to the methods of its application in his own philosophy.

21. See ch. 6 below.

4 Realism

The philosophical theories to which the term "realistic" is customarily applied (a usage I here adopt without comment on the appropriateness of the term) are usefully grouped together not so much on account of any body of doctrine they share as because of their common interest in establishing philosophy as factually grounded knowledge, with a special subject-matter and methods appropriate to its investigation, and conclusions which, whatever their ultimate bearing on human hopes and social uses, are certified by their logical and factual relationship to the objects—"the knowing relation," "mind," "nature," "space-time"—about which they provide information. This interest draws positive support from the dominant intellectual tendencies and academic respectabilities of the early 20th century and philosophical pertinence from its specific opposition to the traditional idealism and currently influential pragmatism of the period. In the course of its extended debate with these philosophies, and in pursuance of its own quest for a factual subject-matter in reference to which the long-standing "problems of philosophy" can be solved by methods approved in non-philosophical inquiries, this philosophic interest found expression in a series of "positions" occupied and defended. These are characteristic *on the whole* of the "realism" of the period and have been taken to constitute its essence. Their bearing on the primary interest in *pinning down* philosophy to a factual subject matter, capable of exploration and analysis by methods of unimpeachable logical purity, must be kept in mind, however, if they are adequately to be understood.

If philosophy is to establish itself as a branch of factual knowledge, the nature of knowledge as a discovery of facts, objects, [and] realities as they are in their own nature and independent of the subjective propensities, interests, and bias of the mind that knows them must first be vindicated. Hence, as R. B. Perry insists, the primary realistic thesis is that "the object of knowledge is always some fact that stands there independent of the knowing of it." [1] This thesis must be defended against both idealism and pragmatism, and in the course of its defence theories of knowledge develop, of bewildering variety and ingenuity—all intent, however, on showing that knowledge, consistently with all that physics, physiological psychology, and introspection can tell us, can be understood as a discovery by "the mind" of real objects as they exist antecedently to inquiry concerning them, and independently of what the mind demands or the heart desires that they should be.

The emphasis on the object, or "the facts," as constituting the ultimate cognitive authority, and hence the final arbiter of philosophic truth, leads naturally to a consideration of the methods by which we come at the facts or the objects in their ultimate and objective purity. In its early phases this often amounted to an inquisition into what we really know, what we are quite certain about when an object is directly presented to the mind. For later realists the sciences provide the model for exact knowledge, and the philosopher, if he is to reach the facts in his own field, must discover a scientific method for his researches. The sciences, however, are many. One can follow the more speculative hypotheses of theoretical physics toward an unsubstantial, hence possibly mental, world of "pointer-readings," or take the suggestions offered by behavioristic psychology and eliminate mental states even from human behavior. Among the sciences, logic, as a formal discipline, has a peculiar place. In scope and generality of application it rivals, and in precision and cogency far surpasses, philosophy as traditionally understood. Even if logic in its modern alliance with pure mathematics is not accepted, as it was by Bertrand Russell, as *the* exclusive method for a properly scientific philosophy, it tends to have special prestige in realistic inquiries and to lend to many of them a flavor which, like that of the Snark, is "meager and hollow, but crisp." Even here, however, there is no consensus. Alexander's* metaphysical speculations are neither crisp nor meager, but it would be quite arbitrary to exclude them from the characteristically realistic investigations of the period. The agreement underlying such differences is to be found at another level—in the common conviction that some method for philosophy must be found, either eventuating in certainty or comparable in adequacy and precision to those of the sciences, and that what this favored method is competent to disclose will be what, as philosophers, we ought to accept as basic, ultimate, or "real."

1. Ralph Barton Perry, *The Present Conflict of Ideals* (New York: Longmans, Green and Company, 1918), pp. 364–65.

* Samuel Alexander, discussed below. The reference, again, is to Lewis Carroll's "The Hunting of the Snark, An Agony in Eight Fits." Ed.

On the side of "the object" a similar multiplicity is apparent. Knowledge discloses "the real," and things are ultimately what in factually reliable investigations they are found to be, quite independently of any "higher synthesis" or pragmatic reduction of their meaning. Thus if we have knowledge in geometry and arithmetic, the objects to which such knowledge refers must really be what the mathematician says they are, and hence must really be. Objects immediately experienced in dreams and hallucinations indubitably are what in such experience they are found to be, and hence indubitably *are*. To domesticate such objects, along with the mermaids of folklore and the round square, which is an object of discourse and is what it is, and therefore *is,* can hardly be an easy matter. Is there a realm of subsistence, or *Being,* more inclusive that that of existence in space and time, which they indefeasibly inhabit? Or can we somehow show that propositions apparently about such objects are, given proper logical manipulation, not actually about them at all, and hence that their truth does not involve the reality or even *being* of such monstrosities, but refers us instead to the finally analyzed constituents of basic facts which only a careful student of *Principia Mathematica* would know how to describe in philosophically acceptable terminology, and even he not yet. Or, finally, can we find, by methods analogous to those of the sciences but more inclusive in scope, some primary reality, space-time, for example, or societies of organisms, to which all that from all sources we know can after philosophical interpretation be referred, and from which all can be shown to proceed? Here, once more, the answers supplied are endlessly various, but the question asked is the same, as are the reasons for finding it important. If knowledge is a disclosure of reality, then reality must be what knowledge, in all its varieties, discloses, and the business of philosophy is so to understand "the real" as to reconcile what is thus disclosed with what, on a philosophical estimate, reality in its basic, or inclusive, or ultimate or otherwise philosophically eligible characters, basically, inclusively or ultimately is. If "realms of being" are left in their apparently irreducible variety, we have the inclusive "pluralism" of early realism. If the variety of objects is reduced, by methods of logical or epistemological analysis, to those held on logical or epistemological grounds to be basic, we have analytic realism. If a synthesis is attempted by reference to some especially ultimate and eligible reality in which all are contained or by which all are generated, we have a return to speculative philosophy in the grand style. In any case we have a coordination of objects known by reference to what, as the outcome of philosophy's own variety of factual investigation, is taken to be "real." Theories that share the conviction that such a coordination and systematization, on the basis of knowledge gained by approved logical or factual methods, is the proper goal of philosophy, will count as "realistic" in this discussion.

The realistic movement, as it was in its earlier and more enthusiastic phases, when it represented a new philosophic gospel, is now out of fashion. There are idealists still with us, and pragmatism has taken a new lease on life. But there are not many philosophers who today would care to call themselves "realists," or present their theories as aspects and applications of the realistic faith. There are good reasons for this, as will later be seen. Its meaning, however, is likely to be misinterpreted. For it may lead to the conclusion that realism is something over and done with, something which, except for historical purposes, we can safely afford to neglect. Nothing could be further from the truth. The problems with which academic philosophy is today for the most part concerned derive directly from the various realistic experiments, and the methods employed in dealing with them are precisely those which "realistic" views about the nature of knowledge, the function of philosophy and the reality to which it refers, rendered natural and plausible. If the outline we followed in earlier chapters were adhered to, and "applications and outcome" of the philosophy discussed included in the same chapter with the statement of the philosophy in question, very nearly all the rest of this book would be comprised in the chapter on "Realism." For realism, in its applications and outcome, is what most recent philosophizing comes to. But here the applications take us into more special fields and are less instances of a doctrine than further developments of methods and explicit consequences of assumptions inherited from theories which, on the whole, no longer command assent. Hence "analysis," "speculative philosophy," and "value theory" are better dealt with as special types of philosophical inquiry than as examples of something generally describable as philosophical realism. They are, nonetheless, what a philosophy that recently rejoiced in that title comes to when some of its consequences have been seen, while others, no less important, still operate as unexamined preconceptions in both analysis and speculation. Whatever the value of the realistic philosophies as show-pieces in the museum of the history of thought may turn out to be, their importance for the present study of what a philosophy in operation amounts to, and what comes out of it, is fundamental.

The Standpoint of Realism
Philosophy and the Facts

To appeal in any cognitive enterprise to "the facts" is ordinarily simply to try to tell the truth about whatever it is that is being investigated. In this sense, of course, all responsible philosophies are concerned with "facts," and realists have no right to assume for themselves any special devotion to fact or any preeminent authority to speak for it. There is, however, a sense in which the appeal to "fact" is a peculiarly realistic procedure. The question here is not simply as to what is true, but as to where primary and philosophically ultimate truth is to be found. For Bradley, as we have seen, change and temporal transition are facts, but they are not "real," and their philosophical purport is not to be understood until they have been so reconstructed as to fit harmoniously into Reality as a whole. In Dewey's logical theory, again, factual propositions have a mediatory and instrumental status. We do not, in inquiry, get at facts for their own sake, but in order to reach a judgment of practical moment, and thus to reconstruct a problematic situation. Here too the philosophical importance of what is factually attested, what simply is the case, is subordinated to some further meaning or significance which attaches to the fact in virtue of its relation to something else. And when this meaning is identified as what "in Reality" it is, or what pragmatically it comes to, its own ultimacy as just the specific fact it is, whatever use may be made of it or whatever Reality as a whole may be, is seriously compromised.

The realistic emphasis on "facts" is, therefore, in the first place, a polemical one. As such it furnishes another instance of the way in which a philosophy develops and defines its position as the spokesman of an aspect of experience felt to be significant and fundamental, which the dominant philosophies of the period will not permit us to describe in language appropriate to its apparent nature. Neither idealism nor pragmatism displays an adequate respect for the cognitive ultimacy of what is simply matter of fact, what apart from philosophical interpretation and embroidery we simply find to be the case. Nor, in consequence, does either attach sufficient value to the moral attitude which faces the facts, however unpleasant they may be, or to the practical sanity which is prepared to say, with Arnold and Woodbridge, that "things are what they are and the consequences of them will be what they will be; why then should we wish to be deceived?" [2] That either idealists or pragmatists were given to mere wishful thinking would, as has been seen, be a caricature. But it remains the case that the philosophical standpoints from which these thinkers *finally* estimate both meaning and cognitive validity are such that literal accuracy of knowledge as a report of matters of fact and the value of an acknowledgement of such factual finality for both theory and practice cannot clearly be made out by them. Hence the feeling "the plain man" of "sound sense" is likely to have with regard to both—a feeling which, though he could not justify it argumentatively, he is quite right in trusting. In these philosophies nothing is ever seen clearly on its own account, it is always on the point of becoming an adjective of the Absolute, or a means to the organism's attainment of non-cognitive satisfaction. Neither Bradley's *Logic* nor Dewey's is logic of the sort that a spe-

2. F. J. E. Woodbridge, "Confessions," in *Contemporary American Philosophy,* edited by George P. Adams and William Pepperell Montague (New York: Macmillan, 1930), vol. 2, p. 421 [quoted by Woodbridge as "one of (Matthew) Arnold's favorite quotations" Ed.].

cialist in propositional forms or the structure of deductive systems would find adequate. For Bradley logic is metaphysics, for Dewey it is an affair of biological background, social consequences, and the procedures which enable the inquirer to pass reliably from dubiety to satisfaction. Each of these theories tells us something about logic, but neither indicates what in its own right it is, for neither is in a philosophical position to do so. When the consequences of such theories come sharply into conflict with what in logic, or common sense belief and behavior, or moral experience, we simply find to be the case, the need is indicated for the emergence of a new philosophy in which the ultimacy of facts and the literal validity of our knowledge of them can adequately be exhibited.

The inspiration for such a philosophy is drawn both from philosophical and non-philosophical sources. In an era of specialization in knowledge, and in an academic atmosphere in which methods of limited and detailed research are preferred to large and elusive syntheses, it is natural to hold that things are *at least* what they are found to be in the course of such special investigation. Wider implications are not denied outright, but there is no specialist licensed to deal with them except the philosopher, and his "field" thus tends progressively to become just what nobody else is prepared to handle with the intellectual instruments which, in scientific practice, are recognized as reliable. Practical consequences, too, are outside the area of respectable inquiry, save on those rather embarrassing occasions when the investigator, mindful of his larger duties, rises, or lapses, into edification. Such matters, on the whole, are best left to deans, university presidents, and the clergy. This situation can be made a theme for ironical observation and it is in certain respects less than ideal. But it does correspond to a genuine fact about the contemporary organization of knowledge. The beliefs best attested in intellectually reputable circles are, on the whole, those attained by just this process of specialization, and in abstraction from wider meanings and social or ethical evaluations. Hence, when the inquirer sensitive to the habits of thought of his time finds in philosophy a reversal of this situation, with the "facts" certified by special inquiry transmuted into mere appearances of the "Whole" or treated as instruments for social adjustment, he is likely to be suspicious of the procedure involved. He may be an idealist or a pragmatist in his preferences and over-beliefs, but in an investigation that pretends to yield *knowledge* he looks for something different.

And since the student and later professor of philosophy is acutely sensitive to just such influences, he, too, is likely to look for something different and to construct it where he does not find it ready-made. The authority of fact-finding in research will find its reflection in the ultimacy of "facts" reached by an approved "technique" in philosophy. Questions of the larger "meaning" of things and of their practical uses will remain, but what the philosopher, as a researcher, can contribute to these is not vision nor imaginative insight nor the social gospel, but information. And since it is the bearing of their hopes and fears on what is ultimately real that people traditionally want from the philosopher, *information about reality* obtained by a reliable technique, and limited in the first instance to the field in which he, rather than his scientific colleagues, is qualified by professional training to speak with authority, will be his goal. R. B. Perry admirably expresses the temper of American realism in the following passage: "The realist assumes that philosophy is a kind of knowledge, and neither a song nor a prayer nor a dream. He proposes, therefore, to rely less on inspiration and more on observation and analysis. He conceives his function to be in the last analysis the same as that of the scientist. There is a world out yonder more or less shrouded in darkness, and it is important, if possible, to light it up." [3] That philosophy must cover a wider area and offer a dimmer illumination than the sciences, Perry recognizes with some regret. But in philosophy, too, we work from parts to wholes, proceeding piecemeal and attaching primary authority to what is factually certified, whatever its implications may be, and at no point allowing preferences or considerations of utility to distract us from the primary purpose of discovering what the facts are and accepting them, as they are, as the basis for philosophy.

The affinity of philosophical realism to political "realism," to "realism" in art, literary criticism, and the like, is much more difficult to make out. If the recognition of "facts," not merely as independent of our wishes, but as, in essence, actually opposed to them, or in conflict with conventional moral standards, is stressed, we get the realism which the literary critics view with wonder or alarm. If the "realities" are those facts which a cynical politician thinks it necessary to take account of in order to get what he wants, we have "realism" in its current political usage. The popular psychologist and lay preacher urges us to "face reality," and has in mind, apparently, a warning against being interested in anything which his own rather pronounced cultural limitations prevent him from considering important. In all these cases a contrast between facts on the one hand and an interpretation of dubious validity on the other is maintained, and so far philosophical realism has something in common with its contemporary verbal associates. But the realistic philosophers who gave the movement its intellectual structure have, with the exception of Bertrand Russell, had little further connection with these realisms. They were as ready to intuit "intrinsic" goodness and rightness as to believe the worst when they saw it. Their moral views were benevolent and optimistic, their politics liberal and progressive. They were, in fact, in most respects, men of the moralistic, progressive pre-war era, and their urge to found philosophy on "facts" was moti-

3. Perry, *Present Conflict of Ideals,* p. 368.

vated, ostensibly at least, by respect for the reliability of factual knowledge. No doubt a Marxist and/or a psychoanalyst could disclose deeper and more disreputable "drives" at work, but since these account for anybody doing anything, and would equally account for his doing anything else, their disclosure is not very helpful in any specific investigation.

The philosophical motive is, of course, simply a response to the challenge, which opposing theories present, to state this doctrine of the ultimacy of facts in a form in which it will meet all reasonable objections. The influence of Bradley and McTaggart in Britain, and of Royce in America, is very considerable. If there were contradictions in $2 + 2 = 4$, taken as literally and ultimately true, then it could not be the case that $2 + 2 = 4$. But it is the case that $2 + 2 = 4$, that events occur, and bodies move, and that there was a world of material objects before any minds emerged to observe it. Hence it cannot be true that any of these statements contradicts itself or anything else that there is good reason to believe. To state what is factually warranted in such fashion that it is also philosophically impregnable, and to expose the sophisms of opposing doctrines is the primary task. Since the opposing doctrines are extremely subtle, and supported by notions of knowledge and "the mind" which it is difficult to reject without at least apparent contradiction, the realist has a large task on his hands, and one to which his powers are admirably suited. The resulting philosophy, while it is intended to vindicate the convictions of the plain man, is not a plain philosophy. Its "strenuous simplicity," to borrow an expression from J. W. Scott, is, at times, a very formidable affair. But its aim is clear enough, and it is not surprising that, whatever the world at large might think of it, in academic circles where ideals of research predominate, it should have seemed an admirable and eminently sensible philosophy.

The "Idiosyncracy Platitude" or "Knowledge Is Knowledge"

The first step in this philosophical procedure of artful innocence is to insist on what John Wisdom has neatly termed the "idiosyncracy platitude." On the title page of his *Principia Ethica,* G. E. Moore inscribed the dictum of Bishop Butler, "Everything is what it is, and not another thing." The quotation was happily chosen, for the principal aim of Moore's book was to show that the answer to the primary ethical question, what does goodness consist in? or how is "good" to be defined? is simply that good is good, a "simple indefinable, unanalyzable object of thought," [4] and is not to be defined in terms of, analyzed into, or identified with anything else whatever. This is in one sense a platitude, and its purpose is precisely to stress the uniqueness or idiosyncracy of the ultimate value predicate. This was felt to be extremely important precisely be-

4. G. E. Moore, *Principia Ethica* (Cambridge: University Press, 1903), p. 21.

cause its recognition enables us to *pin down* moral theory, and to recognize the ultimacy of the primary facts in this field. A naturalistic ethics attempts to reduce ethical to non-ethical predicates; a metaphysical ethics tries to find the basis for value judgments in some character of ultimate reality. In neither case is justice done to the specific meaning of ethical predicates. And when a philosopher has seen the inadequacy of such attempts and why they are inadequate, his pronouncement that "good" is just good and not another thing is not only enlightening but in some respects decisive. For it specifies the area within which the philosophical meaning of ethical notions is to be found. It was, in Moore's use of it, the first major contribution to a realistic ethics. We shall trace its consequences in a later chapter.*

Prichard's statement of the "platitude" for the case of knowledge is equally trenchant. "Knowledge is *sui generis* and therefore a 'theory' of it is impossible. Knowledge is simply knowledge, and any attempt to state it in terms of something else must end in describing something that is not knowledge." [5] This, too, is important. For, as Prichard argues, and as our analysis of both idealistic and pragmatic accounts of thought has shown, the attempt to treat knowledge as an ultimately ineffective attempt to grasp a supra-relational Absolute, or as an instrument for non-cognitive satisfactions, does end by describing something that is not knowledge. Prichard thinks that once knowledge is seen as just knowledge, "It is simply *impossible* to think that any reality depends upon our knowledge of it, or upon any knowledge of it. Knowledge is essentially discovery, or the finding of what already is. If a reality could only be or come to be in virtue of some activity or process on the part of the mind, that activity or process would not be 'knowing', but 'making' or 'creating', and to make and to know must in the end be admitted to be mutually exclusive." [6] This, if true, is important.

The method in these platitudes will now be apparent. They constitute the realist's first line of defense against reductive analysis or too-sweeping synthesis in which the specific facts to be analyzed lose their specific character. And since there are many philosophies in which such analysis and synthesis, with their consequent distortion of the subject treated, have a leading place, the rediscovery of substantial fact as just what it is will seem to many a return to essential sanity, and a protection henceforth against dubious doctrine. When Woodbridge set down as his primary metaphysical principle "the recognition that existence is primarily what it is and can neither be explained nor explained

5. H. A. Prichard, *Kant's Theory of Knowledge* (Oxford: Clarendon Press, 1909), p. 245.

6. Prichard, *Kant's Theory of Knowledge,* p. 118.

* The "later chapter" is original chapter 6, "The 'Problem' of Moral Value," not included herein. Ed.

away," [7] he was making this insight the cornerstone of his philosophy, one of the sanest and soundest America has yet produced.

The Problems of Philosophy

This return to pregnant platitude may seem, on the face of it, a short way of dealing with traditional problems. When Woodbridge assures us that there is no "problem" of knowledge, and when Marvin,* speaking for the "New Realist" group, suggests that "neo-dogmatism" would be an appropriate designation for the attitude toward philosophical criticism that this version of realism recommends, the reader is likely to conclude that the problems of philosophy are simply being brushed aside. There is a sense in which this is true. For, if these philosophers are right, these problems have, at least in considerable measure, arisen from an attempt to reduce, e.g., knowledge to something which is not knowledge and then to inquire how, in this dubious guise, knowledge is really possible at all, and how it is related to "reality." To deny that there is *in this sense* a "problem" of knowledge is not to imply that there are not a great many facts about the conditions and criteria of valid knowing which it would be philosophically useful to inquire into. It is simply to say that knowledge is related to reality by being a knowledge of it, that is, a discovery or apprehension of its nature, and that in consequence "the relation . . . between cognitive experience and what is thereby cognized is simply cognition itself." [8] Similarly the "neo-dogmatists" did not claim that we can dispense with very careful "criticism" of knowledge-claims. What they held was that there is no need or place for the *sort* of criticism supposed, since Kant, to be peculiarly "philosophical" in nature, that, namely, which asks not what we do reliably know in the situations in which we come at facts, but how it is possible, in terms of a theory in which "the mind" gives laws to nature, for thinking to attain "objectivity," "universality," and "necessity." If we do not construct but discover the objective world, then there is no real problem of how such a construction could yield knowledge. To see this is not to evade "fundamental" problems, but to see through them.

There is, however, another aspect to the situation, and a more puzzling one. The "knowing" to which the realist appeals, meaning a discovery of facts, objects, "nature," as they really are, is not exempt from philosophical suspicion. For much that passes for knowledge is found to be deceptive and unreliable. We *seem* to look out through our eyes and see material objects, but "re-

---

7. Woodbridge, "Confessions," pp. 418–19.

8. F. J. E. Woodbridge, *Nature and Mind* (New York: Columbia University Press, 1937), p. 414.

* Walter T. Marvin, "The Emancipation of Metaphysics from Epistemology," in *The New Realism: Cooperative Studies in Philosophy* (New York: Macmillan, 1912), pp. 47–51. Ed.

ally," we have all been told, we are directly aware only of sensations produced in us through the interaction of our bodies with stimuli that impinge upon them. We interpret such sensations as signs of objects and, with an elaborate conceptual machinery, refer to an unperceived external world of which we have no first hand acquaintance at all. Not only is knowledge of it, as Santayana observed, "a salutation, not an embrace," but it is a salutation of dubious propriety, since mind and object have never met. Whether or not this theory is finally true, it has a very considerable body of doctrine to support it—in the facts of physiological psychology, in the discrepancy between the qualities of "data" as immediately inspected and the properties which, on the basis of scientific investigation, we believe externally "real" objects to possess, and in the "constructive" role of thinking in the sciences. In the face of such evidence to affirm that knowing is essentially discovery of what *is,* and that in knowledge the mind confronts the object directly, is a heroic undertaking, and one it will require the utmost dialectical acumen to defend. To appeal to the primary facts seems simple enough, but to maintain their primacy in philosophical controversy is a different matter. Hence the problems of philosophy recur, but in a different form. If we are to abolish epistemology we must construct an epistemology to end epistemologies, or at least a theory of the nature of knowledge and the relation of the mind to its objects which warrants the view that knowing is discovery, and that "reality" is simply what, in reliable knowing, we find to be the case. The technique of realistic theories is quite easy to understand. We take our stand on what, in our non-epistemological moments, we really know. This will be what we are quite certain of in the privileged case where we can confront data, facts, or objects face to face and apprehend them directly as they are. That knowing in this sense does actually occur is only demonstrable, of course, by actually having cases of it, but those who are inclined to be sceptical about it can be refuted by showing that unless we really know *something* in this fashion all further knowledge-claims are involved in endless dubiety and no real criticism of them is possible. For we can only test doubtful claims or measure probable reasonings by relation to what we know to be the case. In order to know that we know, or to criticize knowledge, we must first of all know. All "criticism" comes back, therefore, to what is found to be the case in those instances in which we actually *do* know, beyond all shadow of doubt.

There are, however, painfully few such instances, and much that in the sciences and practical life falls short of this sort of validation is nonetheless commonly held to be a matter of reasonably grounded belief. The problem of knowledge, in its new guise, becomes the problem of showing how such beliefs are related to and logically derivable from what we really or ultimately know to be the case. A philosophical criticism of knowledge, as distinct from the sort any careful inquirer would engage in in the course of his own investigations, involves just this reference to what is *really or ultimately known*. A physicist checks his hypotheses by reference to empirical data, but his "data" are not primary or "hard" data; they do not get us back to the situation in which we are simply acquainted with objects directly present to the mind. The leading principles a biologist uses in organizing his subject are plausible, and useful for his purposes. They are incorporated in theories that provide us with what, in common parlance, passes for "knowledge" of the nature and behavior of living organisms. But they are very far from self-evident; we do not *know* that they are true. Hence we must ask what "probability" attaches to such theories and invoke a logic of probability, itself based on certainties, including the certainty of what is probable, if we are to have any primary or philosophical warrant for accepting them. Here the "problem" of induction emerges. What right have we, what cognitive warrant, to generalize from observed to unobserved instances? It is no doubt convenient to do so, but convenience is no proof of truth, and when we look for a principle of induction whose intrinsic evidence will be sufficient to lend respectability to scientific generalizations, or for a theory of probability which will give formal sanction to procedures actually in use and thus provide a *logical foundation* for methods of empirical inquiry, we have started an investigation that will be long and arduous, if not in principle interminable.

It is in the light of this procedure that the characteristic subject-matter of a realistic philosophy is best understood. Is there an external world, and if there is how do we know it? It is sometimes hard for the uninitiated to see that this is a problem at all. Surely the way we know that there are objects "external" to our bodies is by perceiving them; and the warrant for perception is its *general* adequacy and reliability, when it is understood to be what, in use, it is found to be—a way of seeing things as they look, handling them as they feel, and the like. He might have supposed that this would be a characteristically "realistic" answer to the "problem" of the external world. If so, however, he would have failed to notice a crucial step in the development of this philosophy. The realist is not interested in defending our ordinary means of knowledge-getting as the generally reliable sources of information which, on the whole, they are found to be. He wants to show, in answer to philosophical criticism, that knowledge as discovery or disclosure has a final and absolute warrant. Only thus will its respectability be maintained as the unique mode of access to "the real" which he knows it to be. But what is "known" in this sense is not what, by cognitive tests elsewhere employed, passes for reliable knowing. It is what stands in some peculiar and privileged relation to the mind called acquaintance, or direct apprehension, or, for general principles, self-evidence. Now whether or not we can legitimately claim that perception is *in this sense* "knowledge" will depend on whether it can plausibly be regarded as a case of the immediate presence to "mind" of the perceptual object or a "part" of such object. This will be a question of tremendous moment. For unless the object is thus directly and infallibly present in perception in its real nature we must conclude that what is perceived is not a sufficient warrant for the truth of perceptual judgments. This does not merely mean that we must check one perception by another, and by the reports of other percipients. It means that perception *as such* requires a warrant from some more direct and immediate mode of access to the real. This, it is usually supposed, is had in acquaintance with sensory data. These are known immediately and infallibly. They do not appear, however, save to the very hardy, to be "true parts of the physical world." The "problem" then arises as to how what we really know about objects that are not the perceptual objects of ordinary observation can serve as a warrant for our beliefs that there are such objects and that they have some or all of the properties ordinarily attributed to them. Here perception, in the ordinary sense, will not count as evidence. It must be reduced to sensing plus some sort of belief or quasi-belief about the relation of objects thus sensed to ulterior objects which are never, save as the relata of this questionable relation to sense-data, open to observation at all. *In this context* questions that in ordinary inquiry are of minor moment take on a new significance. It is observed, for instance, that a penny looks elliptical when seen from an angle. What of it? That, under ordinary circumstances, is hardly surprising. It is the way we should expect it to look under the normal conditions of vision, and the observation that we see it thus as it looks would hardly be evidence that we do not see it. Seeing it as it looks is the way in which we *do* see it, and neither the fact that it looks as it does, nor the further fact that under other circumstances it wears a different aspect is in the least anomalous. But all this is far too simpleminded for epistemologically "naive" realism. The penny is really not elliptical, it only appears so. And hence what we see is the appearance of a penny. Is this appearance, which is all that is directly and infallibly given—since in the case of illusory perception there may "really" be no penny there at all—*itself* a "true part of the physical world?" Is the real penny made up of such appearances so that in sensing it we are really, in an extended sense of "part," sensing a part of the real object itself? If so, we can hold that perception is direct, and that what is immediately given is "the object" itself, though we shall have to hold that an object thus containing all its aspects is a different sort of entity from any that the "crude, brick-bat notion" of a material thing has led us to expect. This is a difficult view to defend, but if it were defensible we should have philosophical warrant for the belief, previously expressed, that we know there is an external world because we perceive it.

If, however, we find it too difficult to think that a "real" material object is composed of sensory data, we shall have to say that our direct experience, yielding only such data, does not disclose an external world, and shall have to find some device, from logical construction to animal faith, to give a rational or irrational sanction to the belief that such a world exists. If we don't "*really see*" perceptual objects, then we must seek evidence for their existence not in what in perception we supposed ourselves to see but in what, in fallible acquaintance, we sense, and in what by logical and epistemological ingenuity we can find an excuse for believing. Thus far does the observation that pennies look elliptical when seen from an angle take us into the "problems of philosophy."

It has seemed important to stress this fact at some length, since the remoteness of the disputes in which philosophical realism is for the most part involved from the factual basis to which it appeals, is likely, if the connection is not seen, to appear paradoxical. Actually, to summarize, the connection is this. Knowledge is to be understood in its uniqueness as discovery of what actually (or "really") is the case. For this purpose it must be defended against all the charges made against it. The form in which it is thus found infallibly secure is that in which it amounts to the direct presentation to the mind of the object as in its own nature it is. This, in consequence, is what knowledge is in the cases where we are quite sure we have it. As such, it serves as the basis and measure for the reliability of all other knowledge claims. What cannot be shown to be thus directly given in its intrinsic being is not known in this primary sense. As an object of belief or opinion it must be certified by what is really known. To indicate the relation of our more dubious beliefs to what is thus ultimately reliable will be the task of a critical philosophy. The form this task will take when the reliability of perception as a source of knowledge of the external world is in question has just been seen.

It is not to be supposed that all realists have taken the course outlined above. Some, like Woodbridge, have been content to affirm that we do through the senses acquire knowledge of nature, without allowing themselves to be drawn into any precise statement as to the ultimate logical relation between sensory data and material objects. Their realism thus remains on the prophetic level, and announces a wise conclusion without revealing, save aphoristically, the manner in which it is warranted by the available evidence. For the most part, however, the formulation given above sets the problems on which investigation centers. Realism is a specialist's philosophy, and many of its devotees have been so far specialists as to concentrate furiously on some particular complication of the dispute without much regard to its bearing on wider issues, thus, in Santayana's oft-quoted words, "redoubling their effort when they have forgotten their aim." Is "the datum" identical with the real object which is the *true* objective of knowing or is it not? Do we "transcend" data and, though precariously, reach ulterior objects, or are we confined to a world of actual and possible data? Can we find a logical foundation for empirical generalizations, and thus solve the problem of induction? These, it has been supposed, are plain and sensible questions and a whole generation of acute reasoners has expended its philosophical energies upon them. That they make sense only in terms of a quite special formulation of "the problem of knowledge," and that this formulation may itself be highly questionable in the light of what knowing, outside the realistic debate, shows itself to be, has only recently begun to dawn on the disputants as a real possibility. Our present concern is not with that late and lovely dawning, but with the problems which, in the intermediate period, dominated academic philosophy, and with the standpoint from which that domination could appear as a matter of plain good sense, and of the application to philosophy of those methods of logical rigor and exact analysis which were capable of raising this dubious discipline to the rank of genuine knowledge.

Logic and Philosophy

The questionable status of logic as a philosophical discipline in both idealistic and pragmatic theories has already been discussed. In the growth of realism, logic, as a special source of philosophical enlightenment, came into its own, and perhaps even more than its own. The impact of this development on the "problems of philosophy" as realistically defined was threefold. In the first place, logical inquiry was emancipated from dependence on either metaphysics or psychology and given its autonomous place as an inquiry into the nature of propositional forms and the structure of deductive systems. It was thus enabled to expand in its own proper territory and to establish remarkably fruitful relations with the mathematical sciences to which, as a formal discipline, it obviously was closely allied. In *The Principles of Mathematics,* Russell proclaimed the merger of logic and pure mathematics, and, in the vastly impressive *Principia Mathematica,* was able with Whitehead's collaboration to carry it through to a challenging if not altogether convincing conclusion. Whether or not *Principia* proves, as Russell believes, that "from certain ideas and axioms of formal logic, by the help of the logic of relations, all pure mathematics can be deduced, without any new undefined ideas or unproved propositions," [9] it unquestionably gave a tremendous stimulus to logical research, and set many acute philosophers to specializing in a field which, whatever its connection with more general philosophical problems, has proved a fruitful subject-matter for inquiry on its own account. As psychology grew out of philosophy into a special science, carrying with it into its more limited investigations some of the problems and pretensions its philosophical associations had generated, so

9. Bertrand Russell, "Logical Atomism," in *Contemporary British Philosophy,* edited by J. H. Muirhead (London: George Allen and Unwin, 1924), vol. 1, p. 361.

logic as a formal science is at present growing. It is not surprising that its attempts to clarify its own procedure and free itself from metaphysical encumbrances should prove of such special interest to some philosophers that they have been inclined to regard them as the only appropriate subject-matter for an enlightened philosophy.

In the second place, however, progress in logical research, like progress in any other of the sciences, does have a definite bearing on philosophy in its further activities. For philosophers make use of logical notions and procedures, and if their notions have been narrow and their procedure inept, the outcome could hardly fail to be unsatisfactory. A better understanding of logic is thus likely to bear fruit in a more rational philosophy. If Kant's antinomies are based on logical blunders in reasoning about infinite aggregates, a better mathematico-logical analysis of the subject will be a reasonable basis for philosophical enlightenment as well. If, as Russell alleges, the monism of absolute idealism is based on a "subject-predicate" logic, and if a study of the forms of propositions leads to the conclusion that relational propositions are logically respectable, then the apparent necessity for monism evaporates. And if an eminent metaphysician is led to suppose that because the word "nothing" has an intelligible use, there must *be* a nothing to which it refers and that this "nothing" can be made a theme of profound significance for the meaning of "existence," he ought certainly to inquire further into the nature and use of verbal symbols and be instructed accordingly. In all these cases, a philosophical error can plausibly be supposed to have its basis in a mistake in logical analysis, and a resort to logical analysis, therefore, to be the appropriate method for clearing up *these* problems of philosophy. It would not seem unreasonable to those who took such puzzles and their elucidation as a primary clue to the nature of philosophical knowledge to say that logic is *the* method of philosophy, and that only through its intensive use will a scientific method in this subject be achieved.

In the third place, the special subject-matter of logic and pure mathematics can plausibly be regarded as of peculiar philosophical significance. Here, at least, our aspiration for absolute truth appears to be satisfied. Its formal cogency depends on no "laws of thought" or stipulations of human convenience. All Being is its province and in its timeless validity there is no change, neither shadow of turning. Thus Russell announced that in mathematics reason can "investigate into the heart of all things actual and possible." [10] "The world of

10. Bertrand Russell, *Mysticism and Logic* (2d ed.; London: George Allen and Unwin, 1917), p. 69. [The exact wording Murphy provides is not in the text, though the gist of it is. On page 63, Russell says: "It is in the power of understanding and discovering [general] truths that the mastery of the intellect over the whole world of things actual and possible resides. . . ." And on p. 69: "[M]athematics takes us . . . further from what is human, into the region of absolute necessity, to which not only the actual world, but every possible world, must conform . . ." Ed.].

pure reason knows no compromise, no practical limitations, no barrier to the creative activity embodying in splendid edifices the passionate aspiration after the perfect from which all great work springs." [11]

The philosophical interpretation to be placed on this rhapsodic logical realism is itself one of the "problems of philosophy," and for this theory a major one. The straightforward view, and the one Russell and Moore and their American followers first adopted, was simply to ascribe ultimate ontological status to logical and mathematical objects, and to regard logic and mathematics as means of access to a realm of Being wider and more ultimate than mere space-time existence. The development of this view and the later critical reaction against it are responsible for almost as many realistic "problems of philosophy" as are the puzzles about perception. The earlier stages in the development sound peculiarly antiquated today, but the later and more sophisticated theories have grown so directly out of them, and are so largely determined in their critical conclusions by the views criticized, that to understand the standpoint of realism we must see in outline what the earlier doctrine affirmed and the later has sought, at all costs, to avoid.

Realms of Being

The presuppositions of this theory are that logic and mathematics yield knowledge which is valid in its own right and a primary source of philosophical enlightenment, and that knowledge discloses real facts and objects as they are. "The number 2 is not purely mental, but is an entity which may be thought of. Whatever can be thought of has being, and its being is a precondition, not a result, of its being thought of." [12] The limits of Being are thus remarkably inclusive. "Number, the Homeric gods, relations, chimeras, and four-dimensional spaces all have being, for if they were not entities of a kind we could make no propositions about them. Thus being is a general attribute of everything, and to mention anything is to show that it is." [13] This is in a way surprising, but it seems consistent with the status of thought as discovery. The number 2 is discovered "in just the same sense in which Columbus discovered the West Indies," and its properties and relations depend as little on the mind as do those of physical objects. This does not mean that everything mentionable exists, or is real, if "reality" is used for existence or some other special mode or variety of Being. "The gist of realism," as Holt observed, "is not to insist that everything is real, far from it, but to insist that everything that is is,

11. Russell, *Mysticism and Logic,* pp. 60–61.

12. Bertrand Russell, *The Principles of Mathematics* (2d ed.; London: George Allen and Unwin, 1937), p. 451.

13. Russell, *Principles of Mathematics,* p. 449.

and is as it is." [14] Whether this is a tautology or a profound ontological discovery, or a curious confusion of the two, only subsequent investigation could show. What it *appeared* to be was an introduction to realms of Being which philosophy, with splendid universality and a fine disdain of mere existence, could make its own, and for whose exploration logic, since its laws are not limited to what is physical or mental but apply to all significant being, was a philosophical instrument of particular value.

If the universal terms or concepts which inhabit this wider realm of Being seem unsubstantial, that, no doubt, is a prejudice due to our practical and hence unphilosophical interest in what, in this particular world, happens to exist. But for intellectual analysis, the world of existence itself reduces to the concepts or meanings we find in it. And if this is what analysis shows it to be, then this is what, without further ado, it actually is. In a surprising early article G. E. Moore asserted: "It seems necessary . . . to regard the world as formed of concepts. These are the only objects of knowledge. They cannot be regarded fundamentally as abstractions either from things or from ideas; since both alike can, if anything is to be true of them, be composed of nothing but concepts. A thing becomes intelligible first when it is analyzed into its constituent concepts." [15] Consequently, "an existent is seen to be nothing but a concept or a complex of concepts standing in a unique relation to the concept of existence." [16] A "concept," it should be recalled, is, in this usage, not any sort of mental state ordinarily, but a "universal meaning."

The consequences of this drastic doctrine Moore himself did not draw, but the American new-realists, a decade later, were ready to do so. And why not? After all, thought is essentially discovery of what *is,* and analytic thought deals in concepts, abstractions and general terms. How can we hold, as, considering the new triumphs of logic and mathematics, we must, that these disciplines yield knowledge, unless we are prepared to admit that things really are just what, in such analysis, they are found to be. If mathematical physics analyzes space into extensionless points and time into durationless instants, then space is quite literally made up of points, and duration of instants. For it is not the business of analysis to falsify the world, but to yield knowledge of its structure. But this will carry us, philosophically, a long way. The terms and relations disclosed in a logical analysis are, as such, neither physical or mental; they possess a neutral being, and their further status in a physical system or as elements in a mind is adventitious with respect to their logical standing as terms-

14. Edwin B. Holt, in *The New Realism: Cooperative Studies in Philosophy* (New York: Macmillan, 1912), p. 359.

15. G. E. Moore, "The Nature of Judgment," in *Mind,* new series vol. 8, 1899, p. 182.

16. Moore, "Nature of Judgment," p. 183.

in-relation. Thus analyzed, the substantial things of the external world are "Such stuff as logical and mathematical manifolds are made of," [17] terms and propositions. The simplest entities (logically) in the world are "identity, difference, and number," and into these, with slightly more complex logical entities and secondary qualities, matter can be analyzed without remainder. "Various concepts in combination *are* matter." [18] Consciousness is a cross section of such neutral entities selected by an interested organism, and acquiring in this relation a status they did not previously possess, without surrendering either their inalienable objectivity and neutral being or their material status, if they also belong to complexes which are material things. "Both physical objects and ideas are composed of the same neutral entities, and both physical and mental activity are derived from the activity of neutral entities—the generative activity of propositions." [19]

It is not surprising that logical analysis should thus be considered not only *a* means of access to Being as it essentially is, but for philosophy the preferred one. The terms to which it leads us are ultimate (not open to further analysis), and in their neutral being independent of the mind that apprehends them. As Perry said, "The ultimate *terms* of experience are at any rate independent, whatever may turn out to be the case with certain complexes of these terms. If the knower wishes to eliminate the personal equation and seize on things-in-themselves, his safest course is to sift experience to its elements and thus obtain a sure footing in the independent world. Such elements, whether sensory qualities or logical indefinables, will afford him a nucleus of independence to which he can add such complexes as will satisfy his criterion." [20] Now "Ultimates" and things in themselves independent of the knower are peculiarly elegible ontological and epistemological objects, and if "the generative activity of propositions" should prove sufficient to construct a world, the oldest hopes of philosophy would be realized in a new and impressive fashion. It is no wonder that the new realists surveyed the world of neutral entities with enthusiasm and found it good.

Methods of Analysis

This result, however, has not, on the whole, commended itself to later analysts. That analysis in some fashion leads to truth, that the use of the machinery of terms and "external" relations does not, as Bradley held, lead essentially to a distortion of the ultimate subject-matter of thought but provides the best means

17. E. B. Holt, *The Concept of Consciousness* (New York: Macmillan, 1914), p. 114.

18. Holt, *Concept of Consciousness,* p. 157.

19. Holt, *Concept of Consciousness,* p. 274.

20. R. B. Perry, in *The New Realism: Cooperative Studies in Philosophy* (New York: Macmillan, 1912), p. 128.

we have for organizing and extending our knowledge, and that logic is in some primary sense the organon of such analysis, is still maintained. But it may well be that the truth to which it leads is not quite so simple a reflection of the apparent structure of propositions as Holt and his colleagues had supposed. We do indeed use propositions in which the term "mermaid" occurs, and such propositions are sometimes true. If they are true, moreover, there are facts to which they correspond, and the constituents of the fact can, when the proposition is fully analyzed, be seen to be just the entities to which the terms of the proposition really refer. So, at least, Bertrand Russell held when he took this puzzling matter under further consideration, and this treatment of it was decisive for later "analysis." [21] If then the term "mermaid" really referred to a constituent of the fact [reference] to which makes the proposition about a mermaid true, there would have to be a mermaid, rejoicing in some objective mode of being, though not, of course, that of space-time existence. But there is another alternative. Perhaps the proposition in which the term "mermaid" appears will be found, when fully analyzed, not to contain any such constituent as "a mermaid" to which a constituent in the fact must correspond. In that case the ontological reference is obviated, and we can get along without mermaids, at least in any realm of being of which logic compels us to take account. That would be a considerable balm to our "sense of reality," which assures us that *in fact* there are no mermaids, and would effect a considerable simplification in the philosophy of logical realism. The procedure by which this simplification is achieved will concern us later. The point here is simply to notice its philosophical *raison d'être*. If logical analysis left us with mermaids, or round squares, or the number 2, then there must indeed *be* such entities as constituents of facts and hence as parts of "the ultimate furniture of the world." The logical analysis which rids us of such entities is therefore also an ontological justification of beliefs held on other grounds as to what "the world" ultimately consists of. And it is its utility in this role that particularly recommends it to many of its advocates.

The function of logical analysis in the development of philosophical realism is, therefore, a peculiar one. It is not simply a matter of carrying over into philosophy techniques that have proved their worth in logic and mathematics and might well be supposed to have a wider application. Nor is it just a matter of defending, from a realistic standpoint, the knowledge-yielding value of analytic methods in various types of inquiry. It is also, and essentially, an attempt to reconcile an initial assumption of the ontologically primary status of the results of logical analysis with beliefs held on other grounds as to what the ultimate objects or "beings" in the world really are. Such an attempt may lead,

---

21. See esp. *Introduction to Mathematical Philosophy* (London: George Allen and Unwin, 1919), ch. 16 ["Descriptions"].

as intellectual fashions change, to the conclusion that, as Russell in a later and more chastened mood asserts, "Logical constants, . . . if we are to be able to say anything definite about them, must be treated as part of the language, not as part of what the language speaks about. . . . It will still be true that no constants except logical constants occur in the verbal or symbolic expression of logical propositions, but it will not be true that these logical constants are names of objects, as 'Socrates' is intended to be." [22] Here a more refined "syntactical" analysis has been performed on the basis of which it is possible to separate statements that refer to "extra-linguistic objects" from those which are concerned only with linguistic rules and their consequences. The propositions of logic are held to belong in the latter group. Different in result as this is from the earlier view, it agrees with it in one essential respect. A question of the ontological status of logical entities is settled by means of an analysis of the denotation of terms, the nature of logical rules and the like, and a comparison of the results thus reached with what, on other grounds, is supposed to be actual or existent. The denial that logical constants have an "extra-linguistic" reference, and the claim that they are merely "parts of the language," are just as much statements about the ontological status of the entities concerned as was the previous claim that such entities have a real and inalienable being of their own, quite independent of all "language" and all human thought. They are statements made in the interest of an "empirical" theory which wishes to eliminate from "the world" any objects for which there is not a definite place in sensible experience, or "nature," insofar as sensible experience enables us to discover what it is. To relegate logical objects to language is to say that in "the world" there *are* no such objects, and this is a conclusion congenial to a now fashionable type of philosophical belief. But it is a consequence of logical analysis only when such analysis is taken as a means of separating the "real object" sheep from the "linguistic" goats and enabling us to decide what there is in the world and what there is not.

That this is a different sort of question about logic from either of two others with which it might be confused must be clearly seen if we are to make sense of "analysis" as it has functioned in the philosophies which derive their inspiration from Russell. It is not the same as the question, what is the subject matter and content of logic as a science?—what, that is, would a person *find out* by studying logic? Whether logical constants are linguistic entities merely or names for objects supposed to subsist outside of language, the logical structure of deductive systems remains the same. Nor is it the question, how does the use of logical rules in inquiry help us to gain information or to formulate theories which, in their application, extend our knowledge? That is an extremely fruitful

22. Russell, *Principles of Mathematics,* 2d ed., pp. xi–xii.

question, and anyone innocent of philosophical controversy might suppose that it is what we want to find out about when we ask how logic applies to the real world. But how *is* there any other intelligible question about the meaning and validity of logic, than these two: namely, what does logic tell us on its own account, and, what, with its help, can we find out about matters of fact? Clearly, on the realistic premise that knowledge is a disclosure of *being,* and that the objects to which it really refers are exhibited by logical analysis, there is. It is precisely the question, what is logic (or any other inquiry for that matter) about *really,* and what *are,* e.g., logical constants, not as they function in logic, or as logic functions in further inquiry, but as constituents of the real world? This is not a formal question at all, but one about the sort of entity entitled to count as objective or empirical or extra-linguistic or whatever else in a particular philosophy is held to be the status appropriate to real objects. The satisfaction an "empiricist" gets from the conclusion that logical objects are merely verbal entities is of the same sort that the "rationalist" got from his discovery of a realm of being in which his best hopes were not disappointed, that, namely, of picturing the world in terms congenial to his notion of what a *genuine* object ought to be. Either satisfaction may be warranted, but its warrant is of a different sort from that which the pursuit of logical studies for their own sake can provide. An "analysis" thus designed to rid the world of philosophically undesirable entities and to pronounce a final verdict on what in its ontological status the referent of a sign really is, has an intelligible place in the development of realistic philosophy. Whether it has an equally intelligible place in a genuinely critical philosophy is a question to which we shall recur.

The Place of Mind in Nature

A further impetus to realistic speculation is provided by the desire to harmonize what we know of "the mind," as knower and valuer, with what the sciences tell us of the evolution and natural conditions of mental behavior. So long as idealism held the field this was not, for the philosopher, a primary problem. For the natural world itself was a mere phenomenon or appearance, and while mental behavior as an observable phenomenon has undoubtedly emerged within it, *Mind* as knower and valuer is epistemologically and metaphysically prior to such emergence. We need not account for either Knowledge or Value, for it is in terms of them, as basic, that we explain the objectivity of the natural world from which they were supposed to be derived. When, however, a thorough-going realism has reestablished the cognitive respectability of an antecedent natural environment as independently real, and inclined us to accept the scientific account of the evolution of human organisms as quite literally true, the problem of the relation of the mind to nature is likely to be supplanted by that of the place of mind in nature. Not all "realists" have also been "naturalists"—have attempted, that is, to show that what mind is found to be in its space-time environment (including its relations to other sentient and socially conditioned organisms) is the whole truth about it—but the normal tendency has been in that direction, and reasonably so. For unless we have some independent reason for supposing that the description of mental evolution and behavior given by the sciences is in some essential respect inadequate, we shall naturally be inclined to accommodate our views about mind to what, from these sources, is found to be the case. Religion and philosophy have in the past been supposed to provide such independent reasons. Religion, insofar as it is believed to disclose a non-natural origin and destiny for the soul, still does so. But philosophy, if it no longer need assume a non-natural mind as the source of nature, is now in a position to ally itself rather with the sciences than with religion in this matter. The result of such an alliance, it would be reasonable to hope, would be of benefit to both parties. It would broaden and clarify the view of mental behavior which psychology and the social sciences at present supply by including those aspects of behavior, especially concerned with *values*, about which these disciplines so far have nothing very reliable to tell us. It would provide a sound epistemological foundation for the sciences and thus avoid the agnostic, positivistic, and finally sceptical conclusions into which philosophizing scientists have in the past too frequently been led. And finally, it would provide a general picture of nature and of evolution in which mental phenomena could be exhibited in their essential continuity with the rest of nature and at the same time in their own distinctive characters. The "togetherness and distinctness" of things in a space-time world thus offers the model for a philosophical synthesis of mind and nature which, if it could be consistently carried through, would be a remarkable philosophical achievement.

The most ambitious realistic venture of this sort that we have had is Alexander's imposing *Space, Time, and Deity.* "The Temper of Realism," he had earlier insisted, "is to deanthropomorphize; to order man and mind to their proper place among the world of finite things," [23] a world in which space-time is the simplest and most pervasive reality, and deity that unique emergent quality which beings of any progressively higher levels of space-time structure possess in their relation to that immediately below them. In such a world knowing must find its place as a relation at once distinct from (since minds have the unique emergent quality of mentality) and continuous with the orders of relatedness out of which "minded" organisms have developed. Such is the relation of togetherness in space-time, where one of the terms is a mind selectively aware of the objects around it. "To be aware of a thing is to be caught in the common web of the universe, to be an existence alongside the other existences;

23. Samuel Alexander, *The Basis of Realism* (London: Oxford University Press, 1914), p. 1.

peculiar insofar as this empirical character of awareness is distinctive of a certain order of existence, but otherwise not peculiar, at least for metaphysics." [24]

Any number of developments in the sciences can be used to substantiate this undertaking and to lend empirical content to its speculative interests. The notion of space-time offered rich material for such speculative development, the theory of evolution applied to the natural world as a whole and used to mark out levels of "higher" and "lower" in the order of existents was obviously serviceable, and the behavioristic theories of mind, whether accepted *in toto* or not, were in line with the general tendency to domesticate "mind" in Nature. A philosophy that aspires to be the unifier of the conclusions of the sciences into a coherent and comprehensive whole, in which facts about knowing and valuing, of which idealistic philosophy had hitherto been the custodian, can also find their appropriate place, has thus a remarkably promising subject-matter, and the hope that such a philosophy might, in a reasonably short time, outline the essential structure of nature, and hence of "reality," did not at the time seem extravagant.

Here as elsewhere, however, the proximate subject-matter of philosophical realism was not this natural world as such, but the problems that arise in the attempt to discover its basic or essential nature. What means has philosophy, which the sciences have not, for finding out what this world actually is? That it is a world of space-time, in the sense that a physical description of it makes use of both spatial and temporal coordinates, we know. Is it also and ultimately a world of Space-Time? To affirm that it is, one must go beyond physics. One must meet the objections raised by, e.g., Bradley against space and time as ultimately real, and must show how they can be real on their own account and can characterize Reality in its ultimate nature. In the course of this argument one may well be impelled to impute to Space and Time (or Space-Time), as ultimate, a structure for which physics yields no evidence, and which is, on other grounds, difficult to accept. But this is not surprising, for the truth of statements made about spatial and temporal relations in physical inquiry is one thing, and the adequacy of Space-Time to serve as the basic reality from which all things emerge and to which all are reducible without remainder, is quite another.

Again, the problem of the relation of mind to the rest of nature will take on a special character when an objective synthesis of all that we are empirically acquainted with in a Space-time world in undertaken. "Knowing" is held to be a "togetherness" of mind and object in Space-time. But many of the objects of immediate acquaintance are not usually supposed to occupy places in space at all. Their illusory character depends on just this circumstance. Do they none-

---

24. Alexander, *Basis of Realism*, p. 6.

theless belong to the space-time continuum of nature, and in what manner of location are they to be located there? The question is extremely difficult, and calculated to arouse endless controversy. It is the *sort* of question that need arise, however, only when it is first assumed that direct experience discloses "the object" as it "really" is, and hence that placing the knowing situation "within nature" requires us to attribute to nature, and finally to space-time, all the characters objects as experienced appear to possess. *Given the assumptions,* the "problem" of the place of illusory characters in the one space-time which, for Alexander, is the locus of all natural objects, is indeed a crucial one. Unless they can be thus located they fall outside "nature" altogether, and the world empirically observable ceases to be the objective world to which our thinking claims to refer. Whether it is better to return to dualism at this point and leap with animal faith at a space-time world never open to inspection, or to complicate the world of nature by the inclusion of much that, in a more ordinary usage, does not belong to it, or indeed, to anything, since it is precisely what experienced things sometimes look to be but are not, it is indeed difficult to decide.

How, finally, are "values" to be included in nature? To what objects do value-predicates apply, and are they natural or non-natural predicates? If all that exists is "really" spatio-temporal, then it is of space-time objects, in respect of some of their characters or relations, that value is to be predicated, if it actually belongs to anything at all. Can we suppose that the beauty of a sunset is a real character of the sunset, independently of any relation to sentient organisms? Or do value predicates accrue to things insofar as they are objects of any interest, or of a specially qualified interest? Or, finally, do they perhaps have no "objective" status at all, so that when we call a thing valuable we are saying nothing of it, but only expressing an emotion toward it? These, again, are puzzling questions, and it has seemed natural that they should be raised. They are, perhaps, less closely related to the kind of distinctions we ordinarily have in mind when we make value judgments, and to the validity we claim for such judgments, than to the consequences of a philosophical attempt to predicate of a selected object or set of objects all that, in our total commerce with the world, we find it reasonable to affirm. But they *seem* to be factual questions, capable of a precise and factual answer, and as such they form the basis for the philosophical inquiry to which the realistic standpoint naturally leads.

To summarize: Realism as a philosophy is known by its problems, and by the assumption that a concern with these and an attempted solution of them by recourse to factual information and probable hypothesis is the proper business of philosophers. I have tried to show that this was a natural standpoint from which, given the primary interests involved and the dominant intellectual habits and fashions of the period, to come at the subject. That it is, nonetheless, a very special standpoint and that the plain answer to plain questions it is prone to demand actually are intelligible only from this standpoint, has already been suggested and will later be argued more fully. It is important that it should be seen. For we shall have thought our way through, and perhaps out of, this philosophy not when its more explicit doctrines, already largely out of fashion, have been once more "refuted," but when we have seen through its *problems* and the assumption that they present the issues with which philosophy is or ought to be concerned in the only form in which they can be subjected to clear analysis and (possible) factual solution.

The Dialectic of Realism
The Problem for Realism

It has been suggested in the preceding and will be further argued in the present section that the "problems" the realistic standpoint has bequeathed to philosophy are not in all respects as fundamental or urgent as, from this standpoint, they appear. There is, however, at least one problem this philosophy confronts which is quite genuine and quite fundamental. There really is something problematic about any set of ideas or theories or beliefs in which in the course of knowledge-getting or value-discrimination we have reasonable confidence, when these are taken, as they stand, as competent to disclose the "real" nature of the world, or the nature of the "real" world. To claim this status for them is to raise issues with which in our ordinary use of them we are not concerned, and which may carry us a long way beyond the context of such use and application. Common sense, for instance, is competent to provide us with information about practically relevant features of our material and social environment which is quite indispensible for the maintenance of life in the manner to which we have been accustomed. To doubt that some judgments of this sort in their ordinary usage are veracious, and can be discovered to be so by perceptual tests, would be the intellectual occupation only of "a fool or an advanced thinker," and would merit the criticism G. E. Moore, in his "Defence of Common Sense," * has made of such doubting. But common sense is *prima facie* a limited and fallible affair. Competent to adjust us adequately to perceptually obvious and socially important features of the world, it is likely to become quite misleading if taken as the norm to which scientific inquiry, especially in the social sciences, should conform, and its obvious bias toward the tangible, the familiar, and the readily communicable seems quite to disqualify it as a means for discovering what the "real" world, in its more remote and "transcendent" aspects, really is. What credence ought we to give to common sense

* G. E. Moore, "A Defense of Common Sense," *Contemporary British Philosophy,* edited by J. H. Muirhead (London: George Allen & Unwin, 1924), vol. 2. Ed.

judgments when we are considering them *philosophically* in relation to other means of knowing, and are trying to decide what and how much, on the whole, they can tell us? In one form or another, every philosophy is confronted with this question when it tries to coordinate our various ways of inquiring and to adjust our ideas and preferences in a total reasonable interpretation made in the light of all that, in any fashion, we find to be the case. The contrast between what, in their non-philosophical use, our ideas and valuations tell us and what is to be made of them philosophically is the point of departure for any philosophy that has anything to say and expects to contribute to human experience an element of understanding not elsewhere reliably obtainable. Had the realists not been aware of this problem and primarily concerned to solve it, they would not have been philosophers at all, but only specialists in logic, or psychology, [or] biology, or the pseudo-problems that arise when these subjects are treated in terms of an inexact terminology and a large disregard of contextual limits and empirical reference. In fact they were genuinely and properly concerned with it; and their method of dealing with it was, in the philosophical situation of the time, *prima facie* reasonable.

For, if the outcome of idealism and pragmatism has shown us anything, it is that this philosophical relation of our various types of knowledge and value claims to what on the whole it is reasonable to believe about the world and the place of knowing and valuing in it, is not reliably to be discerned *either* by referring such claims to Reality as a whole, in its ultimate and Absolute nature, or by reducing them to their meaning and use for some special interest or interests held to be empirically ultimate and humanly important. Either of these methods, as has been seen, and as the realists were prepared to show in detail, results in a distortion of the subject-matter examined, and leads us not to make the most of any aspect of experience by seeing it in its effective connections, but to see it out of focus. The first commandment for philosophy, once this has been seen, will naturally be to keep both eyes on the object or objects to be understood, and to see them first of all for what, in their own nature, they show themselves to be. Any philosophical synthesis that breaks this commandment will give us an interpretation not of things as they are, but only as from a biased and inadequate standpoint they appear to be. Good is good, knowledge is knowledge, and it is on such facts *as they stand* and without reductive distortion that a sound philosophy must be built.

Yet this basis in the factual ultimacy of what, antecedently to speculative synthesis and epistemological interpretation, we find to be the case is not easily discovered. For it is philosophical adequacy that has to be established, and this will not be secured by showing that the beliefs, ideas, or valuations in question work reliably for their own primary purposes. Much that thus "works," and that justifies itself in use, is admittedly relative to the interests and special conditions of a particular inquiry or practical activity, and would, as it stands, be a poor candidate for ultimate and final truth about the real world. Hence, not everything that passes for genuine can forthwith be taken to be so in the sense required. The items selected thus to stand as ultimate and unshakable must prove their right to this status by meeting all philosophical objections that can be made against them and vindicating their claim to be real in their own right. And the subsequent organization of experience will have these ultimates as its foundation stones, and will indicate the way in which they support the superstructure of beliefs *in themselves* not final or certain but guaranteed by their relation to the "foundations" on which, in logic, or epistemology, or value theory, or metaphysics, they can be shown to rest.

The structure of philosophical realism is, I believe, best understood when it is thus articulated. The ultimates are "the facts" or the "realities" themselves, as these are found to be by direct inspection, or logical analysis, or empirically controlled hypothesis. These are quite final and ultimate as they stand, and require no external support or interpretation to guarantee their philosophical respectability. And whatever is not thus ultimate or final must be understood in its relation to these. This relation will provide the measure of the philosophical justification for derivative ideas or valuations, as distinct from that which they enjoy in use and for the special purposes of non-philosophical inquiry. It will not be surprising if "knowledge" or "value" or "space-time," thus understood, wears a somewhat different aspect from that which, in other inquiries, we find it to have. For these other inquiries are not concerned with this fundamental question, and it is not to be assumed that what, e.g., "poor, dear common sense" has to say about what we perceive and what we are warranted in believing on the basis of perception will be of much use for an understanding of what in philosophical analysis perception is found to be. The sciences are better, but they too have their makeshifts and their special interests and procedures, and a space-time that will meet all the requirements of theoretical physics may need very considerable retouching before it can pass as a philosophical ultimate, dialectically qualified to withstand Bradley's attacks on the "reality" of space and time, and to maintain itself as in its own right the reality from which all things emerge and of which they are all composed.

Thus philosophy emerges once more with a special subject-matter of its own and special professional methods of dealing with it. A philosophical account of knowledge will differ from an analysis of what distinguishes tested and reliable beliefs and procedures from those not thus tested, as carried out in other types of inquiry. Inductive reasonings in these latter inquiries are justified by examination of the procedures which do and those which do not get ideas into empirically warranted and *cognitively* useful relations with the subject-matter of inquiry, those which do and those which do not prove on the whole reliable means of finding out the order and connection of events. The reason, e.g., for expecting the sun to rise tomorrow and not expecting arsenic to be as healthful as milk could be made out without much difficulty in terms of such a comparison. If, however, a search for the *philosophical foundations of induction* is instituted, considerations of this sort will cease to be of decisive importance. We shall need to know whether there is any ultimate ground for "passing from observed to unobserved instances," whether, for example, there is any principle of induction, either self-evident or at least highly probable on its own account, which warrants more special inductive hypotheses, or whether perhaps some logical manipulation of the frequency theory of probability will do the business. And if neither of these inquiries appears to have any satisfactory issue when it is the probability of *theories,* the ground for regarding one as a more reliable guide to truth than another, that is in question, we shall have to say that there is no ultimate warrant for induction, that we are just guessing, or betting on the future, or the like. From this standpoint the belief that the sun will rise tomorrow, even with the whole of our astronomical knowledge to support it, is *ultimately* no more reasonable (i.e., better grounded in what is ultimately certified) than the belief that the stars have a profound effect on human destiny. This is in some respects unfortunate, for it seems to cancel *philosophically* a distinction between reasonable and unreasonable beliefs which, on other grounds, we should think it very important to make, and it is likely to lead inquirers either to a further fruitless search for formal and metaphysical foundations for reasonings which are not in fact formally or metaphysically grounded but simply found *in fact* to be reliable means of discerning the structure of specific subject-matters, *or else* to suppose that there "really" is no such difference in reliability between astronomy and astrology as we elsewhere find, and that since we must resort to "faith" in either case, one faith is rationally as good as another. But whether unfortunate or not, it is the natural result of an apparently straightforward procedure, and leads at once to the "problems" in which those who specialize in such inquiry have ever since been involved.

Two Sorts of Ultimacy

In order that the specific character and consequences of this procedure may be clearly seen, I propose to contrast it with another, which might, given the same problem, have been adopted, but which in fact is only today being recognized as a possible alternative. It is agreed that there *is* a philosophical problem of the relation of particular inquiries and activities to what, on the whole, it is reasonable to believe and humanly important to take account of. And it is further agreed that what philosophy must take as primary is what in all our commerce with it the world is found to be. What is thus found is *ultimate* as against any interpretative syntheses or analytic reduction, since it provides the material on which the synthesis must build and to which the analysis must apply if it is to conform to anything that we reliably know to be true. In what, however, does this ultimacy consist? Suppose the question concerns what we "really" know and how a philosophical criticism can throw light on this question. And suppose that perceptual knowledge is particularly under examination. Two different ways of dealing with this question will indicate the contrast of alternative procedures I have in mind.

Do we, through perceptual observation, gain knowledge of "the external world"—i.e., of the material objects in our more immediate environment, our own bodies among them? And is this knowledge (if we have it) one of the *ultimates* on which philosophy must build if it is to enhance our understanding of the grounds and reasonable coordination of our beliefs? In one sense, it seems to me, belief based on perceptual observation, on seeing, hearing, tasting, and handling, and testable by reference to further perceptual observation of the same sort and by reports made by others as to what they perceive, is properly describable as "knowledge." It provides, that is, true belief, reached by a method found on the whole to be reliable and one which is self-correcting in that its further use is calculated to enhance the veracity of its particular deliverances. Whether the word "knowledge" is appropriate here is in one sense a trivial question. But whether beliefs thus tested have the kind of reliability which in ordinary experience distinguishes what is reasonably credible from what, as it stands, is misleading and unreliable, is not. For often when we are talking about what we *really* know it is this sort of validity for fact-finding purposes that we intend, and to suggest that perceptually certified beliefs do not possess it and are not cognitively reliable because in some further sense they do not amount to "knowledge," would be seriously misleading.

In one sense, I maintain, such perceptually warranted beliefs are, for philosophy, quite ultimate. For we have no other way of finding out the facts which through perceptual observation we discover, and a philosophy which failed to take account of such facts and of the manner of our assurance of them would simply confuse us about what we can find out and how we test it. We know that there is an external world, as was suggested, because we perceive it, and if we did not perceive it, but had to resort to constructions of sense data or intuitions of pure space or a leap of animal faith in order to warrant beliefs reasonably based on perception, we should still not be able to see how they are warranted in fact, and should be unable to distinguish empirically testable hypotheses from dubious guesses about the way sense data do or do not belong to the surfaces of unobserved physical objects. And since we can make this distinction, and since perceptually warranted hypotheses have a distinctly better standing than epistemological theories about the way sense-data "belong" to material objects, a philosophy which suggested that no such distinction was possible, or supposed that we must logically base our knowledge of the external world on such much less reliable constructions, would be merely confusing. It would send us off in search of ultimate certainties on which to ground perception, and lead us to suppose that we must have them, even when we seem not to, since unless we had them perception could not enjoy the reliability which in our ordinary knowledge-getting and testing we find it to have. Or, for those who see that such certainties are far more dubious than the facts they are supposed to certify, the tendency will be to say that if this be "reason" for belief we want none of it, but can be quite content with procedures which, judged by its standard, are *merely* makeshift and instrumental devices for attaining ends not "really" cognitive at all, since they do not achieve the certainty or logical guarantee required for knowledge as such. This conclusion, though in one respect a gain in enlightenment, will in another be seriously misleading. For it will suggest that if perception has no *ulterior* warrant in ultimate certainty, then it has no reasonable basis at all, and is to be accepted *ad hoc* and independently of its cognitive standing. But there are a great many very dubious beliefs which we are also inclined to accept *ad hoc* and because animal faith or practical convenience recommends them, which nonetheless differ from perceptually testable beliefs in a way that is, for reasonable men, of quite fundamental importance. To suggest that this difference is philosophically of slight importance, or that it is not based on the genuine superiority of empirical observation as a means for finding out what the world around us actually is and what we can expect of it, is to open the door to every sort of obscurantism. Thus do scepticism and animal faith work together to produce confusion on just the issues about which men expect, and have a right to expect, that philosophers will set them straight.

Perceptual observation, however, while in this sense ultimate as a primary source of information of which, in its normal working, philosophy must take account, since it has no other and certainly no better way of getting at the facts thus disclosed, is in another sense not "ultimate" at all. It is in no case infallible or beyond internal criticism. Beliefs based on perceptual observation and subject to perceptual tests are normally reliable and perceptually corrigible, but they may be in error. Hence if we are looking for what is certainly and infallibly "present to the mind" we shall have to distinguish between the datum or sensible appearance which is, or at least can more plausibly be supposed to be, present in epistemological purity, and the ulterior object which is not thus present and hence not *directly* given at all. To realize that, even in perception, things are not always what they seem, and to be prepared to look again and to notice the way in which the appearance of a thing changes in accordance with changes in the percipient and the external medium, is certainly the part of wisdom. But only the most heroic measures will even *seem* to suffice to transform our seeing of things as they look into a direct presence of "real" object to immediate apprehension. Moreover, material objects as perceived are not "the real objects" to which scientific analysis reduces the world of physics, and if perception were supposed to be a way of knowing what the physical world "really" is, where "reality" is identified as the object of a different method of investigation, though one which depends on perception for its factual warrant, it must be held to be seriously defective. We see things as they look and can be manipulated in our ordinary dealings with visible and tangible objects, and what we see is determined by the special relations in which objects stand to our bodies, our interests and our expectations, as well as by their status as antecedent existents. This does not mean that we are not, in perception, observing bodies that exist outside of us, and acquiring the information which enables us to say what characters, as members of an antecedent physical world, we can reasonably attribute to them. It does mean that perceptual observation is not and should not be expected to be direct access to any *other* reality than what the objects with which our bodies are in fairly direct relationships show themselves to be under the conditions of perception. What else is true of them is discoverable by other means, though means which assume the primary reliability of perception as empirical observation, and could not stir a step without it. In short, perceiving is not a strong candidate for the post of infallible awareness of the "real" object, or the true objective of knowledge, on which a total metaphysics or epistemology can be built. If such ultimacy is required we must look beyond perception, either to indubitable sense data and logical constructions, or to ulterior objects intuited in some remarkable way, or, if we surrender "knowledge" to make room for faith, in some transcendent world as a non-empirical equivalent for the natural world with which, through observation and tested hypothesis, we are all the while in reliable but, alas, non-ultimate, cognitive relation.

The failure of perceptual observation to achieve "ultimacy" in the absolute sense does not in the least compromise its primary use as an element in a reasonable philosophical coordination of our knowledge. On the contrary, it enhances it. For when we try to reconcile what we find out in perception with what we find out *about* it and what, on other grounds, we have reason to suppose the world to be, it is perception in its ordinary contextual application that can make good its claim to primacy *in its own field* and to comprehensible relation with the rest of our knowledge, whereas perception gotten up as an epistemologically infallible access to "reality" would be as dubious an entity as the epistemological substitutes and supports for it have proved to be. We learn from physiology and psychology that perceiving is a complex process, involving sensory stimulation and organic response, as well as (probably) the use of images and other psychic content as intermediaries. That such a process should result in a simple and infallible awareness of objects as they are independently of the relations in which in perception they stand to us, would be surprising. But that as a result of such a process, however complicated and "mediate" it may prove to be both physiologically and psychologically, we are able to observe the objects in our immediate environment as they look, to manipulate and measure them, and to form reliable estimates of what, under other conditions they will appear to be, and what, outside the range of observation, is going on which accounts for their appearing as they do, is something not at all "surprising" unless one is already committed to a theory of knowledge as intuition plus belief about the ulterior reference of intuited data—a theory for which there is no empirical warrant. Perception as we now enjoy it may be the result of a process in which the characters of sensory data were first immediately "had" and later referred to objects not then perceived at all. That is a question for speculative psychology to answer if it can. But perception as we have it is not *now* a process of introspecting or intuiting the character of sensory data and referring them to physical objects known only as the dubious referents of this peculiar transaction. If it were, neither psychologists nor physiologists would have any empirical warrant for supposing that their descriptions of the way organisms behave are true of anything whatever. They would, indeed, as Santayana has the great merit of insisting, be talking poetry about the unknowable, of a sort for which our animal behavior gives some practical support but no shred of rational warrant. The only account of perception which can be made philosophically consistent with what we find out in psychology and physiology to be the case, is one which allows psychology and physiology the empirical basis they require if we are to take them seriously at all. What in detail the processes involved in perceiving consist in, is a question about which philosophers as such have nothing useful to say. The matter is one for empirical investigation, and there are investigators at work on it. Nothing could be less helpful than the attempt to settle it by stipulation as to what must be going on if an epistemological theory as to what "the datum" and "the object" must be if we are to have *real* knowledge of *real* objects is true. But whatever it may be, nothing could be more surprising than the conclusion that we do not, in perceptual observation, see objects external to our bodies as they look, handle them and observe their tangible properties, and find that their perceptible properties are reliable guides to what, under other circumstances, they will be and do. If philosophical consistency not only with the conclusions but with the procedure of the sciences is in question, there can be no doubt that the ultimacy of perception, in the relative and contextual sense, and the irrelevance to the procedures of reliable inquiry of epistemological attempts to reduce it to something more "ultimate," can reasonably be made out.

Moreover, and finally, the fact that perception does not *directly* disclose objects as they exist on a scale and in relations remote from those of the perceptual interaction of organism and environment is not in the least anomalous. It is precisely what we should expect *if* we took the perceptual world as in perception we find it, and used what we find it to be as an empirical clue to what objects, under other circumstances, are and do, and an empirical test of the factual accuracy of hypotheses to which observed events have evidential relevance. This is the way scientific inquirers, when they are conducting their research and not engaging in dubious philosophizing, actually *use* perceptual observation, and the connection thus established between the "world of physics" and the "world of sense" is a cognitively warranted one, which epistemological "constructions" of electrons or classes of sense data serve at best to parody.

In summary then, perceptual observation provides us with a physiologically and psychologically mediated method of finding out how our immediate bodily and material environment looks and acts, a method which is reliable and corrigible in terms of further perception, an indispensable basis for further empirical exploration of environing objects, and a philosophically primary source of information, not about ultimate reality, but about what we really and reliably discover about those elements of the world which, *as sentient organisms,* we can see and hear and smell and taste and handle. Nothing we know from other sources gives good ground for supposing that perception has not the cognitive validity which, seen thus in its contextual relativity, it appears to have, and there is no reasonable way in which we can dispense with or derive from more epistemologically eligible organs of cognition the information it provides. The best way of making sense of our experience as a whole, of distinguishing what is genuine from what is spurious in matters of belief, and of taking account of what, as sentient and cognitive organisms, we find interesting and important, is to allow to perception the primary validity it has when thus interpreted, and to resist all attempts to treat it as either more or less than it thus shows itself to be.

This conclusion, if true, is philosophically important. It is not just a way of saying that we perceive what we perceive. It places perception in its natural setting and enables us to see what it contributes to our total cognitive enterprise, and why, in the interests of good sense, we must take its evidence as primary. In the whole history of modern philosophy there has been no single factor so regularly calculated to dislocate in theory our primary cognitive connection with the natural world and, by casting doubt on the validity of this connection, to open the door to every variety of fantastic, arbitrary, and wishful speculation as this epistemological confusion about the nature and validity of *seeing* and *handling* as ways of finding out about the world. It is hardly too much to say that an adequate interpretation of perception is the first requirement for philosophical sanity, or, what is much the same thing in the end, critical good sense in the estimate of evidence. If a realistic theory could bring us back to this basic sanity, its philosophical achievement would be a great one.*

The Realistic Procedure

It will be obvious that the "Ultimacy" to which philosophical realism has in fact resorted has been of the absolute, not of the contextual variety. Its procedure, therefore, has been to take what we find in some one or other of the various contexts of experience as philosophically final or "real," without analyzing its contextual meaning to determine what in its primary nonphilosophical use it is or to what it is relevant. Thus a realistic theory of knowledge becomes an assertion of what the (infallible) datum, the ulterior (or real) object, and the knowing relation which guarantees that our awareness of such data shall somehow be a disclosure or means of knowing about the object, the true objective of inquiry, must be, if we are ever really to *know* at all. And such an account takes philosophical precedence over any inquiry which points out what in fact our means of knowledge-getting are, and what, by their means, we do, in practical experience and the sciences, find out to be the case. This does not mean that these inquiries are not to be viewed with sympathy and respect, but it does mean that since they are not ultimate on their own account, and since it is only by reference to what *is* ultimate whether as certain in knowing or as objectively real in what is known, that their philosophical status is to be made out, they must be interpreted as derivative from or based upon (in knowing) and as aspects or parts or appearances of (in reality) what is in this fashion taken as ultimate and final. The procedure of exhibiting the relation of datum to object in knowledge, of analyzing statements into that final logical form in which they picture the ultimate elements in basic facts, or of describing all experienced objects as literal pieces of that space-time which is the reality or stuff of which all things are made, is the natural outcome of the assumption that there *are* such ultimates—whether intuition or logical analysis or animal faith or empirical metaphysics be the sure guide to their nature—and that the problem of the philosophical status of any aspect of experience is solved when its identity with or derivation from such an ultimate "reality" has been exhibited.

Now there is, so far as I can see, no *a priori* reason for supposing that an undertaking of this sort might not have been successful. The world *might* have been constructed on this pattern, and our knowledge might have paralleled its ultimate structure. And if it had had such a structure, the various realistic ex-

---

* A number of the ideas of this section were later presented, in a different form, in a different context, and to a different purpose, in *The Uses of Reason* (1943), esp. in part 1, ch. 1. Ed.

periments, epistemological, analytic, and speculative, were nicely calculated to disclose it. To regard the undertaking as inherently absurd or unreasonable is quite to underestimate its plausibility. For there *is* a question about the "reality" of anything which carries the inquirer beyond non-philosophical uses and forces him to ask what, for philosophical purposes, or in its place in a reasonable interpretation of experience in all its aspects, is to be made of it. That the way to deal with this question is to discover what is quite final or real *on its own account* and not merely in its specific contribution to what, on the whole, it is reasonable to believe, and then to treat everything else as for philosophy a function or derivative of this, was a plausible assumption, so fully in harmony with traditional preconceptions in this field that it was natural to proceed upon it until experience of its application and results cast serious doubt upon it.

If, however, the world, as by the use of our rational powers we can find out about it, has not such a structure, the attempt to treat it as though it had, to import a spurious absoluteness into what is at best humanly and empirically reliable on the whole, and to exhibit in their relation to such "ultimates" the validity which beliefs, theories, and value-discriminations have in their contextual application, would exhibit its ineptitude in its philosophical consequences. The structure of theories of this type, as we should expect it to appear—not in their properties, but in their performance—if this discrepancy between assumption and fact actually existed, would be the following:

Each such philosophy would have its own ultimates, and their selection would naturally be a somewhat dubious affair. For it would not be the ultimacy which, e.g., in perception, or scientific inquiry, or responsible moral judgment, displays itself in the unique and specific contribution which the activity in question makes to a rationally organized experience and in our inability to get on without it in an adequate total adjustment. That is a relative affair and one which, while reasonably persuasive to a man trying to put his experience together and make the most of it, is far from being either epistemologically or metaphysically absolute. If we want an infallible datum, or a direct feeling of the feelings that constitute the concrete reality of ultimate actual entities, or an analysis which "pictures" the finally analyzed constituents of facts, we must look elsewhere. How we shall know them when we see them, how distinguish the true absolutes from the spurious, of which, since there are many competing pretenders to the position, there must be a considerable number, and how relate them intelligibly to the world as in more pedestrian ways we come at it, are "problems" of a formidable character.

If there are instances of knowing, intuiting, or feeling so infallible in their nature and so favored as means of access to "reality" as such as to provide an absolute basis for philosophical constructions, it is quite right for philosophers to appeal to them. The fact that they are hard to get at and even when pointed out at length remain indiscernible to otherwise competent investigators with different philosophical interests and preconceptions, is unfortunate, but does not prove that some among them are not genuine. Those of us who are unable to attain such insights are in no position to condemn them directly as "mysterious" or "supernatural." The world after all is full of a number of things, and there is no *a priori* reason why apprehensions of this sort and "realities" thus basic should not be among them.

It is, however, reasonable that their credentials should be inspected with particular care. There have in the past been many such claims to infallible knowledge and special access to ultimate reality which, by common consent, are now recognized rather as instances of that tenacity of belief that, as Peirce taught, blocks the path of inquiry, than as esoteric disclosures of the truth. And while the insight itself *if it occurs* is of course incorrigible, the arguments advanced to convince us that there *must* be such absolute knowledge if anything is actually to be known at all, and such final realities if the world is to be comprehensible even in the sense in which in practical and scientific transactions we seem to understand it, are open to inspection and will hardly stand it. If the absoluteness of realistically conceived "ultimates" in knowledge, in analysis, and in reality were of the spurious sort which attaches to experiences or inquiries and their results when these are very strongly felt to be reliable and important, and accepted without any critical awareness of the conditions in which they are reliable and the uses for which they are important, the consequences of their acceptance and the manner of their controversial defence and philosophical authentication would not be difficult to predict. We should expect them to be associated in some special way with the vindication of some special interest felt to be profoundly significant. The assurance that we do *really know* something and that the foundations of knowledge are unshakable is of considerable emotional significance to many thinkers. All the loyalty that properly attaches to the adherence to what can be shown to be the case as distinct from what is merely guessed, opined, or wished, can by an understandable transference be shifted to some primary knowings which are quite certain and thus constitute the norm both for themselves and for all else that claims the truth. Knowing in this sense is referred to in italics and defended in heated tones and with desk-thumping, and any questioning of it will appear, to the faithful, as a laying of profane hands on the ark of the covenant. McTaggart's pronouncement in criticism of William James, "Nobody ever broke with logic but logic broke him," is amusingly paralleled in the slogan chosen by C. B. DeMille for his motion picture glorification of The Ten Commandments—"if you break them, they break you." In all cases in which the importance rightly attached to a system of thought or of morality whose working validity cannot be rejected without serious disruptive consequences is transmuted into an unqualified devotion to some particular absolutes in which that working validity is supposed to be uniquely enshrined, such ultimates will appear and will be defended by the plea that without them the very foundations of knowledge or conduct are undermined. And in these circumstances it is the task of philosophical criticism to distinguish the ultimacy which does in fact attach to reliable ways of knowing and sound principles of conduct in the organization of experience from the dubious absoluteness of certainties, principles, and realities supposed to underlie these and as "foundations" to provide the philosophical warrant for their reliability.

The marks of the spurious absolute, when it is presented not in the report of an infallible intuition but as the basis of a reasoned philosophy, will be two. First, the absolute selected will be found, on examination, to owe its persuasiveness to its alleged relation to activities or interests which are supposed to presuppose it as their foundation; and second, the defense of this absolute against its rivals will assume this relation and proceed to the demonstration that *if it obtains,* a denial of the ultimacy in question entails the rejection of actual procedures, logical, or moral, or empirical, which we cannot do without. This *identification* of the factual genuineness of some selected aspect of experience or inquiry with the absolute reality into which, for philosophical purposes, it is analyzed, and the subsequent claim that in rejecting the analysis and its "ultimates" we are denying the empirical ultimacy of the facts from which it has been questionably derived, is the procedure by which, if our hypothesis is correct, philosophies of this sort must proceed. The outcome will not be a fresh approach to any reality that can be tested in its connection with what, on other grounds, we know. It will be a question-begging debate between the defenders of rival "absolutes" whose mutually exclusive pretensions reflect in a distorting medium the primary and indispensable contribution which the aspects of experience they claim to represent can make to a sound philosophy. Space and time, as pervasive features of the natural world, become Space-Time, and this Space-Time must be the stuff of reality if space and time and nature with them are not to be submerged in the rival absolutes of mind, or supernature, or the like. Logical analysis, as the indispensable instrument for making our ideas clear and [for] knowing what we are talking about, becomes the final arbiter of what the furniture of the world must be if we are to talk about it or picture it in the terms required for an *ultimate* logical analysis. And these terms and their implications we must accept on penalty of violating the laws of logic (or of syntax) and lapsing into meaningless verbiage. The mediate transactions involved in finding out about material objects as they exist independently of the special circumstances under which we perceive them become the sufficient evidence that knowing is *essentially* mediate, the datum never being identical with the object known but always the representative merely of an ulterior reality which is the *true* cognoscendum, and those who find this doubtful as a description of what all empirical inquiry consists in are convicted of subjectivism because they have really denied that *knowledge* can transcend the immediate contents of consciousness. In all such cases the assertion without qualification or contextual reference of something which we find warranted in non-philosophical experience only in a qualified form, which both specifies its primary meaning and gives it an understandable place in relation to much else that is *also* true, *may* be the appropriate means of reaching ultimate philosophical truth. In that case we should expect that out of such a procedure will come a better understanding of what knowing is when we see it in operation, of how logic functions in scientific hypothesis and the like, and of how in space and time experienced things possess their distinctive characters and modes of behavior. But if the procedure is not an appropriate one, we should expect to find its absolutes quite barren apart from their relation to the aspects of experience whose primary meaning they distort, and quite unable to render that connection intelligible. Its fruits will be insoluble problems of how to reconcile the aspect of experience it has taken as absolute with others which its exclusive pretensions render anomalous, but which are quite indispensable to an adequate philosophy; and interminable controversy with rival contenders who can be convicted of denying the "ultimate" truths of its preferential devotion and can in turn convict it of an equally inexcusable rejection of the ultimates to which with understandable ardor they cling. If the development of realism should prove to be of this latter sort, our hypothesis that its procedure is a mistaken one would so far be verified.

The ultimates of this philosophy must not only be controversially identified, but their relation with the procedures of thinking, valuing, and the like, and with the accredited results of these procedures on non-philosophical levels, must be exhibited. If this is actually the way to philosophic wisdom we should expect that as a result of the inquiry these procedures and results would be more clearly understood and more securely established, with their appropriate measure of validity and range of application. What could make the validity of particular judgments of good more comprehensible than the indication of their connection with the ultimate or intrinsic good which is their final warrant? If, however, the procedure is mistaken, the consequence would be that a radical discrepancy would appear between the considerations that warrant good thinking and sound judgment in other instances, and those which connect or ought to connect them with their philosophical foundations. What is secure in the sciences, as a sound though far from infallible or incorrigible working assumption, may be dubious indeed as a first principle or logical derivative thereof; while the ultimate certainties are frequently sublimely irrelevant to anything elsewhere found to be reliable and credible. The result will be that these inquiries must proceed without much regard for the supposed philosophical foundations, yet with a certain sense of insecurity which invites half-baked philosophizing, animal faith, or rigid specialization, as compensations for the failure throughout philosophy* to make clear the connections actually involved in the human situation in which special inquiry has its place and justification. Since these connections are not made out in professional philosophy, the failure to establish them on an intelligible level becomes the excuse for mystical short-cuts, arbitrary appeals to social significance, or for the professional narrow-mindedness which, in reaction against such excesses proceeds to identify the boundaries of specialization with the limits of intelligible discourse. *It* will, in fact, be just that dislocation of "fact" from meaning or philosophical interpretation which is the natural outcome of the unimaginative persistence in an inappropriate method of inquiry.

The dialectic of this situation is quite simple. The "data" of, for instance, scientific inquiry are not the ultimate data of awareness to which knowledge must ultimately appeal. Hence in the theory of knowledge we must reduce the "world" of perceptual observation to the world of "hard" data whose immediate presence, even after earnest critical effort, we cannot persuade ourselves to doubt. These will be what experience really comes to when it is examined with appropriate critical rigor. But we appeal to experience for verification in the sciences, and only what is *really* given can count as empirical warrant for an hypothesis. Thus Russell insists, and quite properly on this basis, that "Verification consists always in the occurrence of an expected sense-datum. Astronomers tell us there will be an eclipse of the moon: we look at the moon, and we find the earth's shadow biting into it, that is to say we see an appearance quite different from that of the usual full moon. Now if an expected sense-datum constitutes a verification, what was asserted must have been about sense-data; or at any rate, if part of what was asserted was not about sense-data, then only the other part has been verified." [25] A sense-datum, it must be noted, is such an item as a colored patch—an existent particular, described as, e.g., the "appearance" of the earth's shadow on the moon, only because it is supposed that this particular is related to others of the same sort, or to some ulterior object, in such fashion as to be, in a more or less Pickwickian sense, a constituent of the object that is said to appear.

There are, then, two empirical "problems" here. One, which concerns the

25. Bertrand Russell, *Our Knowledge of the External World* (London: George Allen and Unwin, 1914), p. 81; 1929 ed., p. 89.

* The phrase "failure throughout philosophy," partly obliterated in the text, could also be read as "failure of a thorough philosophy." Ed.

astronomer, is whether his instruments are adequate to permit the observation of the eclipse predicted, and what this eclipse as observed is evidence for. This is the question of what happens in the external world when we observe it, and what such observed happenings are empirical warrant for believing about objects and events beyond the range of observation. The other is the question of whether there is an external world at all, and how the sensing of a datum not itself an object in this world can afford evidence of what happens in it. We infer from what we observe about the present behavior and position of earth and moon that there will later be an eclipse. Can we in comparable fashion infer from our own "hard data" that there is a world in which earth and moon as material objects actually exist? This seems to be a problem of the same sort, and a fundamental one. For if we do not really observe the eclipse, how can we use such observation as an empirical verification of astronomical predictions. The hypotheses of astronomy seem thus to rest on a foundation in sense data, and until this is safely laid, the whole superstructure will be insecure.

What we get, however, when we try to make out this connection of empirical observation with sense data is not a new inductive hypothesis, empirically grounded, but an analysis of what physical objects ultimately *consist in,* or what statements about them ultimately refer to—an analysis based not on what, e.g., the physical sciences can tell us about them, but on what they must be, and what we must be saying about them, if an experience reducible "ultimately" to sense data is to provide epistemologically sound information about them. A moon that is more than a set of actual or obtainable data would have no verifiable warrant in an experience in which only the occurrence of such data can be verified. Hence if all we were talking about when we appeared to be talking about the moon were such data, then by sensing data we could get the kind of evidence we think we have when we perceptually observe the moon's eclipse. The outcome is not to give us new information about the moon as perceptually observable, but so to redefine it and our knowledge of it as to square with an antecedent assumption as to what is empirically observable. The only evidence for such a theory would be the alleged obviousness of the initial assumption that perceptual observation *must* reduce to infallible sensing plus belief in what such sensing verifiably warrants, together with the dialectical force of the argument that if this is what experience is, then to suppose that the moon or anything else is more than the class of its possible appearances is to make an assumption for which there is no "empirical" warrant. The moon as more than a set of data becomes in this debate a "transcendent" object, a "something I know not what," the Spencerian unknowable, and much else that only a long acquaintance with the language of epistemological vituperation would enable one to catalogue.

The result thus achieved does not help to make the astronomer's predictions and observations more empirically secure in the ordinary sense, or to indicate in what their security consists. In order to attain that end we should have to look again through a telescope, or devise other instruments better calculated, in the material world in which astronomical observation occurs, to disclose precisely what is happening. Increasing precision in observation and care in the testing of hypotheses is one thing, the reduction of sentences that appear to refer to material objects to others that name only colored patches and their sensory associates is quite another. Judged by the epistemologist's tests, the astronomer's belief that there are, or are to be, further data than those now sensed, which could, in a logically intricate fashion, be treated as "appearances" of "the moon," and that these will probably be such as are to be expected if the astronomer's hypotheses are, in common parlance, "true," is an extremely precarious assumption, allowable only on the ground that it would simplify the world if such classes of data occurred and that there is no coercive reason against it. Judged by the standard of empirical inquiry, the prediction that an eclipse will occur can be a highly reasonable one, and the evidence in its favor so strong that no competent investigator would seriously question it. To object to it on the ground that the passage from our own "hard data" to an external world even of classes of such data is a very questionable one would be simply impertinent. We should not be able by reference to such "data" and constructions to exhibit the considerations which *in astronomy* render the prediction highly probable and place some empirically certified conclusions beyond the scope of reasonable doubt.

The two sorts of inquiry must, then, go their several ways, the one that is held to be empirically dubious maintaining itself by increasingly impressive agreement between its predictions and observable occurrences, while the one that is supposed to reach final certainty expends its energy in logical and verbal constructions whose "empirical" warrant is the identification of experience with what is infallibly sensed, and the deduction that what is not thus identifiable is beyond the scope of empirical verification and thus ultimately undiscoverable, or (in a later version) meaningless.

Yet, while the two are essentially distinct in their interests and procedures, they are quite unhappily entangled. For the astronomical inquiry employs a relative and fallible "experience" and thus it is alleged *ought* to have its basis in the logical constructions of sense data. The fact that it does not has little bearing on its empirical procedure, but much on the opinions astronomers and others, in their more reflective moments, will form concerning its validity as knowledge. If it proves very hard to accept the view that the moon is only a class of actual and possible sensory data, even when the alternative to this is a "meaningless" reference to objects with which, on other grounds, we are all perfectly familiar, then the philosophizing astronomer will be inclined to invoke animal faith, or to find spiritual solace in the fact that it is hard to make statements about material objects in a philosophically intelligible way, or to use the general confusion in the matter as an excuse for his own special crotchets or over-beliefs about matters he has never had time or training seriously to investigate. And the general public, believing rightly that astronomers ought to know what they are doing, will find in these vagaries evidence that nothing is too queer to be true, and few emotionally congenial beliefs too disreputable to rank beside the best that the sciences can tell us about the *real* world.

The professional philosopher or logical analyst, on the other hand, will go his way in fine scorn of such popular confusion. It is still his business, is it not, to relate dubious beliefs to their secure foundations? And if ultimate security is to be found in sense-data, he must be prepared to discern in the relations between such data the ultimate referents of scientific statements. He will turn therefore to "logical constructions." But how will he know what to construct? In "ultimate" analysis all data are, as given, whether in dream or empirical observation, equally infallible, and all references beyond data logically unwarranted. Russell tells us that the principle of abstraction which eliminates inferred entities (perceptually observed) in favor of logical constructions "depends, for its use, upon the existence of some fairly reliable body of propositions, which are to be interpreted by the logician in such a way as to preserve their truth while minimizing the element of inference to unobserved entities. The principle therefore presupposes a moderately advanced science, in the absence of which the logician does not know what he ought to construct. Until recently it would have seemed necessary to construct geometrical points; now it is event-particles that are wanted." [26]

There is surely a certain irony in this. It is the independently ascertainable truth, which the sciences by their own methods are capable of reaching, which is to be "interpreted" and "preserved" in the translation. Whatever "entities" the investigator requires are to be supplied him, but baptised in logical terminology which comports with the epistemological proprieties. The effective warrant for such "entities" will be the validity of the theories which refer to them in their scientific use and perceptually observable tests. What thus justifies itself as true is to be accepted as true by the analyst, who is certainly in no position to criticize its factual adequacy. What, then, does the translation give us that we did not know before? Only the language that must be used if these discoveries are to be harmonized with the notion that only sense-data are empirically observable. How do we know that this notion is correct, and that the translation says in its terms what the proposition, already sufficiently understood for scientific purposes and here accepted as true, really meant? They

26. Russell, "Logical Atomism," p. 367.

must "ultimately" mean this if they are not to refer beyond "experience" in a philosophically objectionable sense and to be, in that sense, unverifiable. And why is this further sense philosophically objectionable? Because all our knowledge of matters of fact must be tested in experience, and experience must ultimately be the certain grasping of immediate data. How else should we ever *really know* anything at all?

This procedure is closely analogous to that of the constitutional lawyer who is prepared to square any action the government finds it necessary to take with the intention of the founding fathers and the letter of the Constitution. This performs a useful function, within limits, since it enables us to accept more easily laws which are in any case essential, but which without this sanction would have been in conflict with our notions of ceremonial correctness. And it does no harm, provided that it is understood simply as saying over again what was primarily certified by its necessity for the adequate and orderly carrying on of government business. It has its disadvantages however. For the independent absoluteness that attaches to the constitution as written may lead literalists to insist that what cannot in some fairly direct way be translated into its terms has no warrant at all, and to identify what is thus "unconstitutional" with what is politically and morally inadmissible. And in a similar way, the absoluteness of sense experiences as such can cause confusion when hypotheses actually required for the progress of the sciences and amply justified in their results are excluded by "empiricists" because the objects to which they refer are too remote from infallible sensory givenness for even Russell's logical re-baptism to lend them a sufficiently apparent odor of sanctity.

In any case, the philosophic error in both cases is plain. We do want a political and practical warrant for changes in the constitution, and this is only to be found in the manner in which, in virtue of such changes, the government can more satisfactorily perform those services which are its effective justification. To suppose that this *effective* ultimacy of the claims of government in its contribution to a life on the whole good, and better than could be secured without it, is embalmed in the Constitution as written, is to look for ultimacy where it is not to be found, and to ask us, in squaring this with our actual procedures, to deceive others and perhaps also to deceive ourselves. And equally, to suppose that the empirical warrant which is the cognitive justification of the sciences requires some further certification by reference to what is ultimately given in "acquaintance," and that a ceremonial translation of this sort is therefore somehow essential to the philosophical estimate of the meaning and truth of scientific statements, is seriously misleading. For it impels those who see that such certification is either trivial or highly questionable to be sceptical or cynical about activities which have a perfectly good warrant in their own procedure and in the contribution which, through the faithful use of reliable methods, they are able to make to knowledge and practice. And it invites those on whom it imposes to distort the content and sense of empirical knowledge by reducing it to a status in which its actual worth in inquiry does not appear. If it should prove to be the case that the fruits of realistic theories of knowledge were actually of this character the hypothesis on which we are proceeding would so far be strengthened.

If there were only one such philosophy, we should expect its effects to be chiefly those outlined in the preceding paragraphs. Where there are a number in competition, however, the situation is complicated. For under these conditions, each is likely to deal with problems not primarily as they arise in the philosophical interpretation and organization of experience, as encountered in non-philosophical contexts, but rather as they emerge as difficulties in the systems and arguments of opponents. And here they take on a rather special appearance. If we hold that all knowing is direct (and some realists have held this), and that the datum is itself the object to be known, the "problem" arises of how we can have knowledge of objects of which it is very unplausible to suppose that we are thus directly aware. Now a dualistic realism can solve this problem very well, since it holds that knowing is essentially of objects of which we are not directly aware. And we seem to have such knowledge. That scores a point for the dualist. But there is also a problem of how, if all knowing is indirect, we could ever compare our ideas with the facts and have empirical evidence of their truth. Now a monistic realism which holds that objects are known directly and face to face is not troubled by this problem. And that certainly scores a point for the monist.

The situation can be generalized. *Any* philosophy that takes as ultimate certain phases of experience to the exclusion of others can sooner or later be convicted of having failed to account plausibly for the elements of the world thus excluded. An alternative theory in which the stone *these* builders rejected has become the headstone of the corner will be in a strong position on this point, and will be inclined to stress it at length as providing its own philosophical justification. *Any* philosophy is "concrete" in comparison with a competitor if it includes what the other omits and agrees *so far* with the opinions of the "plain man" who takes account of all these factors without knowing how, philosophically, to coordinate them. But each, in its own ultimates, has subordinated or excluded something else, and must do so where the absolutes of philosophy are the primary aspects of experience interpreted without regard to their contextual limits and connections. Hence there is always opportunity for a new contender, or for an old one temporarily *hors de combat,* to adopt and misinterpret * the interests to which current doctrines do less than justice. Such

---

* The word in the manuscript is "misinterpret." Possibly "interpret" was meant; either one would do. Ed.

a controversy is in principle interminable, for the contestants are all proceeding on a false assumption, and each is incapable of making the discriminations and specifications which would enable us to see not only that all these things are "real" but what they really are and how their being what, outside the controversy, we find them to be is compatible with the equally "real" being of much that is incompatible with the absolute pretensions of their advocates but quite consistent with their own empirical genuineness and reliability.

Whether the development of realism is to be understood as a progress toward the sure apprehension of philosophical (logical, ethical, epistemological or metaphysical) ultimates, or whether it is an endlessly inconclusive debate between contenders each of whom is placed in an indefensible position by his own procedure, and each of whom, therefore, is able to show that his opponents are no better than they should be, is yet to be decided. The evidence that the latter is the case would be of the following sort. We wish, let us say, to analyze "the good." It seems plain, if we appeal to moral judgments, that ethical predicates have a different usage and meaning from non-ethical. To reduce the good to the satisfaction of desire, or the evolution of the species, or the will of the absolute, without asking whether these in their turn are *good* is to have robbed it of specific moral meaning. "Good," we may well say, examining a series of such analyses, is just good and nothing else. And the recognition of this will certainly appear as an advance in philosophical enlightenment. But what is this peculiarly ethical good? To call it a simple unanalyzable non-natural quality is to characterize it primarily with reference to the failure of alternative theories to describe it. In some ways, surely, it is a highly conditioned and relative affair, expressive of human interests and needs and appetites, and, indeed, meaningless apart from them. As a non-natural quality of objects, it is extremely hard to identify as anything more than the postulated objective equivalent for a strong conviction that moral questions are different from other questions and are to be dealt with on their own terms.

If we turn to moral discernment and practical good will, however, we find the situations in which these apply to be affairs of conflicting interests and emotions, of claims and counter-claims, to which the notion of a goodness which would attach to objects or experiences if they existed quite alone seems supremely irrelevant. The introduction of such an ultimate good is no help in practice and the attempt to discover by intuition whether, e.g., pleasure is or is not such a good is much more likely to end in scepticism about the whole procedure than in a better understanding of moral judgments and the conditions of their reliable use. Factors not relevant to the ultimate good—interest, emotion, changes in habit and circumstance—are clearly relevant to the only evaluations we can reliably make, and the philosophical claim to set up a good beyond these, more certainly known and ethically authoritative, is an invitation to dogmatism and controversy that is, in its effects, not helpful.

Hence it is natural that those who feel the insufficiency of such a procedure and wish to relate ethics intelligibly to its human and hence natural basis and to stress the moral relevance of happiness and the satisfaction of wants, should rebel against ethical absolutism. But how, then, are we to analyze "the good"? If we take interest, *de facto* demands and appetites, or the struggle for power as the primary fact in morals, and say that these are "the facts" ethical statements really express, and that whatever cannot be thus expressed, whatever introduces "mysterious" normative notions like right and wrong is analytically unacceptable, the old difficulty recurs. For we shall still want to distinguish those interests and appetites which are *morally* justified from those that are not, and the reduction of moral to non-moral predicates will not enable us to do this. The good is not *just* good, if its being such isolates it from its contextual meaning and use, but it is also not anything other than good, if its being such reduces it to interests and claims whose primary reference does not include the moral distinctions of right and wrong, good and bad, as essential to its meaning. Hence the alternative to dogmatism here appears to be a kind of scepticism in which moral values are mere instruments to, or aspects of, non-moral interests and satisfactions. And we are again not in a position to take seriously in philosophy the moral distinctions without which we can hardly make sense of our conduct.

Between isolation with its accompanying absoluteness and reduction with its sceptical relativism there would seem on this basis no alternative. To what reality are our moral judgments to correspond? If it is just the ultimate and final reality of goodness, we fail to understand it, for its essential connections and conditions are omitted. If it is a reality other than goodness, we fail to understand it, for in relation to this the distinctively *moral* character of our valuations will not appear. If the ethical absolutists triumphed yesterday with Moore, while the relativists are today in the ascendant, we can be confident that tomorrow, when the unhappy consequences of the relativist view have once more become irksome, a neo-absolutism will emerge, comparable perhaps to a new-neo-realism in epistemology, and we shall be off again. The insight needed to turn this controversy into more fruitful channels is on this basis not attainable. We should have to see that philosophically *nothing* either is just what in its "intrinsic" nature and absolute pretensions it is nor yet another thing, but that everything is what in its context and connections it shows itself to be. But for that insight the philosophy we are here considering has no place.

The same dilemma confronts us in logical theory. Do the propositions of logic disclose ultimate logical objects whose eternal and indefeasible being is the objective warrant for the discovery that logic is logic and nothing else, and that what it tells us is sometimes valid. The reaction against such ontological ultimates, and the demand that logical procedures be connected with inquiry, with discourse, with the processes by means of which we organize our thoughts and extend our theories, were clearly justified in what they protested against. But if logical propositions do not correspond to a *logical* reality, to what reality do they correspond? Surely no *other* reality will do, if we are to keep their distinctive logical nature before us. It is not enough to say that logical processes enable us to pass from premises to conclusion in an argument and that this is often convenient. The point is that they enable us to accomplish this passage *logically,* and if we try to distinguish the "conventions" of logical grammar from those not thus logical we shall have to say that they are those in which the rules of logic are embodied, and that these, as contrasted with other conventions, have a quite unique and irreducible cognitive authority. Why should we not say this? Because if we did we should have to recognize that peculiar combination of ultimacy and relativity which is the manifest nature of logical procedures in use, but not in philosophical debate. Insofar as the inquiries of contemporary philosophy follow the pattern thus indicated, they confirm the suggestion that this mistaken procedure is the source of inconclusive argument which can admit of no answer except one that again generates the old familiar difficulties and produces no conviction save in those already persuaded.

The outcome and applications of this philosophy are to be considered in the four following chapters.* Not all the philosophies there discussed are "realistic" in some of the senses in which that term is frequently applied. Hence I have not included the "outcome" in this case under the same heading as the standpoint and internal structure of the philosophy discussed. They belong together because they deal with the problems this philosophy has propounded and keep, in essential respects, within the limits of the debate its standpoint defines. There are some notable exceptions, especially in recent developments in "analysis." These, however, are still in the transitional stage, and closely enough bound up with their antecedents to be profitably discussed in connection with them.

The topics selected do not cover the whole range of current philosophical discussion, but would seem to be fair and extensive samples of its methods and consequences. Particular results here will be found to be as varied as the special issues discussed. One general statement as to their purport can be made in advance. [Their purport] has been such as to shake men's faith in their ability to establish by reasonable philosophical means the connection between what we need to assume and can legitimately use in particular inquiries and what is

---

* That is to say, chapter 5, "The Problem of Perceptual Knowledge" (not here included); chapter 6, "The 'Problem' of Moral Value" (not here included); chapter 7, "Recent Speculative Philosophy," included here as chapters 5 and 6; and chapter 8, "Philosophical Analysis" (not here included). Ed.

"ultimately" true, valid, or moral. This failure to make out the connection philosophers have sought leads, in practice, either to scepticism or to dogmatism, the latter insofar as the ultimates felt to be essential are placed beyond the reach of rational inquiry, the former insofar as the claim to ultimacy is abandoned and makeshift ideas in their frankly makeshift character accepted as the best that we can reasonably expect. The manifestations of these tendencies in popular or non-professional philosophy will be the topic of the final chapter.* They bring us back to the place where in philosophy we actually stand today, and complete the answer to our question as to where the speculations of the past fifty years have brought us.

* "The final chapter" was chapter 9, "The Standpoint of Philosophy"; three of its sections are included here as chapters 7 and 8. Ed.

5   Recent Speculative Philosophy I

What "Speculative Philosophy" Is

In many circles and at several periods in the history of philosophy the expression "speculative philosophy" would have appeared to involve an obvious redundancy. If the aim of this type of inquiry is, as Broad characterizes it, "to discuss the nature of Reality as a whole, and to consider the place and prospects of men in it," [1] then speculative philosophy would seem to many to be simply philosophy itself. One of the more striking features of the philosophy of the recent past is the growing acceptance of the notion that the essential work of philosophy does not, or need not, involve the speculative ventures with which it has traditionally been associated, and that its work of analysis and coordination can be better done without recourse to "ultimate Reality" or "Reality as a whole" than with it. The motives for this distrust of speculation, and the nature of the attempt to reconstitute philosophy independently of it, have already been considered and will be further discussed when we come to deal with recent analytic philosophy.* Our present concern is with the current revival of speculative philosophy in the grand manner, and with the way in which, in opposition to positivism, pragmatism, and analysis, the advocates of this method of solving philosophic problems have reaffirmed their faith, and accompanied it with works of impressive magnitude and scope.

More specifically identified, speculative philosophy is the attempt to solve the problems that arise when the various aspects of experience are understood "not merely piecemeal or in fragments, but somehow as a whole," by discovering some ultimate entity or entities which these aspects all disclose and to which their characters, so far as they are genuine, ultimately belong. To orga-

1. C. D. Broad, "Critical and Speculative Philosophy," in *Contemporary British Philosophy,*" edited by J. H. Muirhead (London: George Allen and Unwin, 1924), vol. 1, p. 96.

* In original chapter 8, "Philosophical Analysis," not herein included. Ed.

nize experience rationally as a whole is then to exhibit the dependence on or derivation from this ultimate reality of everything that for any adequate reason we take to be real or authentic on its own account. Since it is agreed that the sciences and practical life do not disclose such a reality in its finally concrete or ultimate character, the philosopher must, while taking full and respectful account of their teachings, be prepared to go beyond them and to attain, by specifically philosophical inquiry, information about the world in its *ultimate* nature which supplements our ordinary knowledge and enables us to see this in its proper and limited character. It would not be correct or sufficient merely to characterize this type of inquiry by its aim at philosophic wisdom. What is fundamental is the method by which this wisdom is to be attained—by knowledge of a reality which is in its own right, and in explicit contrast to what is discovered elsewhere and by more meager methods, the final or concrete actuality on which all else depends. Nor is it sufficient to say, as Whitehead does, that "Speculative Philosophy is the endeavor to frame a coherent, logical, necessary system of general ideas in terms of which every element of our experience can be interpreted." [2] As his own procedure shows, this generality of application is attained not by finding something common to the objects of our various activities and inquiries as they stand, but by discovering a very remarkable and metaphysically eligible set of objects—"actual entities," [3]—which are "the final real things of which the world is made up" and invoking an ontological principle to justify the claim that "everything in the actual world is referable to some actual entity" [4] and that apart from such final actualities there is "nothing, nothing, nothing, bare nothing." The speculative description offered is, therefore, to apply to everything, but only insofar as it applies preeminently to one sort of thing (in this case "organisms") while everything else is shown to be an aspect, feature, or element of the system of actualities thus defined. A description of everything we know in terms of matter would have unrestricted generality of application, if it applied to matter, and if it could be shown that material objects were the final real things of which the world is made.

This point is not here made as an objection to the method in question, but simply to make plain its special nature. The fact that a description was general enough to apply to everything would not be sufficient to render it eligible for speculative purposes. It would still be necessary to show that what was thus general or pervasive was also ultimate, "concrete," and "fundamental," so that, needing no further speculative warrant on its own account, it could pro-

2. A. N. Whitehead, *Process and Reality* (New York: Macmillan 1929), p. 4.

3. Whitehead, *Process and Reality,* p. 27.

4. Whitehead, *Process and Reality,* p. 373.

vide the standpoint from which the philosophical meaning and genuineness of everything else (or of the more special and limited features of the world) could be understood. Thus Alexander does not merely tell us that space-time relations are pervasive, and that everything empirically discoverable has a place in a space-time order. He announces, and for his purposes it is quite essential, that space-time is, in its own right, the final reality in the universe, and that everything else is to be understood as being constituted of this space-time which is the ultimate stuff of things.

The term "speculation" then has, in this usage, a much more special sense than that of simply taking a "synoptic" view of things, or seeing life steadily and seeing it whole, or entertaining hypotheses of considerable imaginative scope and novelty. It is an inquiry into the nature of objects ontologically eligible, as "concrete," or finally real, to occupy a place of philosophical preeminence, and it is an attempt to organize all experience around the objects thus discovered. If religion, for example, is found to be in harmony with the nature of things as thus disclosed, then religion, in a somewhat sublimated form, no doubt, is thereby vindicated. And if explicit conscious experience and precise intellectual analysis are found—in contrast to the vast and vague experiences that, on speculative grounds, are held to pervade the "real" world—to be but a superficial phase in the aesthetic experience of actual entities, then clarity and distinctness must be set down as meager and unreliable guides to what is deepest in reality and most fundamental in experience. The assumption on which the philosopher works, if he adopts this method of inquiry, is not only that the world can be understood, but that it can be understood *in this way,* that it is in fact stratified into "final" reality and derivative manifestation, and that to understand anything as itself "actual" in this sense, or as an aspect or feature of such actuality, is to see what is "finally" significant or valid in its nature.

There is, of course, nothing philosophically novel in this sort of undertaking. The great philosophical systems of the 17th century followed just this model, and it is not surprising that Descartes, Spinoza, and Leibnitz should provide speculative inspiration for contemporary thinkers of a similar intellectual bent. With speculative idealism the connection is less apparent. The "critical" emphasis in the Kantian philosophy is unfavorable to straightforward ontologizing, and compels its disciples to detour through mind as "foundational" to reach the total Reality that meets the "final" demands of thought. If, however, the critical machinery is omitted, and the advocates of a spiritual universe are prepared to base their claims on what Reality must be in order to be ultimate and actual, rather than on what it must be to be known, the result is, as McTaggart observed, an ontological rather than an epistemological idealism, and one very much in the spirit of the great pre-Kantian system builders. And, in any case, the primary reference of all that requires philosophical elucidation to a "reality" both self-sufficient and sufficient to serve as the basis for the reality of everything else as well is common to post- and pre-Kantians and unites them in opposition to the anti-metaphysical tendencies of much recent "analysis." Finally, the realistic movement moves on naturally into an "objective synthesis" of the sort peculiar to speculative philosophy as here defined; and it is, in fact, out of realism in its more orthodox forms that the most ambitious and original philosophical systems of recent times have developed. A "reality" not contextually specified will inevitably conflict with others no less apparently "real," and the obvious way of resolving such jurisdictional conflicts will be to discover which of the competing realities is in its own right "real," and how the others can be reduced to or predicated of it. If events are *real,* then "events" must become the "stuff" of nature, and apparently enduring things must be exhibited as characters of the changing processes which are the concrete actuality. It will not be surprising if events, in order to support the title thus inherited, take on characters not always associated with them in non-philosophical experience, if, for example, they become sentient organisms in order that the "concreteness" found in our own sentient experience, and surely in its own right "real," may find its appropriate basis in the final actualities of which the world is made up. Speculative philosophy is the natural outcome of realism when its constructive or integrating function as a philosophy is stressed. For the only basis for such integration which "realism," as we have understood it, could provide, would be an object or set of objects competent in their own nature to be the ultimate referents for all that, in any aspect of experience, we claim to know.

The revival of "speculation," in this meaning, is, therefore, by no means a surprising phenomenon. Its present varieties are notable, however, for their close connection with "speculative" developments in the sciences, and for their explicit reaffirmation of what they take to be the perennial principles of philosophic inquiry, against the attacks of skeptics, relativists, analysts, and other questioners of the ultimate verities. And they are for our purposes of crucial importance, since they bring to clear and intransigent expression a tendency which we must understand if we are to see what philosophy in operation has been, and why it has taken the special forms and had the often unhappy consequences which have actually characterized its development. Put as plainly as possible, the *prima facie* case for speculative philosophy is this. Its claim that philosophy aims at wisdom, and that this wisdom, if it is to be more than esoteric insight or miscellaneous edification, must be based on knowledge, appears to be correct. Its further claim that the only kind of knowledge that would serve the purpose is that in which the variegated lessons of experience are coordinated and "interpreted" in their bearing on that which, being uniquely and finally real, is a sufficient basis for all estimates of what is "ultimately" valid or genuine is highly plausible and fits in with prevailing preconceptions and practices. Its determination to discover this final reality, and to exhibit the ontological structure which is the final cognitive warrant for our judgments both of actuality and importance, seems, in consequence, no more than an honest effort to meet its philosophical responsibilities. That the results of "adventures of ideas" in this field should be tentative, inexact and subject to endless critical revision, was perhaps to be expected. The undertaking is a tremendous one and the human mind all too limited in its powers. But so long as the need for philosophical integration is great, and so long as the theories that condemn the search for ultimate truth are seen to be no more than arbitrary refusals to extend the methods of rational inquiry into regions with which the analyst, as a result of his professional preoccupations, would prefer not to deal, the demand for such a synthesis will persist, and new systems, borrowing the latest ideas of the sciences or expressing the dominant preferences of the time, will be developed, in the perennial hope that they will reach at least a little nearer than their predecessors to the heaven of final truth, and that their ruin, when it comes, will, like the mansions of traditional philosophy, provide at least an inexhaustible theme of learned inquiry and cultivated discourse. Whether this speculative revival should be taken as a new proof that man is a metaphysical animal, and that ontology crushed to earth will rise again, or as additional evidence that we have not yet learned to deal with philosophical problems by a method appropriate to their nature, is a further question, and the one which it is a primary aim of this chapter to answer.

Problems and Methods
"Speculation" and "Speculative Philosophy"

If we are to proceed in this inquiry with any measure of accuracy, there is one prevailing confusion which must be got out of the way at the start. In his admirable and inspiring book *Adventures of Ideas,* Whitehead has made himself the spokesman for the claim that general interpretative ideas have an essential role in human history, and that the extension of the range of such ideas is an essential contribution to human progress. His contrast between the pedantic or "scholarly" type of mind and the speculative inquirer intent on refashioning and generalizing current notions in order to broaden the range of knowledge is vividly expressed and undoubtedly corresponds to something genuine. One has only to consider the contribution to mathematical knowledge involved in the generalization of the notion of "number" and the puerility of the pedantic objections to this procedure—that an irrational number is not a number, or that the mathematical theory of infinite aggregates involves ideas inconsistent with more traditional notions of number and hence is "unintelligible"—in order to see the force of his statements. The current generalization in physics of the concepts of space and time is an equally striking instance. In these cases, and the many others which will occur at once to any student of the history of thought, a conflict arises between those who regard a departure from existing usage and a venture beyond respectable limits of inquiry as "nonsense" and are consequently convinced that "space" *cannot* be "curved" or simultaneity relative, and those who are prepared to violate existing usages and ignore prevailing conventions for the sake of a more broadly rational and inclusive theory. If the latter tendency is described as "speculative," as it well may be, then it becomes apparent that the speculators have, on the whole, been on the side of enlightenment, and that the adoption of ideas and methods of analysis which, relative to current usage and professional propriety, are "nonsense," or at best "rash, speculative guesses," since they either violate or stretch to the limit the rules of that usage, is sometimes a thoroughly legitimate and reasonable procedure. For scholars the reasonable topics in the world are penned in isolated regions, *this* subject matter or *that* subject matter. Your thoroughgoing scholar resents the airy speculation which connects his own patch of knowledge with that of his neighbor. He finds his fundamental concepts interpreted, twisted, modified. He has ceased to be king of his own castle, by virtue of speculations of uncomfortable generality, violating the very grammar of his thoughts.[5] In contrast to so unimaginative a pedant, how admirable is the adventurer in ideas, voyaging through strange seas of thought alone, and returning to enrich us all with the fruits of his exploration. Yet, relative to the standards of plausibility and intellectual propriety conventionally accepted, every such explorer was first of all a mere speculator, righteously condemned by his colleagues, depending not on procedures already accredited but on guesses, insights, imaginative ventures. "New directions of thought arise from flashes of intuition bringing new material within the scope of scholarly learning. They commence as the sheer ventures of rash speculation."[6]

If "speculation," in this sense an imaginative venture into the unknown which *commences* as a rash guess but, in the cases in which genius is distinguishable from mere mental vagrancy, does not remain on that level, is identified with the "speculation" peculiar to the speculative philosophy which it is Whitehead's chief interest to defend, then speculative philosophy finds itself in good, and its opponents in bad, company, and those who look with suspicion on the final real things of which the world is composed are shown to be brothers to the earlier critical philosopher who looked with suspicion on the giraffe and asserted its nonentity. And there is, in fact, an element of this sort of obscurantism in some "positivistic" criticisms of speculative philosophy, and of Whitehead's in particular. There is no more objection *in general* to a generalization

5. A. N. Whitehead, *Adventures of Ideas* (New York: Macmillan, 1933), pp. 137–38.
6. Whitehead, *Adventures of Ideas*, p. 138.

of the notion of "feeling" than to that of number, and the proof that statements about the "feelings" of the apparently inanimate world *would be* nonsense, or at least very odd, if the ordinary use of the term "feeling" were intended, does not at all prove that the statements *are* nonsense or less than reasonable in the extended sense which Whitehead, in the interest of philosophic generalization, proposes to give to the term. There is nothing canonical in current usage when the problems dealt with exceed the scope in which that usage has its appropriate application, and the insistence that any speculative departure from it must be "meaningless" is just the type of narrow pedantry to which Whitehead's strictures legitimately apply.

In spite of this, however, the justification of speculative philosophy, in the special sense in which Whitehead's own philosophy is a speculative system, through its association with the *Adventures of Ideas,* is essentially confusing. "Speculation" in this more general sense occurs in every branch of inquiry in which old ideas are refashioned or eliminated as the adaptation of thought to the scope and complexity of its subject matter develops. Indeed, the rejection of "speculative philosophy" as an inadequate and misleading method of getting at the facts primarily relevant to the philosophical organization of experience might well be in this sense an important "speculative" advance in philosophy. The merit of "speculation" is determined not by its "rashness" or "generality" any more than by its conventional impropriety, but by its capacity to develop into a responsible and adequate interpretation of the subject matter to which it is intended to apply. A speculation in this sense "rash" may be an insight of genius, or it may be a silly waste of time. The generalizations of "number" and of "space" have proved their soundness by their subsequent development. The metaphysical speculations to which Whitehead's philosophy of organism is most closely linked have had no similar development. Is there, then, some important difference between some such speculative ventures and others which their grouping as *Adventures of Ideas* serves rather to obscure than to clarify? In order to answer this question we must consider the particular sort of venture which consists in specifying a "final reality," laying down, on philosophical grounds, the constitution of the world in which this reality has ontological preeminence and predicating of the reality thus characterized all that has any claim to be "real" at all. It is fairly apparent that the theory of numbers, though "rash" as a generalization of previously limited notions, is not "rash" as an attempt to continue a sort of activity which, in many previous trials, has culminated in failure and confusion, and which can be seen to rest on assumptions which appear to be out of harmony with otherwise reliable knowledge of the world. It may be that it is this fact that accounts for the success of scientific speculation and the failure, so far, of the particular sort of enterprise on which Whitehead has embarked. *So far,* the term "speculative," as a designation of the sort of inquiry described in the previous section, is intended to suggest neither praise nor blame, but to identify a subject for discussion. What has so far been said is that this subject is not the *general* procedure of advancing knowledge in "adventuring" into new territory, but more specifically the philosophical construction previously identified. If this is clearly recognized a large and handsome but nonetheless fishy red herring will be removed from the path of inquiry.

"Misplaced Concreteness"

Prima Facie *Problems*

The speculative urge, in its specifically philosophical form, does not develop far or fruitfully without fairly definite points of connection with problems arising from our non-philosophical commerce with the world. We ask not "what is Reality, and why?", but "what *really* is the world which our more ordinary methods of inquiry characterize only abstractly and incompletely, yet to which they all somehow apply?" And this question becomes crucial whenever the incompleteness of some particular sort of inquiry is brought sharply to our attention and we feel the need of relating it intelligibly to what lies outside its scope. Now nothing has been more frequently stressed in recent years than the "abstractness" of the description of the world which the more exact sciences supply. That these descriptions somehow apply to the actual world is, in the light of their impressive empirical confirmation, very difficult to doubt. Yet it is equally difficult, as the methods of scientific inquiry become better understood, to suppose that such descriptions can or in their proper scientific use are intended to give a complete picture of the world or even of "nature" as the sequence of events open to perceptual observation. To treat the products of physical analysis as the whole truth about nature would be, in Whitehead's happy phrase, to "misplace concreteness" and to confuse and impoverish our concept of nature accordingly. The "world of physics," if this means the world as physics describes it, belongs to but does not constitute the total actual world of which philosophy, if it is to do justice to all aspects of our experience, must take account. How, then, can the sciences which purvey such abstractions be true, though not the whole truth; and how is the "modern world" to relate those factors that lend concreteness, vividness, and value to experience to what, on scientific grounds, it finds to be the case? These were the questions which chiefly concerned Whitehead in *Science and the Modern World*. There can be little doubt that they are pertinent questions, and that in his survey of the manner of their treatment in European thought in the last four centuries, Whitehead had some remarkably suggestive and striking things to say about them. The success of his book, in spite of its baffling metaphysical interpolations, is striking evidence of the pertinence of the problems with which it dealt.

This problem of philosophical interpretation becomes a problem of speculative philosophy, however, only when a further step has been taken. If we are to say how scientific "abstractions," or any others, stand to what, on the whole, it is philosophically reasonable to believe, we must, Whitehead assumes, say what the concrete reality is from which the sciences abstract, and describe this in its ultimate concreteness. The remedy for misplaced concreteness will then be found in knowledge of the ultimate concrescence in which the becoming of Reality consists. If science gives us only abstractions, then we must look elsewhere for concreteness, and hence for primary reality. Where would this more naturally be found than in such actuality as our own feelings and emotions disclose? And what would be more reasonable, if reality is thus an affair of feeling and striving, than to conclude that an electron, which physics describes but abstractly, in its measurable properties, is concretely or in its own immediacy a pulse of emotion, and that in thus conceiving it we are getting nearer to its ultimate nature than physics in its inevitable incompleteness ever could? It is apparent that in reaching this conclusion we have somewhat altered the verdict we should, on other grounds, have been prepared to render on the comparative cognitive worth of precise scientific analysis on the one hand and feelings of causal dependence on and emotional sympathy with external nature on the other. "The deliverances of clear and distinct consciousness require criticism by reference to elements in experience which are neither clear nor distinct. On the contrary, they are dim, massive and important." [7] In measuring a physical object I reach only its superficial elements, or "appearance." In sympathizing with the emotional states of the elementary organisms that compose it, I am reaching, though "dimly," the *reality*, the actual entity, in its own intrinsic nature. Art rather than science is our best means of access to a reality which is, in its own final nature, a fact of aesthetic experience. For art "unlooses depths of feeling from behind the frontier where precision of consciousness fails," [8] and at its best "reveals as in a flash intimate, absolute Truth regarding the Nature of Things." [9]

Here a philosophical conclusion about the relative noetic values of scientific description and artistic appreciation has been reached by means of a detour which assured us, on speculative grounds, that what we enjoy in art is ontologically more penetrating than what we measure in science; and this is an answer of sorts, though not, I think, of the best sort, to the problem propounded in *Science and the Modern World.* But it is an answer got by shifting the ground from the relative merits and more obvious intent of science and art in their own territory to an estimate of their capacity to disclose concrete reality in its deeper nature. If science and art are properly interpreted philosophically as clues to the nature of actual entities whose feelings we dimly but massively

7. Whitehead, *Adventures of Ideas,* p. 348.
8. Whitehead, *Adventures of Ideas,* p. 349.
9. Whitehead, *Adventures of Ideas,* p. 350.

feel, then this conclusion is a just one. If they are not, its introduction has proved to be a source of serious confusion, one calculated to foster sentimentality and dubious profundity in the appreciation of art, and to lead to the undervaluing of accurate and testable knowledge as the best guide we have to the nature of the external world. But whether it is a proper interpretation or not, it is at least clear that it has been achieved by a speculative transformation of the question originally asked. We began by asking what significance and relative validity ought reasonably to attach to the "abstractions" of science in a philosophical interpretation of experience as a whole. This might have been answered by considering first the special role these abstractions play in scientific inquiry and what reasons we have for supposing that such inquiry is competent, by their use, to establish reliable contact with matters of fact not otherwise discoverable. We might then have proceeded to inquire how far similar methods would be appropriate and probably fruitful in other types of experience, and how far, in consequence, their use might reasonably be extended. It might then have been possible to determine, for instance, what bearing scientific knowledge can be expected to have on aesthetic appreciation, and to what extent the "insight" such appreciation sometimes achieves could rank as a source of information comparable in accuracy or reliability to scientific knowledge. And it might have been even more pertinent to ask why aesthetic insight should be expected to be a revelation of "the nature of things," except, of course, of their capacity to serve as themes for artistic construction and aesthetic enjoyment.

None of these questions has here been seriously asked or considered on its own merits. They have all been subordinated to the supposedly more ultimate question of what "reality" in its inner nature is, and how far our various experiences are capable of disclosing the reality thus specified. It is in this way precisely that a problem of philosophical interpretation has become a problem of the speculative identification of "the real." It was not inevitable in the nature of the case that the search for "wisdom," or at least for good judgment in the reasonable coordination of diverse aspects of experience, should take this form. It is speculative philosophy itself which imposes this form upon it—whether for better or worse, our subsequent analysis will endeavor to determine.

Nature and Naturalism

A problem of comparable philosophical importance receives exhaustive treatment in Alexander's *Space, Time and Deity.* What is the status of "mind" in "nature"? The idealistic philosophy against which Alexander's theory is, in part, a protest, had held that the natural world is "unreal" except in its relation to mind, and that the notions ordinarily employed in its description become contradictory if taken as attempts to characterize reality in its ultimate and philosophically acceptable nature. Hence the need, on the controversial level, of showing that nature can be "real" on its own account, and [that] space and time [are] the primary constituents of this reality. Again, and more fundamentally, there is a real problem involved in reconciling the natural history of mind, and its local and precarious status within the physical world, with its claims to know truly and judge rationally. Is knowledge a "mysterious" intrusion in the world, or is it possible to understand the manner in which an organism of sufficiently complicated structure comes to think, and the bearing its bodily behavior has on its cognitive attainments? This is not merely a request for more scientific information. We must correlate the standpoints of different inquiries and settle questions of philosophical relevance and intelligibility! Is it necessary, if we are consistently to understand human behavior as a "natural" event in a "natural" world, to assert that thinking is merely "aptness of the body," and that any statements about a mind which cannot be translated literally into statements about the bodily behavior of the "minded" organism are incompatible with an enlightened philosophy? Is teleological behavior, in which the apprehension of an end as right and reasonable appears to be a cause-factor in subsequent conduct, "supernatural" and unworthy of a truly "naturalistic" philosophy? Are introspective data parts of "nature"? If so, where do they belong in it, and if not, what status can introspection have in a naturalistic philosophy? It is obvious that "nature" can mean many things to many men and that the questions thus ambiguously asked have an endless variety of possible answers. But they are not therefore trivial questions. What is wanted is an interpretation of "nature" that will make it the adequate referent for all empirically testable and cognitively respectable statements about the world in which our bodies have spatial positions. Opposed to "nature" here is "the supernatural" in either a religious or a metaphysical guise, and the philosophies that take their stand on "nature" are mainly concerned, I think, to show that it is possible philosophically to understand all that is humanly testable or reliable in the claims of "mind" by reference to its function and prospects in the world as we know it, independently of recourse to the supernatural in either of these senses. Where the boundaries of "nature" are to be drawn is evidently, for such a philosophy, a matter of considerable importance. If they are too narrow we shall be compelled to rule out as "supernatural" much that is actually essential for an understanding of human behavior. On that level simplification is achieved by vituperative exclusion of anything held to be "non-material" or "mysterious" or discontinuous with the specification of nature stipulated in advance as canonical for all enlightened minds. Biology, sociology, and psychology, to say nothing of philosophy, have suffered much in the past from this variety of "naturalism." If, on the other hand, the boundaries are too wide, "nature" becomes a non-discriminating term and a source of verbal comfort rather than philosophical understanding. A theory that could, in a reliable way, indicate the manner in which the special capacities of organisms with minds develop and find their appropriate objects in a space-time world which needs no religious revelation or metaphysical underpinnings to render it rationally acceptable would be a very considerable contribution indeed to the philosophical organization of experience. Only insofar as such a theory is obtainable can we be reasonably assured both that the demands of our "higher" nature will not lead over into mystification, and that our experience will not be distorted and impoverished to conform to an oversimplified and arbitrarily determined "nature" into which in fact it does not fit. What constitutes "mystification" and what "oversimplification" in these matters can only be decided philosophically when we see what, in particular, we are committed to by the theory in question, and how far we can maintain it consistently with what, in our non-philosophical activities, we find the world to be. A "mystification" is a theory which can only maintain itself at the cost of disconnection and final dissociation from the rest of experience, in the way in which the man who believes himself to be Napoleon finds that, whatever the inner significance of the hypothesis, it cuts him off from effective social relations with those who are, and on the whole remain, of a different persuasion. An oversimplification is a theory that gains its authority from methodological stipulations rather than empirical adequacy, and is in fact (though not officially) abandoned whenever we are forced to deal at first hand and independently with the situation to which it was supposed to apply. A philosophy that avoids both these errors is greatly to be desired, and such a "naturalism" as Alexander's promises to be that sort of philosophy.

Here, again, however, a speculative transformation ensues. The mind is to be exhibited as a part of nature, but what is nature *really?* If its metaphysical being is to be discovered, we shall have to come at it in a rather peculiar way. Space and Time are known to us as pervasive features of the external world, and we might reasonably be inclined to identify nature as the system of events in time and space (with some reservations as to the spatial character and locus of mental events). Is the natural world, then, *space-time?* Is space-time sufficient in its own nature to serve as the stuff of all things and the matrix of all becoming; and is mind itself a configuration of space-time or motion, which "knows" other objects insofar as it is together with them in this one space-time and can respond to them in a manner appropriate to its distinctive level of space-time complication? It is by no means easy to give a plausible affirmative answer to these questions, though Alexander's attempt to do so is a masterpiece of constructive ingenuity. And it is just such an answer that is required when "nature" is speculatively identified on the basis of its capacity to serve as an ontological ultimate, and when the "natural" status of anything becomes in consequence a matter of its place in and/or emergence from the only reality of which all things are made and to which they are reducible without remainder. Is mental behavior reasonably understandable as a factor in the world of space-time events? Is a mind a piece of the ultimate stuff of things which is space-time? It was not evident *prima facie* that the first of these questions was reducible to the second, or that such reduction was the most sensible means of getting an answer to it. It is, however, what speculative philosophy makes of it, and our estimate of the satisfactoriness of its procedure will determine what we are to make of speculative philosophy.

The World of Physics and the World of Sense

A third problem with which speculative philosophers have recently been concerned is a natural development from the confusion about perception that we have already considered.* All that we know empirically about the physical world is what our perceptual observations tell us. And all that is "really" given in perceptual observation, all that we can be quite sure of, are the sense-data we cannot, even after much effort, bring ourselves to doubt. So runs the argument. [But] what is the status of these data in the physical world that we suppose, on their evidence, to exist? This is not at all the question as to what the objects ordinarily supposed to be perceptually observed are, and what, through observation of their behavior, we can find out about more remote objects. The object observed is here the datum itself, and this, Russell believes, is most plausibly interpreted as an event happening in a brain. Its proximate causes are there, if physiology is right, and how could it, without a "preposterous kind of discontinuity," be supposed to be in a space-time region remote from its cause? If this is true, however, it is very heartening. For while in scientific theorizing about matter we come at it only remotely and externally, this immediate awareness of sense-data enables us to observe "matter" at first hand, though the "matter" observed is that of our brains and not the external objects usually supposed to be perceived. If we could further say that other physical objects are composed of such elements as these data, and hence that in observing such data we are directly aware of the "stuff" of nature, our inference from what is perceived to unperceived physical objects would seem much less precarious than it does if data are not themselves parts of the physical world. This world, in respect of its ultimate elements, though not of the manner of their combination, then becomes a fairly simple and homogeneous affair. Russell offers in "neutral monism" a theory which deserves to rank with the other major speculative undertakings of the period. It involves the characteristic elements: a substitution of a more philosophically eligible object for the one with which, in

---

* In original chapter 5, "The Problems of Perceptual Knowledge," not herein included. Ed.

perceptual observation, we are concerned; an identification of the stuff or "ultimate" constitution of the objects usually classified as material which makes such eligible objects ontologically fundamental; an attempt to solve the *prima facie* problem of the relation of perceptual to scientific objects by relating them to these ultimate elements. It may hardly seem an adequate compensation for failure to observe objects external to our bodies that we should be assured of the remarkable power of immediately inspecting the stuff of our own brains, and guaranteed that what is thus observed is, in a somewhat unusual sense, an actual constituent of the physical world to which external objects also belong. It is, however, an appropriate speculative offering, and it is by just such gifts that speculative philosophy proposes to enrich our store of knowledge.

The Nature of Philosophical Intelligibility

Those who come to speculative philosophy with idealistic rather than realistic preconceptions have been more inclined to emphasize the demands that ultimate reality must meet if it is to satisfy our minds than [they have been] to take the sciences, "nature," or the "stuff" of the brain as their point of departure. And such demands, if they are held to determine not only what we must think but what reality in its own intrinsic nature must *be,* provide a sufficient basis for speculative systems of a very impressive sort. In *The Nature of Existence,* McTaggart has been able to deduce from certain highly general but allegedly evident propositions about what substances and their parts must be, the necessity that reality must have a structure which, so far as we can see, it only could have if it were a society of timeless spiritual centers or persons, eternally related in mutual perception and love. The deduction is speculative in that it is based not on the observed nature of persons as we elsewhere discover it, or on the place such persons occupy in the material world, but on self-evident knowledge of what any substance *must* be, to exist at all, and hence on an ultimate assurance as to what the "substances" we misperceive as, e.g., material objects actually are, in spite of all appearances to the contrary. It is possible that McTaggart was encouraged in this conclusion by his earlier philosophical discovery that "our nature can make no demand, can set no aim before itself which will not be seen someday to be realized in the world, which is therefore righteous." [10] But the deduction itself employs the terminology of Cambridge analytic realism, and its conclusions are supposed to derive none of their cogency from the (for McTaggart) cheerful picture they present. The light they shed on the ultimate nature of the real is a cold and intellectual light, and the fact that they confirm views about the eternity of persons, the primary onto-

10. J. McTaggart Ellis McTaggart, *Philosophical Studies* (London: Edward Arnold, 1934), p. 211.

logical status of love, and the unreality of time which are extremely congenial to their author's antecedent convictions is an impressive proof that independent speculative inquiry can lead to highly acceptable conclusions. The world at long last meets the demands of McTaggart's nature and provides him with a satisfying ontological status for the things he values most, but it is speculative philosophy that provides the sanction for this. It is this speculative sanction which will concern us here.

Finally, C. S. Peirce, in his strikingly original and suggestive theory of the logical criteria of a good philosophical hypothesis, has interpreted the demands of "reason" or explanation in a typically speculative fashion and used them to support a "world view" which in imaginative daring certainly deserves a place among the outstanding theories of the period. The roots of this theory were indicated in a previous chapter [chapter 3]; its consequences will provide an instructive instance of what philosophical "explanation," interpreted as a speculative generalization about the basic kinds of being and the order of their evolution, can actually tell us about the world.

The Dialectic of Speculative Philosophy
The Identification of "the Real"

The peculiar and distinctive object of speculative philosophy is reality itself, in its ultimate or final nature. How is this object discovered? Other and more limited inquiries may deal with reality under one aspect or another, but only in philosophy do we gain that concrete or ultimate grasp of its nature which enables us to correct the "abstractness" of, e.g., scientific knowledge and to see it as it really is. Has philosophy then some privileged method of access to "the Real," some source of information as to its nature elsewhere unavailable? The mystics have claimed to possess intuitive insight or immediate experience of ultimate reality, and Bergson has maintained that what can be thus intuited—the immediate data of consciousness in their felt duration—is peculiarly "real" in a metaphysically eulogistic sense. Where such claims pass from an esoteric to a rationally examinable level, however, the problem that is paramount is that of justifying the title of what is disclosed in mystical insight, immediate sensible experience, or elsewhere, to the ultimate and metaphysically primary character assigned to it. There is, after all, much in "experience" that is not thus ultimate, yet which claims to be in its own fashion real or authentic. Hence the task of a speculative philosophy, so far as it is a reasoned system, is to show that something or other, accepted as *the* unique reality, can maintain this claim against rival contenders, can "save the appearances" by including in its own nature all that on philosophical grounds we are obliged to recognize as genuine in experience as a whole, and finally, can provide us with the sort of wisdom philosophers, and notably speculative philosophers, seek.

The only materials available for speculative construction are those discovered in some special phase or aspect of experience, whether it be religious illumination, space-time measurement, or the introspective enjoyment of mental states. As Whitehead says, speculative generalization involves "the utilization of specific notions, applying to a restricted group of facts, for the divination of the generic notions which apply to all facts." [11] These specific notions will, in the context in which they are first encountered, normally appear to have a limited application. It is, in fact, just this apparent limitation and the need of relating what is thus special to what, through other channels, we learn about the world, that gives rise to philosophical reflection. There certainly *seem* to be actual facts, e.g., about "inanimate" objects and their behavior, which are not primarily facts of aesthetic experience at all. If, however, aesthetic experience possesses the "concreteness" required for a final fact, and if *final* facts are finally the only facts there are, we shall be impelled, in the interests of speculative generalization, to say, as Whitehead does, that "The final facts are, all alike, actual entities; and these actual entities are drops of experience, complex and interdependent," [12] and to support this by showing, not that what passes for factual by *other* tests has this character, but that anything that is finally or ultimately *actual* must have it, and that apart from such actuality there is nothing.

It will, of course, be true that in this process of generalization some of the more special features of more specific notions will be eliminated. Such generalization "seizes on those characters of abiding importance, dismissing the trivial and the evanescent." [13] Thus, if we wish to find in the unity observed in personal experience the clue to the continuity imputed to physical nature, we must be careful not to insist on unessentials. "In mathematical studies, where there is a problem to be solved it is a sound method to generalize, so as to divest the problem of details irrelevant to the solution. Let us therefore give a general description of this personal unity, divesting it of minor details of humanity." [14] And, more generally, as an able and enthusiastic advocate of this type of speculative philosophy has said, "The philosopher must rob empirical facts of their specificity to make them universal, must dislocate accepted truths from their settings in limited domains so as to understand the universe in its eternal character." [15]

There is, as has been said, no *general* objection to this procedure. But we must be very sure that this generalization, since it has evidently ceased to mean

11. Whitehead, *Process and Reality,* p. 8.
12. Whitehead, *Process and Reality,* p. 28.
13. Whitehead, *Adventures of Ideas,* p. 301.
14. Whitehead, *Adventures of Ideas,* p. 240.
15. Paul Weiss, *Reality* (Princeton: Princeton University Press, 1938), pp. 6–7.

what the specific concepts it employs originally meant, has some definite meaning and reliable application of its own. Dislocated from their original settings, these ideas must find some new setting in which they do intelligibly fit. If none is provided, then there is serious danger that the plausibility such notions appear to possess will actually be borrowed from the original meaning no longer appropriate to them, and that, for example, the "minor details of humanity," from which the notion of "personal" unity has abstracted, will actually provide all the speculative cogency the term "personal" in its generalized usage retains, while at the same time we are compelled to say that *in this sense* the *generalized* unity described is not "personal" at all. A generalization which extends our knowledge of the world and can secure confirmation through its applicability to independently ascertainable fact is a great contribution to our knowledge. A generalization which depends upon an ambiguous terminology to import into its descriptions a "concreteness" due to association with human personality, emotions and the like, to which, as thus generalized, they are not entitled, is less helpful. I do not yet contend that a speculative philosophy normally involves this confusion, though I shall later try to show that it does. But I think it is clear, at this stage, that it is peculiarly liable to it. For it has avowedly robbed its terms of the specificity which determines their ordinary usage, and is therefore not entitled to depend on *this* usage, and its known application, for the elucidation of its own meaning, except where it can specifically be shown that the new or generalized usage warrants the application in question. If "Time" is the "mind" of "Space," as Alexander assures us, and if "Mind" is here used in a much more general and speculative sense than that which normally distinguishes the mental from the non-mental, then *in that usage,* one event-particle in space-time may "know" another in virtue of their merely spatio-temporal relations. What this has to do, however, and whether indeed it has anything very enlightening to do, with "mind" and "knowing" on the human level has still to be determined. It would be a great mistake to suppose that since "mind" as exemplified in mental behavior is spatio-temporal, and since all spatio-temporal actualities "know" each other in virtue of their togetherness in space-time, the problems of the status of *human* knowledge in the material world are thereby solved. What we have is simply a set of terms dislocated from their antecedently known usage and application, and presumably to be provided with another in which they will be adequate, as they previously were not, to describe the final actualities of which the world is made.

There is, moreover, a new set of requirements which the entities to which these terms in their generalized usage are to apply must meet. These entities, as "finally" real, must be capable of meeting all the objections that can speculatively be brought against them as candidates for ontological supremacy. Since, in their ordinary or non-philosophical usage, the entities designated by these terms made no such pretensions, it was not necessary, *in that usage,* to consider such objections. It was enough, for purposes of perceptual observation and scientific analysis, that the objects investigated should be described fairly exactly in terms of their spatial and temporal relations, and that some tests be provided which would enable the inquirer to know what was being asserted and what application was intended when terms like "same length," "same time" and the like were used. It was not required that the space and time referred to be capable of constituting, in their association with each other, the self-contained and self-existent reality of the universe. It is evident that when they function in this capacity we may have to attribute to them characters not otherwise discoverable, but required if space-time is to be the stuff of which all things are made. So, again, the requirements for an "actual entity" which is in its own nature "concrete," and hence possesses all the characters speculatively required in the object to which all that we value in experience is somehow to be attributed, will be different from those which define a "fact" in scientific usage. By ordinary tests there actually are entities which, so far as we can tell, have no feelings or subjective experiences of their own. But such objects cannot be actual entities in the speculative sense, for they would be only "vacuously actual" [16]; they would have no metaphysical insides, no being for themselves, or self-enjoyment. "An entity is actual, when it has significance for itself" [17]; "self-functioning is the real internal constitution of an actual entity," [18] and short of this nothing can be a *res vera,* a final actuality. This actuality is not, in ostensibly inanimate nature, to be discerned by ordinary processes of observation and experiment, though it can be sympathetically enjoyed in our vast and dim, but fundamental, feelings of our derivation from our causal past. But it is held to be the speculatively basic truth, because only entities thus capable of enjoying, conceptually valuing, and aesthetically harmonizing their experiences would be fully concrete and actual.

Now this, again, *may* be true, for anything we have yet proved to the contrary. It is emphasized here in order to stress once more the difference between the usage and tests for validity of the statements of speculative philosophy and those which its terms, in their more specific application, antecedently possessed. To prove by ordinary tests that a chair is actually a society of aesthetically selective organisms would be very difficult indeed. Even our sympathetic powers of feeling the feelings of external objects would here carry us only a little way, since these are admittedly too vague to yield very definite information, and there are, until they have been speculatively guaranteed, too many grounds on which their reliability as sources of information might be impugned

---

16. Whitehead, *Process and Reality,* p. 43.
17. Whitehead, *Process and Reality,* p. 38.
18. Whitehead, *Process and Reality,* p. 38.

to warrant much confidence in them. To prove that an "actual entity" must be an organism, however, that actual entities are the only finally real things, and that in consequence a chair must, so far as it is actual at all, be such an entity or combination of them, is a very different matter. It is with the latter type of proof that we are speculatively concerned, and the meaning of the statements made must be understood in this connection and with this application.

What then are the tests for metaphysical ultimacy, and how shall we know a final real thing when we meet it? It must be (a) such that it possesses in its own nature whatever we take to be most *important,* or significant or genuine, and (b) such that whatever can truly be said of anything whatever can "ultimately" be said of it. The first requirement is necessarily vague. What *being* in the fullest sense is it is difficult to say in any general way. It is a matter for ultimate judgment that only what exists for itself or enjoys its own existence is fully actual. To those who doubt such an ultimate the reply is that a merely "vacuously actual" object would have less than the metaphysical maximum of actuality, and hence would not be the *final* reality we are seeking. There may of course be many such actualities, no one of them self-complete. But in the system defined by their mutual relations, if there are many, and in isolated ultimacy, if there is but one such being, all that is philosophically certifiable as genuine is somehow contained. Otherwise how could we say of such a "reality" that it was *final* and *absolute,* and that apart from it there was nothing?

I suggest, therefore, that the characters we should expect to find in the ultimates of speculative philosophy are those the particular philosopher is strongly predisposed to regard as supremely significant. If, like Alexander, his main interest is in a "reality" that will include, as parts of "nature," all that is humanly significant, space and time as the *pervasive* characters of the natural world will recommend themselves as candidates for speculative ultimacy. If, like Whitehead, he has reacted strongly against the "abstractness" of a one-sided philosophy of nature, he will be inclined to stress the concreteness of aesthetic experience, not only as *also* "real," but as peculiarly and preeminently real, and hence as possessing special philosophical status. An actuality in whose nature such concreteness is not to be found will not be *ultimately* actual at all. If, like Russell, he has previously, for epistemological reasons, reduced the world as verifiably known to sense data, it will be plausible to hold that these cognitive ultimates are also the stuff of the physical world and that, in consequence, the world is, at least in spots, more qualitatively continuous with such data than might otherwise be supposed. If, like McTaggart, he is persuaded that the timeless love of disembodied persons is what a rational universe ought to disclose, it will not be surprising that the necessary requirements for substances and their parts turn out to be those which, so far as we can see, only such a society of persons could meet. In each of these instances, and many others like these, the entities in question—space-time relations, aesthetic experience, sensations, persons related by love—will originally have been encountered in a different context. In that context, however, they will fall short of the finality which, it is assumed, their speculative vindication would require. Hence each is transformed, generalized, and equipped with whatever additional properties may be required to meet this further requirement. An "ultimate reality," if this hypothesis is sound, is the intended referent of a term like experience, "person," "force," or "space-time," in the meaning it acquires when this operation has been performed. Whether or not, in this usage, it still has a rationally certifiable application, has still to be determined.

Saving the Appearances

How could such a theory possibly be tested? It would be quite unfair to impose on it the tests appropriate to a different inquiry, that of scientific research for example, since it is not science and does not pretend to be. The tests wanted will be those appropriate to its own aim and subject matter. To repeat the quotation from Berkeley's *Dialogues* which Whitehead set on the title page of his *Principles of Natural Knowledge,* "I am not for imposing any sense on your words. Only, I beseech you, make me understand something by them." It is not an imposed meaning, but that which speculative philosophy in its own intent and by its own usage of terms determines, that is to be understood.

The sort of confirmation offered for such theories is, in fact, their capacity to solve the traditional problems of philosophy, to meet the objections brought against them by opposing theories, and to provide the basis for a reasonable integration of experience. Their success in these respects is what is claimed by those who put them forward, and it is what constitutes the evidence, so far as there is any evidence, of their truth. Suppose space-time were the stuff of things. Should we then be able better to understand how mind can act on body and body on mind? Is the space-time described invulnerable against the attacks of Bradleyan dialectic? And is the "naturalism" it would guarantee a sound basis for an estimate of man's place and prospects in the world? Or, on a different line, suppose that actual entities were all sentient organisms whose emotional responses to and aesthetic harmonization of their feelings of other feelers constituted their "formal" actuality. Should we then be able to answer Hume's challenge to "point to the impression" on which our idea of causal connection is based? Are such entities "concrete" enough to repel all suspicion of "vacuous actuality"? And would the assumption that the world is made up of such entities help us to achieve that "deeper understanding" ever "confronting intellectual system with the importance of its omissions," [19] and thus to make the most of our experience? If these questions can be answered in the affirmative, the speculative hypothesis has so far served its philosophical purpose of effect-

19. Whitehead, *Adventures of Ideas,* p. 60.

ing a rational coordination of the several aspects of experience and it is by its fruits in this undertaking that it is to be judged. Apart from such testing its pronouncements are merely claims to esoteric knowledge, which might, for all we know, be true, but in which, unless one happened to be blessed with the insight in question, there would be no reason to believe. It is at this point that we reach the dividing line between those works on metaphysics which deserve to rank as serious contributions to philosophy and those, placed so disturbingly near them on library shelves, which are explicitly concerned with the occult. Fortunately it is with the former only that we are now concerned.

Among the criteria thus specified, a further discrimination should be made. The problems of philosophy, as we have already seen, are of two rather different sorts. There are those which arise inevitably from the attempt to relate special sorts of information and claims to validity to all that, as rational animals, we find ourselves concerned with. These are quite genuine and profoundly important. There are also those that are the consequences of the speculative translation of the first sort into problems about being or reality as such and its essential attributes. The genuineness of these is suspect until we have some independent reason to believe that they are more than the unhappy by-products of an inappropriate method of inquiry. It reflects no special merit on a theory that it solves the "mind-body problem," if that "solution" is only a laborious device for eluding the implausible consequences of unwarranted assumptions. Again, the proof that a metaphysical ultimate can stand against its rivals is only of philosophical importance if there is good reason to believe that such ultimacy is required by the nature of the entity in question. To show that the concepts of space and time employed in exact science are not self-contradictory is very useful, for we need those concepts in responsible inquiry, and if they were self-contradictory in this usage we should have no logical right to employ them. Whether, on the other hand, space-time as the stuff of all existence is ontologically respectable, is a less crucial question, since its validity or invalidity in this guise would neither support nor compromise the logical correctness of the concepts ordinarily employed. On this level the merits of one speculative philosophy as compared with another are so largely bound up with assumptions which these philosophies share, but for which no independent evidence is offered, that it is very difficult to estimate their validity.* It is not

* At this point in the manuscript the following lines are crossed out, apparently by the author, possibly by someone else: "William James somewhere recounts as a philosophical parable the story of the jurisdictional conflict that arose when one clergyman had got as far in the performance of appropriate rites as to announce, 'I am the resurrection and the life,' only to be countered by a rival cleric arriving late but firm in the knowledge of his prerogatives, with the dictum, '*I* am the resurrection and the life.' The dispute on this level seems very largely a private fight, and to those possessed of antecedent doubts of the ultimate authority of both pretenders, of less than vital importance." Ed.

enough to be assured that matter cannot be the final reality of things and *there-fore* spirit must have its way, if we are still unconvinced that there need be any discoverable object in *this* sense "final." "A plague on both your houses" is the ostensibly appropriate comment on such a situation.

If this apparent irrelevance of the problems and debates of speculative philosophy is to be avoided, a further step must be taken. It must be shown that the "reality" that is speculatively discerned is the very same that, in other inquiries, we lay claim to. We do want to know something more about the objects of any special inquiry than a conscientious use of the methods and tests *internal to* the inquiry can tell us—we want to know what bearing the inquiry itself and its results have on what, elsewhere, we find to be the case. There are material objects, to be sure, if science is to be believed, but physical science itself is an abstraction, and until we have corrected this abstraction by reference to the more "concrete" reality from which the sciences abstract, we shall not know what matter really is, or how far what science tells us about it is to be taken as a reliable guide to its total nature. Hence, an estimate of the interpretation it is reasonable to put on the findings of science requires a knowledge of the actuality from which science abstracts, and this knowledge is within the keeping of speculative philosophy. The "reality" which speculation reaches is the reality at which science aims, insofar as it claims to be rationally defensible knowledge and not just a useful technique for securing "practical" results. The reasonable organization of our beliefs must therefore proceed by way of knowledge of the "final reality" to which all beliefs refer, and if it could be shown that space and time were speculatively unacceptable it would follow that the world the sciences purport to describe does not really have the properties they attribute to it and that they are, therefore, unreliable guides to its nature. The credence to be accorded to scientific statements as more than useful calculating devices will then depend on the speculative warrant they can secure. And since, as has been seen, it is difficult to make sense of our various knowledge claims except on the basis of a recognition of the *cognitive* validity of scientifically certifiable beliefs, this speculative warrant becomes a matter of considerable importance. And equally, if we find it in our hearts to believe that poetry is somehow truer than science, the demonstration that the actual entities at which poetry and science both aim are "really" more like what the poet tells us than what the scientist, with his more "abstract" intellectual procedures, can discover, will be a noteworthy contribution to the support of what, without it, was merely a dubious preference.

In summary, then, the situation is this. The relevance of speculative constructions to problems that arise outside the range of speculative controversy is determined by the fact that the "reality," "authenticity," or reliability which it is philosophically reasonable to assign to special inquiries and interests is held to depend on their agreement with and adequacy as manifestations of the *reality* which is speculatively identified. If this were the case we should expect that a speculative theory which "saves the appearances"—which is able to exhibit the objects of religion, art, perceptual observation, and scientific knowledge as aspects, functions, or phases of the "reality" selected—would provide a sound basis for the philosophical integration of experience. It would enable us to see in each of the "aspects" considered what is distinctively "real" and reliable in it, to understand their mutual relevance, and to set each in its proper place, without special bias, and without distortion, in a view of the world which corresponds, on the whole, to what in all our reliable dealings with it we find it to be. In a pedestrian way, I think, this corresponds to Whitehead's eloquent statement of the function of philosophy. "It is our business . . . to re-create and re-enact a vision of the world, including those elements of reverence and order without which society lapses into riot, and penetrated through and with unflinching rationality. Such a vision is the knowledge which Plato identified with virtue. Epochs for which, within the limits of their development, this vision has been widespread are the epochs unfading in the memory of mankind." [20] This is nobly said, and, if allowance is made for some rhetorical flourishes, it does state the end toward which philosophy, as a reasonable organization of the several aspects of experience, is working. Insofar as a speculative philosophy contributes to this sort of reasonable vision, it is justified by its fruits.

If, however, the reference to ultimate reality does not perform this function, if its elucidations are found to be based on contextual confusion, its coordinations the sterile products of tautologies masquerading as factual statements through an equivocal use of terms, and its final "vision" a rationalization of antecedent preconceptions very much in need of rational criticism, then its claims are not confirmed, and its merit as a method of philosophical inquiry becomes extremely questionable. The business of a speculative philosophy is to "save the appearances" in the manner described, and it is by its adequacy in this capacity that we must judge it.

The "Objective Synthesis"

The procedure by means of which this integration is achieved will be examined specifically in the case of each of the speculative systems to be considered. It will, however, be convenient to have a somewhat simplified model which will suggest their method of operation. This, as it stands, is not a precise representation of any of the theories in question; its only justification is the help it may later give in following a complex and subtle argument. Suppose, then, that we are brought by a process of reflection, however initiated, to consider the "real"

20. Whitehead, *Adventures of Ideas,* p. 126.

nature of Cleopatra, Queen of Egypt. There is a familiar saying to the effect that the length of Cleopatra's nose was one of the factors affecting the destiny of nations, and we can understand the sense in which this is true. Now the length of Cleopatra's nose was a physical fact and the queen herself a physical object, subject, like the rest of us, to the laws of physical nature. But Cleopatra herself was not merely a physical object, she was also, it appears, a socially potent and humanly desirable woman, possessed of a "spiritual" quality of charm which, though dependent on her physical make-up, is not adequately expressible in terms of physical or even of biological laws. How is this situation to be understood? If we follow the approved methods of speculative "naturalism" must we not say, with Samuel Alexander, that Cleopatra as a natural object is reducible without remainder to a space-time configuration, and that when we know fully how and under what conditions instants of time occupy points in space we shall be able to express in philosophically ultimate terms all that a good biographer could tell us about Cleopatra? This, her final reality, is one with the reality of which all things are made, and in knowing it we know what is "fundamental" about her as well.

This somehow seems unplausible, and for a fairly obvious reason. Cleopatra is no doubt *also* a space-time configuration, and this is very interesting; but there are things we want to say about her which do not get expressed in any statements we know how to make about points and instants. Even if her charm could be correlated with some special complexity of space-time we should still know that this particular warp in metaphysical geometry was charming only if we can know it in a different way from that in which we respond to point-instants in their proper spatio-temporal characters. We should have at least to say, as Alexander does, that the qualities that render the Queen of Egypt charming, though ultimately reducible *without remainder* to space-time, which is all there is for Cleopatra or anything else to be, are also unique and distinctive in their qualitative character, and this addition, though it in some measure saved the appearances, would have the look of a flat contradiction which only natural piety could bring us to accept. Our hesitancy to deal with Cleopatra, metaphysically, merely on the space-time level might be removed if we were told that time, as the source of change and evolution in space-time, was the mind of space, and hence that Cleopatra and pure space-time, being both "minded," were not after all so different as they appeared. If, however, we were further reminded that being the mind of space is only being a mind in a very general sense, in that, namely, in which an instant, by changing its place in space, can be a source of novelty, we might well feel that the proffered assuagement was more verbal than real, and that for all we could see the "mind" of space was only time under an alias, and behaving very indiscreetly at that.

An alternative method would be to deny that Cleopatra was just space-time, to brand any such treatment of the friend of Caesar as "misplaced concreteness," and to emphasize the fact that Cleopatra as a physical or spatio-temporal object is a mere abstraction, since what we know about her in this way, compared with all that in other respects we take her to have been, is less than the whole concrete truth about her. It is as a datum for aesthetic appreciation and emotional response that Cleopatra is most fully and concretely known. This, then, is her "reality," and the abstractions of science are but meager things compared with it. This works fairly well for Cleopatra, though not without a pardonable emotional overemphasis. But we are, as speculative philosophers, intent on generalization. If the description will work for Cleopatra, why not for the barge she sat in? This, too, is a physical object, and in its case the social and emotional relations which complete its "reality" are somewhat less obvious. Must we then say that the barge, as perceptually observed and physically measured, was an inanimate object and let it go at that? We have already learned that a physical object is an abstraction from a more concrete reality. In the case of Cleopatra and ourselves we know that this reality is aesthetic and emotional. And it is these aspects that lend [this reality] its concreteness. Must we not correct the abstractness of our knowledge of the barge in a similar fashion? An *actual entity* is a unity of aesthetic experience, and the barge, in its concrete reality, not its physical abstractness, is an actual entity or combination of them. It is true that our social relations to these actual entities do not easily appear in conscious or reflective experience. But at a deeper level we reach them at least darkly, and in poetry we have, in flashes of insight, an awareness of the deeper truth.

We must not, of course, expect to find these elementary organisms possessed of feelings, concepts, and the like in the full sense in which *we* have them. Our measure of sentience seems to be dependent upon a quite special bodily structure which in these cases can hardly be present. It is feeling, emotion, and conceptual awareness in the generalized sense that belong to them. And in this sense feeling is something more than we can expect the barge, as externally observed, to manifest, and something less than we suppose Cleopatra herself to have possessed. It is, in fact, a very puzzling sort of feeling, and one which, apart from our aesthetic experiences, interpreted as cognitive disclosures of external objects in their intrinsic nature, and from the special requirements of our theory of actual entities, we should have seen no reasons at all to impute to it. The assurance that it is there, and that our poetic feelings are thus profound sources of ontological information, may even seem, on other grounds, a puzzling and disturbing conclusion, more likely to foster confusion and cryptic utterance than to eventuate in reliable knowledge. But such is the procedure, and in giving feelings to the barge we have at least made sure that Cleopatra actually has them, and that our appreciation of her will not be impoverished by pedantic omissions.

It is to be doubted, I think, that either of these lines of inquiry has added a single factual element to our understanding of Cleopatra or her entourage. Each has rather the appearance of an attempt to tell everything about the situation in terms specifically appropriate to only some of its elements, an attempt which is intelligible enough in the light of the philosophical interests involved, but which does not render the facts described more intelligible. On the contrary, each theory appears to be required to follow up an arbitrary and inadequate identification of "reality" with extremely implausible speculative postulations, and to justify these in turn by an equivocal terminology which saves the appearances only by appearing to say more than its specific subject matter will warrant. The outcome is not a better organization but a progressive disorientation of our knowledge, asking us to believe the incredible in order to have a warrant for what, on other grounds, we know to be true, or to trust, for its speculative profundity, the cognitive claims of a type of insight that elsewhere seems peculiarly unreliable. If it should be the case that speculative philosophy is, though in a far more subtle and devious way, an essentially similar enterprise, we should have some grounds for doubting its cognitive worth. But we must turn, now, to these philosophies themselves.

6 Recent Speculative Philosophy II
Applications

Whitehead's Philosophy
The Philosophy of Nature

The background of Whitehead's speculative system is to be found in his earlier and admirable examination of *The Concept of Nature*. The problem primarily dealt with is that of understanding the statements made in the physical sciences as the truth, but not the whole truth, about the natural world which we observe in perception through the senses. The standpoint from which the inquiry is made is a straightforward one. "I am maintaining the obvious position that scientific laws, if they are true, are statements about entities which we obtain knowledge of as being in nature; and that, if the entities to which the statements refer are not to be found in nature, the statements about them have no relevance to any purely natural occurence." [1] Thus if we can accurately describe physical happenings in terms of the behavior of material particles at points of space and instants of time, there must be something in the world described to which these statements correspond and which they truly represent. But, equally, it is clear that statements of this sort do not tell us the whole truth about this world of events. We perceive the world around us as colored, odorous, and more or less solid to touch. We cannot attribute these qualities directly to the objects described by physics, for there is no reason to suppose that these objects possess them. But we must attribute them to the natural world with which physics is concerned. The alternative to this would be a "bifurcation" of nature, in which the world perceptually observed and the world physically described fall apart and we are left without any reliable way of connecting them. Again, the events we observe are not punctual and instantaneous; they all possess extension both spatial and temporal, and overlap or are connected in virtue of their extensive

1. A. N. Whitehead, *The Concept of Nature* (Cambridge: University Press, 1920), pp. 45–46.

relations. If the space and time of physics stand in any intelligible relation to the extended and enduring events perceived, it ought to be possible to exhibit this relation and thus to show how the statements of the physicists can apply in the "nature" that we observe through the senses.

A natural way of stating this relationship would be to say that space and time, as physics refers to them, are abstractions from the world of events. They therefore disclose some of its features without expressing its total nature, and when we see their place in the natural world we can understand both how the statements of physics are true and also how, being selective and abstract, they leave the way open for alternative descriptions which emphasize those qualities and relations which physics, for its own purposes, need not consider, but which are nonetheless factors in nature, as it concretely is. The concrete entities of which the sciences supply an abstract description are events. Such events actually possess, in their relations to percipient organisms, the qualities they are observed to have. The red of the sunset is "really" in the sky, *from the standpoint of the percipient,* and the transaction, including the response of the percipient's body to external stimuli, which determines this "inherence" is as much a natural fact as any other. And sets of such events, in their extensive relations, possess the properties required for points, instants and event-particles, so that what is said of these entities can truly be said of such events. The method of extensive abstraction by which this is demonstrated is for the non-mathematician a complicated affair, but its philosophical purpose is clear. Nature as a system of extended events we know. Nature as scientifically described must be some aspect of this natural world if we are to credit its descriptions with a valid application. Therefore the indication of the relations between extended events which provide a valid empirical interpretation for statements involving "points" and "instants" is a substantial contribution to our understanding of the place of science in the natural world.

Two quotations will make Whitehead's position at this time clear. "By saying that space and time are abstractions, I do not mean that they do not express for us real facts about nature. What I mean is that there are no spatial facts or temporal facts apart from physical nature, namely that space and time are merely ways of expressing certain truths about the relations between events." [2] And, "to be an abstraction does not mean that an entity is nothing. It merely means that its existence is only one factor of a more concrete element of nature." [3] The traditional puzzles of epistemology have arisen from neglecting the "more concrete elements" and supposing that the abstractions *by themselves* constitute the natural world. It is then impossible to find a place for the factors which these abstractions do not include, and, since the world perceptu-

2. Whitehead, *Concept of Nature,* p. 168.
3. Whitehead, *Concept of Nature,* p. 171.

ally observed obviously includes such factors, the relation of perceived nature to causally "real" nature becomes anomalous. The correction for such "misplaced concreteness" is to recognize that nature in its concreteness is more than this, that "nothing in nature could be what it is except as an ingredient in nature as it is. . . . An isolated event is not an event, because every event is a factor in a larger whole and is significant of that whole. There can be no time apart from space, and no space apart from time; and no space and no time apart from the passage of the events of nature." [4] Our motto, in the philosophy of nature, must be "seek simplicity and distrust it." [5]

The merits of the construction Whitehead offered as the basis for a philosophy of nature cannot here be examined. I have elsewhere given reasons for questioning the efficacy of "the event" in Whitehead's usage as the concrete entity to which the space-time structures of physical theory can be referred.[6] The point of interest here is that it sets a plausible pattern for a more ambitious philosophical venture, and one on which Whitehead was not slow to enter. There *is* a philosophic need for relating what physics tells us to what, in other ways, we know. And this has seemed to be met, in the case of "space," "time," and events, by showing that physics presents an abstraction, and philosophy interprets this by showing the more concrete reality to which the abstraction belongs. Here, at least, philosophy is the critic of abstractions, and its right to serve as critic depends upon its knowledge of the concrete reality from which abstraction is made. Generalized, this becomes the leading principle for all Whitehead's later speculations. "It is the task of philosophy to work at the concordance of ideas conceived as illustrated in the concrete facts of the real world. It seeks those generalities which characterize the complete reality of fact, and apart from which any fact must sink into an abstraction. But science makes the abstraction, and is content to understand the complete fact in respect to only some of its essential aspects. Science and philosophy mutually criticize each other, and provide imaginative material for each other. A philosophic system should present an elucidation of concrete fact from which the sciences abstract." [7]

"Abstract" and "Concrete"

This statement and its application provide our primary clue to the structure of Whitehead's philosophy, its initial plausibility and promise, and its final confusion. Philosophy is to elucidate the concrete fact, but where is it to find such facts, and how will it be able to vindicate their metaphysical adequacy? Obvi-

4. Whitehead, *Concept of Nature,* p. 141–42.
5. Whitehead, *Concept of Nature,* p. 163.
6. A. E. Murphy, "What is an Event?" *The Philosophical Review* 37.6 (1928): 574–86.
7. A. N. Whitehead, *Adventures of Ideas* (New York: Macmillan, 1933), p. 187.

ously, if "concreteness" is to include all that it is reasonable to take account of philosophically, it will have to find a place not only for those elements in nature from which physics abstracts, the secondary qualities for example, but also for those emotional responses and aesthetic enjoyments not usually attributed to material objects and events but nonetheless vividly present in our experience.

We cannot take account of all that we find meaningful, genuine, and desirable in experience without considering events in the special aspects they take on when they are enjoyed, valued, and artistically arranged by a human organism intent on making the most of its experience. In vividness, immediacy, and fullness of satisfaction, what is apprehended when we stand in those special relations to our environment which enable us to sympathize with its feelings, enjoy its beauty and the like, is certainly a completer fact than anything an abstract and analytic description can give us. The "concrete" is here a fact of aesthetic experience, and it is on such facts that philosophy, as the critic of abstraction and guardian of the concrete or total fact, is now to base itself.

But this concrete fact is also, if Whitehead is right, the actuality from which physics abstracts and which constitutes the inner nature of all that is actual. "The notion of physical energy, which is at the base of physics, must then be conceived as an abstraction from the complex energy, emotional and purposeful, inherent in the subjective form of the final synthesis in which each occasion completes itself. It is the total vigour of each activity of experience. The mere phrase that 'physical science is an abstraction,' is a confession of philosophic failure. It is the business of rational thought to describe the more concrete fact from which that abstraction is derivable." [8] From this it is evidently but a short step to the insight that what science measures as wave-lengths and vibrations are, in their own concrete nature, "pulses of emotion," and that the transmission of energy is an abstraction from the "creativity of the world," which is "the throbbing emotion of the past hurling itself into a new transcendent fact." [9] This, if true, is quite remarkable information about the external world which neither perceptual observation nor scientific inquiry seemed at all able to warrant, and in supplying it speculative philosophy has not only extended our knowledge in a very striking way but has also provided a standpoint from which we can estimate the comparative reliability of physical science and romantic poetry as clues to ultimate truth.

"Actual Entities"

Evidently we have here moved rapidly and far. But it will be advisable to pause for special attention to one particular step in the process. We have proceeded

8. Whitehead, *Adventures of Ideas*, p. 239.
9. Whitehead, *Adventures of Ideas*, p. 227.

on the basis of "the philosophic generalization which is the notion of a final actuality conceived in the guise of a generalization of an act of experience," [10] but is this generalization a well-grounded one? We did not reach this important information about physical energy by a further examination of the way in which such energy is found to behave when we are observing external nature. What we did was to say that what can be learned from this *sort* of observation is an abstraction, and its result, therefore, not, for philosophy, a "final actuality." We then looked into our own experience to find out what finality *these* consisted in, in the quite different sense of that which was most immediate, vivid, and fully satisfying in human experience. What has this got to do with the inner nature of physical objects, or of the reality which physics abstractly describes? An emotional experience is vivid and actual for us because we are sentient organisms responding in a rather special and complicated way to a biosocial environment. There is not much empirical evidence independent of aesthetic insight and speculative philosophy, to warrant the conclusion that apparently inanimate nature is made up of organisms with bodily structures capable of such responses. There is doubtless much more going on in the world than physical science describes, but where our only reliable means of getting information about such events is that which physical science provides, it seems *prima facie* reasonable to say not that the objects described are "abstractions," but that our knowledge of them is schematic and incomplete, and that we have no reliable means of finding out what *else* is true of them. That does not convict the world described of metaphysical deficiency, but simply points modestly to the channels of information available and asks us not to expect to know more than by these means we can find out. What *else* may be the truth about such objects we could only know if we had further relations with them on which cognitive conclusions would properly be based. If I could enter into sociable communication with an electron, I could doubtless apprehend it more vividly and aesthetically than is at present possible. But it would surely be a mistake to postulate such social relations in order to assure myself that an electron "concretely" is what my neighbors are found to be, centers of feeling and emotion, when I know *them* most concretely. So far, such an assumption seems quite unnecessary in order to recognize either that we know objects incompletely when we know only their physical properties or that some objects, sentient organisms, known in virtue of more special relations in which we stand to them, have feelings, and that this fact is philosophically important for a complete or "concrete" understanding of *them* and of their value for our lives. And this is really all that the abstract-concrete contrast has served to establish.

It is here that the "actual entity," "res vera," or *final* actuality performs its

10. Whitehead, *Adventures of Ideas*, p. 304.

speculatively indispensable function. We ask not what electrons actually are, so far as we can tell, or what conscious experience actually and "concretely" is, but what anything *must* be to be finally or fully actual at all. The criteria for ultimacy are, as previously observed, not easy to determine, but in Whitehead's theory they evidently reflect his preference for the aesthetically immediate and emotionally vivid. "An actual fact is a fact of aesthetic experience." [11] Such a fact is peculiarly eligible metaphysically, it has "being for itself," since it is a center of feeling; it is concrete; it embodies in its nature a teleological process of becoming, and process and telic activity are clearly important factors in the world; it agrees with what we observe when we see the world at first hand, in our own aesthetic and emotional experience. If we are to have a final reality that includes in its own nature all we regard as philosophically important and [that] will serve as the primary referent for all that, outside philosophy, we need to take account of, [then] the actual entity as a sentient organism—feeling sympathetically the feelings of other organisms, valuing them as possible components in an aesthetic harmony of its own experience, and aiming purposively at a final harmonious feeling of its world, which is an aesthetic achievement—is a formidable contender.

It is not enough, for speculative purposes, to assume that there are such entities, as constituent elements in even apparently inanimate objects. We must further stipulate that *ultimately* these, with their characters and relations, are all there are. "According to the ontological principle there is nothing which floats into the world from nowhere. Everything in the actual world is referable to some actual entity." [12] " 'Actuality' means nothing else than this ultimate entry into the concrete, in abstraction from which there is mere nonentity." [13] Since this entry into the concrete means presence as a factor in the experience of sentient organisms it follows that "nothing is to be received into the philosophical scheme which is not discoverable as an element in subjective experience." [14]

If such entities are all there are, then clearly it is with such entities that physical science deals, though abstractly. "Physical science is the science investigating spatio-temporal and quantitative characteristics of simple physical feelings." [15] The causal efficacy of A on B (where A and B, of course, are sentient organisms, though possibly of a rudimentary type) is simply B's feeling of the feelings of A, including both the datum as felt and the emotional response to that datum. Simple physical feelings are feelings of the feelings of other actual entities as these are objectified in the experience of the sentient

11. A. N. Whitehead, *Process and Reality* (New York: Macmillan, 1929), p. 427.
12. Whitehead, *Process and Reality*, p. 373.
13. Whitehead, *Process and Reality*, 321.
14. Whitehead, *Process and Reality*, p. 253.
15. Whitehead, *Process and Reality*, p. 364.

organism, and to feel the feeling as *derived from* the antecedent feeler is to apprehend causal efficacy in its primary expression. "The primitive form of physical experience is emotional—blind emotion—received as felt elsewhere in another occasion and conformally appropriated as a subjective passion. In the language appropriate to the higher stages of experience, the primitive element is *sympathy,* that is, feeling the feeling *in* another and feeling conformally *with* another." [16]

If this is true, we must quite revise our previous notion that we have no reliable means of getting into social relations with an electron. On the contrary, "[W]hen we observe the causal nexus, devoid of interplay with sense-presentation, the influx of feeling with vague qualitative and "vector" definition, is what we find." [17] Compared with this vague, but profound, assurance, the measured results of scientific investigation are precise and superficial. We should hardly expect to find in them a witness to concrete actuality as authoritative as the primary assurance of a world of feelers and their feelings for which more primitive emotional experience is our guarantee. Speculative philosophy has here directed us to the insight into "concreteness" where it is to be found and thus corrected the superficiality of our abstractions in a very striking way.

The sanction thus provided is, however, a rather dubious one. The primitive physical experience, in my own case at least, remains incurably vague and dim even after I have made very earnest efforts to sympathize with primary actual entities, and its *cognitive* content derives almost wholly from its vague adumbration of what Whitehead's *Process and Reality* assures us is true. If I did not know on speculative grounds that a "concrete" reality must be a feeler of feelings, I should find it very difficult indeed to place any confidence in the dark deliverances of my emotional responses in these matters. And the speculative warrant is itself somewhat tenuous. It seems to depend almost wholly on an antecedent determination to describe everything in terms obviously appropriate only to some rather special sorts of thing; and to do this for no better reason than that these are "concrete," as humanly vivid and satisfying, that what is "concrete" is alone finally actual, that what is finally actual is all that there ultimately is in the world, that therefore a description applicable to such actualities is somehow applicable to everything, and that in consequence, if this is what everything actually is, the vague emotional responses which lend equivocal support to an animistic view of things are the deepest knowledge of reality that we have. But was this really a convincing procedure?

Of course, if we *identify* concrete actuality with what, as human beings, we find most humanly significant, what we can respond to with emotional satisfac-

16. Whitehead, *Process and Reality,* p. 246.
17. Whitehead, *Process and Reality,* p. 268.

tion, then we shall have to say that everything finally is, in a general way at least, what our emotional strivings and valuations have been found to be. Since our "sympathy" with objects depends on the social relations in which we stand to them, it will be convenient to conclude that sociality is more pervasive in nature than might otherwise have been supposed. But, equally, since it is difficult to believe that the qualities that render our experience concrete could pervade the natural world except in a very attenuated form, it will be necessary to water down terms like "feeling," "conceptual valuation," and the like in such fashion that there will be at least a measure of plausibility in talking of "feelings" in the form in which they would be appropriate to the ultimate constituents of objects perceived, and to speak of perceptible objects, in their "concrete" nature, in the terms that romantic poetry employs. All this will be the normal consequence of the speculative identification, and this identification is plausibly motivated by a desire to show that what is humanly "concrete" is also ontologically fundamental, and that what we enjoy in aesthetic experience and "insight" is also the deepest truth about the universe. "The teleology of the Universe is directed to the production of Beauty." [18] It is doubtful, however, whether the right to say such inspiring things has not been purchased, philosophically, at a prohibitive cost.

The Human Standpoint

The primary difficulty one is likely to feel with this philosophy is that it shifts in a misleading and unprofitable way the critical basis for a reasonable estimate of the reliability of different sorts of experience. We know, of course, that the world looks menacing to a worried man and friendly to a cheerful one, that the poet's heart dances with the daffodils, and that "The instinctive interpretations which govern human life and animal life presuppose a contemporary world throbbing with energetic values." [19] But we have grown accustomed to discounting such aspects as reliable sources of information about objects, except in the special emotional relations in which they stand to the percipient. The basis for this was the discovery that nature in many of its aspects appears to be profoundly unconcerned with the emotions it inspires in sentient and sensitive "actual entities," and that by "abstracting" from these emotional overtones we get a more literal and reliable picture of what is happening on a scale of physical interaction to which our hopes and fears have little direct relevance. Each of us remains, of course, at the center of his world, and nothing can be fully concrete or satisfying to him that eliminates the special characters the world takes on as an object of his enjoyment and concern. But he may still learn to

18. Whitehead, *Adventures of Ideas,* p. 341.
19. Whitehead, *Adventures of Ideas,* pp. 281–82.

realize that this vivid world is a peculiarly human one, deriving its emotional satisfactoriness from just those features of things which are least generalizable. The part of philosophical good sense, grounded on this reliable experience of the special and limited character of the human standpoint, would seem to be to distinguish what is in this way "concrete" and humanly precious from what is pervasive and ubiquitous in nature as a whole. To identify "concreteness" with ultimacy and ultimacy with pervasiveness is at once to generalize and to attenuate the human standpoint, and to affirm once more that the aspect things wear in their relations to the wants and preferences of human beings is the most reliable guide we have to the nature of the non-human world. On any basis but that of a speculative stipulation this seems to me an uncommonly difficult position to maintain in the face of our ordinary commerce with the world. It "misplaces concreteness" in a more fundamental way than does the theory Whitehead earlier criticized, for it spreads the emotional coloring of human concern (here identified as concreteness) over all nature, and attributes to all that is actual the constitution an "actuality" must have in order to measure up to its all too human demand for fullness of being. Certainly a wise philosophy will not impoverish experience by rejecting as "unreal" those aspects of things which only a human response can elicit. The world *is* beautiful if in aesthetic enjoyment we find it so, and its beauty is for us an important fact about it. Our experience would be incomplete without this element of aesthetic satisfaction, and no reasonable organization of experience can afford to neglect it. But, just as surely, a reasonable philosophy ought not to identify with reality or actuality as such what it thus finds important. To do so is to identify the humanly significant with the ontologically ubiquitous, and that is an unfortunate identification on both sides.

The consequences for nature are not particularly damaging. For all we know to the contrary, electrons *might* be pulses of emotion in some very general sense. This would presumably be quite consistent with their continuing to behave in a peculiarly unfeeling way as scientifically discoverable. Their enjoyment of their own immediacy and their sympathy with ours would have no consequences that conflict with any scientific findings, since feeling is apparently to be so generally interpreted as to be consistent with anything that science, by its more superficial means, can discover. Some scientific terms are more verbally congenial than others to such generalization; it is easier to think of an electron, which is a peculiarly lively object in any case, as inwardly sentient than to have a like conception of a stone. But this is a matter of imaginative facility, not of scientific verifiability, in either case; and it is as unlikely that the philosophy of organism will be refuted as that it will be confirmed by further physical research. For, after all, philosophy is concerned with the concrete reality from which the sciences abstract, and will doubtless continue to abstract for their more limited purposes. If anyone wishes to believe without scientific warrant that the world is full of feelings, he is at liberty to do so.

The philosophical danger of the theory comes from a different quarter. As an imaginative over-belief, a world of diffused sentience is an innocent fantasy. The trouble is that speculative philosophy wants to support this belief with substantial evidence, and in order to do so, invites us to treat as cognitively authoritative sources of illumination not, on any other showing, very reputable. In our more precise observations of nature we find no very good evidence that we are feeling the feelings of the elementary constituents of matter. This, however, can be explained. "Mentality is an agent of simplification; and for this reason appearance [the world as apprehended in our processes of comparison, analysis and the like] is an incredibly simplified edition of reality. There should be no paradox in this statement. A moment's introspection assures one of the feebleness of human intellectual operations, and of the dim massive complexity of our feelings of derivation." [20] These feelings of derivation, it will be recalled, are the emotional experiences in which the causal efficacy of the antecedent world is directly apprehended. And "reality" for any "actual entity" is the real antecedent world *as thus given.* Our mental operations may transform the datum as thus given in such a way as to depart from its nature or they may not. If in the final phase of experience into which the operations of mentality have entered the characters attributed to the data are those which belong to them as, in the primary phase, they are given, the relation is "truthful." If not, it is "falsifying." [21] In any case the reality to which, in our more complicated mental inquiries, we are trying to conform, and about which our statements must be true, is what is given in this vague and dim primary experience, *as it is thus given.* But this seems actually to subordinate our best tested intellectual instruments, as means for discovering truth, to the intuitions of emotional sympathy in primary physical feeling.

Whitehead seems actually to say this, in a disturbing passage. "Consciousness is the weapon which strengthens the artificiality of an occasion of experience. It raises the importance of the final Appearance relative to that of the initial Reality. Thus it is Appearance which in consciousness is clear and distinct, and it is Reality which lies dimly in the background with its details hardly to be distinguished in consciousness. What leaps into conscious attention is a mass of presuppositions about Reality rather than the intuitions of Reality itself. It is here that the liability to error arises. The deliverances of clear and distinct consciousness require criticism by reference to elements in experience which are neither clear nor distinct. On the contrary, they are dim, massive,

20. Whitehead, *Adventures of Ideas,* p. 273.
21. Whitehead, *Adventures of Ideas,* p. 344.

and important. These dim elements provide for art that final background of tone apart from which its effects fade. The type of Truth which human art seeks lies in the eliciting of this background to haunt the object presented for clear consciousness." [22]

There is a sense in which this is true and harmless. It would be a mistake to hold, philosophically, that the world is limited to what we can clearly and distinctly perceive. Any hints from vague sources which enable us to piece out what is distinctly apprehended are philosophically welcome, so long as they are employed with a proper sense of their relative unreliability as compared with what is more exactly ascertainable. But that is not what is here said. When "reality" is identified with what is given in vague emotional experience, then this becomes the norm to which critical reflection ought, so far as it aims at truth, to conform. The world is then best and most reliably known in vague and dim intuitions, and the best products of conscious reflection are, philosophically, on a lower level. This view, if taken seriously and applied consistently, would run contrary to every reliable principle of rational discrimination in matters of knowledge, and invite a deluge of romantic nonsense in the guise of philosophical insight. Whitehead himself is an eminently reasonable man, and there is no likelihood that he will take his theory seriously outside its abstruse and speculative limits. But if it is philosophically sound it *ought* to be taken seriously, and some of the younger Whiteheadeans are intent, apparently, in going the whole humorless way with it. In this guise, that in which its consequences can best be been, it amounts, I believe, to a radical disorganization and dislocation of the orderly structure of our knowledge. The speculative identification has not here done its philosophical work reliably or well. It has simply found ultimate reality in the object of its preferential interest and, in order to be able to say ontologically inspiring things about objects of considerable human concern, has been compelled to treat factually certifiable knowledge as a superficial "aspect" of the reality revealed through the "intuitions" and "insights" in which its animistic implications find their questionable authentication.

"Process and Reality"

In this consideration of Whitehead's philosophy I have neglected what might well appear to be its most essential element, the remarkable systematic elaboration into the speculative system of *Process and Reality* of the categories, principles, and "categoreal obligations" it employs. As a work of constructive imagination this book ranks very high indeed, and a study of its internal articulation is a fascinating business for those with the patience and dialectical ingenuity to follow it through. It is not a subject, however, that permits of short

22. Whitehead, *Adventures of Ideas,* pp. 347–48.

and clear statement in a work of this sort. The categories must be explained in some detail and the subtleties required to exhibit their supposed application in, e.g., the extensive continuum are endless. We should, however, expect that in spite of the genius of its author, the system must inevitably prove inadequate to its speculative responsibilities. It is not an easy matter to describe the entities of which everything must finally be true if it is true at all in such a fashion that even a fraction of what we have reason to accept as true can be predicated of them. Whitehead is amazingly fertile in the invention or discovery of metaphysical gadgets with which to equip his ontological ultimates. The process of perception, in order to supply the information that perception must supply if it is to tell us the things about the external world that on Whitehead's view we ought to perceive, develops into a combination of immediate awareness of the causal efficacy of our bodily organs in producing sensa, infallible intuitions of contemporary *space* into which the sensa are projected, and symbolic reference of the sensa thus projected to the objects supposed to occupy this space but themselves apprehended only as the probable successor* of causal antecedents of our bodily states. All this, of course, is ultimately expressible in terms of feelings of feelings—"we enjoy the green foliage of the spring greenly" [23]— and both the green in the foliage and that in our verdantly qualified appreciation of it exist only as characterizing feelers and their feelings. Only feelers feeling greenly the green (and greenly felt) feelings of other feelers are finally appropriate subjects for the green that, as perceptually noticed, appears to belong to trees and plants. It will be evident that the attempt to assess a theory of this kind by an internal criticism of its assumptions and their consequences would carry us a long way from what, in otherwise reliable perception, we find the observable world to be.

Yet there are one or two complications that may perhaps be mentioned, and whose elucidation would be an excellent subject for future doctoral dissertations.[24] One curious consequence of Whitehead's identification of causation

23. Whitehead, *Adventures of Ideas,* p. 321. [Cf. "Annihilating all that's made / To a green Thought in a Green Shade" (Andrew Marvell, "The Garden"). It is almost inconceivable, given his extensive learning and his love of poetry, that Whitehead did not know this poem; his words here seem a reflection of it. Although Murphy often quoted poetry, I do not know whether he knew Marvell. Ed.]

24. There is an admirable work on this subject by John Blyth, which, I hope, will shortly be published. Nothing that has yet appeared as an examination of the structure of Whitehead's *Process and Reality* approaches it in thoroughness and penetration. [Not long after these words were written, this work was published: John W. Blyth, *Whitehead's Theory of Knowledge* (Providence, R.I.: Brown University, 1941), 101 pp., with a foreword by Murphy. This was originally, or is based on what was originally, a doctoral dissertation defended at Brown University in 1936. Ed.]

* The handwritten words inserted after "only as the" can be read either as "probable succession of" or as "probable successor of." Ed.

and "objectification" is that all experience is retrospective, each actual entity being wholly concerned with its causal past. "In order that an entity may function as an object in a process of experiencing: (1) the entity must be *antecedent,* and (2) the entity must be experienced in virtue of its antecedence; it must be *given.*" [25] The whole experience of a subject is concerned with data thus given. It can conceptually prehend and value them, it can contrast their actual characters with those they might have had, it can simplify and transmute, in the more complicated phases of experience it can make judgments about these data, and, finally, it can organize its feelings of them into an aesthetically harmonious whole. But, from first to last, the only *subjects* of its concern are the data given in physical feeling as antecedent actual entities, objectified through the subjects' feeling of their feelings. There is, in fact, something surprisingly Proustian about actual entities; their whole existence is summed up in their effort to get aesthetically adjusted to their past. "All relatedness has its foundation in the relatedness of actualities; and such relatedness is wholly concerned with the appropriation of the dead by the living—that is to say, with 'objective immortality' whereby what is divested of its own living immediacy becomes a real component in other living immediacies of becoming." [26] This is an unfortunate conclusion, since Whitehead also holds that contemporary actual entities, not thus related, form an extensive continuum, and that this is directly apprehended in "presentational immediacy." The attempt to avoid the apparent contradiction of these two views leads to labyrinthine complications and is not, I think, at all successful. For, on his own principles, an actual entity can be concerned only with its own causal antecedents and there is no experiential togetherness in which contemporary actualities can coexist. There must be more in the world, on Whitehead's own showing, than his "actual entities" can contain.

The principle of process, which *identifies* the formal or intrinsic being of an actual entity with its becoming, also causes trouble. An entity aims at a "satisfaction" in which its various feelings will be harmoniously reconciled. But this final achievement is no part of its actual becoming; when it occurs the process of its coming to be has been completed, and the entity *as a process* has ceased to be. The satisfaction would then appear to be no part of the *being* of the entity in question. Nor is it a part of its "objective immortality" or effect, for an actual entity is perceived (prehended) by subsequent actualities as it was, i.e., as a process of becoming, and in this process the satisfaction had no place. So long as the process is going on the satisfaction which is its completion has not been achieved, and it is "objectified" in others as it was when it was going

25. Whitehead, *Adventures of Ideas,* p. 229.
26. Whitehead, *Process and Reality,* p. ix.

on. It simply never did attain a satisfaction as an actual state of its own being, and it cannot correctly be "prehended," even by God, as other than it was. "The notion of 'satisfaction' is the notion of the 'entity as concrete' abstracted from 'the process of concrescence'; it is the outcome separated from the process, thereby losing the actuality of the atomic entity, which is both process and outcome." [27] This is very puzzling. In an entity whose essential being *is* process of concrescence, how can we abstract from the process and have any actuality left? The entity surely *is* not its outcome if in the outcome the process which defined the entity does not exist, and if, moreover, its outcome is simply its objectification for others as it was before it had an outcome. Whitehead seems at times to realize that there is something very curious here. "In the conception of the actual entity in its phase of satisfaction, the entity has attained its individual separation from other things; it has absorbed the datum, and it has not yet lost itself in the swing back to the 'decision' whereby its appetition becomes an element in the data of other entities superseding it. Time has stood still—if only it could." [28] I can only understand this as a whimsical way of saying that the "satisfaction" never actually occurs at all, it is like other entities dear to devotees of process, evermore about to have been. Since the teleology of the universe consists in the striving of actual entities for satisfaction, this seems an unfortunate result. It was, however, to be expected. When actuality is *identified* with process, whatever is not a phase in becoming is thereby robbed of being and becomes an entity which time would have to stand still to actualize—if only it could.

There is evidently a great deal more that could be said on all these points, and it may be that in these comments I have missed some subtlety in Whitehead's construction which would serve to explain away my difficulties. But that, even if true, would have but little bearing on the central thesis of this section. This speculative machinery was intended to be more than an elaborate dialectical construction. It was supposed to contribute to that philosophical understanding of the world which enables us to see its various elements in their appropriate relations. I cannot see that it has done so. It has offered verbal comfort to our all too human tendency to see the world essentially in its emotional relation to ourselves. But it has compromised this satisfaction by extending the meaning of its terms so far that their comforting connotation is no longer legitimate, while without it they lose the "concreteness" which was their primary excuse for speculative authority. It has assured us of the fundamental place of Beauty in the world, and of the rather subordinate but still important status of truth. But in order to justify this it has had to subordinate

27. Whitehead, *Process and Reality*, p. 129.
28. Whitehead, *Process and Reality*, p. 233.

reflective knowledge to emotional insight at its vaguest and least reliable. And its world of actual entities, in their emotional concern for their past and [their] aim at satisfactory feelings about it, remains lamentably remote from the actuality of the world that in practice and tested knowledge we are elsewhere concerned with. By the tests appropriate to a speculative philosophy it appears, therefore, to have failed to justify itself.

Alexander's *Space, Time, and Deity*
The Speculative Requirements

On the face of it, Alexander's speculative undertaking is strikingly different from that of Whitehead. The "ultimate" to which he appeals is, with respect to "concreteness," at very nearly the opposite pole from Whitehead's "actual entities," and the philosophical function it serves is "to deanthropomorphize," to show that there is in nature "a more fundamental plan of which we are only the highest known empirical illustrations,"[29] a plan which has its basis in pure space-time and its progressive fulfillment in an order of emergent qualities to which mind, though so far as we know the latest, is by no means to be the last addition. Deity, the next higher quality in the order of evolution, will not be merely "mental" or "spiritual," but will stand above mind in rank, as mind stands above "mere" life. Within this hierarchy mind is to find its place, definitely lower than the angels. Its capacity for knowing is "an instance of the simplest and most universal of all relations"[30]—that of compresence in space-time. Its mental quality is an exemplification of the character which time, itself the "mind" of space, brings into being at any level of emergent development, a quality at once "new" and reducible without remainder to its "bodily" and finally spatio-temporal basis. Its values are the expression, on the mental level, of "the supremacy of the adapted over the unadapted types,"[31] which finds a particularly lucid illustration in natural selection on the level of biological adaptation. "Realism" here joins forces with naturalism in the demand that mind, and all that is uniquely human, be put in its place and treated as a special but in no wise metaphysically preeminent instance of a structure which nature as such and in virtue of its primordial space-time constitution everywhere displays.

In spite of such differences, however, the structure of the two philosophies is in essential respects the same, and their outcomes by no means as divergent as the identification of the one with "naturalism" and of the other with ontological animism might suggest. We should not be surprised to find irreconcilable differences in the metaphysical ultimates of the two theories. For, after all,

29. Samuel Alexander, *Space, Time, and Deity* (London: Macmillan, 1920), vol. 2, p. 70.
30. Alexander, *Space, Time, and Deity*, p. 82.
31. Alexander, *Space, Time, and Deity*, p. 310.

the considerations that lead a philosopher to identify one feature of the world rather than another as preeminently real are to a large extent preferential and personal; the taste in absolutes is quite as variable as that in styles of art, and while there is endless dispute about taste, the imponderables which actually dictate a decision are very difficult to evaluate in any rational way. Once the ultimate has been selected, however, the intellectual responsibilities of its defenders will lead them along a familiar path. Their absolute must be shown to be capable of functioning as a "concrete" reality in the sense of possessing, in its own intrinsic nature, all that is required to constitute it as "finally" real and the ground for the reality of everything else. This will require a speculative reconstruction in which it loses those characters which distinguished it in its merely limited or contextual application but [which] are judged unfit for speculative hypostatization, and acquires others essential to it as a "final" reality. There is as great a gap between the spatio-temporal events with which Alexander starts and pure Space-Time,* as there is between Whitehead's "actual entities" in their metaphysical concreteness and the (in a different sense) concrete world of human experience. Then it will be essential to show that what *apparently* falls outside the scope of this speculative identification can really or ultimately be derived from or predicated of the ultimates specified. "Mind" is simply a geometrical complication of space-time stuff, and in consequence the distinctive feature of mind must already be present in pure space-time. This makes mind more spatio-temporal than is sometimes supposed, but it also makes Space-Time more like mind. For Time is the mind of space and "all finite existence is alive, or in a certain sense animated." [32]

In a certain sense only, however, for the temporal process analogous on lower levels to "mind" must obviously be more general than what we know as consciousness in our own experience if mind is in this fashion to be generalized. Consciousness is a new quality in the order of emergence, but it is also "ultimately" reducible without remainder to space-time, as it must be if the speculative identification is to be maintained. And it is as difficult to say quite precisely what this generalization actually implies as it was to say what "feeling" in its generalized sense was supposed to convey for Whitehead. For in each case the purpose of the generalization is not *prediction,* in which case precision would be an asset, since it would tell us what exactly we were to expect to find if the theory were true, and how in consequence to test its truth by further observation, but *predication,* the right to attribute what, from other

---

32. Alexander, *Space, Time, and Deity,* p. 67.

* Between "Space-Time" and "as there is," the following typed words appear, lined through though not totally obliterated, possibly by the author, possibly by someone else: "in which instants occupy points in space and in combination with their spatial positions constitute the point-instants which are the limiting cases of motion and the stuff of the physical physical [*sic*] world,". Ed.

sources, we already know, to an ultimate reality which can own all its varied aspects in a simple and satisfying way. For this purpose it is very helpful to say that space-time is already in a certain sense animate, since an animated reality is a more acceptable subject of which to predicate "ultimately" what we observe in living organisms than is one which is in its "final" characters lifeless. A certain imprecision here is a definite advantage, since it enables us to talk of everything in the terms normally appropriate only to rather special sorts of thing and thus to increase our speculative riches by debasing our intellectual or terminological currency. An actual entity that "feels," even if only in the general sense in which the constituent of an ostensibly inanimate object might be supposed to feel, may, for experimental observation, be indistinguishable from one that does not, but it is a far more eligible "actuality" to which to refer the whole nature of the world as we know it. For we must get mind in somewhere, and if to vindicate its genuineness is to show its status in ultimate reality, then ultimate reality must be of such a sort as finally to receive it.

Finally, Alexander's Space-Time, like Whitehead's actual entities, must be many things at once and play many parts. For it is ultimately all there is, and, as all there is, is quite a lot. An *identification* of the whole with one of its more obvious aspects is likely to lead to at least apparent contradictions, and to endlessly ingenious efforts to avoid them. The result is more likely to be remarkable as an heroic effort to avoid the unfortunate consequences of arbitrary assumptions than as a usable contribution to the philosophical understanding of experience, the speculative detour having served to add a fabulous dimension to actuality, to which the rest is very dubiously assimilable, and not, as was hoped, to provide a reliable standpoint for the reasonable organization of what, in non-philosophical inquiry, we find the world to be.

In presenting Alexander's philosophy as primarily a specimen of this type of speculative adventure I am, of course, doing less than justice to its total value. Rereading *Space, Time, and Deity* after a period of a dozen years,* I am again impressed with the fine breadth and wisdom of the mind that constructed it. There is no problem of philosophy that Alexander discusses about which he does not have something original and enlightening to say. The book, one feels, ought to have started lines of inquiry along which a whole generation of more pedestrian inquiries could fruitfully have worked. We and our students should be turning again and again to the titanic work of this great mind for enlightenment. Such, however, has not been the case. Instead, less than twenty years after its publication, *Space, Time, and Deity* stands already as a lonely and rather fantastic landmark in the development of speculative realism, still loom-

---

* This reference suggests that this material was written some time in the period 1937–39 and confirms that it was no later than 1940. Ed.

ing impressively on the landscape, but rarely visited save by industrious PhD's collecting relics of a "movement" already played out and superseded by more modish "trends" in speculative adventure. The reason is plain enough. The edifice, for all its grandeur, was unsoundly built and would not hold together. If it seems ungrateful, in one who profited from the work and greatly venerated its author, to emphasize once more the defects in its structure, the justification must be that great gifts could be put to better uses, and that perhaps, if the principles of speculative construction are understood, we shall in the future be able to proceed more securely.

Space-Time

In the world of natural events we can discern different "orders" or levels of existence. There are matter, secondary qualities, life, mind, intimations of an order higher than mind, and space-time in which all the rest are together and whose pervasive structure is repeated at every level of empirical existence. If we were to look for some underlying plan in terms of which the whole existent world could finally be understood, would it not be in this pervasive spatio-temporal aspect of things that we should expect to find it? In that case, if we follow the route of speculative identification, we should go on to ask whether that space and time, in addition to being empirically pervasive, "may be in some peculiar fashion basic to all being."[33] If this were the case we should have an answer to the perennial problem of metaphysics—the nature of being as such and its essential attributes—and a standpoint from which the empirical diversity of things could be ordered and unified in a remarkable way. If nature in its primary being is space-time, then mind, as a part of nature, is a derivative from, and an instance of, the nature space-time as such possesses. It should then be possible, if we understood the fundamental structure of space-time, to see how a mind is related to its body, to objects known, to the categoreal characters which all things, as spatio-temporal, possess, and to the next emergent quality which, in relation to our own level of existence, will characterize its possessors as deities. The flower in the crannied wall is not, except in a poetic sense, a promising subject from which to discover what God and man are, but space-time seems, in this speculative interpretation, a much more eligible candidate.

The candidate, however, must save itself before it can save others, and for this purpose must put on incorruption in a familiar fashion. It is evident, at this point, that we are leaving the level of spatio-temporal fact in its more ordinary manifestation. That the natural world is spatio-temporal, that this is a philo-sophically significant fact about it, and that much is to be learned by taking this

---

33. Alexander, *Space, Time, and Deity,* p. 30.

fact very seriously indeed, seems true, even on the factual level. The way, for instance, in which our notions of cause and substance are tied up with spatial and temporal relations is decidedly pertinent to philosophical elucidations of the puzzling notion of "substance." Here, however, we are to be concerned with the world not insofar as it is spatio-temporal, but insofar as it is Space-Time, a stuff of which finite things are made, a being which "logically, and in fact, precedes finite things which are differentiations of that stuff." [34] "Just as a roll of cloth is the stuff of which coats are made but is not itself a coat, so Space-Time is the stuff of which all things, whether as substances or under any other category, are made." [35] This would be nonsense if space-time meant simply the spatio-temporal structure of a material world. Things are not made of their positions and relations. Here, however, the spatial and temporal determinations of events have been superseded by point-instants which are pure events on their own account, and a point-instant is the occupation of a point in space by an instant of time. Such occupation is not static, to be sure. A point-instant is the "limiting" form of a motion, and motion—pure motion—is a forward dating of points of Space in Time; it is the change in date of spatial positions. In pure Space-Time the instants differentiate points by endowing them with various dates, while the points lend "togetherness" to time by enabling instants to be repeated at various spatial positions. In this combination, Space is the basis of continuity, and hence, while Space or Time by itself would be a mere abstraction, Space-Time, or pure motion, the structure in which the occupation of points by instants permits of both "togetherness" and "distinctness," is a self-complete reality possessing in its own right all that is requisite for Being as such.

It is hardly necessary to remark that while this conception owes something to the notion of space-time as a physical constant, it is in fact, as Alexander clearly sees, of a quite different order. What is asserted is not that temporal as well as spatial coordinates are required for the location of events, and that the temporal as well as the spatial specification will vary with the relative motion of the observer, though this, of course, is not denied. Alexander is maintaining that instants themselves occupy positions in space, and hence their order does not constitute a new dimension but "repeats" that of the spatial positions occupied. "Time with its distinctive features corresponds to the three dimensions of Space, and in a manner of speech Time does with its one-dimensional order cover and embrace the three dimensions of Space, and is not additional to them. To use a violent phrase, it is spatially, not temporally, voluminous." [36] A

34. Alexander, *Space, Time, and Deity*, pp. 48–49.
35. Alexander, *Space, Time, and Deity*, vol. 1, p. 341.
36. Whitehead, *Space, Time, and Deity*, vol. 1, p. 59.

one-dimensional order could not, to be sure, be voluminous in its own right. The violence is clearer when one says, "Time is spatially, not temporally extended." Or, as Alexander adds, "metaphysically . . . it is not therefore a fourth dimension of the universe, but repeats the other three." [37] The term "metaphysical" here is important. The reason for holding that Time "repeats" the three dimensions of Space is that instants of time have here been turned into literal occupants of space and these, naturally, have the position of the places they occupy, and not independent positions of their own. A table is spatially, not "tabularly," located and extended. And this was necessary because, according to Alexander, in *pure* space-time something must occupy positions to "differentiate" them, and there is nothing but instants of time to do it. I have tried elsewhere to show that the results of this transformation are not happy. Temporal positions turned into spatial occupants lose their status as positions in a *temporal* order, and this metaphysical geometry of pure events becomes a very puzzling affair.[38] The transformation, however, was required by the speculative demands of the system, and its outcome is largely predetermined by the demands for "ultimacy" with which the system began.

The further development for space-time can only be suggested here. Motion is identical with Space-Time; what moves in space is Time itself. There are "perspectives" of space from the standpoint of any instant as located at a point, space from this standpoint being marked out by the lines of advance or motions which lead up to that point-instant, and variously dated accordingly. And there are perspectives of time from a point. Space and Time in this intricate interconnection constitute the matrix of Being and the source of all Becoming. The categories, universality, causality, substantiality, and the rest are the characteristic features of anything just so far as it is made of space-time stuff. We can know, therefore, that the categories will be exemplified in all actual existence, just as we can know that if anything is made of rubber it will stretch. Evolution is accounted for by the inherent restlessness of Time; the qualitatively novel forms of existence are begotten by Time on Space, and are all, in the end, identical with spatio-temporal configurations.

Emergence

The primary device by means of which the empirical diversity of things is reconciled with the underlying identity speculative identification requires is that of "emergence." This notion has played a useful part in recent philosophy

---

37. Alexander, *Space, Time, and Deity*, vol. 1, p. 59.

38. [Arthur E. Murphy, "Alexander's Metaphysic of Space-Time,"] *The Monist* 37. 3, 4 (July, October 1927): 357–84, 624–44; 38.1 (January 1928): 18–37.

and it is necessary to distinguish its present usage from others which might be confused with it. In describing the behavior of living beings it is sometimes useful and legitimate to ascribe to them characters and modes of behavior which could not appropriately be predicated of their physico-chemical elements. If only these elements, as they occur in isolation or in other combinations, were known, it would not be possible to deduce from this knowledge the special qualities or modes of functioning characteristic of the living wholes which, in *this* combination, they constitute. The "emergent" view as a descriptive generalization is, as Broad says, that "the characteristic behavior of the whole *could* not, even in theory, be deduced from the most complete knowledge of the behavior of its components, taken separately or in other combinations, and of their proportions and arrangements in this whole." [39] There is no great mystery about this, in the instances where it is descriptively useful to assume it, though a mystery can be made of it. The characters attributed to the elements of such wholes are those required to explain their behavior as they function in physico-chemical processes. And in such processes, except when organisms of a certain complexity are involved, the specific properties of living behavior are not manifest. There is no need to smuggle vitality into the carbon molecule in order to justify the claim that sentient organisms, as living, behave in ways we should not have expected if we had known only their physico-chemical constitution and not *also* their special modes of organic behavior. Nor is it "superstitious" to suppose that living organisms have ways of behaving which no knowledge of their components would have led us to expect. The question is one for empirical investigation rather than philosophical vituperation to settle. Meanwhile a research biologist is entitled to use such explanatory hypotheses as his specific subject-matter requires without either intimidation from mechanists who find anything nonmechanical "supernatural," or edification from "spiritualists" who accept this "supernatural" as a philosophic revelation. It is perfectly possible that some forms of living behavior may be genetically derivative from non-living matter, without any non-natural dispensation, and at the same time analytically irreducible to them. Moral behavior has developed in a species genetically nearer the ape than the angel, but the nature of morality could not be discovered by observing the behavior of apes, or any interested organisms other than those moved by specifically moral considerations. If "emergence" expresses this theoretical warrant for an inquirer to follow the lead of his subject-matter without preliminary commitments as to the form

39. C. D. Broad, *The Mind and its Place in Nature* (London: Routledge and Kegan Paul, 1925), p. 59.

a good explanation in his field *must* take in order to square with assumptions that the later in evolution is or is not essentially reducible, in its nature and mode of behavior, to its evolutionary antecedents, then there is much to be said for it.

This is not, however, the use Alexander makes of it. In his view there are genuinely new qualities in the world, and it is the special function of Time to bring these qualities into being. But equally, "Each new type of existence when it emerges is expressible completely or without residue in terms of the lower stage, and therefore indirectly in terms of all lower stages; mind in terms of living process, life in terms of physico-chemical process, sense-quality like colour in terms of matter and its movements, matter itself in terms of motion." [40]

The relation between the new quality and the collocation of elements on the next lower level is that of identity. "Mind and its corresponding body are indissoluble and identical." [41] And in other cases, "following the clue of the relation between mind and its body," we "identify the quality with its peculiar form of body." [42] This has proved very puzzling to critics of this view, as is not surprising. If the emergent quality is expressible without remainder in terms of processes on a lower level it is very hard to see what is unique or novel about it, and if we actually *identify* the two the situation becomes even more difficult. It is, of course, true that if "body" here means body with mind, no reduction is required, for the two are identical. But that would not say what Alexander wants to say. Mind in its "novelty" must be identical with body on the level below mind, and so on down, if the final identification of reality with Space-Time is to be secured. It is this speculative identification that causes the trouble, and so long as it is retained I can see no way out of the apparent contradiction involved. If mind is "emergent" in any useful sense then it is *not* "reducible without remainder" to what is not distinctively mental, and it is precisely what is novel in it that is not thus reducible. But it must be thus reducible if we are finally to talk about everything in the terms appropriate to one special sort of thing, namely Space-Time. The hypothesis of emergence serves here, therefore, to enable us to have the matter both ways, to identify the very empirical features of things which are held, in their qualitative novelty, to be irreducibly distinct, and to invoke "natural piety" to justify this questionable procedure. It is very much to be hoped that *this* form of "natural piety," which only extreme devotion to a speculative theory could condone, will not be confused with that

40. Alexander, *Space, Time, and Deity,* vol. 2, p. 67.
41. Alexander, *Space, Time, and Deity,* vol. 2, p. 39.
42. Alexander, *Space, Time, and Deity,* vol. 2, p. 47.

respect for the discovered complexities of existence which "emergence" in the other sense seeks to justify.

Space-Time and Mind

The difficulties one speculative device caused can, however, be alleviated by another, which is its appropriate complement. To *identify* mind with body, and body finally with Space-Time, is not so disturbing after all, if Space-Time itself has a mind-like character. "The body or stuff of each new quality or type of soul has already its own type of soul, and ultimately the body of everything is a piece of Space-Time, the time of which is the soul-constituent which is identical with the body-constituent. Beginning with spatio-temporal finites, there is a continual ascent to newer and more developed existents, so that the course of Time issues in the growth of ever new types of 'soul,' and in this way all existence is linked in a chain of affinity, and there is nothing which does not in virtue of its constitution respond to ourselves, who are but the highest known illustration of the general plan; so that there is nothing dead or senseless in the universe, Space-Time being itself animated." [43]

This situation Alexander sometimes expresses by saying that "Time is the Mind of Space," or, more precisely, "Qualities form a hierarchy, the quality of each level of existence being identical with a certain complexity or collocation of elements on the next lower level. . . . Mind and body do but exemplify, therefore, a relation which holds universally. Accordingly Time is the mind of Space and any quality the mind of its body; or to speak more accurately, mind and any other quality are the different distinctive complexities of Time which exist as qualities." [44] This interpretation is "an extension downwards, made without concealment, of what can be derived from considering mind." [45] It is a natural result of this extension that motion is "the first form of animated body." [46]

This does undoubtedly provide us with the feeling that we understand things better. For all existence is at least verbally linked in a chain of affinity, and it is much easier to "understand" how like can act on or be produced by like than to work out in detail the de facto connection of things. A. C. Garnett has followed Alexander in this matter. The mind-body relation has long been a puzzling one. He believes that in Mind, or in Time which is the mind of the universe, we have "the connecting link which makes their interaction intelli-

43. Alexander, *Space, Time, and Deity*, vol. 2, p. 69.
44. Alexander, *Space, Time, and Deity*, vol. 2, p. 428.
45. Alexander, *Space, Time, and Deity*, vol. 2, p. 52.
46. Alexander, *Space, Time, and Deity*, vol. 2, p. 50.

gible." For "Time is the Mind of the Universe, and time is found in motion as well as in conation. The problem is that of the relation between two forms of process and structure, those of matter and those of will. The difference between these two forms is not that one is mental and the other is not. Mind, or time, belongs to both." [47] I find it hard to see much in this. If we are clear that to call both processes mental is only to say that they both occur in time, their interaction is not made much more intelligible. We knew that much from the start. If we *call* time "mind," and say that both processes are mental since both are temporal, this *sounds* more enlightening, since we have only to deal with one sort of process, mental events, and not two, mental and material. But it only retains its explanatory efficacy so long as being mental is supposed to mean more than just being temporal. If we remember that processes *in this sense* mental may still differ in all the ways in which mind and matter have always been supposed to differ, the "connecting link" is seen to be a purely verbal one. But if we go on to suppose that motion, being temporal, and hence a form of mind, is therefore like mind in some *other* ways that had not been previously anticipated, we shall find no empirical warrant for the view. It is very much as if I asserted that one could conveniently cross the Sahara in a steamboat and offered as evidence the fact that a camel is the ship of the desert and that what is possible for one sort of vessel is *in principle* equally possible for another. So long as we keep to the minimum meaning the verbal identification lacks explanatory value; so soon as it comes to suggest a further affinity it loses all factual warrant. We shall see, I believe, that the assertions of Alexander quoted above belong in this familiar speculative category. They retain their explanatory value only so long as their specific meaning is forgotten.

Thus Alexander holds that each point-instant in pure space-time infallibly "knows" all the rest in virtue of their spatio-temporal connection.[48] Small wonder, then, that mind, when it emerges, should be able to "know" its appropriate objects, knowing being but "an instance of the simplest and most universal of all relations." [49] But what does this spatio-temporal "knowing" amount to? Only being "compresent" with other things in space-time, lying on lines of advance that connect point-instants with each other through the changes of date in points. To know infallibly *in this sense* is just to stand in these spatio-temporal relations. This is really very little help when we come to deal with the kind of knowing which consists in a sentient organism making reliable judgments on the basis of its perceptual observations. Alexander has tried to con-

47. A. Campbell Garnett, *Reality and Value* (New Haven: Yale University Press, 1937), pp. 140–41.

48. Alexander, *Space, Time, and Deity*, vol. 2, p. 200ff.

49. Alexander, *Space, Time, and Deity*, vol. 2, p. 82.

nect the two by showing that all appearances are literal spatio-temporal parts of the external world and thus, that in seeing things as they look to be and are not I am just being together with other objects in space-time, with the added peculiarity, since I am a sentient organism, of being selectively aware of such objects. The attempt is heroic, but futile. Not only must we "misplace" appearances on this view to account for "mere" appearances and illusions, but we must actually misplace places, which are the ultimate substances to which "appearances" belong. And that is really very difficult.[50]

The point is, of course, that the kind of "togetherness" that constitutes knowledge on the human level involves relations, like that of "appearing," which have no place in the togetherness of point-instants in their purely space-time relations. The attempt to treat the former on the basis of the latter is, when worked out, quite misleading, and when left on the level of general verbal association, an incitement to loose thinking and illusory speculative satisfactions.

Again, if motion is a form of animate body, it is no wonder that an organism, which is a complex of motions, is alive. But the animation of motion amounts merely to the fact that points are changing their dates, and thus that there is a restlessness in pure space-time which, if this theory is correct, eventually brings forth beings "animated" in the more usual sense. The "source" of novelty is the time in which all things are produced, no doubt, but the source only in a very tenuous sense—the condition without which nothing could change or be produced. In the same way time is the source of war and peace, and everything else. The observation is more poetic than informative, unless it is linked with Alexander's speculative hypotheses, and in that form it is very difficult to find any evidence of its truth.

Nor is it exact to say that the relation of mind to body is in any very important respect like that of time to space. "Mind and its corresponding body are indissoluble and identical. Space and its Time are in like manner not two things but one, and there is no Space without Time nor Time without Space."[51] Alexander elsewhere holds, of course, that Time is not identical with Space; if it were it could not differentiate it or play the distinctive role which enables Alexander to speak of Time and not Space as the "source" of movement. If any one of these striking statements were taken in the sense it would have to possess to be of speculative use in identifying things we know to be different, it would be false, or rather, nonsensical, since it would attribute to points and instants characters and connections which, as points and instants, they could not possibly possess. If they are reduced to the sense they must bear to be even possibly

50. I have discussed this fully in "Alexander's Metaphysic of Space-Time," *The Monist*, cited above, note 38.

51. Alexander, *Space, Time, and Deity*, vol. 2, p. 39.

true, the assertions that there is change in the inanimate world and that this change is more closely associated with its temporal than with its purely spatial character, that organisms that behave mentally are physical bodies and hence certainly spatio-temporal, that the organism that thinks is the very same organism that is a physical object, though its thinking is not a physical property of it, and that mind is like time in that mind is a novelty in the natural world and time a source of novelty, are innocuous, but inadequate. It is to such considerations that we must appeal if we are to give the hypothesis any reliable sense. Yet we must, by speculative transformation, import into them a different meaning, if we are to make a metaphysics of them. We can, as a result of this transformation, observe with a show of sense that a sentient organism ultimately is a piece of space-time, that in this space-time "configuration" the unique mental constituent is identical with an arrangement of instants among points and that such point-instants know infallibly the whole space-time universe, such knowing consisting in the spatio-temporal togetherness of the entities concerned, thus exhibiting "knowing" as a pervasive natural relation. This, I take it, is a very model of speculative identification, the use of an equivocal terminology to suggest a metaphysically satisfying conclusion which the facts adduced do not warrant, but which can be deviously derived from them by a systematic misapplication of terms.

It would be profitable to consider Alexander's theory of value, and his brilliantly imaginative philosophy of religion. These, however, would add nothing new, though they would, I believe, substantiate the account so far given of this philosophy as a speculative system. And to this we must for our present purpose confine ourselves.

The Confusion of Tongues in Russell's *Neutral Monism*
The World of Physics and the World of Sense

As an advocate of "scientific method" in philosophy, Bertrand Russell may seem to stand at a considerable distance from the speculative undertaking we have just been considering. And in some of his philosophical moods he has criticized such speculations very pointedly. His attempt, however, to "analyze" mind and matter into "entities which are metaphysically more primitive," [52] and to unify our knowledge by showing that the statements made in physics and psychology are ultimately about such "entities" and the manner of their interconnection, follows the same pattern as do the theories of Whitehead and Alexander: [this attempt] involves the same sort of contextual distortion, speculative identification of the *ultimate* existents in terms of which physics and psychology are true, and terminological virtuosity which, by making statements about one type of object in the terms appropriate to another, lends an

---

52. Bertrand Russell, *The Analysis of Matter* (London: Allen and Unwin, 1927), p. 9.

appearance of profundity to assertions which, in fact, are incurably confused. If it can be shown that, in this very different context, the structure we have found elsewhere to be characteristic of speculative philosophy is verifiably present, and productive of just the consequences anticipated, our hypothesis will be substantially confirmed.

In *The Analysis of Mind* Russell formulated his doctrine of "neutral monism" as follows: "The stuff of which the world of our experience is composed is, in my belief, neither mind nor matter, but something more primitive than either. Both mind and matter seem to be composite, and the stuff of which they are compounded lies in a sense between the two, in a sense above them both, like a common ancestor." [53] Or, "mind and matter are neither of them the actual stuff of reality, but different convenient groupings of an underlying material." [54]

We must be critically attentive at once when such expressions as "the actual stuff of reality" confront us. We know the sense in which woolen goods is the "stuff" of which coats are made, and in the previous section we encountered a more questionable sense in which Space-Time was alleged to be the "stuff" of all existence. The outcome of that investigation, however, was to suggest that when divorced from its more reliable applications and put to speculative uses, "stuff" is more closely linked with nonsense than even colloquial usage might have led us to suppose. An intelligible meaning *may* be assignable to the term "stuff of reality" such that it will be significant and possibly true to say that electrons are *made up* of groups of ultimate particulars of which our percepts are the only members directly known to us, and that these same percepts constitute the "stuff" of mind. Until it has been assigned, however, we shall not know what the author is talking about or what, beyond a vague sense of profundity, his remarks are intended to convey.

Actually, of course, so competent a thinker as Russell has something in mind when he makes these statements, and intends to use them in a theory which will clear up philosophical problems of some importance. In order to see what this usage is, however, we must begin our inquiry on a more empirical level. It has always been one of Russell's primary concerns to establish an intelligible connection between "the world of physics" and "the world of sense." The connection wanted is one that will harmonize what from physics we know about matter with what, introspectively and behavioristically, we know about mind, and, what is more important, will enable us to see how perception, as psychologically described, can afford the kind of evidence we require as empirical verification of the truth of statements in the physical sciences. This last point, for Russell, is fundamental. "All empirical evidence consists, in the last analy-

53. Bertrand Russell, *The Analysis of Mind* (London: George Allen and Unwin, 1921), pp. 10–11.

54. Russell, *Analysis of Mind*, p. 35.

sis, of perceptions; thus the world of physics must be, in some sense, continuous with the world of our perceptions, since it is the latter which supplies the evidence for the laws of physics." Hence, if we want to understand the empirical basis of physical knowledge, "we must . . . find an interpretation for physics which gives a due place to perceptions; if not, we have no right to appeal to the empirical evidence." [55]

Now this seems to be a fairly straightforward problem. We are asking for the empirical evidence that physical hypotheses are true, and for an "interpretation" of physics which shall enable us to give this evidence in theory the weight we do in any case attach to it in practice, i.e., in the procedures of inquiry in the physical sciences. Ought we not to give as straightforward an answer? The empirical evidence for physics is just the observable facts to which physicists themselves appeal, the results of laboratory experiments, for example, as confirmation of their theories. And the reason for supposing that this evidence is reliable is that it is based on perceptual observation, under controlled conditions, of the behavior of the very objects about which reports are made, in this instance the objects that exist in laboratories, and whose behavior can be fairly closely inspected. To give "a due place to perceptions" is here to recognize that perceptual observation is a normally reliable means for discovering how objects behave under some conditions, and provides a sound empirical basis for checking the factual adequacy of hypotheses whose consequences can, in this way, be compared with the occurrences which ought, if they were true, to confirm them. The "world of sense," so far as it serves as the empirical basis for physics, is that part of our bodily environment open to perceptual inspection. The "world of physics" is those features of it which are described abstractly and schematically, but in a way which so far corresponds to the facts as to be capable of impressive verification by the physical sciences. The epistemological connection between the two required in order to make our cognitive claims "intelligible" is simply that observed objects can suggest to an inquiring mind hypotheses about the behavior of objects on remoter and more minute levels which can be indirectly confirmed by further observation. And the physical connection is just whatever in the physical sciences is found to be the structure and causal interrelation of the objects investigated. Such, as the outcome of the chapter on "Perception" indicated, is a sensible answer to Russell's question.* It will be observed that it requires no reference at all to the ultimate stuff of reality.

This, however, is not at all the answer that Russell is prepared to give. It

55. Russell, *Analysis of Matter,* pp. 6, 7.

* The "chapter on 'Perception'" referred to is original chapter 5, "The Problems of Perceptual Knowledge," not included herein. Ed.

would, from his point of view, be a very naive and unsatisfactory one. We must not credit the claims of perception until we have analyzed it to see what is "really" given, and what, on the basis of this, we can really suppose the physical world to be. What is wanted here is not the sort of "datum" physicists actually employ, but a more *ultimate* datum to which, in epistemological stringency, we ought to resort. And the information about the physical world we shall get in this fashion is not the sort the sciences give us, but something more "concrete." For considered as physiological and mental events, percepts will turn out to be parts of the stuff of our brains, and thus "by examining our percepts we obtain knowledge which is not purely formal of the matter of our brains. This knowledge, it is true, is fragmentary, but so far as it goes it has merits surpassing those of the knowledge given by physics." [56] The most "concrete" statement we can make about electrons is that percepts are, in some cases, among the ultimate particulars that make them up.[57] Thus we are offered introspective knowledge (since it is in introspection or "self observation" that percepts as sensible events are most certainly known) of the concrete and ultimate constituents of the material world. Such knowledge would indeed have merits surpassing those of physics, but we must be speculative philosophers to appreciate them. If this shifting of the problem of the empirical warrant for physical hypotheses from the context in which the connection is in fact established in inquiry to that in which percepts, as directly observed events, are supposed to belong as constituents to material objects whose "stuff" they constitute, proves to be philosophically enlightening it will have justified itself in operation. If it does not, it must be pronounced an unwarranted distortion and dislocation of elements in our experience contextually identifiable and in their contexts reliably connected. But whether justified or not it must at least be clear that the shift has been made, and that it is only on the new level which Russell's philosophical preconceptions have determined that "neutral monism," as a theory about the way in which events introspectively observable can be constituents of material objects and thus provide immediate and concrete knowledge of the "stuff" of the physical world, has a significant application. It answers the question initially, and reasonably, asked by proffering a theory according to which non-physical knowledge (i.e., knowledge not derived from physical inquiry) can be had about the concrete or ultimate stuff of physical objects, knowledge which will tend to show that such objects are qualitatively much more like the data of introspective psychology than physics itself gave us any reason to suppose. If we also hold that the only epistemologically respectable data for physics are such sensory events, this assurance will be encouraging,

56. Russell, *Analysis of Matter,* p. 382.
57. Russell, *Analysis of Matter,* p. 320.

for it will assure us that we are not making such a very big assumption in supposing a material world to exist, since this world, after all, is not very different in respect of some of its ultimate constituents from what our data themselves are known to be. Theories or constructions of this sort will, as Russell says, "have the merit of making the inference from perception to physics seem more reliable, since they save us from the necessity of assuming anything radically different from what we know," [58] though of course they will not be certified by any recognized principles of scientific inference. Whether this seeming reliability can be made out in the actual constructions offered, and whether, at its best, it would be more than the speculative shadow of the actual reliability which perception as observation and physics as empirically grounded inquiry actually possess, remains to be determined.

The Perceptual Data

What is actually given in perceptual observation? This is a question to which some attention has already been given,* but it will be necessary to refer to it again if the nature of Russell's philosophical ultimates is to be understood. An astronomer is said to "observe" the position and general appearance of the planet Jupiter as seen through his telescope. But he may be mistaken in this observation, in any one of a variety of ways. Thus, "when we think we see Jupiter, we may be mistaken. We are less likely to be mistaken if we say that the surface of the eye is being stimulated in a certain way, and still less likely to be mistaken if we say that the optic nerve is being stimulated in a certain way. We do not eliminate the risk of error completely unless we say that an event of a certain sort is happening in the brain; this statement may still be true if we see Jupiter in a dream." [59] It follows, therefore, that what the observer *really* observes when he supposes himself to be seeing external objects is an event in his own brain, since this is all that is certainly happening when his perceiving occurs. The rest is mere hypothesis. Hence the paradoxical but natural consequence that the aspects of matter we most reliably observe are not external to our bodies, but events in our own brains. When a physiologist is dissecting a brain, his percept is an event in his own brain, not in the one supposedly observed. The latter is the remote causal antecedent of the former— and about this antecedent only abstract and mathematical knowledge is scientifically available. "The physiologist sees what he is observing only after the light waves have reached his eye; therefore the event that constitutes his seeing

58. Russell, *Analysis of Matter,* p. 271.

59. Bertrand Russell, *Philosophy* (New York: W. W. Norton, 1927), p. 132 [Published in England as *An Outline of Philosophy* (London: George Allen and Unwin, 1927), p. 138. Ed.].

* This question is discussed in omitted original chapter 5, "The Problems of Perceptual Knowledge." Ed.

comes at the end of a series of events which travel from the observed brain into the brain of the physiologist. We cannot, without a preposterous kind of discontinuity, suppose that the physiologist's percept, which comes at the end of this series, is anywhere else but in the physiologist's head." [60] The crucial point here, of course, is the shift from the physiologist's ostensible datum, the observed brain, to "the event which constitutes his seeing" as the *ultimate* datum for perception, on the ground that this alone is certainly actual when the perceiving occurs. Now "all verification of causal laws consists in the occurrence of expected percepts. Consequently any inference beyond percepts (actual or possible) is incapable of being empirically tested." [61] Here at one stroke the meaning of empirical has been altered from "perceptually observable" to "occurrent as a percept," and it is thereupon assumed that whatever is empirically warranted in the first sense must have its whole basis in what is "empirical" in the second. Thus "the facts of physics, like those of psychology [and, of course, of physiology as well] are obtained by what is really self-observation." [62] Such percepts, in their immediate givenness, are "sensa" or sensations. "The passage from these sensations to nerves and brain as physical objects belongs really to . . . the theory of physics, and ought to be placed in the reasoned part, not in the part supposed to be observed." [63] All that is actually observed is sensation or percept, as an event, and our whole empirical warrant for physics must be found in "the connection" we can establish between such events, as data of self-observation, and the objects of physics. If this line of thought is accepted, we cannot expect to ground the scientist's knowledge *empirically* in the way he himself would expect to do so, in the course of his scientific business. Since he "really" has for empirical data only events occurring in his head we must ask him how from self-observation thus interpreted he proposes to get the evidence he needs to establish, say, a physical theory. He will hardly be prepared to answer, since the query so disorients the whole basis and intent of his inquiry as to be insoluble by its means. But Russell is prepared to answer for him.

The Causes of Our Percepts

He proceeds on the assumption that, since percepts are events, we can gain from an observation of their nature and the order of their occurrence, some information as to their causes. "In drawing inferences from percepts to their causes, we assume that the stimulus must possess whatever structure is possessed by the percept, though it may also have structural properties not pos-

---

60. Russell, *Philosophy*, p. 140 [*Outline of Philosophy*, p. 146. Ed.].
61. Russell, *Philosophy*, p. 290 [*Outline of Philosophy*, p. 301, Ed.].
62. Russell, *Philosophy*, p. 172 [*Outline of Philosophy*, p. 180. The bracketed phrase is Murphy's. Ed.].
63. Russell, *Analysis of Mind*, p. 299.

sessed by the percept. The assumption that the structural properties of the percept must exist in the stimulus follows from the maxim 'same cause, same effect' in the inverted form, 'different effects, different causes,' from which it follows that if, *e.g.,* we see red and green side by side, there is some difference between the stimulus to the red percept and the stimulus to the green percept." [64] There is thus a formal or structural correspondence between effects and causes, but this tells us nothing about the intrinsic nature of the cause. In fact, "the only legitimate attitude about the physical world seems to be one of complete agnosticism as regards all but its mathematical properties." [65]

This is a conclusion worth keeping in mind, and we shall later see that Russell might well have been faithful to it. Obviously, it is a long way from statements as to what the ultimate stuff of the physical world, as known in self-observation, concretely is. But just as obviously, it takes us only a little way. *Some* structural correspondence mathematically expressible could be established between our sensations and *any* sort of external reality, between, for instance, McTaggart's society of spaceless and timeless persons related by eternal love and their perceptions of each other which are misperceived as sense-data. If we really knew no more than that about material objects we should know much less about brains, nervous systems, light waves, and the space-time relations of sensations and other brain events than Russell throughout *The Analysis of Matter* regularly supposes himself to know. Insofar, however, as such knowledge is based on what a brain or any other material object looks or acts like when it is observed, and this, in turn, is not further "empirically" grounded in the relation of percepts as brain-events to their inferred causes, it has no empirical warrant. It is no wonder that, having substituted for perceptual observation reasoning about the otherwise empirically unknown causes of percepts, we should have no basis left for the scientific view of the material world which perceptual observation indicates and supports.

How Percepts Are Inside Our Heads

There is, however, one ray of hope. It is reasonable to suppose that our percepts are inside our heads, and that there is this one point at least at which we have "concrete" and "non-formal" knowledge of physical nature. "Whoever accepts the causal theory of perception is compelled to conclude that percepts are in our heads, for they come at the end of a causal chain of physical events leading, spatially, from the object to the brain of the percipient." [66] And it would, as previously observed, involve a "preposterous kind of discontinuity"

64. Russell, *Analysis of Matter,* p. 400.
65. Russell, *Analysis of Matter,* pp. 270–71.
66. Russell, *Analysis of Matter,* p. 320.

to suppose that the effect was anywhere in physical space-time save at a place contiguous to that of its cause. It must be remembered here, though Russell himself seems to have forgotten, that the causal theory of perception now has two rather different meanings. One is that which physiological psychology, working with the view of the material world which perceptual observation warrants, normally affords. The other is that to which Russell himself has been driven, which assumes *some* structural or formal correspondence between effect and cause and, beyond that, professes complete agnosticism. To say that in physical space-time "the percept must . . . be nearer to the sense-organ than to the physical object, nearer to the nerve than to the sense-organ, and nearer to the cerebral end of the nerve than to the other end," [67] will have a different meaning, according as one or the other of these interpretations is accepted. In the first sense it sounds very enlightening, and seems to locate percepts very comfortably in a world of material things. But if one looks for the percept somewhere between the cerebral end of the nerve and the other end, he will assuredly not find it there. He will, in fact, on Russell's theory, find no nerve or brain at all, but only more of his own percepts. Whether the causes of his percepts are in space at all we do not know, nor what interpretation of "in" and "nearer" ought to be given to make the statement quoted say what is true. To be "in" the brain in the only sense in which Russell's theory has given us any reason to suppose that percepts are there, namely to stand in some structural correspondence to otherwise unknown causes, is not a very substantial sort of physical relation.

How, then, *is* the percept in the brain according to Russell, and what epistemological or speculative enlightenment can we derive from this location? It is clear that to say that it is "in" it simply in the way in which an effect must be in the same region as its cause gets us nowhere until some further meaning has been assigned to the causal relation than that which Russell in his "formal" mood is prepared to offer. And it is not at all clear how he can beg* the causal theory of perception in the more usual sense as a basis for our knowledge of the external world when his own theory has undermined the empirical basis of this causal theory. It is further patent that, even when this more empirical causal theory is assumed, our percepts are not in our heads in the way in which our brains are there. They could not be located there by any process of physical or physiological investigation. They do not take up space there, or qualify other entities that do. They must, in short, be "there" in some other sense, and it remains to be seen what this sense is and whether it can offer any aid and

67. Russell, *Analysis of Matter,* p. 383.

* I am not certain "beg" is the word wanted, but that is how I read the handwritten word inserted at this place in the typescript; of course it will do. Ed.

comfort for the connection between percepts and material objects that Russell must establish to provide even the semblance of plausibility for the claim that perception, as he interprets it, provides knowledge of physical objects.

The Constituents of Matter

One way in which the relation between percepts and physical objects is further expounded by Russell is encountered when he says that percepts or sensations are constituents of the matter of the brain. It might be supposed that since the material constituents of a material object are in the place where the object is, the *ultimate* constituents of matter are in the place where the material object is, and that in knowing them we are knowing the "concrete" nature of the thing at that place. This supposition, however, requires careful examination in the light of the meaning which "constituent" in this usage must have. If this light, however fitful, proves sufficient also to indicate the sense in which self-observation can supply concrete information as to the inner nature of electrons, we shall be able to proceed with circumspection in this dark subject. In *The Analysis of Mind,* Russell said that "the ultimate constituents of matter are not atoms or electrons, but sensations, and other things similar to sensations as regards extent and duration." [68] And in *The Analysis of Matter* he holds that "a percept is an event or group of events, each of which belongs to one or more of the groups constituting the electrons in the brain" [69] and that "our percepts and 'mental states' are among the events which constitute the matter of our brains." [70] Now, to say that the ultimate constituents of matter are not electrons but sensations *sounds* like saying that the sum of 7 and 5 is not 11 but 12, that is, as though the solution offered were the correct answer to a question for which an incorrect answer had been given. It is in fact much more like the statement that the United States is made up not of mountains, plains, and sea-coasts but of the psychological ties that bind its people together. In the sense in which a piece of matter might be supposed to be constituted of electrons, it could not possibly be made up of sensations; just as America is not geologically formed of democratic good will in the way in which it is made up of contiguous parts of the earth's surface. This may appear to be a trivial point, but it is quite fundamental. For Russell seems frequently to suppose that when he says that matter *is* made up of such entities as percepts he is giving a more profound or ultimate answer to the question usually answered by saying that it is made up of protons and electrons. And that would be speculative nonsense. It may be possible to translate statements about electrons into statements about

68. Russell, *Analysis of Mind,* p. 121.
69. Russell, *Analysis of Matter,* p. 320.
70. Russell, *Analysis of Matter,* p. 322.

sensations "without loss or gain of meaning," as some analysts hold, but what would then be said about sensations would not be that they stood to each other, and to material objects, in the relations in which electrons had been supposed to stand. Until a meaning for "constituents" which says exactly what Russell means by it in his usage has been specified we have no right whatever to assume that the ultimate constituents of matter stand to it in one sort of spatial relation rather than another, or, indeed, in any spatial relation at all.

The "Aspect" Theory

Russell's earlier view about the perceptual constituents of matter was that they are what would usually be described as its appearances, connected together according to the laws of perspective. Each such perspective aspect or appearance is "in" two places, the place of the perspective from which it appears, and the place of the object of which it is a constituent, since it is a member of the group [of aspects] which together *are* the object. A percept can be said, on this interpretation, to be at the place where a brain is, meaning that it is the appearance an object not a brain (unless it is another brain that is being observed) has from the place where there is a brain. It would seem only a short step from this to the conclusion that since the percept is at the place where the brain is, it is in the brain. And if this seems odd, we can add that it is "in" it as one of the constituents which together constitute the brain. But this will not do. For the constituents of the brain *in this sense,* its perspective aspects, are not at the place where the brain is at all. The appearance at that place is a constituent (aspect) of an object at another place, and the constituents of the brain itself are the aspects which from other places, it has, and which are not where it is, but where the brains of other percipients are. The appearances "where the brain is" are therefore in this theory not constituents of the matter of the brain, and its constituents are its aspects from other places. In short, the percepts that are said to happen "in a brain" are not among its perspective aspects and hence not the constituents of the "matter" of the brain itself; they are the aspects of other things as, by the aid of a brain, one is now able to observe them.

On this interpretation, to say that we know "concretely" what a material object is would be to say that we are aware of what, e.g., it looks like, and that this reveals what it is, since this aspect together with others obtainable *are* what it is. There would be no question here of knowing matter "from the inside" or getting at its ultimate stuff in the awareness of our own brains. For the "stuff" of matter is simply what it appears to be, and we know this, as a rule, much *less* adequately and concretely in the case of our own brains than in that of externally observable objects. The percepts "constituting" it would, obviously, not be its inner elements, as electrons might in some sense be supposed to be, and there would be no need whatever to take an agnostic attitude toward the material world in respect of its non-formal elements, since these would be of all things most readily open to inspection.

The "Event" Theory

In his later philosophy Russell has abandoned the principles of this theory without giving up its terminology and implications. He now treats sensible appearances not as aspects of observable objects but as events happening to a percipient and in a brain. These events can be said to constitute the brain in the sense that they make up its history and it simply is the events that would usually be said to happen to or in it. This puts the whole matter in a quite different light. In the earlier theory percepts were parts of the physical world because they were constituents of the object perceived, in the later, because they are constituents of the percipient, happening in his body. In each case there is an intersection of physical and mental causal lines, and the percept, as a member of each, is neither, exclusively or in itself, and hence is neutral between them. But previously, it was the aspect of, e.g., a penny, which, as an aspect, was one of the constituents of the penny and, as experienced, an element in the biography of the perceiver. Now it is the occurrence of a percept which as happening in or to a brain is part of the history of the brain, one of the constituents that "make it up," and also is, as a sensation, a link in a chain of experiences. The percept is still a constituent of matter, but of a different piece of matter, and in a different sense of "constituent" than before.

Can this latter theory yield a valid interpretation of Russell's view that percepts are elements in the "stuff" of reality? In this case we are defining a thing as the group of what would ordinarily have been called its "states," and by this, Russell holds, "we alter nothing in the detail of physics." [71] Perhaps not, but we alter a great deal in the substance of neutral monism. Can it be said that a percept is an event in the history of an electron in a human brain? Only in a very dubious sense. When Russell wants an illustration of an "event" in the history of an electron he instances the scintillation that occurs when it comes in contact with a material object like a screen. It is this sort of event which is referred to when the causal laws of electronic behavior are stated. The fact that the sentient organism of which this electron is a constituent is perceiving something, and that the percept occurs as an effect of the responsive behavior of the organism in question is, if we choose, an event in the history of the electron, but a rather remote one. To suppose that it discloses in any peculiar way the stuff or inner nature of the electron is as plausible as the supposition that the Roosevelt administration's devaluation of the dollar is a peculiar disclosure of my inner nature since it happens to a political organization of which, in a sense,

71. Russell, *Analysis of Matter*, p. 284.

I am part, [and that it] is therefore an event in my history and a constituent of the "stuff" that makes me what I am. There is no objection to anyone speaking in this manner if he chooses, but unless he is choosing to be oracular or obscure it is difficult to see much point in it.

More particularly and fundamentally, however, the relevant consideration here is that to say that percepts are *in this sense* parts of the stuff of the material world, is to say very little indeed. They are what happens when a sentient organism is stimulated and responds in a particular way and are thus elements in the history of a material object—the sentient organism itself. There is no reason at all, however, to suppose that they afford a good guide to its content as a material object. On the contrary, since so far as we can tell they are what happens only to a very special and complex sort of material object, it is rather likely that the other events that make up the history of this object, or the electrons in it, are considerably different from those that have this special connection. We find these peculiarly interesting, of course, for they are the empirical clue to what is going on elsewhere. But they serve thus as clues, not as samples of "concrete" elements in the "stuff" of material things; [they are] only effects of material objects from which, by the aid of perceptual observations of the further behavior of such objects, some probable knowledge of their causes may be gained.

The Speculative Dividend

In other words, and to make a long story as short as possible, all that this theory, precisely interpreted, can tell us is that from the nature of perceptible events and the manner of their occurrence we can learn something of the nature of their causes, and of the events occurring or likely to occur elsewhere. But there were two (at least) very different ways of saying this. One was to refer directly to the observations on which our knowledge of brains, nervous systems, and the physical world is based, and inquire how far these warrant the conclusions they are supposed to support and how our knowledge of, e.g., brains is likely to be further extended by further research into their nature and manner of functioning. This was in one sense "unphilosophical," since it accepted the general reliability of perceptual observation [and] the probable truth of physics, and asked only how each is to be understood in its relation to the other, physics in its empirical reference, perception as a means of exploring the physical world. Its merit was that it appeared to make sense of their actual interrelation and thus to answer the question as to the connection of physics and perception originally asked.

The other and ostensibly more profound way was to reduce perception, for the sake of ultimacy, to self-observation, and to regard the physical world as simply the cause of such percepts, a cause not otherwise perceptually known.

The result was to leave us without the information on which our knowledge of the external world is normally based, and to lead to the futile effort to find some other and more "concrete" source of information about it. This was to be done by indicating a special relation of percepts to brains, a relation in virtue of which they were peculiarly endowed to provide information as to the ultimate stuff of the physical world. This relation has now been seen to owe all its speculative efficacy to the use of a terminology which suggests conclusions to which its users are by no means entitled. The percept was to be very close in physical space-time to its antecedent brain event. But this did not serve to locate it physically, nor even to indicate what, in a causal world known only in its formal "structure," "very close" could mean. It gained a meaning only when the ordinary and observationally grounded relation of sensation to its cerebral conditions was assumed, and then it served not to locate the percept in the brain in the sense in which its physical parts are in it, or to provide any other information about it than that conveyed by saying that it had a brain state for its proximate cause. The percept, again, was to be an ultimate constituent of the matter of the brain. If this was intended in the sense in which electrons are constituents of it, the claim was nonsensical. If it was intended in the sense in which the aspects of an object may be said to be constituents of it, it was clearly false. If it was intended in the sense in which a thing is constituted by its history and the effects it produces are thus constituents of its physical nature, it is quite trivial, since the particular constituents or effects in question can be supposed to provide knowledge of the further "stuff" (history) of the physical thing in question only insofar as they enable us to infer its nature in the usual way. It is only when it bears something of all these senses at once, borrowing from the agnostic strain the suggestion of a "concrete" nature for matter not scientifically discernible, from the aspect theory the sensible "constituents" of matter which would allow percepts to constitute this concreter nature, and from the "event" theory the connection with the brain which would make location in it a certificate of membership in the physical world, that it can even begin to bear its speculative burdens. Since these senses are incompatible, it cannot, even thus, be expected to bear them far.

All the plausibility that the account finally possesses, then, it borrows from the accepted reliability of perceptual observation and scientific theory, and from the capacity of the former to provide empirical evidence for the latter. In lifting the discussion to the heights of speculative ultimacy, in which the ultimate stuff of reality is disclosed by the percept as a constituent of matter, no progress has been made. The speculative version has not added one iota of intelligibility or clarity to the previous diagnosis. What it has done is *first* to create an illusory difficulty by reducing perceptual observation of material things to self-observation of mental and brain states, in the interests of an arbitrary theory of knowledge, and *second* to offer an illusory satisfaction by talking about percepts as though they possessed a status as "constituents" of matter, to which in fact they are not entitled. The first step tends to shake our confidence in processes of inquiry which are better grounded than anything else we know and which ought reasonably to be trusted. The second invites us to take sensible effects for ultimate constituents of the physical world. Their combined effect is thus to disorganize and disorient our knowledge in an unnecessary and misleading way. At the end of the process we know no more, and by no other means, than we knew before. We have simply employed a set of concepts which promise more than they can perform without losing all reliable meaning in an effort to alleviate the discomfort in which a mistaken analysis of perception had left us, and to bestow an irrelevant blessing on processes which find their actual warrant elsewhere. And this, I take it, is the normal method and outcome of a speculative solution of our cognitive problems.

Sellars' "Physical Realism"
The "Ontological Concept" of the Brain

With [Roy Wood] Sellars' version of the theory that consciousness, "the total field of a person's experiencing," including both mental processes and "content" (visual, auditory, etc.) is in the brain, we can deal much more briefly. Compared with Russell's devious doctrine, it is straightforward and clear. It is developed in support of an "evolutionary naturalism," and is an attempt to connect mind with its organic basis and natural environment in a way which shows it genuinely to be a part of nature. Sellars is anxious to do justice to the distinctive characters of mind and also to place mental functioning unmistakably within the physical world. The motive is a reasonable one; the task is pursued with much learning and a thoroughness and brings to light much that is of interest in relation to the organic conditions of conscious behavior.

I am here concerned with the theory only as a variant of the type of speculative identification of "the real," and [the] consequent demonstration that whatever is actual is predicable of or localizable in the "reality" thus identified. To show, in the philosophy of "physical realism," that mental behavior and mental "states" are parts of the natural world, it is necessary to locate consciousness *inside* the organism as a physical object. This is imperative because Sellars holds that "[t]he physical is but another term for *being*—for existence." [72] Again, "That which is physical is real, and that which is real is physical." [73] This, obviously, is a speculative identification in our sense, as the terms "real" and "being" indicate. If it were successful it would accomplish a considerable simplification of philosophical problems. To locate "consciousness" in nature would then be to place it inside of, or adjacent to, some physical

---

72. Roy Wood Sellars, *The Philosophy of Physical Realism* (New York: Macmillan, 1932), p. 6.
73. Sellars, *Physical Realism*, p. 13.

object or objects. And in knowing it, as we are peculiarly able to do in introspection, we should be knowing the physical objects to which it belongs in a unique way and should at last possess that introspective knowledge of physical objects which has already been seen to have remarkable speculative attractions.

The *prima facie* difficulty with this identification and consequent speculative enlightenment is that there is another use of the term "physical" in which it is not true that all that has "being" or that we need philosophically to take account of, is physical. That is, we can distinguish the physical properties of an object, as these are identified first in practical manipulation and later and at a different level in the physical sciences, from others which are not in the same sense physical at all. When we speak of the brain as a physical object we may be referring to what it is insofar as (a) it is a material space-occupying object inside our heads and spatially related to the skull, spinal column, etc., and/or (b) it is found to be "composed" of more minute entities, molecules, atoms, and finally electrons and protons. When it is said that all visual data, by which Sellars means all that in any literal sense is seen as colored and extended, are in the brain, we must not suppose him to mean that they are in it as it is in the head or as brain cells are in the brain. If we are to regard the brain as the "reality" to which consciousness belongs, we must speak of it in a way quite different from that which would be appropriate when, in the more ordinary scientific sense, we describe it as a physical object. Sellars is quite explicit on this point. Consciousness, we are told, is an event "adjectival . . . to the organism"—"the qualitative dimension of a brain-event." [74] This receives further elaboration: "If we assert that visual data are *in* the visual center of the brain, we must make it clear that the 'inness' here is of a kind peculiar to sense-data in their relation to the brain, an ontological 'inness' which we may indicate by such phrases as intrinsic to the brain, a feature of the *content of being* of the brain, a *quale* of a brain event." [75] It is because of this special manner of ontological occupancy that we "participate in the being of brain-events. Here, and here alone, are we, as conscious beings, on the inside of reality." [76]

It is recognized that the physical sciences lack this special access to physical reality and hence can supply us with no assurances of being thus on the inside of reality. Thus, "science cannot taste, or participate in, the veritable substance of physical systems; and, if our own experiencing suggests to us that the organism does have a sentient tang and a conscious dimension, there is nothing in science to contradict it." [77] Hence we are justified in "an enlargement of the ontological concept of the brain beyond that which grows up in us when we

74. Sellars, *Physical Realism,* p. 414.
75. Sellars, *Physical Realism,* p. 415.
76. Sellars, *Physical Realism,* p. 414.
77. Sellars, *Physical Realism,* p. 421.

are completely dominated by the kind of descriptive knowledge the external sciences contribute." [78] And thus we come once more to the conclusion that "in each one's consciousness he *participates in* that physical reality called the brain." [79]

Now all this has a very familiar sound. We start with the statement that the natural world is physical, and this sounds important. For in the sense in which we can scientifically identify "the physical" it is true that "mind," "consciousness," and their kin are functions of a sentient organism which is a physical object, and that the nature of this organism as sentient and conscious depends on its structure as a physical object, and more particularly, on the structure of the brain and nervous system. To realize that human consciousness, so far as we know in any reliable way of its existence, is existentially dependent on this sort of physical structure and could probably not occur without it is to reach a philosophically important conclusion. But speculatively we wish to go further. If the physical is in this sense fundamental, may it not be the final reality for which philosophers have looked? Should we not identify it with *being* itself? But if it is all there is, then consciousness must be physical too and, like all that is physical, occupy a place in the space of material objects. It does not appear to do so, by the usual tests. But if we enlarge our concept of the physical, provide ourselves with a brain with ontological as well as physical dimensions, we shall be able to say that the "inness" of consciousness in the brain is an ontological inness and thus we shall have reached our speculative goal, though by means of a detour with which we are now familiar. Just as "feeling" must be more than feeling, "space-time" more than space-time, and the "stuff" of matter more than its material composition, so here "the brain" must develop into an ontological object that physics and physiology know not of, but whose "reality" we can taste and participate in by enjoyment of our own mental states. And thus while reality may all turn out to be "physical," it will not be physical in the way in which the physically identifiable properties of things are so.

Now, as was previously observed, there is no *a priori* objection to an extension of terms with a known use beyond the context on which that usage depends for its meaning, *provided* that a new meaning is assigned to them and that we can in some way identify the objects to which they are now supposed to apply. If some spatial relations more complicated than those ordinarily dealt with could be discovered between sense-data and physical objects like brains, we should be glad to hear of it. And if we could find out by introspection something about our brains that we should not otherwise have known the information will be welcome. What would be disastrous would be a proffered

78. Sellars, *Physical Realism,* p. 415.
79. Sellars, *Physical Realism,* p. 415.

usage which provided the *semblance* of intelligibility by allowing us to speak of mental states *as if* they were physical and of introspection *as if* it were inside information on objects physically identified, but borrowed all its cogency from a meaning of "physical" and "knowledge" to which, in this extended sense, it was by no means entitled, thus achieving a verbal unification at the cost of literal applicability and determinate contextual meaning. It remains for us to determine whether Sellars' ontologizing of physics and physiology belongs to the latter sort of enterprise or to the former.

The Relation of "Ontological Inness"

A red sense datum, Sellars tells us, is in the brain *as an event* adjectival to the brain, and its relation to the brain as a physical object is such that in being aware of it we know the brain *from the inside* and "participate in its being." These are the statements we want to understand. Some clarification is necessary. An event is usually said to happen *in* a location when it happens to something in that location. If I say that a murder happened in this room, I mean that it happened somewhere and to something in the room. Is a red sense-datum something that happens to a brain or some part of it? Not in the sense that the brain or any part of it becomes red, or that any physical object in the place where the brain is becomes red. On the contrary, "a sense datum is in the brain participatively and not as a surface quality known." [80] Nor is it one of the events which in their mutual relations *constitute* the brain as a physical object. Sellars is definitely opposed to any attempt to reduce physical objects to events in that fashion. Nor, of course, is it there in the sense in which my toothache is *in* my tooth, so that the place at which the physiological happening is located is correlated with the place at which a feeling is sensibly located. If asked to point to the place where the seen red was I should certainly not point to my head as, if asked where my toothache was, I should point to my tooth. To what other method of location can we appeal? Sellars offers a suggestion. Consciousness, he tells us, is "ontologically inseparable from the kind of integrative patterns and processes which are taking place in the brain and which we call nervous or mental almost interchangeably." [81] And this connection is such that "careful introspection should disclose the mode of working of the brain." [82] This relation we must further explore.

"Ontological inseparability" is a hard concept. I am inclined to think that much that Sellars has to say, and all that physiological psychology will warrant, could be expressed more accurately in terms of *existential* inseparability. If

---

80. Sellars, *Physical Realism*, p. 436.
81. Sellars, *Physical Realism*, p. 441.
82. Sellars, *Physical Realism*, p. 410.

mental states have brain states as their indispensible antecedents, then mental states cannot occur unless a physical brain is functioning adequately, and they may in a loose sense be said to be "adjectival to," i.e., dependent on, the brain. Moreover, a knowledge of mental states would be a source of information as to the nature of the brain, since from the nature of the effect we can sometimes make probable inferences as to the nature of the cause. In the same sort of way President Roosevelt's political charm is existentially bound up with his vocal powers and, once the correlation was established, I might be able from a knowledge of the charm disseminated to determine, even if I had not heard him, whether the President was still in good voice. It would, however, appear excessive to add that in some further sense the effect was adjectival to its cause, or that a knowledge of it enabled me to participate in the *being* of its cause. Obviously, then, this sort of existential dependence and causal correlation are not all that is meant by ontological inseparability and introspective awareness of physical being.

Yet when I try to find out what *more* than this the alleged connection is supposed to be I am quite baffled, unless I accept the hypothesis that it is simply this relation dubiously described in the terms that would lend color to the speculative identification with which Sellars began, but for which there is no empirical warrant. An "ontological inness" would then be seen to be simply a relation which is not one of location in any of the more usual senses at all, but one of existential dependence spoken of as though it were a relation of spatial inclusion or occupancy in order to warrant the conclusion that the *being* of consciousness is physical and as such participates in the *being* of the physical object on which it obviously is causally dependent. This has the advantage of suggesting that the world is one in a fashion we should otherwise hardly have suspected, but it has the disadvantage that this suggestion is supported solely by a dubious terminology whose vestigial meaning is carried over from a context in which, as thus extended, it has no reliable application. It therefore permits us to be speculatively instructed only as long as we remain conceptually confused.

There is still the claim, however, that in introspection we know physical reality "from the inside." Here the outside-inside contrast has reference to the abstractness of the scientific account of the brain as compared with the immediacy and concreteness of our acquaintance with mental states. This contrast is a genuine one, and there is no doubt that in introspecting mental states we know more ultimately what *they* are than, by external observation of a brain, we know what *it* is. The question is, however, whether in knowing our mental states we know more concretely *what a brain is* than in knowing what, e.g., physiology can tell us about it. Sellars, in making the claim, spoke of participating in the *being* of the brain, tasting its veritable substance. This, unless it implies a mystical theory of knowledge as identification of knower and known, seems to me very misleading. For surely, the only way we can taste a substance is to taste its flavor and the only way to feel its inner nature is to feel its feelings—if it has them. This tells us what its taste is, what its feelings are, and what *it* is, qua tasted and felt. It does not tell us what its *being* is, and, indeed, it is hard to see what merely human cognitive process could convey that information.

Now, if a brain has sentient experiences or mental states, then in being aware of these we are aware of the brain as sentient. But what we are then aware of is not the "inner" nature of the brain as physical but its feelings as sentient. It would seem to me much more accurate to say that the organism has feelings than that the brain as a physical object includes them as occupants adjectival to its being. But even if the latter locution is preferred, it still remains the case that in enjoying these feelings we learn what "the brain" is only so far as it feels or is sentient, and what *else* may be true of it as a physical object is to be discovered by the usual process of causal correlation. And in the case of physical objects which are not *also* sentient, there is no good reason to suppose that any such "inner being" exists. In plain language, awareness of the mental states of a physical object that is also sentient provides information as to the mental experiences of a physical object, and, *directly,* nothing else, whatever. Indirectly, and by causal correlation, it provides probable knowledge of the physical structure required to produce these mental states. But that the physical structure thus known has for its inner reality the sort of qualitative content introspectible in mental states there is no reason to suppose. The "physicalizing" of life and mind has here, as usual, led to the ascription of an "intrinsic" reality to physical objects for which there is no evidence, in order that we may be able to predicate of such objects, as *speculatively* or *ontologically* physical, characters which, in their empirically reliable manifestation, they do not possess.

It may be that in this exposition I have missed some further meaning Sellars' theory could be given, and in terms of which the ontological "inness" of consciousness in the brain and the introspective knowledge of the inner being of physical objects can have some securer cognitive status. Here, as always, the account given is to be treated as an hypothesis the reader may test for himself in further inquiry. I conclude this section by summarizing the interpretation of Sellars' theory I am offering. If I am right, the speculative structure of this theory is the following: it is to be proved that to be is to be physical. This will not work if "physical" retains its common sense or scientific meaning. Hence "physical" must *ontologically* mean more than this, and a "more" that physics and physiology, by their external methods, cannot locate. This something more is the *being* of a physical object but not its being (in the normal sense) as physical. What then? In the favorable case in which we get at it directly and *participate* in its reality, it proves to be its *being* as sentient. But if its being as sentient is its *inner* being, then in apprehending this we are participating in the reality of the physical object itself, and not merely in the sentient experience of the special sort of physical object which happens also to be sentient. Hence mental states as felt are participatively in the physical brain as an ontological reality, and consciousness, in this peculiar sense, is "in" the brain. Whether this conclusion is to be regarded as a contribution to our reliable knowledge of the physical world, or as the illegitimate offspring of the unhappy mating of physical fact with metaphysical verbiage the reader must decide for himself.

McTaggart on "The Nature of Existence"
Personal Idealism

The main conclusions to which the intricate and elaborate reasonings of *The Nature of Existence* finally lead had been stated and defended by McTaggart many years earlier as the reasonable outcome of the Hegelian Dialectic which he then accepted and, with great ingenuity, defended. That the universe must be spiritual and righteous was taken as proved by Hegel's Logic. The final category of that logic, the one that must be applied to all to which the category of Being is applicable, on pain of dialectical contradiction, is that of the Absolute Idea, and this, rightly interpreted, assures us that "Spirit is ultimately made up of various finite individuals, each of which finds his character and individuality by relating himself to the rest, and by perceiving that they are of the same nature as himself. In this way the Idea in each individual has as its object the Idea in other individuals." [83] Only in such a system of related individuals can the requisite unity of Reality be combined with the requisite differentiation. These individuals, being themselves "spiritual" centers, are "persons," and we conclude that "the only eternal reality is related persons." [84] The relation between such persons is further seen to be that of love—"passionate, all-absorbing, all-consuming love." [85] For "it is by love only that we can fully enter into that harmony with others which alone constitutes our own reality and the reality of the universe." [86] Persons, thus related, have no beginning or end in time; *sub specie temporis* they must be held to have existed previously to their present life, and to be due for endlessly continued future existence. In its

---

83. J. McTaggart Ellis McTaggart, *Philosophical Studies* (London: Edward Arnold, 1934), p. 214.

84. J. McTaggart Ellis McTaggart, *Studies in Hegelian Cosmology* (Cambridge: University Press, 1918), p. 53.

85. McTaggart, *Philosophical Studies*, p. 223.

86. McTaggart, *Philosophical Studies*, p. 266.

own nature, however, this Reality is changeless, and the apparent temporal change must be taken as a manifestation of the eternal character of that which is timelessly real. These conclusions are held to be spiritually very good. They agree with and elucidate the doctrine that the world must satisfy every demand our nature truly makes upon it.

In *The Nature of Existence* McTaggart departed to a very considerable extent from the method of his earlier works. The logic by which he proceeds is orthodox, not dialectical, and the analytic devices employed to facilitate its progress owe more to Russell and Moore than to the British Hegelians with whom McTaggart had formerly been associated. Yet the destination finally reached is the familiar one. The world consists of persons, eternally related in all-absorbing love, and of nothing else whatever. Time is unreal, but the order misperceived as temporal is such that each eternal person appears to have an endless existence through all time, so that it is *as* true to say that I have existed before and will exist after my present life as that I exist at present. And the states of myself that appear as future culminate in a good so great that the heaven of orthodox belief is in some respects a poor thing compared with it. To know this, again, is very good, but we are warned not to let our hope that it may be so at any point relax the rigor of our critical analysis. Reason and reason alone must warrant this desirable conclusion. It is fortunate that there are at least two quite different ways by which it does so, the Hegelian already noted, and the speculative deduction now to be examined.

Our concern with McTaggart is not primarily with his conclusions, impressive though they are, nor with the elaborate development of his reasoning, which Broad has expounded with such care and at such length in his *Examination of McTaggart's Philosophy* that there is no excuse for a less tireless critic to make a long story longer. There are, however, certain features of McTaggart's procedure which shed considerable light on the methods and consequences of speculative philosophy as we have so far been considering it. The fact that in other respects his theory is, as will be obvious, very different from those of Alexander and Russell makes their agreement on essential points a striking illustration of the way a speculative system retains its spots even, to mix the metaphor, on a horse of another color.

The Requirements for Existence

The primary step in such a speculative undertaking is the identification of the "reality" in its own right "ultimate" and the exclusive basis for everything else that claims in any sense to be real. McTaggart's method differs from that of Whitehead and Alexander in that while they explicitly start from some aspect of the experienced world and generalize this, he bases his demonstration on characters and relations which anything existent must possess, and these are arrived at not by examining particular sorts of existence, an empirical procedure in which McTaggart has but little confidence, but by contemplating the evident truth of certain very general propositions about substances, their "parts" and "sufficient description" and deducing the consequences which follow from these propositions about the nature of everything that exists. It is only after the general structure of reality has been securely settled that we turn to the question of the particular sort or sorts of entity there may be in which this structure is exemplified. It turns out that disembodied persons related in timeless love provide the only eligible exemplification of it that we can even imagine, and that it is in consequence very likely that they, and they alone, are "real." But this is not supposed to have anything to do with the decision as to the structure existence must have. Thus in McTaggart we encounter a more ostensibly *a priori* determination of "reality" than any so far encountered.

Whatever exists, we are asked to see, must be a substance, or a group of substances, or a part of a substance, or a quality or relation of substances. A substance is that which has qualities and stands in relations without being itself either a quality or a relation. It is held to be evident that all substances have parts that are substances and that any substance is thus infinitely divisible in at least one dimension. It is further evident, though hard at first to see, that substances, being diverse, must be dissimilar as well and that every substance must have a description that applies to it alone and is specifiable in terms of its original qualities and relations. This requirement, however, proves to be incompatible with the infinite divisibility of substances unless we assume that a relation of "determining correspondence" holds which is such that a sufficient description of any substance can be secured when its place in a determining correspondence system has been specified, and that this specification can be made without a "vicious" infinite regress. The statement of what a determining correspondence system is like is extremely abstract and difficult to follow. It finally becomes clear, however, that a system of persons perceiving their own perceptions, other selves and their perceptions, with an intensity, directness, and adequacy which makes "love" the most appropriate term for the connection, would be a determining correspondence system, and that nothing else that we know of would be. Nothing that is material, or temporal, or spatially extended would meet the requirement; hence it is impossible to hold that anything whatever, even the data of direct perception, can actually be temporal, material, or extended. It is therefore necessary to hold that the perception of anything as changing, extended, or colored (since color presupposes extension) is a misperception, and thus the greater part of our experience, in its most empirically insistent characters, simply a mistake. This may appear to be hard doctrine, but there is held to be no logically possible alternative to the recognition that existence *must* have the characters in question and that nothing material, temporal, or extended can have them and, as McTaggart long ago observed, "Nobody ever broke with logic, but logic broke him."

Now this is a very formidable conclusion to have reached with so little empirical evidence, and we cannot but wonder at it. So much to have come from so little, and, in a different aspect, so little from so much, since from all the empirical richness of the universe only disembodied persons and their all-absorbing perceptions and emotions appear to have survived.

How, more precisely, has the substitution of this anaemic but emotionally potent changeling for the world of natural existence been achieved? Clearly, everything turns on the evident truth of such propositions as that every substance must have parts that are substances and hence be infinitely divisible. Here "substance," it will be recalled, is *anything* that has qualities and stands in relations without being itself a quality or relation. A sneeze is in this sense a substance, and so [also] is a perception, and we are later asked to believe that every perception has "parts" in this sense to infinity. Is it evident that a self is a substance which has parts, that perceptions are parts of such substances, capable of endless division? Is it even clear that "part" here has the same sense as that in which one could say, as McTaggart does in a favorite illustration, that Great Britain is a substance of which the counties of the island kingdom are a set of "parts"? Can we know a priori that every substance in this very general sense must have a "sufficient description"? For those who find the further pursuit of these inquiries a fruitful subject, Broad's commentary will provide a useful guide. What he shows in detail, and what a hastier critic might have concluded with less elaboration, is that the general notions here employed are extremely vague and that when any possible precise meaning is given them there is no sufficient, nor even any plausible, reason for supposing that existence must be a determining correspondence system in McTaggart's sense. And that is fortunate, too, since it was pretty clear on the empirical evidence we elsewhere regard as trustworthy that it is not.

A Priori *Knowledge or Tenacity of Belief?*

A particular instance of McTaggart's procedure, which does not involve the machinery of "determining correspondence," will illustrate his method. It can be shown, he believes, on quite unshakable evidence, that time is unreal, in the quite straightforward sense that nothing can have the characters it must have to be an event in time, or a change or a process, without self-contradiction, hence that nothing *has* these characters, and that in consequence we are mistaken in perceiving anything as temporally earlier than, simultaneous with, or later than anything else, or in believing that anything has ever occurred, changed, or ceased to exist. The evidence for this is that any event in a temporal series must possess the temporal characteristics of presentness, pastness, and futurity, and that nothing can have all these characters, since they are incompatible.[87] It will not do to say that an event *was* future, *is* present and *will be* past, and that there is no contradiction in this. For being present must be analyzed into having the character of presentness at a moment of "present" time. But every moment in the series of events is present, past, and future as well, and if we say of it that it is present in present time, past in past time, and future in future time the difficulty simply recurs on a new level. At no point are we allowed to say of anything that it *was* past or *will be* future with primary reference to the "now" directly apprehended. We are compelled to say that it *is* past or *has* pastness, and since of anything that has pastness in this temporally unqualified sense, it is also true that it has presentness and futurity and that these are incompatible, there is no way out of the dilemma. Broad states the position clearly. McTaggart "assumes that what is meant by a sentence with a *temporal copula* must be completely (and more accurately) expressible by a sentence or combination of sentences in which there is no temporal copula, but only *temporal predicates* and non-temporal copulas." [88] Thus it seems to be a contradiction to say that an event *has* pastness, presentness, and futurity, while there is no contradiction in saying, in the sense we normally understand, that it *is* present, *was* future, and *will be* past,* where the verb has a definitely temporal sense, *unless* it is assumed that these statements *must* be philosophically translated into McTaggart's self-contradictory substitute and hence that "time is unreal." The regress McTaggart finds vicious "arises because there remains at every stage a copula which, if taken as non-temporal, involves the *non-temporal* possession by a term of certain temporal predicates which could belong to it only *successively.*" [89] There is, of course, a problem in trying to generalize the meaning of "now" when in fact it has a specifically "indexical" element and can be understood only in its use in specific transactions of communication. It *sounds* like a contradiction to say that "Queen Victoria is *now* alive" is a proposition that was true and has in the course of time become false. Actually, however, what a person was asserting if he said, in 1890, "Queen Victoria is *now* alive," has not become false, and what I should be asserting if I said today "Queen Victoria is now alive," was never true and never will be. What is asserted in

87. See McTaggart's argument in *The Nature of Existence* (Cambridge: University Press, 1927), vol. 2, ch. 2, and [C. D.] Broad's discussion of it, *Examination of McTaggart's Philosophy* (Cambridge: University Press, 1938), vol. 2, part 1, pp. 309ff.

88. Broad, *Examination,* p. 314.

89. Broad, *Examination,* p. 314.

* After some hesitation I decided that this is, or may be, just what Murphy intended to say. However, if not, the requisite shift is obvious. Ed.

each case is understandable only when the relation of the assertion to the situation *indicated* by the speaker is understood, as, in its context, we all do understand it. So equally the "*is* present" of the assertion McTaggart finds contradictory is a temporal "is" and not the timeless "is" of the historical present which he attempts to substitute for it. The contradiction has arisen only as the result of an inept analysis, arbitrarily imposed.

What is noteworthy here is not that the "reality" of time has been rescued, but that McTaggart was prepared to maintain the analysis he offered even at the cost of surrendering the most empirically reliable facts we know, that we perceive ourselves as temporal beings in a world that changes. Such allegiance to ostensible *a priori* necessity, even when it conflicts with the whole run of experience, evidences a remarkable state of mind. It may be described as devotion to "reason." But it is more justly described, I think, as sheer tenacity of belief, refusing to reexamine its preconceptions even when confronted with their evident inapplicability to the subject-matter concerned. At no point in the argument, long and infinitely ingenious as it is in *The Nature of Existence,* does it seem seriously to occur to McTaggart that the fact that the notions of "substance," "whole and part," "sufficient description," and the like cannot be applied without self-contradiction to anything whatever that we empirically know or scientifically discover, might indicate that there is something seriously wrong with these notions so far as they are supposed to apply to what actually exists. They were, after all, derived from *some* sort of commerce with the world, even if only that which the study of traditional metaphysics and a strong feeling for the values of personal affection provides. If they prove, in speculative elaboration, to lay down requirements which nothing but the "substances" of traditional metaphysics, united by the ties of affection which McTaggart finds extremely valuable, can meet, that may quite possibly testify as much to the poverty of the initial experience and to a trained incapacity to be instructed by further knowledge of the world, as to the profundity of the speculative insight involved. Even "persons" have to be made over, disembodied, eternalized, and deprived of the power to make judgments and assumptions in order to become elements in a determining correspondence system, for judgment and assumption have not the directness the relation specified demands. But without one deviation into empirical good sense we move relentlessly on to the system which Hegelian logic and McTaggart's conviction of a spiritual universe had long since marked out. Is it not at least fairly probable that the concepts and assumptions required to bring about this happy outcome owed their cogency in McTaggart's mind as much to their association with the "spiritual system" with which he started and to which he clings throughout, as to their *a priori* necessary application to all that actually exists? If this were so we should have once more, and in a striking form, the speculative *identification,* here most elaborately bolstered by *a priori* evidence, of all that exists with the particular sort of existence the philosopher is inclined to prefer, and the consequent conclusion that everything that exists *must* really be this if it is to be anything at all. The reader must judge for himself, and from a closer examination of the system than is here possible, whether this is not in fact the case.

Reality and Appearance

The dislocation of experience produced in this philosophy by its speculative identification is impressive. Not only must we say that there is no material world and that nothing exists in time, we must go on to say that insofar as we perceive anything given as extended, colored, or changing, we are misperceiving it. Our errors in these matters cannot be laid to mistakes in judgment, since on this view there are no judgments, or supposals, and to perceive one's own state of mind as a judgment is to misperceive it. "When we say that a perception appears as a judgment, we mean that another perception perceives it as a judgment." [90] Since there can *be* no judgments, this is of course a misperception, and the extent of this misperception of what one could hardly have supposed himself to be mistaken about in his own experience is alarming. I may suppose myself to judge a man to be very evil and to hate him accordingly. Actually, however, I do not hate him at all, or make any judgment about him. My actual relation to him is one of perception or misperception and "when a perception appears as a judgment, assumption, or imagining, with certain emotional and volitional qualities, we have no reason to suppose that the perception has those qualities." [91] We have, on the contrary, good reason to suppose that it has not. For in ultimate reality, which is all the reality that there is, the emotional relation between "substances" is one not of hatred but of love.

Consider, then, the judgment that every substance must have parts that are substances and so on endlessly. Might I have been mistaken even about this? It is now clear that I was mistaken about it if I supposed it to be a judgment, or to assert anything, or to be other than a timeless misperception of a self or part of a self. It certainly seemed to be a judgment occurring in time and *about* entities many of which are not perceived at all. If I could be wrong in supposing it to have these characters *might* I not also be mistaken in supposing that what it *appeared* to assert is self-evidently true? No, says McTaggart, for when a perception is misperceived as a judgment this misperception is partly true and partly false. And it may be that only the part that is true is noticed. Then the

90. McTaggart, *Nature of Existence,* vol. 2, p. 300.
91. McTaggart, *Nature of Existence,* vol. 2, p. 335.

inaccurate perception appears as a completely true judgment. And it is on such that, in the ruins of perceptual observation and introspection, we must rest our confidence.

Yet even the self-evidence of perception, to which judgment has been reduced, is radically compromised. For if anything *seems* evident it is the temporal character of what we perceive. And yet about this we are always mistaken, according to McTaggart. Now, "No one has ever asserted that the self-evident correctness of a perception meant more than that it was self-evident that the perceptum was as it was perceived *while* it was perceived. If time is unreal, this must be restated in order to get a proposition which is not merely phenomenally true, but really true. And in that case there seems nothing improbable about the theory that the reality which appears as a perfectly correct perception occurring at a certain time is really a timeless perception which is only partially correct." [92] This seems to mean that if we can be mistaken about the fact that our perceptions are temporal we can be mistaken about anything and that what *seems* most reliable by all ordinary tests can nonetheless be radically mistaken. When it is recalled that the correction of our perceptions is here made on the basis of a theory about what we *really* perceive, [which theory] owes its cogency to such propositions as that the perceptions of the parts of a whole are parts of the perception of the whole, the full disorientation of the criteria of knowledge will be evident.

The Good Time Coming

It may be said, however, that McTaggart's system is not in this respect essentially different from any other reasoned view of the world. For "no philosophy—with whatever intentions it may have set out—has been able to treat the Universe as being what it appears to be." [93] And if the outcome of this philosophy is in one respect disconcerting it is in another highly significant and comforting. For it assures us that reality in its ultimate nature is very good, and that the order of existence, misperceived as temporal, is such that each of us will appear to exist through all future time and to achieve a culminating state which will appear to begin and never end, and which if not wholly good is at least overwhelmingly better than the present. "If we know that we shall, in a finite time, reach an endless state which is infinitely more good than bad, we know what is doubtless a very important fact—perhaps the most important fact— about the future." [94] We know that our lives are approximating to a "reward," a final good, that they will reach, a state in which we shall know nothing but

92. McTaggart, *Nature of Existence,* vol. 2, p. 341.
93. McTaggart, *Nature of Existence,* vol. 2, p. 341.
94. McTaggart, *Nature of Existence,* vol. 2, p. 473.

love. The early Christian hope of a good time coming when time shall be no more is thus substantiated, though perhaps not in a form which they would have wholly appreciated. McTaggart's most serious doubt about the validity of his theory seems to be inspired by the fear that it is too good to be true.

This optimism, however, is pretty clearly based on a mistake. We do *not* know, if this theory is correct, that we shall reach this happy state, but only that we shall *appear* to do so. The reality underlying this appearance is a timeless series of misperceptions, of which our "present" experiences are members, ordered from less to more adequate in a sense which makes the less adequate appear to be past and the more adequate to be future, and having as a final term a perfectly correct perception, with all the happy insight such a correct perception enjoys. What I actually know, therefore, if I accept McTaggart's argument, is that my "present" experience is an eternal and incorrigible misperception in such a series. I cannot think that *this* constitutes good news, or, whether true or not, [that it] is too good to be true.

As McTaggart observes, "It is very difficult to get anything like a clear idea of what a timeless and eternal state of consciousness would be, since we always in our present state misperceive states of consciousness as being in time." [95] Now, on his theory, "we"—if we identify ourselves with what in present experience we find ourselves to be—shall never be in any other state than this, nor achieve any more satisfying relation to the selves of which we are eternally part and which, in respect of their timelessly correct perceptions, are eternally very happy indeed. Such a timeless self seems capable of a remarkable degree of mental dissociation, since the only elements in it of which "we" shall ever be conscious are misperceptions coexisting with correct perceptions of the same objects and possessing no evidence, save that which McTaggart's philosophy provides, that they belong to a larger spiritual unity which is eternally very good. The "I" with which I empirically identify myself has no such satisfactions and never will have, and small comfort is to be got from the assurance that it will *appear* to have them, since only McTaggart's philosophy gives us this assurance and it equally provides us with the evidence that what renders the appearance comforting is simply a mistake.

This fairly obvious implication of the theory is missed by McTaggart through a liberty of speech which he allows himself but to which he is not entitled. Instead of saying that the self appears to have an endless existence, he says that it "has, *sub specie temporis,* an endless existence." [96] And when he is arguing for immortality he observes: "It is as true (of the self) that it exists endlessly in future time as that it exists at the present. Neither sort of existence is real but

95. McTaggart, *Nature of Existence,* vol. 2, p. 456.
96. McTaggart, *Nature of Existence,* vol. 2, p. 376.

there is an appearance of each which is a *phenomenon bene fundatum.* And I think it would be generally admitted that if it is as true that I shall live endlessly in the future as that my body will die at some future time, then I may properly be called immortal." [97] But this would be generally admitted only so long as we supposed that the one statement was surely true and the other, therefore, being as true as it, was also true. It is no assurance to be told that what we want to believe is as true as something else commonly held to be true if we are also told that this something else is false.

As for the *phenomenon bene fundatum,* McTaggart himself has insisted that "it is essential to remember that what is phenomenally true is not really true, but really false," [98] while the foundation for the "appearance" is a relationship which guarantees no other fortune for our "present self" than what it now and eternally possesses, that of being in some way which it is extremely difficult to understand a set of misperceptions in a changeless self whose happy state in other parts and as a whole has curiously little bearing on anything that, in these incurable misperceptions, we are at all able to identify.

The point I wish to make is that empirical actuality here has its revenge on the speculative system that superseded it. So far from McTaggart's "reality" being something finer and more desirable than the world we know, it is only by borrowing from this world and its temporal "appearances" a suggestion of the possibility of a real future progress to which it is not at all entitled, that it is able to maintain the significance its author attaches to it. This is more apparent still in the case of McTaggart's eloquent remarks about "love." What the relation that exists between timeless disembodied selves and their parts, and the selves that perceive or misperceive them, can be, I find it hard to see. But it must in any case be something almost unimaginably different from the fellowship of men that perish, and the creaturely complex but very precious ties that grow out of common appetites and needs and shared purposes and meaning in a changing and risky world. I could not, for my own part, regard the assurance that my experience was a part of a self which in this metaphysical fashion loved others and was loved by them as more than a most unlikely statement about a highly questionable and humanly unimportant relationship. It *seems* to be more, because we forget that "love" as we ordinarily value it is, for better or worse, a thing very different from this and, I suspect, a far more valuable one.

The pattern we expected of a speculative philosophy is here completed, down to the final irrelevance of "reality" to the very experience it set out to dignify with ontological preeminence. The speculative discovery that the world is made up of nothing but persons and their mutual affection is not a substantial addition to our knowledge, nor one that can clarify experience and enlighten

97. McTaggart, *Nature of Existence,* vol. 2, pp. 188–89.
98. McTaggart, *Nature of Existence,* vol. 2, p. 206.

practice. It is simply an elaborate way of speaking about everything as if it were a case of personal love. That does not tell us more about everything, since most of what we know is found not to have the character in question and to be non-existent in consequence. Nor does it tell us more about personal affection, or how we can understand it better and value it more justly, for in this speculative transformation the thing we valued and needed to understand has become unrecognizable and incredible. It is, in fact, so far as I can see, to tell us nothing at all that has any reliable application outside the talk in question, or any profounder insight to offer than that of the incongruity between the dialectically ingenious consequences of tenaciously maintained stipulations about existence on the one hand and the manifest nature of the observable world on the other. Which of these is to be accepted as genuine and which rejected as "appearance" is an issue of philosophical good sense on which the verdict, I believe, is not difficult to reach.

C. S. Peirce on "The Logic of the Universe"
The Categories
No philosopher of recent times has criticized more searchingly the attempt to base philosophy on deductive reasonings from self-evident principles than has Peirce.* Equally pointed and cogent is his rejection of the "ultimates" to which metaphysicians traditionally appeal and of the certainties, arbitrarily maintained, which block the path of inquiry. In these respects Peirce's theory of the role of hypotheses in reasoning, and of the kind of explanation that a logical survey of our means of knowing would lead us to expect a sound philosophy to provide, promises to serve as a useful antidote to the speculative vagaries we have so far been considering. If, in spite of this promising approach to the subject, and in spite of the impressive logical acumen of Peirce himself, the result of his speculative venture proves to be unhappily similar to those already examined, we shall be led to conclude that the factors which actually determine the development of such a philosophy are more fundamental than the logical machinery indicates, and that these factors, here as elsewhere, have their fruits in an equivocal and untenable verbal substitute for reliable knowledge. It is this conclusion that the following analysis serves, I believe, to warrant.

Peirce's theory of the nature of a good philosophical explanation has its basis in his account of the pervasive categories which, he holds, are exemplified in all phenomena. These he denominates, not very happily, "firstness," "secondness," and "thirdness." Any phenomenon, anything at all on which conscious attention can be directed, can be considered simply for what it is in itself, as a "first"; in its *de facto* connection with any second thing with which it is in fact

---

* As previously indicated, chapter 3, "Peirce's Pragmatic Metaphysics," can be regarded as a preface to this section. Ed.

connected, in abstraction from* any reason which might or might not be found for the connection, as a second; or, in respect of the law or reason which it manifests, as an instance of mediation or "thirdness." Feeling is offered as the obvious instance of "firstness," and, Peirce tells us, "by a feeling I mean an instance of that sort of element of consciousness which is all that it is positively, in itself, regardless of anything else." [99] Brute fact or force is his favorite instance of secondness. "It may be said that there is no such phenomenon in the universe as brute force, or freedom of the will, and nothing accidental. I do not assent to either opinion; but granting that both are correct, it still remains true that considering a single action by itself, apart from all others, and, therefore, apart from the governing uniformity, it is in itself brute, whether it show brute *force* or not. . . . In like manner, if we consider any state of an individual thing, putting aside other things, we have a phenomenon which is actual, but *in itself* is not necessitated. It is not pretended that what is here termed fact is the whole phenomenon, but only an element of the phenomenon—so much as belongs to a particular place and time." [100] Of thirdness, or "efficient reasonableness," we shall hear much as the discussion proceeds.

It should be born in mind that the distinctions thus introduced do not appear, at this stage, to refer to distinct sorts of entity which are, in their own nature, exclusively "firsts," "seconds," or "thirds." On the contrary, Peirce says explicitly, "The universal categories . . . belong to every phenomenon, one being perhaps more prominent in one aspect of that phenomenon than another, but all of them belonging to every phenomenon." [101] And again, "Not only does Thirdness suppose and involve the idea of Secondness and Firstness, but never will it be possible to find any Secondness or Firstness in the phenomenon that is not accompanied by Thirdness." [102] What is maintained is rather that there is an *aspect* of in-itselfness, of factual actuality and of reasonableness or mediation in everything. The primary importance of this is not that it introduces us to new realms of being, but that it indicates the kind of question it is reasonable to ask when anything mentionable is considered under one or another of these aspects. For the firstness of anything *as first* no reason can be given, and none is required. Thus "to ask why a quality is as it is, why red is red and not green, would be lunacy. If red were green it would not be red; that is all." [103] If this seems a hard saying one has only to recall that what would be asked about red,

99. Charles Sanders Peirce, *Collected Papers* [hereafter cited as CP], edited by C. Hartshorne and Paul Weiss (Cambridge: Harvard University Press, 1931, 1932), 1.306.
   100. CP, 1.428.
   101. CP, 5.43.
   102. CP, 5.90.
   103. CP, 1.420.

* "For" in the original is replaced here with "from." Ed.

in an intelligible question, would be the place of red in a continuum of qualities or the reason for something or other being red, that is, for the law that its redness manifested. Of its qualitative being *as such* it is sensible to ask only what it is, not why it is such. And to the actuality of fact as such, no question can reasonably be put save that of what is in fact the case. As we are here abstracting from the further question of a possible reason, that question obviously does not here arise. To have insisted, as against Hegel and other philosophical idealists, that the actual world has always this element of *de facto* actuality about it, and that the reasons why a thing should be do not tell us that in fact it exists unless we can set up some reliable connection between logic and brute fact, was a noteworthy contribution to philosophical enlightenment.

The bearing of this on Peirce's theory of the nature of explanation is at once apparent. "Indeterminacy . . . or pure firstness, and haecceity, or pure secondness, are facts not calling for and not capable of explanation. Indeterminacy affords us nothing to ask a question about; haecceity is the *ultima ratio,* the brutal fact that will not be questioned. But every fact of a general or orderly character calls for an explanation; and logic forbids us to assume in regard to any given fact of that sort that it is of its own nature absolutely inexplicable." [104] Hence Peirce's dictum, which furnishes the key to his whole speculative philosophy, that "Law is *par excellence* the thing that wants a reason." [105]

Since only "thirdness" can provide an answer to a reasonable request for explanation, and it is also "thirdness" or uniformity as an evidence of effective reasonableness that needs to be explained, we must look to this category and its applications for all the speculative enlightenment we are to secure. What does Peirce mean by "thirdness"? The reasonable element in things, he frequently tells us, is embodied in the "habits" they manifest. "Habit is a generalizing tendency, and as such a generalization, and as such a general, and as such a continuum or continuity." [106] In continuity, then, is the answer to our demand for explanation. Phenomena are reasonable and understandable so far as they are continuous in character, and thus are instances of a generality which operates to determine their uniform behavior in the way a habit operates in human conduct. "Real regularity is active law. Active law is efficient reasonableness." [107] To see the world as reasonable, therefore, is to see it under the form of continuity, where this, in turn, is the manifestation of an active tendency to take [on] habits. And since it is the business of a good hypothesis in philosophy to explain, we shall expect it to find its justification in the discernment of just such continuity in the nature of things.

104. CP, 1.405.
105. CP, 6.12.
106. CP, 6.204.
107. CP, 5.121.

The extremely important role of generality in fruitful reasoning is hardly to be questioned, after Peirce's demonstration of the nature of probable reasoning and the impossibility of judging the goodness of argument by the specification of what, in the particular case, happens to occur. Reason deals with "would be's," with contrary to fact conditions, and with the ideal long run; and to rob it of this generality of reference is to rob it of its meaning in use. So much has been dealt with in an earlier section on Peirce [chapter 3], and there is no need here to call it in question. The generality of reasoning is indispensable. And the world, insofar as our reasonings are applicable to it, must be such that we can know, with reasonable probability, what it would be or would have been, as well as what it is. It is from this point that we now diverge into speculative philosophy, and by a deceptively plausible route. We understand things rationally in terms of their general habits of behavior. There must, then, be real generality in them. But what is the mode of being of such generality and how does it operate to determine the uniform behavior of its instances? This is not a question for logic, but for metaphysics, where metaphysics, as Peirce precisely says, "consists in the results of the absolute acceptance of logical principles not merely as regulatively valid, but as truths of being." [108] Now, the "being" of habits, tendencies, or laws is not the existential being of the events that exemplify them. "A *third* has a mode of being which consists in the Secondness [events] that it determines, the mode of being of a law, or concept." [109] Peirce likens his claim that such thirdness has a real and distinct sort of being to that of scholastic realism. Anyone who holds that hardness "is really and truly in the hard things and is one in them all, as a description of habit, disposition, or behavior," [110] is held to be a "realist" in this sense.

We seem to have taken only a short step in this progress from logic to metaphysics, but it is one that will determine a vast difference in our results. To ask whether the behavior of things can be understood in terms of discoverable laws which are exemplified in actual events and whose consequences can so far be anticipated as to enable us, by their aid, to explore further the structure of the world, is reasonable. To ask whether this *aspect* of structural uniformity has a metaphysical status of its own, such that it constitutes a unique kind of being which, by its own rational efficacy, determines events to act in accordance with it, is *prima facie* a less reasonable inquiry. The former question could be answered by considering the way in which reasoning applies and justifies itself in use in those fields of experience in which it has a clear application. The latter leads on, *via* the dictum that "thought" is the "mirror of being," to the conclusion that, since effective reasonableness rules the world "the end of being and

108. CP, 1.487.
109. CP, 1.536.
110. CP, 1.27 (note).

highest reality is the living impersonation of the idea that evolution generates." [111] And this idea is thirdness, reason or evolutionary love, the becoming of continuity and harmony, at work in the world. And it is very difficult to find evidence for this, or even a precise meaning, outside the limits of the speculative manipulations we are now to consider.

The parting of the ways is, evidently, at the point at which a choice has to be made between a contextual and a speculative use of Peirce's categories. In the former, "generality" would be understood in terms of the way it functions in reasoning. General ideas do have a significant application beyond actual instances, and there is reason to believe that the laws in which such "ideas" are embodied are sometimes in substantial accord with the structure of the facts examined. What, then, is the "reality" to which generality corresponds? Precisely the fact that these ideas, in use, say what is true, namely that things insofar as they have a certain character will behave in a certain way, and that they *would* behave in this way, under altered or unobserved conditions, insofar as the laws in terms of which we describe their behavior are true statements of their general nature. And there is good reason to believe that, within limits, they are true. Statements involving generality are not to be reduced to statements about the *de facto* character of particular matters of fact, and there is reason to believe that, in the contexts in which reason functions reliably, statements involving generality are sometimes true. There is no "nominalism" in this—no attempt to say that all that is meaningfully asserted *must* be reducible to statements about the characters particular things actually possess. And there is equally no metaphysics in Peirce's sense.

If, however, forgetting the original introduction of thirdness as an *aspect* of phenomena, we turn it into a being or agency operating on particulars and determining the manner of their behavior, we are embarked on metaphysics, and the familiar steps in speculative deduction are before us. We must first identify this unique reality as possessing a metaphysical potency which its contextual derivatives hardly manifest. Generality, being an object of particular philosophical concern, must become a unique "reality" and the basis for order and harmony in the world. In order to make this out, however, it will be necessary to use our speculative categories in a very loose way, and it will be extremely difficult to say that the startling results achieved by their manipulation are more than the verbally misleading fruits of emotionally colored and inexact discourse. And, finally, in order to get into the reality thus ostensibly determined the "concreteness" required to make it a plausible substitute for the world otherwise known, we shall have to attribute to habits in their generalized form animistic properties there is no good independent reason to suppose they possess, and to find "love" at work in things in a manner which, in

111. CP, 1.487.

our non-philosophical commerce with things, it is difficult to identify. This will add, no doubt, to the mental comfort of those who wish to feel at home in the cosmos; but it is a disappointing outcome for a theory about the nature of reason. It is, however, logic on the loose which Peirce achieves as the final fruit of his "pragmaticism," when this is subjected to the familiar speculative transformation. It is also, as the analysis will show, what we find.

Synechism

The name Peirce selected for his theory was "synechism." He explains the theory as follows: "Synechism is founded on the notion that the coalescence, the becoming continuous, the becoming governed by laws, the becoming instinct with general ideas, are but phases of one and the same process of the growth of reasonableness." [112] It is this growth of reasonableness that requires an explanation. If we are not to regard it as a brute fact—an illegitimate assumption, since it would treat what requires an explanation as inexplicable and thus "block the path of inquiry"—we must regard it as a result of some more general "thirdness" or tendency to form habits. Thus we have to combine the fact that law requires an explanation with the fact that nothing but a law can be an explanation. The explanation for generality is more general generality. Even this, however, is not enough. So long as any uniformity is present in things there is still something to be explained. Hence, "If we are to proceed in a logical and scientific manner, we must, in order to account for the whole universe, suppose an initial condition in which the whole universe was non-existent, and therefore, a state of absolute nothing." [113] This state of affairs would be a suitable starting point, since it would presuppose nothing that in its turn required to *be* explained. And it would not *really* be nothing after all. It would at least have "firstness," for this requires no reason for its being, and, while "nothing" determinate or actual in the way in which an ordered world is actual, has the sort of "freshness" or spontaneity out of which a world might arise. Hence the development in which the logic of the Universe as "first," "second," and "third" is seen to be mirrored in the course of its actual history, is the following: "The very first and fundamental element that we have to assume is a Freedom, or Chance, or Spontaneity, by virtue of which the general, vague, nothing-in-particular-ness that preceded the chaos took a thousand definite qualities. The *second* element we have to assume is that there could be accidental reactions between those qualities. The qualities themselves are mere eternal possibilities. But these reactions we must think of as *events*. Not that *Time* was. But still, they had all the here-and-nowness of events." [114] So far,

112. CP, 5.4. But see 6.169ff.
113. CP, 6.215.
114. CP, 6.200.

however, we have simply the aspects of firstness and secondness, predicated of peculiar *beings,* which are assumed to evolve in an order of development corresponding to their logical complexity. In such a world a tendency to form habits could occur, since anything could occur. And, once occurrent, it would grow. Thus "it is clear that nothing but a principle of habit, itself due to the growth by habit of an infinitesimal chance tendency toward habit-taking, is the only bridge that can span the chasm between the chance-medley of chaos and the cosmos of order and law." [115]

And thus is exhibited the logic of the universe, to which human logic, metaphysically interpreted, naturally leads.

Of the nature of this habit-forming tendency, to which all the determinate order in the world is due, much more can be said. In our habitual behavior we find much more than uniformity of sequence. "To say that mental phenomena are governed by law does not mean merely that they are describable by a general formula; but that there is a living idea, a conscious continuum of feeling, which pervades them, and to which they are docile." [116] Here we have a clear instance of the way generality operates. "Habit is that specialization of the law of mind whereby a general idea gains the power of exciting reactions." [117] It seems venturesome at first to extend this special efficacy of "ideas" in human behavior to the inanimate world. But the difficulty is overcome "when we remember that mechanical laws are nothing but acquired habits, like all the regularities of mind, including the tendency to take habits, itself; and that this action of habit is nothing but generalization, and generalization is nothing but the spreading of feelings." [118] Matter, in fact, is simply "effete mind," and the process by which evolution in the natural world has been achieved is not the purposeless operation of mechanical laws, but rather the growth of harmony "by virtue of a positive sympathy among the created springing from continuity of mind." [119] The true account of evolution is an "agapastic" one. "Love, recognizing germs of loveliness in the hateful, gradually warms it into life, and makes it lovely. That is the sort of evolution which every careful student of my essay 'The Law of Mind' must see that *synechism* calls for." [120]

Logic on the Loose

There are three steps in this somewhat rapid progress which merit special attention. The first is the remarkable derivation of that which needs an explanation—law—from that which needs no explanation—chance or spontaneity.

115. CP, 6.262.
116. CP, 6.152.
117. CP, 6.145.
118. CP, 6.268.
119. CP, 6.304.
120. CP, 6.289.

This is one of the most striking attempts to get something out of nothing with which the history of philosophy provides us. The second is the efficacy of generality as such, or "habit-taking" as an explanatory principle. And the third is the credibility of the peculiar form habit-taking assumes when identified with the spread of feelings and with "evolutionary love." We shall consider these in order.

To understand the actual world as evolved from "the general vague nothing-in-particular-ness" of non-existent spontaneity may seem hazardous. Peirce thinks, however, that it has a clear logical basis. We simply start with the question: "What elements of the universe require no explanation? This [is] a simple question, capable of being decided by logic with as much facility and certainty as a suitable problem is solved by differential calculus. Being, and the uniformity in which being consists, require to be explained. The only thing that does not require it is non-existent spontaneity." [121] It may seem a long way from this simple logical principle to the love that rules the course of evolution, but the connection is clear. For "synechism amounts to the principle that inexplicabilities are not to be considered as possible explanations; that whatever is supposed to be ultimate is supposed to be inexplicable . . . and that the form under which alone anything can be understood is the form of generality, which is the same thing as continuity." [122] Only an explanation which did derive order from the antecedent chaos would explain uniformity, which needs an explanation, and leave unexplained only that which does not need an explanation, namely, spontaneity. And nothing but "continuity" or "habit-taking" will provide an intelligible agent in the growth of reason. To appeal to any other considerations is to offer an hypothesis *as* an explanation that does not explain. And that is logically inadmissible. Q.E.D.

This sounds formidable, but in its specific meaning is less formidable than it sounds. Uniformity or law, we are told, requires an explanation. And this in a sense, is true. *De facto* uniformity is what suggests the presence of causal laws, and the purpose of inquiry is to determine whether such laws can be formulated, and whether, in terms of them, we can reliably anticipate a further structure in events which subsequent inquiry, directed by this formulation to look for results that would otherwise not have been anticipated, can confirm. If so, we have explained observed uniformity by reference to the structure in question and distinguished a causal sequence from a merely casual one. But the explanation here is the law itself, or the order it indicates, and to suppose that we can get behind the discernment of order and achieve an explanation of order from something that does not contain it is as chimerical as it is unnecessary. No actual order is accepted as final and inexplicable, but what we look for

121. CP, 6.604.
122. CP, 6.173.

when we try to explain it is some further order with which it can be reliably connected. Only when "thirdness" is wrenched violently from the context of its explanatory use and related instead to the other "modes of being" from which it is supposed to evolve, is this obvious and fundamental fact concealed.

And even here it is only very flimsily concealed. For it is not from chaos as such, but from the *order* which would exist in a chance world that the derivation is made. As Peirce says, in a revealing passage, "I only propose to explain the regularities of nature as consequences of the only uniformity, or general fact, there was in the chaos, namely, the general absence of any determinate law." [123] It is precisely because the structure of a chance world is a determinate structure that it serves Peirce's speculative needs. Such a world is a very special sort of world, and mathematicians can make the possibilities it presents a theme for very fruitful investigation. But it is not what is spontaneity in it, but what is order, that warrants the assertion that in such a world a tendency to habit-taking would occur, and that there would be "room" for it to develop. The derivation of something from nothing is, as usual, a most equivocal generation.

It might, however, be said that Peirce has got the world, if not from nothing, at least from very little. The mere chance for a habit-forming tendency to occur and develop is not much to ask of the universe, and that is all he has to ask. This brings us to our second special question, that of the explanatory value of "thirdness" as such. Peirce has certainly, if this hypothesis is tenable, got the more special structure of the world out of something very general indeed—the mere tendency to habit-taking. But this brings us back to a point which, one might have supposed, the progress of modern thought has securely established. Generality *as such* explains nothing. Where the observation that things are alike in certain ways leads us to expect a further structure in terms of which reliable prediction can be made, it is an important addition to our knowledge. The explanatory value of generality here depends on its fruitfulness in indicating some further connection than that which the mere fact of observed likeness already constituted. The appleness of apples, the tabularity of tables, and the horsiness of horses are "true generals," to be sure. But they have no explanatory value whatever unless they serve as clues to some further structure in things which accounts for the likeness observed. To take this likeness itself as a reason and to transform it into an agency determining the manner of behavior of its instances is just the mistake of which an earlier Scholastic "realism" was guilty. It is a striking, though lamentable, confirmation of this essential resemblance of Peirce's theory to that doctrine that he too, once he has taken generality as such as his explanatory principle, falls into the same mistake.

For what synechism actually tells us is that order develops through a ten-

123. CP, 6.606.

dency of things to become orderly. And "chance" or diversity is accounted for, in spite of Peirce's own view that it required no explanation, by a tendency to diversification. How these agencies differ in principle from the dormitive virtue in opium it is difficult to see. Consider the following: "Now, to say no process of diversification takes place in nature leaves the infinite diversity of nature unaccounted for; while to say the diversity is the result of a general tendency to diversification is a perfectly logical probable inference. Suppose there to be a general tendency to diversification; what would be the consequence? Evidently, a high degree of diversity. But this is just what we find in nature." [124] Of course, Peirce adds, this does not explain why any specific diversity occurs in nature rather than any other. What it explains is the universal fact of diversity, just as habit-taking explains the universal fact of law. "To explain diversity is to go behind the chaos, to the original undiversified nothing. Diversificacity was the first germ." [125]

This seems to me a bad hypothesis, and the model of an "explanation" which, since it is obviously compatible with anything that we might expect to find beyond the observed diversification with which it starts, is incapable of providing any other information than that which the word "diversificacity," a pseudonym for any and all diversity treated as the cause of itself, can be supposed to convey. Habit-taking is no better. The most it might lead us to expect is that we should find less "order" in the past than in the present in the Universe as a whole. But this, considering the largeness of the Universe and the hopeless vagueness of "order" as exemplified in uniformity, reasonableness and love, is obviously unverifiable. What it does succeed in doing is to endow "generality," in abstraction from its predictive function in research, with a wholly illusory explanatory value and thus to permit us to believe that we understand the world best when we say very sweeping and inexact things about it. The explanatory form has, here, been divorced from its explanatory function, and the tendency to habit-taking explains the supposed fact that things are becoming more orderly by the statement that they have a tendency to increasingly orderly behavior. That so eminent a logician as Peirce should have found such a theory satisfactory requires explanation. And the explanation is that when generality *as such* is to be understood as a *being* whose agency is required to account for the uniformity in things, such a theory is presupposed. It is at least admirable in Peirce that he accepted the consequences of his speculative assumptions.

Reason and Anthropomorphism
A further apparent significance, of course, lent to "synechism" by the fact that "habit" and "continuity" carry over into their general application the special

124. CP, 6.613.
125. CP, 6.613.

content which belongs to them when habits are human responses. Continuity thus means a spread of feeling, and the growth of uniformity in behavior can without serious incongruity be referred to as "love." If we could suppose that the habit-taking that accounts for order in the universe could be equated with "evolutionary love" in such fashion as to encourage the hope that the world is, on the whole, nearer to our hearts' desire than in its more special manifestations it often seems to be, the result would be of philosophical importance. Does Peirce's theory give us any reason to suppose this? It certainly is intended to do so, and it is this, I suspect, that accounts for the gladness with which, in some quarters, it has been received. Peirce has had some very useful things to say about "chance" in his logical papers. But when he has attained the speculative heights he speaks of it in a different way. "Chance itself pours in at every avenue of sense; it is of all things the most obtrusive. That it is absolute is the most manifest of all intellectual perceptions. That it is a being, living and conscious, is what all the dullness that belongs to ratiocination's self can scarce muster hardihood to deny." [126] It is through thirdness as an agency in what is general, determining its instances to orderly behavior by the sort of causation which a general idea, in the behavior of a rational being, exhibits, that uniformity is achieved. And this, so far from being a mere tautology, assures us that "the idea . . . will create its defenders," [127] and that truth crushed to earth shall rise again. The objection that this sort of explanation is anthropomorphic is one that Peirce has anticipated, and to which he has a vehement reply. He holds that "every scientific explanation of a natural phenomenon is a hypothesis that there is something in nature to which the human reason is analogous; and that it really is so all the successes of science in its application to human convenience are witnesses. They proclaim that truth over the length and breadth of the modern world. In the light of the successes of science to my mind there is a degree of baseness in denying our birthright as children of God and in shame-facedly slinking away from anthropomorphic conceptions of the Universe." [128]

This is courageously said, but what does it mean? It would indeed be "base," in the light of the achievements of science, to deny that the human mind can, by reasonable procedures, find out a good deal about the world. But the progress of science is the best evidence we have that the best way of finding out, and thus showing that nature is "analogous" to the human reason, in the sense that what we find out about it by reasonable methods is true, is *not* to assume that the physical world has an animistic structure, or that the motives most obvious in human conduct are also primary causal factors in the order of nature. The world of quantum physics is a world which "reason" has shown itself

126. CP, 6.612, p. 425.
127. CP, 1.217.
128. CP, 1.316.

competent to explore, but it is not a world whose behavior is in any important respect analogous to the behavior of human beings engaged in responding to ideals and becoming increasingly continuous in mutual love. There was no *a priori* reason for supposing that the behavior of electrons would be of the special sort we have discovered. The love that was once supposed to move the stars might have manifested itself in electro-magnetic fields. There is nothing *initially* superstitious in anthropomorphism. The trouble with it is that the world does not seem in fact to behave that way, and to *persist* in the assumption that it does despite the failure of reliable research to support the assumption, requires a resort to speculative hypotheses which reinstate an animistic language, but with so equivocal an application that its virtues are rather those of emotional appeasement than of cognitive accuracy. The customary compensatory dogmas, hostility to free inquiry, and deliberate narrowing of experience in order to maintain a view of the world which our widest and best attested knowledge does not support are happily not at all in evidence in Peirce's anthropomorphism. He was able to find in speculation the adjustment of fact to an animistic standard of "rationality" which he required. It was a device common in his generation, and perhaps necessary to minimize the gap between the world to which men were emotionally committed and that which their investigations were progressively disclosing. But such a use of "reason" is not, I think, that which best embodies the human faculties of which we are most justly proud.

For what information do statements about chance as a living being and order in nature as "evolutionary love" actually convey? We know love in specific contexts, and if the becoming of the universe were loving in *this* sense, we should be glad, in these gloomy days, to hear of it. But if we looked to the course of events for love of this sort, we should be disappointed. For the special organic situation which makes *human* love effective does not seem to be cosmically pervasive. If we look for love in *this* sense in the general course of evolution we shall almost certainly not find it. There seems hardly enough of love to go around in the purely human situations in which it is normally manifest. What then *shall* we find that confirms the speculative hypothesis? Just an increasing uniformity in behavior conceived as the cause of itself. Does this, then, enlighten us? Not if we keep to the very general sense to which alone we are cognitively entitled. If, however, we think of love once more as a mental agency, our feeling of familiarity and congeniality returns. But there is clearly no basis for it in the speculative demonstration offered. Thus we are back again in the verbal delights of a theory whose empirical basis will not warrant the meaning that must be placed upon it if it is to serve its speculative purpose. It is here that the specific outcome of synechism brings us to the result which our hypothesis led us to expect.

It may, of course, be true that ostensibly inanimate objects are in their actual constitution and behavior more like living organisms than we ordinarily suppose. An hypothesis, empirically confirmable, which indicated the nature of this resemblance would be a perfectly legitimate contribution to biology. We know too little of the world to say dogmatically that it *cannot* be as full of feeling as "synechism" asserts. There are suggestions in Peirce's papers on "the law of mind" which may prove useful to pioneers in this line of inquiry. An open mind, a lively imagination, and an enthusiasm for the further exploration of the "twilight zones" of present knowledge are excellent adjuncts to [the] work of inquiry. What is not so legitimate is a theory which offers as a reason for accepting an hypothesis for which there is at present no sufficient evidence, the speculative identification of uniformity with "habit," of habit with "efficient reasonableness," and of reasonableness with "love." Such an identification allows us to speak as though we possessed a supply of information which we have not got, and to substitute equivocal statements about natural processes for a balanced and soundly based philosophy.

To sum up: The attempt in this philosophy to put a categorical classification of the aspects of phenomena to speculative uses and thus to find a reason for the order in things which *is* their reasonableness is trebly futile. Insofar as it suggests a derivation of law from what is not law, it is mistaken. Insofar as it treats generality as such as an explanation it simply endows the pervasive features of things with a tendency to produce themselves. And insofar as it borrows content from terms with familiar "anthropomorphic" associations, it leads us to expect the world to be more like a sentient organism than there is at present any independent reason to suppose it to be. Peirce's theory reaches its goal only by a combination of these three procedures, and is consequently unsatisfactory.

This does not mean that the world is not "rational" or that we need despair of finding out much more of it than we already know. It does mean, however, that it is to be understood on its own terms, not on ours. To show that it is not explicable in a particular way, by the speculative use of categories to which we are habitually and perhaps emotionally addicted, is not to block the path of inquiry. It is rather to remove from its path misleading signposts which, so long as they remain, will too frequently lead even the ablest thinkers into blind alleys.

7 The Ironical Wisdom of Santayana

The Standpoint of This Philosophy

In his preface to *Scepticism and Animal Faith,* Santayana has strikingly characterized the intent and method of his philosophy. After commenting on "the great ferment in natural and mathematical philosophy" and his own incapacity, for want of special training, to explore its implications, he adds, "For good or ill, I am an ignorant man, almost a poet, and I can only spread a feast of what everybody knows. Fortunately exact science and the books of the learned are not necessary to establish my essential doctrine, nor can any of them claim a higher warrant than it has in itself; for it rests on public experience. It needs, to prove it, only the stars, the seasons, the swarm of animals, the spectacle of birth and death, of cities and wars. My philosophy is justified, and has been justified in all ages and countries, by the facts before every man's eyes; and no great wit is requisite to discover it, only (what is rarer than wit) candour and courage. Learning does not liberate men from superstition when their souls are cowed or perplexed, and, without learning, clear eyes and honest reflection can discern the hang of the world, and distinguish the edge of truth from the might of imagination. In the past or in the future, my language and my borrowed knowledge would have been different, but under whatever sky I had been born, since it is the same sky, I should have had the same philosophy." [1]

This initially modest claim, as its further development indicates, is in fact a remarkably ambitious one. Philosophers are, at least by verbal association, characterized as lovers of wisdom, and wisdom, as Santayana here suggests, is

1. George Santayana, *Scepticism and Animal Faith* (New York: Charles Scribner's Sons, 1923), pp. ix–x (Triton edition, vol. 13, p. 7).

This chapter is a section from original chapter 9, "The Standpoint of Philosophy"; the title of the chapter has been supplied. Most of Murphy's references are to the Triton edition of Santayana's works, issued by Scribner's in 1936–37. Where possible I have transcribed these references to more readily accessible editions. Ed.

something different from learning and spiritually more difficult to achieve. It has its basis not in special information which, as we have seen, is too frequently an incitement to philosophical one-sidedness, but in the candour, courage, and sanity which, surveying the order of nature and the place of man and his ideals in it, can judge the claims and achievements of the human spirit without illusion and without cynicism and, seeing them for what they are, value them at their true worth as elements in a rational life. It is wisdom thus grounded which Santayana offers as the content of his philosophy. The methods by which he reaches his conclusions are not always clear, and on more than one occasion, a winged word, a pregnant paragraph, or even, in later years, a purple passage has bridged a logical gap before which a more academic inquiry might well have halted. It is not surprising therefore that his one-time professional colleagues viewed his results with somewhat qualified approval. But "plain men" who were also reflective and cultivated have always heard him gladly. And in recent years the younger generation of philosophers has owed much to his teachings. This, many have felt, is what a philosophy ought to be and do, and in a period in which more systematic theories have failed to achieve a comparable insight, a glowing sentence from Santayana has frequently represented the best that a philosopher could say about issues on which men ask for philosophic enlightenment and only infrequently obtain it.

This philosophy presents, therefore, an instance of crucial importance for our inquiry. It comes nearer in its first intention, and in its occasional achievements, than any other theory of the period, to doing what we have concluded that a philosophy ought to do, that is, to provide a standpoint from which the rational organization of experience can be understood for what in its relative, precarious, but nonetheless humanly indispensable function, it is, and its achievements assessed at the value which, as elements in that organization, they are found to possess. Nor is this agreement by any means fortuitous. It was from Santayana's *Life of Reason* that I first learned what a sane, generous, and comprehensively reasonable philosophy could be. The project which this volume attempts laboriously to carry forward is the one which his eloquent pages seemed to me to propose.

Yet it soon became apparent that the standpoint which Santayana recommended was one which he was never able consistently to maintain, and which, in his later years, he has increasingly abandoned. From *The Life of Reason* to *Scepticism and Animal Faith* and from rational ethics to that "disintoxication with value" in which the "spiritual life" is now, in his philosophy, supposed to reach its loftiest expression, was a disillusioning progress. Yet, as Santayana has properly insisted, the elements of his later view were already present in the earlier, and, for better or worse, the position at which he has now arrived is one to which, by his initial preconceptions and assumptions, he was from the start committed. If it should prove to be the case, as I shall try to show that it is, that this later view, in its combination of sophistication and primitivism (or scepticism and animal faith) and its aesthetic acceptance of ideas which in fact require reasonable justification and, in this philosophy, cannot secure it, is basically misleading and unsound, it will be particularly important for our purposes to understand the causes of the incoherence and instability of this initially hopeful standpoint, and of the consequent failure of this beautifully phrased philosophy to exemplify in its own development the clarity and just discernment which it has so eloquently described.

The explanation suggested will be, as the reader may by this time have suspected, an application of the hypothesis thus far employed. The philosophic standpoint which, in *The Life of Reason,* Santayana seemed to recommend had in fact no sound basis or clear articulation. It was an attitude assumed by a highly acute and sensitive mind for persuasive aesthetic and moral reasons, but it was an attitude which was never able to come to terms with the structure of the world, or with* the specific reference and application of our ideas about the claims upon it, and it was therefore unable to maintain itself philosophically. It has consequently taken on an increasingly detached, arbitrary, and aesthetically precious character, the result, as I think it can be shown, not of increasing penetration into the profundities of esoteric "Realms of Being," but of a growing dislocation of "cognitive" and "spiritual" claims from the contexts in which their meaning and justification are actually to be found. The "rationality" that in the earlier works promised to be a mastery of experience in terms of a world philosophically understood, has remained an attitude merely, at times almost a pose, and Mr. Santayana in his ironical detachment has become increasingly aware that there are other attitudes which the free spirit may profitably assume and which can serve, if not as substantial elements in the life of reason, at least as inexhaustible themes for mellow reflection and uniformly elevated discourse.

In substance, the analysis offered amounts to this. Santayana, in his earlier works, combined a strong aesthetic attachment to rational form, especially when this was manifested in the work of an earlier age with which he found himself spiritually *in rapport,* with an inadequate understanding of the rational *function* and application of ideas and beliefs. He was thus led to accept in terms of aesthetic finality those products of human reason whose worth depends in essential part on their representative function and use. But this "ideal" acceptance actually leaves us without the capacity to discern what it is in the work of reason, in the several aspects of experience, that actually tests and justifies our ideas; consequently, if we continue to attach a unique value to *rational*

---

* "Of" in the original is replaced here by "with." Ed.

procedure, and to place our confidence in its products, it will be on *rationally* irrelevant grounds. Animal faith will be needed to provide the warrant for knowledge which tested evidence could not supply. "Normal madness" will condone our acceptance of socially useful beliefs which cannot claim the title of knowledge, and the "illusions" which do duty for principles of rational discrimination can be enjoyed as "bright pictures" even when their philosophical authority has been understood. For, "after life is over and the world has gone up in smoke, what realities might the spirit in us still call its own without illusion save the form of those very illusions which have made up our story?" [2] And if we are thus condemned to content ourselves with the surface of things and to conclude that in a world whose existential actuality is intrinsically arbitrary and irrational "there should be none but gentle tears and fluttering tip-toe loves," [3] we can at least reflect that this surface immediately intuited is pure essence, with an eternal and ontologically primary being of its own, and that our grasp of its tautologically indefeasible self-identity renders it an inalienable spiritual possession.

The result of this sort of philosophy is not in fact, as it was in intention, to clarify and elucidate the major "orthodoxies" in terms of which men of candour and courage have in all ages lived well, but rather to undermine the authority of those principles of philosophical discrimination through which these "orthodoxies," in their primary meaning and limitations, could adequately have been integrated and understood. The standpoint from which they are interpreted is not what would justify itself in all ages and countries. It is that which appealed to a quite special cultural group whose aspirations Santayana was peculiarly qualified to express. The rational goods he recognized were the products of a civilization, "catholic christianity," to which he found himself spiritually attached but from which he was, in "Puritan" New England, geographically and factually (since he could not accept the beliefs by which that culture lived) isolated. They survived as cultural ornaments in a society that could not have produced them. Sensing their disconnection, and his own, from the moving forces and ideas of the world in which he found himself, Santayana was led, in affirming his allegiance to them, to identify *detachment* as the condition for rational discrimination with disconnection from the executive order of things, and to regard as "servile" and unspiritual that concern with use and application which is essential to reason in operation. Thus the fruits of "reason" which should have been recognized as achievements, organizations of

2. George Santayana, *The Last Puritan* (New York: Charles Scribner's Sons, 1936), p. 602 (Triton ed., vol. 12, p. 345).

3. George Santayana, *Soliloquies in England* (New York: Charles Scribner's Sons, 1923), p. 144.

existential material, came here as gifts from a more aesthetically congenial age, to be enjoyed for their immediate satisfactoriness and used philosophically as a means of "liberation" from a world in which the spirit can never be at home. The basic peculiarity of Santayana's philosophy, the celebration of the aesthetic finality of rational goods, independently of their representative and rational validity, is the mark, if this hypothesis is correct, of an era of cultural dislocation, and its "wisdom" reflects that bias.

Such an attitude had much to recommend to it sensitive men in the 1910s and 20s. It is precisely the attitude of a perceptive outsider, enjoying the spectacle of a performance with which he has not been able, save perhaps historically, to identify himself. Thus one appreciates the music, the color, the measured dignity, of religious ceremonies at once delightful and incredible, accepting as an aesthetic display what he could not share in as an act of worship and reflecting in spiritual homesickness on the happiness he might have achieved in an age when he could have taken quite seriously the practices to which his sensibilities are so nicely attuned.

This is not the attitude of wise men in all ages, or under the open sky. But it is the attitude in which the cultural difficulty of many Americans in the last generation found a moderately satisfying solution. America* in those days had not come up to their aesthetic expectations. They moved to Greenwich Village† for spiritual liberation and some, more subtle and ingenious, were even prepared for the longer and chillier journey to the "realm of essence." For here at last they found that identification of spiritual freedom with moral and existential disconnection from an "irrational" world and "servile" concern with it which made articulate and philosophically justifiable their own cultural dislocation. Santayana's philosophy is a beautiful monument to that period and its aspirations. If it serves rather to ornament the confusions than to enlighten the judgment of those who accept it, that, perhaps, is hardly surprising.

So much for a preliminary characterization of the standpoint of a philosophy whose adequacy is now to be examined in more detail. If philosophy were, as the disciples of Santayana for the most part take it to be, an affair of taste and preference, of arbitrary acceptances and nobly phrased observations which those of cultivated sensibility will know how to appreciate, then there would be little more to be said about it, save that it is a lovely specimen of its kind and finely adjusted to the needs and sentiments of many cultivated and sensitive

---

* "Americans" in the original is replaced here by "America." Ed.

† The typescript has the following: "They moved to Greenwich Village, to the _____, for spiritual. . . ." Since the author never filled in the blank space left by the typist, the phrase has been omitted, and the reader may fill it in with whatever seems appropriate. The typing of the last chapter of the original (hence this chapter and the next in this work) apparently received no further review from the author. Ed.

persons. If, however, a philosophy is more than that, if, as Santayana told us, it intends to "discern the edge of truth" from the "might of imagination" and to ground the life of reason on foundations that will stand, we shall need to criticize the attitude thus assumed in reference to its adequacy as an interpretation of the types of experience whose rational import and value it proposes to estimate, and the reasonableness of its own "ironical" detachment as the basis for a philosophical integration of experience.

Animal Faith and the Life of Reason

In his earlier works Santayana was profoundly appreciative of the rational form which experience takes on when the outcome of activity is ideally represented, this represented outcome serving to give foresight and harmony to the present organization of impulses, preferences, and beliefs. That this organization is a late and derivative affair, working with materials not in their own nature rational and directed to ends which, at best, are but incidental [harmonies]* in the vast and indifferent course of nature, detracts not at all from its value, when this value is properly understood. For its justification is to be found neither in its causes nor in its effects, but in its nature. The whole value of ideas is ideal, but it is precisely where the mind discerns such ideals and is able to maintain against the world some ideal interest to which, in the knowledge of its own true good and attainable happiness it is pledged, that life justifies itself to the human spirit. The knowledge of the finality of such rational satisfaction, in the midst of relativity† and conditionedness of the situation within nature in which happiness is precariously and temporarily achieved, is the wisdom in terms of which the worth of ideas and ideals is philosophically to be estimated. It was this wisdom, at once perfectly honest and disillusioned in its recognition of the animal basis and natural conditions of the life of reason, and justly appreciative of its unique value in dignifying and bringing to harmonious satisfaction the appetites and impulses on which it supervenes, which Santayana's philosophy seemed to embody. No philosopher of our time, certainly, was better qualified by the catholicity of his interests and the shrewdness of his penetration of sham profundities to celebrate with sympathy and discrimination the spiritual goods in which reason in operation finds its appropriate expression and sufficient justification.

Unhappily, however, this enthusiasm for the form and fruits of "reason" is not enlightened and supported, as it should be, by any adequate theory of the way in which rational inquiry, at its critical best, can yield knowledge of the world. In *Reason in Common Sense* Santayana strove heroically but unsuccess-

---

* Reading "harmonies" for "harmonine." Ed.
† Here I have replaced "relatively" with "relativity." Ed.

fully to show how the "constructions" through which the work of thought proceeds can accurately characterize the independently existing reality or "substance" which, as he has never doubted, is the true objective of our knowledge of nature. The epistemological machinery of "concretions in existence" and "concretions in discourse," of a "reality" composed* apparently of sensational elements yet "constituted in its ideal independence by the assertive energy of thought," [4] was simply not sufficient to make an intelligible connection between the antecedent world out of which, on this view, thought with its constructions and "assertive energy" has developed and the ideal goal of its rational endeavors. Santayana was able to find many virtues in reason, but he was never able to credit it with the simplest and most essential virtue of all, that of providing, on occasion, the plain truth about the world of nature.

Since, however, the conviction of the existence of this world remains, and is, in fact, indispensable to the philosophic standpoint from which *The Life of Reason* was written, some warrant for it must be found. To retain this conviction, even when one's theory of knowledge ought, if persisted in, to lead to a sceptical relativism, is to honor one of the great "orthodoxies" of human thought, dogmatically no doubt, since "criticism" here has been seen to lead to an impasse, but none the less wisely, since in these matters literal knowledge is hardly to be expected and "animal faith" must justify an attitude which animal, and hence human, adaptation requires. It seems in some respects a long way from *Reason in Common Sense* to *Scepticism and Animal Faith,* but the nature of the development is not difficult to understand. The acknowledgment of an independent world of "existence," and the belief that the constructions of human reason are designed, not to disclose this world in its substantial reality but to reflect, from the standpoint of an interested organism, the manner in which we act upon or enjoy it, are present throughout. What has changed is primarily the degree of explicitness with which the inadequacy of reason, thus conceived, to provide knowledge of nature, thus understood, save in a "pragmatic" and all-too-human perspective, has been recognized. The consequent attempt to find in the "orthodoxy" of common sense and, finally, of animal faith, the warrant for a belief in "substance matter" or whatever the unknowable objective of knowing is supposed to be, is natural compensating adjustment to the exigencies of a situation with which "reason" has shown itself incompetent to deal.

There is a disarming frankness in this appeal to plain good sense to settle

4. George Santayana, *Reason in Common Sense* (New York: Charles Scribner's Sons, 1905), p. 82 (Triton ed., p. 73).

* Reading "composed" for "compacted." Ed.

a question on which the epistemologists have gone so frequently and so far astray, which is very attractive. *Of course,* we are inclined to agree with Mr. Santayana, the material world exists. We know what it can do to us, and what we can do to it, whatever the philosophers may say, and to rescind our active commitment to the belief in it, which all adaptive behavior presupposes, would be a piece of preposterous sophistication. Nor does this "orthodox" belief in "matter" commit us to anything metaphysically recondite. The intrinsic structure of the material world will doubtless always elude us. But, as Santayana genially observes, "whatever matter may be, I call it matter boldly, as I call my acquaintances Smith and Jones without knowing their secrets: whatever it may be it must present the aspects and undergo the motions of the gross objects that fill the world: and if belief in the existence of hidden parts and movements in nature be metaphysics, then the kitchen-maid is a metaphysician whenever she peels a potato." [5]

This has a very persuasive sound. If a critical philosophy cannot get us as far as the kitchen maid's sensible assurance of "matter," then so much the worse for critical philosophy. How much wiser to take our stand, ironically, perhaps, but nonetheless benevolently, on the side of the "orthodoxy" she represents and to share with her, and with Mr. Santayana, the feast of what everybody knows, leaving squeamish epistemologists to starve themselves on the niceties of "ideal constructions" and "sense data" if they will. Matter is matter after all, and everybody knows it. The child that cries for the moon (to cite another of Santayana's epistemological witnesses), knows little enough of the intrinsic nature of the object of his desire, but he is enough of a realist to be well aware that there is something there beyond his reach which, though he cannot literally possess it, is plainly identified as an object of present desire and possible knowledge. "He is a little philosopher; and his knowledge, if less diversified and congealed, is exactly like science." [6] In these matters, it appears, we should do well to become as little children.

So far so good. A philosophy that cannot recognize and take account of the palpable validity of "common sense" assurances on their own level and in their own primary usage is in so far a failure. We needed no epistemology to tell us what the kitchen maid and the crying child already know, and certainly none to call in question what, in their own simple way, they have found to be true. What we did need, however, was a philosophy which could retain these elementary assurances and at the same time enable us to understand, along with them, a good many facts about knowledge, scientific knowledge in particular, which

5. George Santayana, *Scepticism and Animal Faith* (New York: Charles Scribner's Sons, 1923), p. viii (Triton ed., pp. 5–6).

6. Santayana, *Scepticism and Animal Faith,* p. 173 (Triton ed., p. 155).

Mr. Santayana's trustful confederates had probably not thought about at all. The "orthodoxy" of common sense, if it is to maintain itself as an element in a reasonable whole of knowledge, needs the assurance that what it takes to be true *is true,* not because it was antecedently sure of it, but because the best that, through all our cognitive faculties, we find out about the world, leaves it standing as a reasonable means of finding out about its intended objects. If this sort of justification is not forthcoming, we get a very different sort of "dogmatism" from that with which we began, a tired and rather cynical dogmatism which retreats to elementary assurances in the knowledge that reason has failed in its wider task and must borrow from primitive credulity the sort of justification common sense should have found as an element in a reasoned and reasonable philosophy. Nothing is more charming than the faith of children; few things are sadder than the credulity of adults escaping from the responsibilities of maturity into the rudimentary assurances of an adolescence they have never really outgrown. It remains to be seen whether the artful simplicities of Santayana's philosophy are nearer to the former than to the latter variety of procedure.

The parting of the ways is very soon reached. The kitchen maid, interrupted in her eminently sensible business to serve as a witness to the reality of "matter"—i.e., the inside of potatoes—would doubtless be inclined to say that she knew well enough what a potato was and that its "hidden parts," so far as these are identified in her operational commerce with it, can by fairly simply manipulation be brought into view. And even the crying child would very likely be appeased, if something tangible, brightly colored and, preferably, edible, were given him in place of the more remote object which, as a little philosopher, he had identified. Philosophers of Santayana's persuasion are committed, in their cognitive efforts, to crying for the moon in a rather different sense. For the "matter" of both the moon and the potato is—on the theory that Santayana inherited and never seriously questions—intrinsically inaccessible, and neither peeling nor crying will ever get us nearer to it. Nature in its vast immensity is evidently beyond us. If we suppose that matter in *this* sense is the primary object of our cognitive aspirations, we shall have to say that since, in perception, we get only the aspects of things on the human scale, and since these are but adventitious appearances, "bright pictures," predicable only symbolically of their material causes, matter in its *own* nature must remain unknowable. It is there, of course, as the antecedent cause of our existence and our behavior is directed on it, but the representations we devise of it are but essences, terms of discourse, on a scale remote indeed from the executive order of nature. Hence "we conceive these realities fantastically, making units of them on the human scale, and in human terms."[7] Where our bodies are fortunately adapted

7. George Santayana, *The Realm of Truth* (New York: Charles Scribner's Sons, 1938), p. 52.

and our "bright pictures" do not mislead us in behavior, such a representation may be called a "normal madness," a pardonable illusion, and we may even as philosophers concern ourselves more with the show of appearance than with the ulterior reality, provided that we never forget the fact that the "essences" or appearances actually apprehended "never were and never will be the essences of things." [8]

It will be apparent that we lost the kitchen maid and the crying child some way back. What we have here is not an elucidation of the contextual usage and meaning of their claims, which would make sense of what they were after and still leave the way open for an integration of their simple assurances with the rest of our knowledge. It is the translation of those cognitive claims (and all others) into the terminology of a remarkably clumsy theory of knowledge in which "matter" has become the occult referent for knowledge unspecified save in its independence of what, by the various methods of inquiry at our command, we can find out about the world—all this, of course, being mere "bright pictures" as compared with its transcendent actuality—and "essence" the designation for anything that appears, simply *as* an appearance and without regard to its evidential value as information about the natural world. It is not surprising that between "matter," thus identified, and "essence" or appearance, reduced to sheer immediacy and hence no longer an appearance of anything at all, the cognitive connection should be a dubious one. But we may well suspect that it will need more than the common sense of simple folk to lend philosophical warrant to a knowledge claim thus interpreted.

But what else, when we view the world with courage and candor, could we have expected? Surely "matter" in its ultimate substance and occult parts will keep its secret to the end. Even if these occult parts were exposed to view we should still see only their appearances, essences on the human scale. And even if science successfully described them in terms of laws which applied with remarkable precision to the course of events in nature, all we should have would be a description—essence again, and not existence. A theory of knowledge which predicated of substance thus identified the traits known to be possessed by objects of knowledge in its more usual applications would certainly be mistaken. And if this comes as a stern and disillusioning doctrine, we may reply, in words that Santayana puts in the mouth of Democritus in one of his more successful dialogues: "What would you ask of philosophy? To feed you on sweets and lull you in your errors in the hope that death may overtake you before you understand anything? Ah, wisdom is sharper than death and only the brave can love her. . . . Shed your tears, my son, shed your tears. The young

---

8. George Santayana, *The Realm of Essence* (New York: Charles Scribner's Sons, 1937); in *Realms of Being,* 1942 "compact edition," issued 1942, p. 136 (Triton ed., p. 134).

man who has not wept is a savage, and the old man who will not laugh is a fool."[9]

"What would you ask of philosophy?" It is a fair question and those of us who are tempted both to laugh and weep at the pass to which this analysis of knowledge has brought us, in our pursuit of the life of reason, must reply. We expected, in the first place, some accurate notion of what the intended object of knowledge in any authentic inquiry actually is, and what the criteria are for reliable knowledge of it. To treat such knowledge claims as though they re-ferred—or must refer if they were to count as more than "animal faith," "sym-bolically" sufficient to guide the human organism's adaptive behavior—to "substance" as here identified, is simply to mistake their nature, and to shift the criticism of knowledge claims from the territory in which the distinction between reasonable belief and unwarranted opinion can reliably be made out, to the windy heights of substance and essence where nothing apparent exists and nothing existent can "literally" be characterized in terms of its manifest nature. We do not question that once this shift has been made Santayana's con-clusions follow. We ask why, in the name of both common sense and philoso-phy, it should have been made, and we claim that its outcome is not, as it purports to be, a defence of the major human orthodoxies, but rather a combi-nation of the kitchen maid's confidence with the scholastic metaphysician's ter-minology which does justice neither to orthodox usage nor to philosophical interpretation. *Of course* we shall go on believing in material objects, as we must, even after this debauch in the attempted rational organization of experi-ence, but the "animal faith" introduced to compensate for the inadequacies of an inept analysis will be less admirable and less enlightening than the more specifically human faith in the powers of human reason which Santayana once taught us to admire.

The result of this procedure, and of the animal faith it recommends, is simply a reinstatement, as the norm of our cognitive relation with the world, of the situation in which such obscure assurances as an animal might express are the best that we can say about it. We are back with "ambushed powers," "hidden potencies," "lurking forces." These correspond, however, not to a deeper wis-dom which identifies the ultimate object-substance, matter or God—to which even scientific knowledge is symbolically and fictionally* addressed—but to a peculiarly human and confused response in which the normal objects of knowl-edge are characterized primarily by our incapacity to discriminate their more specific and reliable characters. Surely there is a disastrous inversion here in the philosophical estimate of reliable knowledge. To be assured that "we are

9. George Santayana, *Dialogues in Limbo* (New York: Charles Scribner's Sons, 1937; Triton ed., vol. 10, pp. 47–48).

* Reading "fictionally" for "pictionally." Ed.

surrounded by enormous, mysterious, only half-friendly forces" [10] and that it is these which, by their "secret operations," kindle experience is not to receive the gift of philosophic wisdom, but only to objectify in literary loose talk the confused emotions which a resort to epistemological primitivism has engendered. And it is with such an objectification that the attempt to characterize matters in terms not of our most accurate knowledge but rather of our "animal faith" finally leaves us.

Scepticism and the Spiritual Life

Yet if knowledge of nature is, at its best, only faith mediated by symbols, and if it justifies itself not by its literal and verifiable truthfulness but by its pragmatic adequacy in the furtherance of animal wants and necessities, how are we any longer to distinguish the edge of truth from the might of imagination, or prefer "the paradise of truth" to the "paper flower" of convention? [11] As a spiritual attitude Santayana still recommends the love of "the inevitable, all-comprehensive, eternal being of truth." [12] Since no reliable means, however, has so far been offered for penetrating its nature, our "constant speculative reverence" for its "divine immensity" [13] would appear to be not only "sacrificial," as Santayana elsewhere characterizes it, but positively superstitious. To be nobly disillusioned in a world in which there is no longer any secure basis for rejecting as illusions the superstitions from which the free mind has emancipated itself, is, after all, a somewhat forlorn procedure.

To understand this aspect of Santayana's philosophy we must turn directly to his account of what, in his later philosophy, he has characterized as "the spiritual life." The sceptic who refuses to commit himself spiritually to a world in which only animal urgency and concern involve us, takes his stand not on knowledge of matters of fact but on intuition of essence. It is to these that his soul is initially addressed, and in refusing to go beyond them to a precarious commitment in the world of nature he is fulfilling an urge proper to pure spirit as such, though not wholly prudent for the animal body in which this spirit happens to be incarnate and to whose appetites and anxieties it finds itself unequally yoked. Pure spirit, wholly free and disillusioned, would surrender "every doubtful claim and every questionable assurance" and stand at last "unpledged and naked, under the open sky." [14]

It is not surprising that in a philosophy in which the whole cognitive and *representative* worth of reason has been reduced to an "animal" concern for

10. George Santayana, *Obiter Scripta,* edited by Justus Buchler and Benjamin Schwartz (New York: Charles Scribner's Sons, 1936), p. 170.
11. Santayana, *Realm of Truth,* p. 58.
12. Santayana, *Realm of Truth,* p. 130.
13. Santayana, *Realm of Truth,* p. 140.
14. Santayana, *Obiter Scripta,* p. 283.

the absent and remote, spirituality should be identified at last with sheer disconnection from anything remote or ulterior and should find its purest satisfaction in the "transparent" enjoyment of sheer immediacy. It is simply the other side of the same mistake, a mistake in which the "spiritual" fruits of reason have been divorced from its representative and practical function, leaving the latter, though essential to survival, animal and for the "free" spirit servile, and the former "intrinsically indefeasible" and, as I am constrained to add, magnificently inane.

The terms in which Santayana describes the "spiritual" life are frequently rhapsodic and difficult to translate. Spirituality* is "perfect candour and impartial vision," achieved when an experience is enjoyed simply in its immediacy and for its own sake, independently of any concern for its antecedents, consequents, or conditions. The life of reason is, of course, in this sense something less than spiritual. For it looks before and after, it is concerned with the fortunes of the sentient organism, it judges between right and wrong, better and worse, and attempts to subordinate present enjoyment to a represented good. But the spiritual life, in its emancipation from animal cares, achieves a "disintoxication with values." For the spirit, surveying all things impartially, "human morality . . . is but the inevitable and hygienic basis of one race of animals," [15] and why should the free spirit concern itself with one animal species rather than another?

The immediacies to which spirit addresses itself are pure essences, each of which eternally is what it is and none of which is anything but exactly what, as intuited, it presents itself as being. Since existence involves more than this, a *de facto* connection and implication in the flux of nature, existence is never given, and nothing given exists. Concern with existence is primarily animal, not spiritual. But where the freedom of immersion in essence has been achieved, the incarnate spirit has at least momentarily won that peace which supersedes understanding. "Piecemeal, amid the accidents of existence, ultimate good is attained whenever the senses and the heart are suddenly flooded by the intuition of those essences to which they were secretly addressed: synthetically, for pure recollection, it is realized by the contemplative intellect absorbed in pure Being." [16]

The realm of Being thus spiritually possessed—though alien to existence and also, as such, to truth, since truth is "the complete ideal description of existence," [17] and of existence and its description pure spirit has no knowledge

15. George Santayana, *Platonism and the Spiritual Life* (New York: Charles Scribner's Sons, 1937; Triton ed., vol. 10, p. 193.

16. Santayana, *Realm of Essence* (1942 "compact edition"), p. 61 (Triton ed., p. 61).

17. Santayana, *Realm of Truth*, p. 14.

* Reading "spirituality" for "spiritually." Ed.

or concern—is not without its ontological compensations. "This eternal aspect of things is also their immediate aspect, the dimension in which they are not things but pure essences; for if belief and anxiety be banished from the experience of any object, only its pure essence remains present to the mind. And this aspect of things, which is immediate psychologically, ontologically is ultimate, since evidently the existence of anything is a temporary accident, while its essence is an indelible variation of necessary Being, an eternal form." [18]

This ontological ultimacy is an affair of some profundity. "Of all the meanings of the word *is*—existence, substance, equivalence, definition, etc., the most radical and proper is that in which I say of anything that it is what it is." [19] And essence in this sense "more truly *is* than any substance or any experience or any event," [20] since these come to be and pass away while it eternally, indefeasibly, and tautologically is what it is and could not be otherwise. Hence, "considered in itself, essence is certainly the deepest, the only inevitable, form of reality." [21] In contrast to its transparent necessity, all existential change must be set down as an irrational accident. There is nothing in the nature of any essence which necessitates its occurrence or existential linkage with anything else. The emergence of one form rather than another in Nature is therefore absolutely groundless and change is "a perpetual genesis of the unwarrantable out of the contingent, mediated by a material continuity impartial towards those complications." [22]

It is not surprising that spirit, presented with so rationally unpromising a world, is tempted to take flight altogether into the heaven of ideas and immediacies. Is not the warfare* of "spirit" and matter, of ideal and actual, an old story? Santayana is at once benevolent and firm with this volatile element. It does not do to ignore altogether the animal basis of the spiritual life. Spirit is existentially linked with matter and can occur only when the propitious organization of a natural body makes it possible. But, equally, it is only in spirit that vital adjustment attains its appropriate fulfillment. "Life triumphant is life transmuted into something that is not life—into union with essence, with so much of the eternal as is then manifested in the transitory." [23] It is to this un-

---

18. Santayana, *Realm of Truth,* p. 14 [?] [This is the page number given in the text, but the passage quoted is not on p. 14 and I have not been able to find it, which shows that I do not know *The Realm of Truth,* nor, indeed, *The Realms of Being,* by heart, though of course it says nothing about my knowledge of the realm of truth. Ed.].

19. Santayana, *Realm of Essence* (1942 compact ed.), p. 5 (Triton ed., p. 7).

20. Santayana, *Realm of Essence,* compact ed., p. 23 (Triton edition, p. 24).

21. Santayana, *Realm of Truth,* p. 14 (Triton ed., p. 16).

22. Santayana, *Realm of Truth,* p. 81 (Triton ed., p. 80).

23. Santayana, *Realm of Truth,* p. 12 (Triton ed., p. 14).

* I have replaced "welfare" in the original with "warfare." Ed.

certain linkage of spiritual intuition of tautologically inalienable immediacies with animal concern for ulterior existences and hidden powers that the logic of this standpoint has finally brought the author of *The Life of Reason.*

It is now quite easy to see why any knowledge that pretends to transcend immediacy, or to attain any more questionable assurance than that embodied in the recognition that what is infallibly possessed enjoys the ontological privilege of being eternally whatever it speciously and transparently is found to be, must remain spiritually suspect. The arbitrary, the "irrational" are* on that side of the dualism set up in Santayana's theory of knowledge, and for such commitments the warrant is animal necessity, not spiritual light. The free spirit, being now disillusioned, will accommodate itself urbanely to such necessities, but is not likely to be imposed on by them. Its kingdom is not of this world.

What are we to say of this, and how, philosophically, to estimate its adequacy? As a "position" which can intelligently be assumed and from whose lofty vantage point a high critical tone can be taken toward more mundane philosophies, it has its advantages. The intuition of essence, as Santayana has described it, is a perfectly possible achievement in intellectual dissociation and one which, as the apostles of "phenomenology" have taught us, has its uses. Anything one notices is surely what *as noticed,* or as an immediate datum, it is, and if attention is paid to nothing else, if we deliberately "bracket" all further connections of implications, that is all that will be seen. The ontologically "deep" being such "essences" rejoice in is simply that which the most trivial tautology possesses, and its (ironical) eternity is the result simply of its provisional disconnection from any date—and not of its superiority to time,† change, and circumstance. One might as well claim for himself, as identified by a number‡ in a telephone book, a noble indifference to animal passions and fleeting desires, since none are there specified, as look for spiritual peace in that "realm" of ontologized tautology which the "spirit" achieves whenever it limits its attention to the surface of its experience in deliberate abstraction from all possible significance. The impressive fact is not that anything mentionable should be, in respect of its mentioned character, what it is and not anything else, but that a free spirit should be supposed to find in the certainty with which this trivial assurance leaves it, the appropriate satisfaction of its highest spiritual demands.

For consider what, on Santayana's showing, this spiritual achievement actually amounts to. There is detachment here in good earnest. But it is a detach-

---

* "Be" in the original is replaced here with "are." Ed.

† Reading "time" for "hire"; "ontologically" at the beginning of the sentence replaces the typed "autologically," a misprint that appears throughout the work and was occasionally corrected by the author in earlier chapters. Ed.

‡ Reading "member" for "number." Ed.

ment from all those commitments and connections through which the ideal goods Santayana once celebrated are made actual and secure. The reason that, in this lofty mood, we know nothing of nature is that we have refused to have recourse to the procedures through which in fact knowledge of nature is secured. It is not clear that such a refusal to make use of the agencies through which nature is observed testifies more to the "purity" of "spirit's" aspirations than to the inanity of its cognitive equipment. We are disintoxicated with values, and with the animal concern which defines, within nature, a standpoint for preference and reasonable satisfaction. But why should we regard such "disintoxication" as spiritual? For the peculiarly inadequate reason apparently that we have confused the disinterestedness which marks the maintenance, among competing interests, of a just and reasonable preference, and which is in fact a spiritual achievement of the highest order, with the "disinterestedness" which simply dissociates itself from moral issues altogether and is actually indistinguishable from the attitude of the callous, the irresponsible, or the merely numb. We are free spirits at last, when this process of dissociation is completed, but have we any reason to suppose that such freedom is more than the unhappy outcome of an arbitrary and inept procedure?

Actually, I think, Santayana's description owes its persuasiveness to the association of its terms with a view of the "spiritual life" to which, in their present usage, they are quite inappropriate. It is difficult to believe that a doctrine so nobly phrased and able to draw so potently on our attachment to those spiritual goods which it appears to celebrate, can really have led us to so barren a conclusion. Yet it is only necessary to translate its statements into their literal equivalents in terms of "essence," "intuition," "substance," and the rest, to see that such is the case. The freedom of the mind for which men have reasonably sacrificed much was not the liberation which ensues when, believing nothing and retreating from the situation in which the distinction between truth and superstition can be made out, we are content to find in the terms of discourse, aesthetically enjoyed, the exclusive objects of spiritual concern. It was the freedom to find out, by reasonable means, what the truth is, and to proclaim it. The detachment valued was that which masters conflicting claims in a reasoned harmony, not that which loses itself in aesthetic immediacy. And the intuition of the mystics, to whom Santayana appeals as masters of the spiritual life, was a claim on existence and eternal life, not on essence or "appearance" and the "eternity" of incomplete verbal specification. What has happened in all these cases is that Santayana has asked us to assume toward "essence" an attitude appropriate only to the spiritual mastery of existence through effective connection with that which can in fact satisfy the questionings of the mind and the aspirations of the heart. And he has done this because he has not himself been able to make those connections either in his philosophy or his valuations and has therefore been compelled to treat as "arbitrary" and "irrational" those very commitments in terms of which reason, theoretical and practical, justifies itself in "operation" and to eulogize as "spiritual" the dislocated fragment of actuality which is all that the retreat to immediacy actually leaves him as a secure possession. In this shift of philosophical standpoint the terms employed have lost their primary content but retained their lofty associations. It is in this mood that one is able to be at once disillusioned and edifying and to assume an attitude of incredulous acceptance toward a world whose content has not been specified and whose structure has not been understood.

The Philosophical Use of Reason

The moral of this account, and it is for the sake of the moral that it has been given, should now be apparent. The philosopher who makes himself the spokesman for the great "orthodoxies" of human experience and attempts with clear sight and courage to reconcile their cognitive and spiritual claims with the nature of the existent world and the possibilities of human happiness in it, must accept the responsibilities of this* great undertaking. If the standpoint from which his interpretation is made is a narrow or biased one its inadequacy will show itself in the arbitrariness and disconnection of the results achieved. There will then be no reasonable basis for a philosophical integration of the primary usages and acceptances through which our reasonable adjustment to the world is made. There will be, as Santayana likes to say, no "reason" (philosophical) for "reason" in its non-philosophical uses, and dogmatism or scepticism, or a paradoxical combination of the two, will be the final answer to the question which asks for a reason on the philosophical level and cannot find it.

If, on the other hand, our philosophical standpoint is soundly based and discerningly developed, we should expect to find, as its justification, a reason for reason, namely, a set of considerations which exhibit the primary, non-philosophical uses of such ideas as are, in their own contexts, intelligible and reliable, and to indicate the specific contributions they are competent to make to a reasonably integrated interpenetration of the world and adjustment of our responses to it. If I were not a sentient organism, responding adaptively to the stimuli and solicitations of my material environment, I should not be able to observe it perceptually as I do. *In that sense* "animal faith" or appropriate bodily adaptation is the precondition for knowledge of nature. But to credit philosophically the results to which perceptual observation leads when its conditions and limits are born in mind is not an act of animal faith, nor is it an arbitrary commitment for which no reason can be given. It is, in the light of my knowledge of nature and my means of finding out about it, an eminently sen-

---

* Replacing "his" in the original with "this." Ed.

sible procedure and one which justifies itself in its cognitive fruits. Compared with it, the "spiritual" attitude which refuses to credit as reasonably warranted anything beyond the intuition of essence can be seen to be an obviously arbitrary and fruitless pose and one which it is quite impossible consistently to maintain in practice or to use as a basis for the understanding of scientific procedure or plain common sense. Reason in operation justifies itself *as it proceeds* in its harmonization of its several elements or instruments and neither dogmatism nor scepticism but only a reasoned and judicious philosophy is required to render its achievements "spiritually" acceptable. It is through such a philosophy that the life of reason can be understood, and those of us who learned from Santayana the possibilities of such a philosophy are not likely to be content with the handsomely decorated substitute he has more recently offered as its "spiritual" equivalent.

8 Reason and Philosophy

The Revival of Metaphysics?

In a remarkable work on *The Unity of Philosophical Experience*, [Etienne] Gilson has pursued a method and arrived at conclusions which in some respects are very similar to those of the present inquiry, in others radically different. The two are in agreement in believing that "the history of philosophy makes philosophical sense," [1] and that it should be possible from a study of it to arrive at a reliable conclusion as to the nature of philosophical knowledge. The period Gilson surveys covers the whole development of medieval and modern thought, and his conclusion, that the characteristic philosophical mistake has been to treat some one aspect of Being, or some limited method of characterizing or investigating it, as though it were adequate to Being as such, bears an obvious analogy to the criticism of one-sided theories so frequently reiterated in this volume. Moreover, his appeal for a return to a confidence in philosophical reason as an alternative to the destructive scepticism in which so much of recent philosophizing appears to have eventuated is in substantial harmony with much that has been said in the present work.* It would be fortunate if we were able to claim this support on further issues as well. On these, however, the divergence is fundamental, and an indication of its nature will serve, I believe, to clarify by contrast the nature of the return to philosophy here recommended.

After observing the recurring resurgence of philosophical inquiry after periods of scepticism and positivism, Gilson offers as a "law" of "philosophical" experience" that *"Philosophy always buries its undertakers."* [2] The reason, he believes, is [that] "by his very nature, man is a metaphysical animal," the need

1. Etienne Gilson, *The Unity of Philosophical Experience* (New York: Charles Scribner's Sons, 1937), p. vii.
2. Gilson, *Unity of Philosophical Experience*, p. 306.

This chapter consists of the last two sections of the original last chapter, chapter 9, "The Standpoint of Philosophy." Ed.
* Replacing "chapter" in the original with "work." Ed.

248

which metaphysics satisfies having its basis in "the very structure of reason itself." [3] This need is further specified. "Philosophy is the only rational knowledge by which both science and nature can be judged." [4] Modern philosophy, however, by its subservience to scientific method, has surrendered this fundamental function of judging the world of scientific matter of fact in terms of first principles that transcend it. It has, in consequence, been unable to find any basis for limiting the pretensions of the sciences or maintaining [a] rational foundation for morals. "Thus left without any set of philosophical convictions concerning man, his nature and his destiny, they have nothing wherewith to oppose the progressive encroachments of science on the field of human facts." [5] The result has been either an acceptance of fact as such as its own justification, and this is the way to subservience to mere power, or else a "liberal" scepticism which attempts to find in the insecurity of all points of view an excuse for accepting the responsibilities of none. Hence "what is now called philosophy is either collective mental slavery or scepticism." [6]

That the "liberalism" of intellectual irresponsibility cannot long endure is obvious. There are too many faiths "animal" and "social" demanding to take its place. "Against the crude, yet fundamentally sound craving of Marxism for positive and dogmatic truth, the scepticism of our decadent philosophy has not a chance." [7] It can only be reliably met by something "more rational and more comprehensively constructive." "The time of the 'as ifs' is over; what we now need is a 'This is so,' and we shall not find it unless we recover both our lost confidence in the rational validity of metaphysics and our long-forgotten knowledge of its object." [8]

The nature of the appeal to "reason" in philosophy [that is] recommended now becomes apparent. Metaphysicians differ on many points, but all "agree on the necessity of finding out the first cause of all that is," [9] an "ultimate ground for all real and possible experience." "Scholastic" philosophy long since found this ground in Being. For "each and every aspect of reality, or even of unreality, is necessarily conceived as being or defined in reference to being" and "the understanding of being is the first to be attained, the last into which all knowledge is ultimately resolved, and the only one to be included in all our apprehensions." [10] Not only is it ultimate in its own right, but the knowledge of

3. Gilson, *Unity of Philosophical Experience*, p. 307.
4. Gilson, *Unity of Philosophical Experience*, p. 277.
5. Gilson, *Unity of Philosophical Experience*, pp. 291–92.
6. Gilson, *Unity of Philosophical Experience*, p. 294.
7. Gilson, *Unity of Philosophical Experience*, p. 294.
8. Gilson, *Unity of Philosophical Experience*, pp. 294–95.
9. Gilson, *Unity of Philosophical Experience*, pp. 306–7.
10. Gilson, *Unity of Philosophical Experience*, p. 313.

it enables us to enunciate such useful [principles]* as "that being only comes from being, which is the very root of the notion of causality," [11] and that "all that which is, down to the humblest form of existence, exhibits the inseparable privileges of being which are truth, goodness and beauty." [12] We get back at last, to be sure, to the ultimate question why there should be "something rather than nothing," [13] but for that, too, there is a metaphysically and theologically satisfying answer. In short, metaphysics supplies knowledge of the first principle and of everything else in the light of the first principle, and thus supplies the philosophically indispensable standpoint for that rational interpretation of the special aspects of experiences of which we, as well as philosophers of the Roman church, have seen the need.

The impressive metaphysical system once reared on these foundations which Gilson and his associates wish now to reinstate as the standpoint for a rational philosophy deserves a much fuller examination than we shall here be able to give it. Its place among the great systems of philosophy is secure, and there will, no doubt, always be those who find in it a welcome refuge from the complications and claims of a world to which Being as such and its inseparable privileges of "Truth, goodness, and beauty" seem curiously irrelevant. That, perhaps, is the world's fault, and those who have surrendered it for the theological and metaphysical comforts of a "transcendent" reality narrow and secure enough to meet their cognitive and emotional demands have been as unsparing in their condemnation of this world as is Gilson in his characterization of modern philosophy. For those who can accept the dogmatic limitations which eliminate disturbing elements and recreate by artifice and authority the intellectual environment in which this metaphysics was once the best that human reason could make of its world it will still have potent attractions. Their philosophical problems, once the initial acceptance has been made are, for the most part, easily solved, and verily, they have their reward. I have not introduced this theory here in order to debate the ontological perfections of that "being" which all reality and all unreality are alleged to possess—the discerning reader will have seen by this time what, in terms of our hypothesis, the appropriate comment would be—but rather to make as clear as possible the very different sense in which the appeal to reason and to philosophy is here recommended.

11. Gilson, *Unity of Philosophical Experience,* p. 314.
12. Gilson, *Unity of Philosophical Experience,* p. 317.
13. Gilson, *Unity of Philosophical Experience,* p. 318.

* The word "principles" has been inserted in the blank space between "such useful" and "as 'that being.'" Ed.

The Life of Reason

The constant standpoint for philosophy, we have said, is simply that of the rational organization of experience, in which each element is seen for what, in its primary meaning, it reliably is, in which the possibilities of harmonious integration of its several aspects are explored without the distorting preconceptions which at present limit our awareness of their nature, and in which each candidate for philosophical preeminence is judged for what it might contribute to such an integrated whole.

Such a philosophy can hardly claim the transcendent authority and cognitive preeminence to which a knowledge of "the first principle" of being entitles Gilson and his associates. It is a precarious and derivative affair, borrowing its content from a developing body of knowledge, and limited in its interpretative scope by a highly variable range of social emphasis and appreciations. It is hardly likely that it can rise much higher than the general enlightenment of the period in which it functions. Its ivory tower is in fact no more than a lookout station for forces on the march, commanding a somewhat wider view of the terrain than would otherwise be attainable, and enabling those prepared to make use of it to proceed with a clearer notion of where they are going. If it pretends to be more than this it loses its responsible connection with non-philosophical actuality and becomes in fact what its critics have so often accused it of being, a sterile manipulation of concepts which have lost their primary meaning while retaining their emotional and verbally congenial associations and which, employed without any independently ascertainable test or application, serve rather to comfort or appease the mind with the formal semblance of rationality than to provide it with the clear sight and just discrimination through which the rational mastery of its experiences might progressively be achieved. There is no reason to believe that the categories of scholastic metaphysics, in spite of their long association with a highly valued religious faith, are more than a fairly obvious instance of just such sterile manipulation and factually inapplicable appeasement. Their revival at this time proves not, as Gilson supposes, that man is by nature a metaphysical animal, but rather that man in his blundering but persistent attempt to be a rational animal, has still not found a way to bring the integrative principles which reason demands into effective connection with the specific subject-matters that require integration.

Yet there is in this no excuse for either scepticism or dogmatism (whether Marxist or ecclesiastical) at the philosophical level. The validity of reason does not rest precariously on the possibilities of a metaphysical synthesis which becomes increasingly unplausible as our knowledge of the work of thought proceeds. We know "reality" in the way in which it can reliably and satisfactorily be known in every accurate perception or tested hypothesis or shared experience which performs what it promises and *is,* in its appropriate use, the means through which reason operates and maintains itself. The standpoint from which such experiences are condemned as philosophically superficial or unreliable is an arbitrary and unreasonable one and its sceptical consequences the fruits of inept procedure, rather than ironical penetration. Whatever else the world may be, and its vastness will always be an appropriate theme for philosophic wonder, it is at least what it shows itself to be in our primary means of access to it, and those who cannot see this, and use it as a foundation on which to build, are not wise.*

Nor do we require a compensatory dogmatism to bolster our confidence. If dogmatism means the affirmation as true of what beyond reasonable doubt is established, then it is a welcome attitude. But dogmatism on the philosophical level has not meant that. It has been rather the attempt to bolster a faith or doctrine, whose reasonable basis could not be made out, by excluding from the area of intellectual inquiry the considerations which, if reasonably entertained, would normally lead us to question its claims. It is not the natural confidence of the mind, as it proceeds, in the condemned applicability of its ideas where they are found, on the whole, to apply, but the defensive reaction of tenacious belief, when that application has failed, against the disturbing factors which have upset it. A metaphysical philosophy must resort to such dogmatism, whether dialectical materialism or being and its perfections be its theme, for its claims are in fact too sweeping for the world in which it is supposed to apply. It is no wonder that the scholastic and the Marxist here understand each other's craving in a way in which neither would understand or accept the more tentative philosophy here suggested.

There need be nothing in the literal validity of any set of ideas which can actually make out its claim in its reliable contribution to a total reasonable adjustment which excludes the literal validity of other ideas used to deal with a different situation, so long as neither is made the basis for a metaphysical overstatement. The scepticism, compensatory dogmatism, and recurrent disillusionment which have marked the history of philosophy are not the inevitable accompaniments of a rational organization of experience; they are the by-products of a bungling method which we should by this time have learned to correct, and which can be corrected if we know what we are doing and how our ideas can apply to the world they intend to characterize.

When this is realized, and when *philosophical* reason is put in its place *within* the work of human understanding and adjustment, we shall not need, I

---

* The phrase "are not wise" is lame, would almost certainly have been replaced by some sweeping and serpentine phrase if the author had revised this chapter. Ed.

think, to be terrified or bewildered any longer by the "rivals and substitutes for reason,"* now so fashionable among us. For if the work of philosophy is to interpret, to harmonize, and to adjust, within the growing body of our knowing and valuing, there is no substitute for its full or rational employment which is not a confused, inept, or one-sided pretender to the authority which only a reasoned philosophy could provide. Where such doctrines are maintained by bluster, threat, or oracular pronouncement the problem they present is educational or political rather than philosophical. But where they claim to find, in some unique and favored aspect of experience, the clue to an "actuality" deeper than the ought† and more ultimate than the world to which our procedures of reliable inquiry apply, that claim can be at once understood and exposed—understood for the modicum of truth it contains and which an opposing over-simplification had arbitrarily excluded, and exposed in its own flimsy absolutism as the unenlightened spokesman of an interest whose pretensions to ultimate authority will not stand fair and comprehensive examination.

Exposure and refutation, to be sure, are not enough, though in this volume they have received preponderant emphasis, since our purpose has been critical and exploratory, to prepare the way for the apprehension of constructive possibilities which the present philosophical set-up has served rather to obscure than to elucidate. In some instances we have seen, I think, how aspects of experience frequently set in destructive opposition, e.g., "the world of physics" and "the world of sense," can be intelligibly related and the contribution of each to our knowledge of the other understood at its proper worth. In other cases the suggestions made have been tentative and schematic, requiring a much more detailed examination of the special subject-matters to be related than would here have been appropriate. It is this work especially in the troublesome field of the social sciences and their concern with "value" that, for my own part, I propose in the future to pursue. What is philosophically needed is not more information of the type the sociologists are so industriously acquiring, though of course, we shall need all the relevant information we can get, but a standpoint from which the specific meaning of explanatory categories in their application to social phenomena, and the legitimacy in the light of what from other sources we know of employing in *this* field the special categories which the subject-matter seems *prima facie* to demand, can be determined. Such an undertaking would require a philosophy, if only to avoid the philosophical morass in which contemporary theorists are so largely engulfed, and

* The title of a chapter in Morris R. Cohen's *Reason and Nature* (1931), mentioned earlier in the original chapter. Ed.

† The phrase "than the ought" may be exactly what was meant; it may also be something else garbled in transmission. Ed.

it would, if successful, be a contribution to philosophy, different in many respects from those discussions of the place of value in "reality" considered in
the chapter on Idealism, but pertinent, as they were not, to the requirements of
the situation which Idealism strove unsuccessfully to master.

It is not likely that a procedure of this sort, if it were widely adopted, would
develop as many or as startling "isms" as the recent past has provided, or
provide as facile a subject for literary criticism and equivocally edifying discourse. The work of reason is for the most part a more pedestrian affair, proceeding line upon line and precept upon precept, here a little and there a little,
to make intelligible and humanly usable the experience which is our commerce
with the world. To the life of reason, wisely and generously lived, it would
make its unique and indispensable contribution. And that, if we have been right
so far, is its final and sufficient justification.

When Faust despaired of the possibilities of life and knowledge he was visited by a chorus of spirits in the air, and their song, though instrumental in the
first instance to the plot of Mephistopheles to keep Faust alive for his own
purposes, was on the side of life and reason in a fuller sense.

> We bear them away,
> The shards of the world,
> We sing well-a-day
> Over the loveliness gone,
> Over the beauty slain.
>
> Build it again,
> Great child of the earth,
> Build it again
> With a finer worth,
> In thine own bosom build it on high!
> Take up thy life once more:
> Run the race again!
> High and clear
> Let a lovelier strain
> Ring out than ever before.[14]

To an inquiry described by [a] discerning and not unfriendly critic as an
essay in philosophical "debunking" I want to append these lines as a juster
indication of its primary interest, not, to be sure, that I should regard the implications of this volume, even if it had fully made out its case, as of the same
cataclysmic order as those to which the spirits refer. But it is essential to insist
that so far as the result here reached is negative, it is also preliminary. We must

14. Translated by F. M. Stawell and G. Lowes Dickinson, in *Goethe and Faust: An Interpretation* (London: G. Bell and Sons, 1928), pp. 90–91.

build again the structure of philosophical reason, whether it is sceptical analysis or the unenlightened procedure of its well-meaning practitioners which has brought it to its present unhappy state. The task of philosophy is essential to the harmonious development of human reason, and well we cannot surrender it without surrendering much of what is best in ourselves. It is a preliminary but essential factor in this work of construction that we should learn from past experience what we are doing and what the structural requirements are for a [building]* that will stand.

* Reading "building" for "binding." Ed.

Bibliographical Notes

Index

Bibliographical Notes

In Part I below I list, sometimes with annotations, some works by Murphy especially relevant to the topics of this book. In Part II I list works by others that either comment on something by Murphy or have the special relevance mentioned.

I

Some of the following works by Murphy, though not all, are referred to herein, either in the text (by the author) or in the introductory matter (by the editor). The date listed is usually that of publication; where publication was some time later, it is that of writing.

1943 *The Uses of Reason* (New York: Macmillan).
1963 *Reason and the Common Good,* edited by William H. Hay and Marcus G. Singer (Englewood Cliffs, N.J.: Prentice-Hall), abbreviated *RCG.* Some of the papers listed below were first published in this collection; a number of others are reprinted in it.
1965 *The Theory of Practical Reason* (La Salle, Illinois: Open Court). Murphy's Carus Lectures (tenth series), edited by A. I. Melden, whose introduction is very illuminating.
1988 "Emerson in Contemporary Thought," *Transactions of the Charles S. Peirce Society* 24:309–16.
1993 "Pragmatism and the Context of Rationality," *Transactions of the Charles S. Peirce Society* 29.2, 3, 4:123–78, 331–68, 687–722. This was chapter 3 of *Contemporary Philosophy,* the original manuscript of the present work.

There is a bibliography of Murphy's writings in *Reason and the Common Good.* The following items, grouped partly chronologically and partly by reference to topic, are all listed therein. Some of the items listed here have special relevance to the topic of this book, or are studies in which some of the points of the present book are developed independently or in which some of the ideas of the present work achieved earlier publication. Murphy published very little more on the topics of reality and speculative philosophy after 1943, when his attention turned away from metaphysics and epistemology to moral and social philosophy.

1926 "Ideas and Nature," *Studies in the History of Ideas* (Berkeley: University of California Press), pp. 193–213.
1927 "Substance and Substantive," *University of California Publications in Philosophy* 9:63–87.

Three additional papers on objective relativism are the following:

1927 "Objective Relativism in Dewey and Whitehead," *The Philosophical Review* 36:121–44; *RCG,* pp. 49–66.
1940 "What Happened to Objective Relativism," *RCG,* pp. 67–78. Extracted from the original manuscript of the present book, this forms the last section of original Chapter 5, "The Problems of Perceptual Knowledge." Murphy called it the "analysis of the old faith," and an "antidote" to it.
1959 "McGilvary's Perspective Realism," *Journal of Philosophy* 56:149–65; *RCG,* pp. 79–92. A twin doctrine under another name; in Murphy's view, an example of speculative philosophy.

The following two papers are cited in footnotes in the present work:

1927 "Alexander's Metaphysic of Space-Time," *The Monist* 37:357–84, 624–44; 38 (1928): 18–37.
1928 "What is an Event?" *The Philosophical Review* 37:574–86.

The following are on themes and doctrines similar to the currents of then contemporary thought discussed by Murphy in this work, or else provide other examples of speculative philosophy:

1929 "The Anti-Copernican Revolution," *The Journal of Philosophy* 26:281–99.
1931 "Mr. Lovejoy's Counter-revolution," *The Journal of Philosophy* 28:29–42, 57–71.
1932 Introduction to *The Philosophy of the Present,* by George Herbert Mead, edited by A. E. Murphy (Chicago: Open Court), pp. xi–xxxv.
1933 "A Rejoinder," *The Journal of Philosophy* 30:354–58. A rejoinder, and a rather feisty one, to Lovejoy's reply to "Mr. Lovejoy's Counter-revolution" (1931); see part II below, Lovejoy, 1932.
1933 "When Physicists Philosophize," *The New Humanist* 6.5:22–27.
1934 "Reason, Logic and Scientific Method," *The New Humanist* 7:13–22.
1935 "A Program for a Philosophy," in *American Philosophy Today and Tomorrow,* edited by H. M. Kallen and Sidney Hook (New York: Lee Furman), pp. 356–74.
1937 "The Fruits of Critical Realism," *The Journal of Philosophy* 34:281–92.
1937 "A Critique of Positivism," in *Proceedings of the Ninth International Congress of Philosophy* (Paris: Hermann et Cie), vol. 4, pp. 70–76.
1945 "Naturalism and Philosophic Wisdom," *The Journal of Philosophy* 42: pp. 400–17; *RCG,* pp. 200–14. Cf. *RCG,* pp. 213–14: "The naturalists, who have so much that is good to offer, still lack and need a philosophy—not a 'position'

(for that they have already), but such working principles of balance, perspective, and discrimination as will keep their devotion to 'scientific method' from narrowing their appreciation of the actual richness and complexity of the human spirit in all its activities and will give their criticism the comprehensive justice which philosophical self-knowledge can supply. There is as yet . . . no 'ism' that can claim that kind of philosophic wisdom as its exclusive possession. But it operates, more or less, in all of them, to the extent that each attempts to maintain and justify its chosen position *philosophically,* and to make it adequate to the whole range of meaningful experience. . . ."

On critical philosophy:

1938   "Two Versions of Critical Philosophy," *Proceedings of the Aristotelian Society,* vol. 38 (London: Harrison and Sons), pp. 143–60; *RCG,* pp. 95–107.

1942   "Moore's Defence of Common Sense," in *The Philosophy of G. E. Moore,* edited by P. A. Schilpp (Library of Living Philosophers, vol. 4; Evanston: Northwestern University), pp. 301–17; *RCG,* pp. 108–20.

On speculative philosophy:

1941   "Whitehead and the Method of Speculative Philosophy," in *The Philosophy of Alfred North Whitehead,* edited by P. A. Schilpp (Library of Living Philosophers, vol. 3; Evanston: Northwestern University), pp. 353–80; *RCG,* pp. 142–62.

1943   "Can Speculative Philosophy Be Defended?" *The Philosophical Review* 52: 135–43. One of three symposium papers on the topic of the title, the others by W. T. Stace (pp. 116–26) and Ralph M. Blake (pp. 127–34), written for delivery at the meeting of the American Philosophical Association in December 1942, a meeting that was "cancelled owing to [war-time] difficulties of transportation." The point of departure was Murphy's 1941 Schilpp volume essay on Whitehead. In his paper Stace attempts to draw a distinction between metaphysics and speculative philosophy, not a very happy one.

Two more on Whitehead:

1930   "The Development of Whitehead's Philosophy," *New World Monthly* 1:81– 100; *RCG,* pp. 126–41.

1961   "Whitehead's Objective Immortality," *RCG,* pp. 163–72.

Three on Dewey:

1939   "Dewey's Epistemology and Metaphysics," in *The Philosophy of John Dewey,* edited by P. A. Schilpp (Library of Living Philosophers, vol. 1; Evanston: Northwestern University), pp. 195–225.

1940   "Dewey's Theory of the Nature and Function of Philosophy," in *The Philosopher of the Common Man, Essays in Honor of John Dewey* (New York: G. P. Putnam's Sons), pp. 33–55.

1960   "John Dewey and American Liberalism," *Journal of Philosophy* 57:420–36; *RCG,* pp. 247–61.

On related themes or referred to in the present volume.

1945   "The Rewards of Learning," *Ethics* 56 (1945): 49–59; *RCG*, pp. 385–97.
1947   "Reason and the Conflict of Philosophies," in *Approaches to Group Under-standing*, edited by L. Bryson, L. Finkelstein, and R. MacIver (New York: Harper and Row), pp. 632–50; *RCG*, pp. 296–308.
1950   "Community of Understanding," in *Perspectives on a Troubled Decade*, edited by L. Bryson, L. Finkelstein, and R. MacIver (New York: Harper and Row), pp. 453–74; *RCG*, pp. 309–26.
1947   "Collingwood's Idea of History," *The Philosophical Review* 56:587–92; *RCG*, pp. 121–25.
1947   "The Philosophic Mind and the Contemporary World," *RCG*, pp. 365–75.
1957   "On Kierkegaard's Claim that 'Truth is Subjectivity,' " *RCG*, pp. 173–79.
1959   "Jonathan Edwards on Free Will and Moral Agency," *The Philosophical Review* 68:181–202; *RCG*, pp. 183–99.
1960   "Pronouncements, Propaganda, and Philosophy," *RCG*, pp. 376–84.

On tangentially related matters, or referred to earlier in prefatory matter:

1945   *Philosophy in American Education*, with B. Blanshard, C. J. Ducasse, C. W. Hendel, and M. C. Otto (New York: Harper and Row).
1953   "American Philosophy in the Twentieth Century," *RCG*, pp. 215–46.
1953   "Reasons in Ethics," *RCG*, pp. 35–46.

Murphy reviewed an extraordinary number of books, especially in the 1930s, when he was book editor of *The Journal of Philosophy* (*JP*) and also regularly reviewed books for the *International Journal of Ethics* (now *Ethics*) and *The Philosophical Review* (*PR*). Listed here are some longer reviews from this period that relate fairly closely to the topics of this book:

1929   A. N. Whitehead, *Symbolism: Its Meaning and Effect*, *JP* 26:489–98.
1930   L. Brunschvig, *Le Progres de la conscience dans la philosophie occidental*, *PR* 39:423–29
         A. S. Eddington, *The Nature of the Physical World*, *PR*, 39:502–8.
         E. Meyerson, *Identity and Reality*, *The Symposium* 1:409–13.
         A. N. Whitehead, *Process and Reality*, *Ethics* 40:433–35.
1931   M. R. Cohen, *Reason and Nature*, *The Symposium* 2:404–8.
         A. O. Lovejoy, *The Revolt Against Dualism*, *Ethics* 41:265–67.
1932   George Boas, *A Critical Analysis of the Philosophy of Emile Meyerson*, *Ethics* 43:118.
         M. R. Cohen, *Reason and Nature*, *Ethics* 43:70–72.
         E. Meyerson, *Du cheminiment de la Pensee*, *Ethics* 43:72.
         F. S. C. Northrop, *Science and First Principles*, *The New Humanist* 5:22–26.
1933   G. Santayana, *The Genteel Tradition at Bay*, *Ethics* 43:231–32.
         California Publications in Philosophy, vols. 13, 14, 15, *JP* 30:71–77.
1934   A. C. Ewing, *Idealism: A Critical Survey*, *JP* 31:352–53.
         W. T. Feldman, *The Philosophy of John Dewey*, *JP* 31:583–84.

C. Hartshorne, *The Philosophy and Psychology of Sensation, JP* 31:387–88.

F. C. S. Schiller, *Must Philosophers Disagree? JP* 31:719–20.

W. T. Stace, *The Theory of Knowledge and Existence, JP* 31:298–300.

A. N. Whitehead, *Nature and Life, JP* 31:329–30.

1935   R. G. Collingwood, *An Essay on Philosophic Method, PR* 44:191–92.

G. H. Mead, *Mind, Self, and Society, JP* 32:162–63.

Possibility: University of California Publications in Philosophy, vol. 17, *JP* 32:437–38.

J. Wisdom, *Problems of Mind and Matter, JP* 32:135–36.

1936   A. F. Bentley, *Behavior, Knowledge, Fact, JP* 33:165–66.

G. H. Mead, *Movements of Thought in the Nineteenth Century, JP* 33:384–86.

Philosophical Essays for Alfred North Whitehead, JP 33:219–20.

The Problem of Time, University of California Publications in Philosophy, vol. 18, *JP* 33:250–51.

E. G. Spaulding, *A World of Chance, JP* 33:302–4.

1937   A. C. Garnett, *Reality and Value, JP* 34:281–92.

D. W. Gotshalk, *Structure and Reality, JP* 34:687–91.

Studies in the History of Ideas, vol. 3, *PR* 46:97–98.

F. J. E. Woodbridge, *Nature and Mind, JP* 34:243–45.

1938   *The Problem of the Individual, University of California Publications in Philosophy,* vol. 20, *JP* 35:188–91.

W. C. Swabey, *Being and Being Known, JP* 35:20–21.

1939   G. H. Mead, *The Philosophy of the Act, JP* 36:85–103.

P. Weiss, *Reality, JP* 36:299–302.

From this point on the number of reviews falls off dramatically. Some post-1940 reviews on themes connected with this work are the following:

1944   P. A. Schilpp, ed., *The Philosophy of Bertrand Russell, The New Leader* 27:11.

1945   R. W. Church, *Bradley's Dialectic, PR* 54:271–74.

1946   R. G. Collingwood, *The Idea of Nature, PR* 55:199–202.

1947   J. Dewey, *Problems of Men, PR* 56:194–202.

R. Bretall, *A Kierkegaard Anthology, PR* 56:702–4.

A. N. Whitehead, *Essays in Science and Philosophy, PR* 56:709–11.

1955   E. E. Harris, *Nature, Mind, and Modern Science, PR* 64:484–87.

1958   N. Lawrence, *Whitehead's Philosophical Development, PR* 67:261–64.

1961   R. Wollheim, *F. H. Bradley, PR* 70:254–57.

II

Here follows a list of writings by others cited or alluded to in prefatory matter, writings on Murphy, and useful or interesting discussions of topics dealt with in this book.

Blanshard, Brand. *The Philosophy of Brand Blanshard.* Edited by P. A. Schilpp, pp. 214–16. La Salle, Illinois: Open Court, 1980. On the distinction between critical and speculative philosophy.

Broad, C. D. *Scientific Thought,* ch. 1. London: Routledge and Kegan Paul, 1924.

Broad, C. D. "Critical and Speculative Philosophy." In *Contemporary British Philosophy,* edited by J. H. Muirhead, vol. 1, pp. 82–100. London: George Allen and Unwin, 1924.

Broad, C. D. "Some Methods of Speculative Philosophy." *Proceedings of the Aristotelian Society,* supp. vol. 21 (1947): 1–32.

Cohen, Morris R. *Reason and Nature.* New York: Harcourt, Brace, and Company, 1931). Pointed to by Murphy as an early statement of objective relativism: "Two statements which, taken abstractly, are contradictory may both be true of concrete existence provided they can be assigned to separate domains or aspects. A plurality of aspects is an essential trait of things in existence. . . . When opposing statements are completed by reference to the domains in which they are true, there is no logical difficulty in combining them" (p. 166).

Creighton, James E. *Studies in Speculative Philosophy.* Edited by Harold R. Smart. New York: Macmillan, 1925.

Hahn, Lewis E. *A Contextualistic Theory of Perception.* Berkeley: University of California Press, 1942.

Hay, W. H. "Arthur Edward Murphy and His Concept of Ultimate Reality and Meaning." *Ultimate Reality and Meaning* 16.1–2 (1993): 73–86.

The Journal of Speculative Philosophy, new series, 1.1 (1987), "To the Reader," pp. 1–5, by Carl R. Hausman, Henry W. Johnstone, Jr., and Carl G. Vaught, the editors. The prospectus for the resurrection.

Lovejoy, Arthur O. *The Revolt Against Dualism.* n.p.: Open Court, 1930. A defense of dualism, discusses objective relativism in chapters 3 and 4. Murphy discussed this in 1931 and 1933, reviewed it in 1931.

Lovejoy, Arthur O. "Dualisms Good and Bad." *The Journal of Philosophy* 29 (1932): 337–54, 375–81. Reply to Murphy's 1931 discussion; Murphy's 1933 "Rejoinder" is to this.

Mays, W. "Whitehead's Account of 'Speculative Philosophy' in *Process and Reality."* *Proceedings of the Aristotelian Society* 46 (1946): 17–46. Very illuminating.

Moore, G. E. "A Defence of Common Sense" (1925), in G. E. Moore, *Philosophical Papers* (London: George Allen and Unwin, 1959), pp. 32–59; originally published in *Contemporary British Philosophy,* edited by J. H. Muirhead, second series (London: George Allen and Unwin, 1925), pp. 193–223.

Nagel, Ernest. Review of Murphy, *The Uses of Reason. JP* 41 (1944): 665–69.

Oliver, W. Donald. "The Logic of Perspective Realism." *JP* 35 (1938): 197–208.

Passmore, John. *A Hundred Years of Philosophy.* London: Gerald Duckworth, 1957. An excellent overall source for the period, with independent and pithy discussions of each of the philosophers discussed by Murphy in this work, as well as many others.

Peirce, C. S. "How to Make Our Ideas Clear," *Collected Papers,* edited by C. Hartshorne and P. Weiss (Cambridge: Harvard University Press, 1934), vol. 5, pp. 248–71; originally published in *Popular Science Monthly* 12 (1878): 286–302, as the second in the series of six papers having the combined title "Illustrations of the Logic of Science." The set as a whole was published, seven years after Peirce's death, in C. S. Peirce, *Chance, Love, and Logic,* edited by Morris R. Cohen (New York: Harcourt, Brace and Company, 1923), pp. 7–153.

Perry, Ralph Barton. *Present Philosophical Tendencies.* New York: Longmans, Green, and Company, 1912. An earlier work bearing some similarities to this one, though not primarily or even mainly about speculative philosophy. What makes it relevant is Perry's discussion, pp. 64–65 and 271 and in chapter 8, of "the speculative dogma," the "uncritical assumption that [the] speculative ideal is valid . . . the assumption of an all-general, all-sufficient first principle." Thus: "[The speculative dogma] arises from the tendency to anticipate that complete unification toward which knowledge appears progressively to move. Absolutism is the expression of this motive in its purity. It is the formulation of the goal of knowledge from an analysis of the process and trend of knowledge; and the assertion of that goal as necessary. So that while absolutism is allied with naive naturalism in its acceptance of the speculative ideal, it is distinguished therefrom by its method. It regards the speculative ideal *as* an ideal, and expressly formulates it as such. This absolutism is not merely *monistic,* as is naive naturalism; but is also *normative,* in that its cosmic unity is the limit or standard of the activity of thought" (pp. 165–66).

Post, John F. "Objective Value, Realism, and the End of Metaphysics." *The Journal of Speculative Philosophy,* new series, 4.2 (1990): 146–59. Contains a nice attempt to define metaphysics.

Ramsperger, A. G. *Philosophies of Science.* New York: F. S. Crofts, 1942. By a convinced objective relativist—see especially chapters 9 and 10.

Reck, Andrew J. *Speculative Philosophy: A Study of Its Nature Types and Uses.* Albuquerque: University of New Mexico Press, 1972. The only study of its kind that I know of. Contains comments on Alexander, Bosanquet, Bradley, McTaggart, Peirce, Russell, Santayana, R. W. Sellars, and Whitehead, among others, and also comments on the various realists. Reck does not hazard a definition of speculative philosophy, is content to let the meaning of the term be generated by consideration of the "many speculative philosophies" (p. 9). Two other points to note: (1) Reck does not distinguish between metaphysics and speculative philosophy; so far as I can see, he uses the terms practically interchangeably: "[S]peculative philosophies are usually metaphysical systems, so that the present study of speculative philosophy is inevitably a study of metaphysics," although, operating with Strawson's distinction between descriptive and revisionary metaphysics, he holds that "because of its innovative function, revisionary metaphysics is essentially speculative" (p. 12). And (2) Reck considers speculative philosophy as starting with Thales, or perhaps Plato, and does not treat that starting with Hegel, or post-Kant, as distinctive. Cf. Thompson, below.

Robischon, Thomas. "What is Objective Relativism?" *The Journal of Philosophy* 55 (1958): 1117–32. An acute analysis of "objective relativism" and of Murphy's views on the matter prior to the 1940 piece "What Happened to Objective Relativism" (published in 1963), arguing that there is a crucial ambiguity at its heart, that Murphy confuses relativity with relatedness.

Stedman, R. E. "A Defence of Speculative Philosophy." *Proceedings of the Aristotelian Society* 38 (1937–38): 113–42. It is nice to have a defense of speculative philosophy; this one, however, though it provides a defense against the sort of criticisms brought by logical positivism and analytic philosophers, does not come near the sort of criticism brought by Murphy.

Thompson, Manley. "Metaphysics." In R. Chisholm, H. Feigl, W. K. Frankena, J. Passmore, and M. Thompson, *Philosophy* (Englewood Cliffs, N.J.: Prentice-Hall, 1964), pp. 125–232. Its first two sections are on "Metaphysics as Speculative Philosophy" and "The Possibility of Speculative Philosophy," pp. 133–82. Contains a discussion of contextual analysis, pp. 199–202. Cf. Reck, above.

Index